AQA Science

Exclusively endorsed and approved by AQA

Jim Breithaupt

Series Editor: Lawrie Ryan

GCSE Physics

Nelson Thornes
a Wolters Kluwer business

Published in 2006 by:
Nelson Thornes Ltd
Delta Place
27 Bath Road
CHELTENHAM
GL53 7TH
United Kingdom

06 07 08 09 10 / 10 9 8 7 6 5 4 3 2 1

A catalogue record for this book is available from the British Library

ISBN 0 7487 9647 9

Cover photographs: wave by Corel 391 (NT); static electricity by
Photodisc 29 (NT);
astronaut by Photodisc 34 (NT)
Cover bubble illustration by Andy Parker
Illustrations by Bede Illustration, Kevin Jones Associates and Roger
Penwill
Page make-up by Wearset Ltd

Printed and bound in Slovenia by Korotan – Ljubljana Ltd

Welcome to AQA Physics

How to use this book

This textbook will help you throughout your GCSE course and to prepare for AQA's exams. It is packed full of features to help you to achieve the best result you can.

Some of the text is in a box marked HIGHER. You have to include these parts of the book if you are taking the Higher Tier exam. If you are taking the Foundation Tier exam, you can miss these parts out.

The same applies to any Learning Objectives, Key Points or Questions marked [Higher].

HIGHER

a) What are the yellow boxes?

To check you understand the science you are learning, questions are integrated into the main text. The information needed to answer these is on the same page, so you don't waste your time flicking through the entire book.

LEARNING OBJECTIVES

By the end of the lesson you should be able to answer the questions posed in the learning objectives; if you can't, review the content until it's clear.

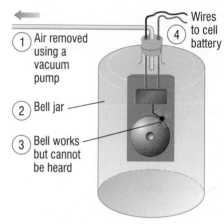

① Air removed using a vacuum pump
② Bell jar
③ Bell works but cannot be heard
④ Wires to cell battery

Figure 1 Key diagrams are as important as the text. Make sure you use them in your learning and revision.

Key words

Important scientific terms are shown like this:

observation or **anomalous**

You can look up the words shown like this – **bias** – in the glossary.

Avoid common mistakes and gain marks by sticking to this advice.

KEY POINTS

If you remember nothing else, remember these! Learning the key points in each lesson is a good start. They can be used in your revision and help you summarise your knowledge.

PRACTICAL

Become familiar with key practicals. A simple diagram and questions make this feature a short introduction, reminder or basis for practicals in the classroom.

E.g.

Geiger tube

Figure 2 Using a Geiger counter

DID YOU KNOW?

Curious examples of scientific points that are out of the ordinary, but true…

FOUL FACTS

Some science is just too gruesome to ignore. Delve into the horrible yet relevant world of Foul Facts.

At the start of each unit you will find a double-page introduction. This reminds you of ideas from previous work that you will need. The recap questions and activity will help find out if you need some revision before starting.

SCIENCE @ WORK

When will you ever use science in 'real life'? Check this feature to find out.

SUMMARY QUESTIONS

Did you understand everything? Get these questions right, and you can be sure you did. Get them wrong, and you might want to take another look.

The ideas in 'How Science Works' are covered in the first chapter. You will need to refer back to this chapter as you work through the course.

This first chapter looks at 'How Science Works'. It is an important part of your GCSE because the ideas introduced here will crop up throughout your course. You will be expected to collect scientific evidence and to understand how we use evidence. These concepts will be assessed as the major part of your internal school assessment. You will take one or more 45-minute tests on data you have collected previously plus data supplied for you in the test. These are called Investigative Skills Assignments. The ideas in 'How Science Works' will also be assessed in your examinations.

What you already know

Here is a quick reminder of previous work with investigations that you will find useful in this chapter:

- You will have done some practical work and know how important it is to keep yourself and others safe.
- Before you start investigating you usually make a prediction, which you can test.
- Your prediction and plan will tell you what you are going to change and what you are going to measure.
- You will have thought about controls.
- You will have thought about repeating your readings.
- During your practical work you will have written down your results, often in a table.
- You will have plotted graphs of your results.
- You will have made conclusions to explain your results.
- You will have thought about how you could improve your results, if you did the work again.

RECAP QUESTIONS

Helen wrote this about a practical she did:

I wanted to find out how strong an electromagnet could be with different lengths of wire wrapped around an iron bar. I thought that the more wire there was, the more iron filings the magnet would pick up.

I had to wear safety glasses to stop any iron filings getting in my eyes. I took an iron rod and wrapped a coil of wire around it. I connected the ends of the wire to a battery and then picked up some iron filings. I put the rod on an empty tray and switched the battery off. Then the iron filings dropped into the tray and I weighed them.

I then repeated this with 12 coils when I got 2.1 grams; 15 coils when I got 3.0 grams and 8 coils when I got 1.5 grams. With 6 coils I gathered 1.2 grams. I used the same battery throughout.

It was difficult because I couldn't scrape off all of the iron filings.

1 What was Helen's prediction?

2 What was the variable she chose to change? (We call this the **independent** variable.)

3 What was the variable she measured to judge the effect of varying the independent variable? (We call this the **dependent** variable. Its value *depends* on the value chosen for the independent variable.)

4 Write down a variable that Helen controlled.

5 Write down a variable Helen did not say she had controlled.

6 Make a table of her results.

7 Draw a graph of her results.

8 Write a conclusion for Helen.

9 How do you think Helen could have improved her results?

How science works for us

Science works for us all day, every day. You do not need to know how a mobile phone works to enjoy sending text messages. But, think about how you started to use your mobile phone or your television remote control. Did you work through pages of instructions? Probably not!

You knew that pressing the buttons would change something on the screen (*knowledge*). You played around with the buttons, to see what would happen (*observation*). You had a guess at what you thought might be happening (*prediction*) and then tested your idea (*experiment*).

If your prediction was correct you remembered that as a *fact*. If you could repeat the operation and get the same result again then you were very pleased with yourself. You had shown that your results were **reliable**.

Working as a scientist you will have knowledge of the world around you and particularly about the subject you are working with. You will observe the world around you. An enquiring mind will then lead you to start asking questions about what you have observed.

Science moves forward by slow steady steps. When a genius such as Einstein comes along then it takes a giant leap. Those small steps build on knowledge and experience that we already have.

Each small step is important in its own way. It builds on the body of knowledge that we have. Galileo was able to demonstrate how an object accelerates and he called the acceleration 'g'. Sir Isaac Newton was able to show how 'g' could be calculated from his laws of motion and gravitation. Many years later, Henry Cavendish proved Newton's law of gravitation by experiment and used it to make the first scientific measurement of the mass of the Earth.

Thinking scientifically

Figure 1 Playing basketball

ACTIVITY

No matter how good a player you are, if the ball is not properly inflated then you cannot play well. As the balls get used during the game it is possible that some of them will get soft. They should all bounce the same.

How high the ball bounces will depend on lots of variables. It will depend on:

- what the ball is made of,
- how much air has been pumped in,
- what the temperature of the ball is,
- what the floor surface is made of, and
- how hard you throw it.

It is impossible to test all of these during a match.

The simple way is to drop a ball from a certain height and see how high it bounces. Can you work out a way to see how changing the height from which a ball is dropped can test how high it bounces? This could then be used as a simple test during the match to see if the balls are good enough.

You can use the following headings to discuss your ideas. One person should be writing your thoughts down, so that you can discuss them with the rest of your class.

- What prediction can you make about the height the ball is dropped from and the height it will bounce to?
- What would be your independent variable?
- What would be your dependent variable?
- What would you have to control?
- Write a plan for your investigation.
- How could you make sure your results were reliable?

H2

Fundamental ideas about how science works

LEARNING OBJECTIVES

1 How do you spot when a person has an opinion that is not based on good science?
2 What is the importance of continuous, ordered and categoric variables?
3 What is meant by reliable evidence and valid evidence?
4 How can two sets of data be linked?

NEXT TIME YOU...

... read a newspaper article or watch the news on TV ask yourself if that research is valid and reliable. (See page 5.) Ask yourself if you can trust the opinion of that person.

Figure 1 Student recording a range of temperatures – an example of a continuous variable

Science is too important for us to get it wrong

Sometimes it is easy to spot when people try to use science poorly. Sometimes it can be funny. You might have seen adverts claiming to give your hair 'body' or sprays that give your feet 'lift'!

On the other hand, poor scientific practice can cost lives.

Some years ago a company sold the drug thalidomide to people as a sleeping pill. Research was carried out on animals to see if it was safe. The research did not include work on pregnant animals. The opinion of the people in charge was that the animal research showed the drug could be used safely with humans.

Then the drug was also found to help ease morning sickness in pregnant women. Unfortunately, doctors prescribed it to many women, resulting in thousands of babies being born with deformed limbs. It was far from safe.

These are very difficult decisions to make. You need to be absolutely certain of what the science is telling you.

a) Why was the opinion of the people in charge of developing thalidomide based on poor science?

Deciding on what to measure

You know that you have an independent and a dependent variable in an investigation. These variables can be one of four different types:

- A **categoric variable** is one that is best described by a label (usually a word). For a magnet, its type is a categoric variable, e.g. horseshoe magnet or bar magnet.
- A **discrete variable** is one that you describe in whole numbers. The number of coils on an electromagnet is a discrete variable.
- An **ordered variable** is one where you can put the data into order, but not give it an actual number. The strength of different magnets compared to each other is an ordered variable, e.g. one bar magnet is stronger than another bar magnet.
- A **continuous variable** is one that we measure, so its value could be any number. Distance (as measured by a ruler, tape or distance sensor) is a continuous variable, e.g. 37 cm, 43 cm, 54 cm, 76 cm.

When designing your investigation you should always try to measure continuous data whenever you can. This is not always possible, so you should then try to use ordered data. If there is no other way to measure your variable then you have to use a label (categoric variable).

b) Imagine you were testing a solar cell, what would be better:
   i) putting a light bulb into the circuit to see how bright it was, or
   ii) using a voltmeter to measure the potential difference?

Making your investigation reliable and valid

When you are designing an investigation you must make sure that others can get the same results as you – this makes it **reliable**.

You must also make sure you are measuring the actual thing you want to measure. If you don't, your data can't be used to answer your original question. This seems very obvious but it is not always quite so easy. You need to make sure that you have *controlled* as many other variables as you can, so that no-one can say that your investigation is not **valid**. A valid investigation should be reliable *and* answer the original question.

Figure 2 Road sign which uses solar cells

c) State one way in which you can show that your results are valid.

How might an independent variable be linked to a dependent variable?

Variables can be linked together for one of three reasons:

- It could be because one variable has caused a change in the other, e.g. the longer the heater is on the more energy is transferred. This is a *causal link*.
- It could be because a third variable has caused changes in the two variables you have investigated, e.g. there is a relationship between the time of year and the energy produced by wind turbines. This is because there is an *association* between the two variables. Both of the variables are caused by the increased amount of wind at certain times of the year.
- It could be due simply to **chance**, e.g. increased use of mobile phones and increased rates of diabetes.

d) Describe a causal link that you have seen in physics.

Figure 3 Different room heaters

SUMMARY QUESTIONS

1 Name each of the following types of variables described in a), b) and c).

  a) People were asked how efficient each of five different heaters was: 'cheap and hot', 'cheap, but not much heat', 'it was fine', 'great, kept me warm' were some of the answers.
  b) These people were asked which ones they would buy. They put the five heaters into order.
  c) The five heaters were tested by measuring their energy input and output.

2 Research on the possible harmful effects of mobile phones states that 'Little research … has been published in the peer-reviewed literature'. What does this statement mean?

KEY POINTS

1 Be on the lookout for non-scientific opinions.
2 Continuous data is more powerful than other types of data.
3 Check that evidence is reliable and valid.
4 Be aware that just because two variables are related it does not mean that there is a causal link between them.

H3 Starting an investigation

Figure 1 A wind turbine

Observation

As humans we are sensitive to the world around us. We can use our many senses to detect what is happening. As scientists we use observations to ask questions. We can only ask useful questions if we know something about the observed event. We will not have all of the answers, but we know enough to start asking the correct questions.

If we observe that the weather has been hot today, we would not ask if it was due to global warming. If the weather was hotter than normal for several years then we could ask that question. We know that global warming takes many years to show its effect.

When you are designing an investigation you have to observe carefully which variables are likely to have an effect.

a) Would it be reasonable to ask if the wind turbine in Figure 1 generates less electricity in the rain? Explain your answer.

Amjid was waiting to cross at a zebra crossing. A car stopped to let him cross while a second car drove into the first car, without braking. Being a scientist, Amjid tried to work out why this had happened . . . while the two drivers argued! He came up with the following ideas:

- The second driver was tired.
- The second car had faulty brakes.
- The first car stopped too quickly.
- The second car was driving too fast.
- The second car was travelling too close.
- The second car had worn tyres.
- The first car had no brake lights.

b) Discuss each of these ideas and use your knowledge of science to decide which three ideas are the most likely to have caused the crash.

Observations, backed up by really creative thinking and good scientific knowledge can lead to a **hypothesis**.

What is a hypothesis?

A hypothesis is a 'great idea'. Why is it so great? – well because it is a great observation that has some really good science to try to explain it.

For example, you observe that small, thinly sliced chips cook faster than large, fat chips. Your hypothesis could be that the small chips cook faster because the heat from the oil has a shorter distance to travel before it gets to the potato in the centre of the chips.

c) Check out the photograph in Figure 2 and spot anything that you find interesting. Use your knowledge and some creative thought to suggest a hypothesis based on your observations.

When making hypotheses you can be very imaginative with your ideas. However, you should have some scientific reasoning behind those ideas so that they are not totally bizarre.

Remember, your explanation might not be correct, but you think it is. The only way you can check out your hypothesis is to make it into a prediction and then test it by carrying out an investigation.

Observation + knowledge ⟹ hypothesis ⟹

prediction ⟹ investigation

Figure 2 The Tacoma Narrows bridge in the USA twisting just before it collapsed!

Starting to design a valid investigation

An investigation starts with a prediction. You, as the scientist, predict that there is a relationship between two variables.

- An **independent variable** is one that is changed or selected by you, the investigator.

- A **dependent variable** is measured for each change in your independent variable.

- All other variables become **control variables**, kept constant so that your investigation is a fair test.

If your measurements are going to be accepted by other people then they must be valid. Part of this is making sure that you are really measuring the effect of changing your chosen variable. For example, if other variables aren't controlled properly, they might be affecting the data collected.

d) Look at Figure 3. Darren was investigating the light given out by a 12V bulb. He used a light meter in the laboratory that was set at 10cm from the bulb. What might be wrong here?

Figure 3 Testing a light bulb

SUMMARY QUESTIONS

1 Copy and complete using the words below:

   **controlled   dependent   hypothesis   independent
   knowledge   prediction**

   Observations when supported by scientific ...... can be used to make a .... This can be the basis for a .... A prediction links an ...... variable to a ...... variable. Other variables need to be ....

2 Explain the difference between a hypothesis and a prediction.

KEY POINTS

1 Observation is often the starting point for an investigation.
2 Hypotheses can lead to predictions and investigations.
3 You must design investigations that produce valid results if you are to be believed.

H4 Building an investigation

LEARNING OBJECTIVES

1 How do you design a fair test?
2 How do you make sure that you choose the best values for your variables?
3 How do you ensure accuracy and precision?

Figure 1 Racing car travelling at speed

Fair testing

A **fair test** is one in which only the independent variable affects the dependent variable. All other variables are controlled, keeping them constant if possible.

This is easy to set up in the laboratory, but almost impossible in fieldwork. Imagine you are studying the acceleration of different racing cars. You would choose the same race track and try them at the same time. This means that all of the many variables (e.g. weather) change in much the same way, except for the one you are investigating.

a) How would you set up an investigation to see how the wing setting on the rear of the car affected its top speed down the straight?

If you are investigating two variables in a large population then you will need to do a survey. Again it is impossible to control all of the variables. Imagine you were investigating how much electricity different sized families used. You would have to choose families from the same sized house, with the same level of insulation to test. The larger the sample size you test, the more reliable your results will be.

Control groups are used in investigations to try to make sure that you are measuring the variable that you intend to measure. When investigating the effects of using a mobile phone, the control group would be a similar group of people who did not use a mobile phone.

Choosing values of a variable

Trial runs will tell you a lot about how your early thoughts are going to work out.

Do you have the correct conditions?
Suppose you have a small water heater to test. You want to find out the best voltage to use. You test different voltages but only very small changes in temperature were recorded. This might be because:

- the heater was not left on long enough.
- too much water was being heated.
- the heater was not powerful enough.

Have you chosen a sensible range?
If there is a big temperature change, but the results all look about the same:

- you might not have chosen a wide enough range of voltages.

Have you got enough readings that are close together?
If the results are very different from each other:

- you might not see a pattern if you have large gaps between readings over the important part of the range.

Accuracy

Accurate results are very close to the *true value*.

Your investigation should provide data that is accurate enough to answer your original question.

However, it is not always possible to know what that true value is.

How do you get accurate data?
- You can repeat your results and your mean is more likely to be accurate.
- Try repeating your measurements with a different instrument and see if you get the same readings.
- Use high quality instruments that measure accurately.
- The more carefully you use the measuring instruments, the more accuracy you will get.

Precision and reliability

If your repeated results are closely grouped together then you have precision and you have improved the reliability of your data.

Your investigation must provide data with sufficient precision. It's no use measuring a person's reaction time using the seconds hand on a clock! If there are big differences within sets of repeat readings, you will not be able to make a valid conclusion. You won't be able to trust your data!

How do you get precise and reliable data?

- You have to repeat your tests as often as necessary.
- You have to repeat your tests in exactly the same way each time.

A word of caution!

Be careful though – just because your results show precision does not mean your results are accurate. Look at the box opposite.

b) Draw a thermometer scale showing 4 results that are both accurate and precise.

The difference between accurate and precise results

Imagine measuring the temperature after a set time when an immersion is used to heat a fixed volume of water. Two students repeated this experiment, four times each. Their results are marked on the thermometer scales below:

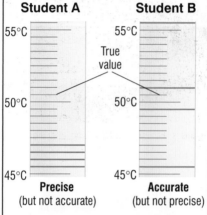

- Precise results are grouped closely together.
- Accurate results will have a mean (average) close to the true value.

SUMMARY QUESTIONS

1 Copy and complete using the following terms:

      range   repeat   conditions   readings

Trial runs give you a good idea of whether you have the correct ......; whether you have chosen the correct ......; whether you have enough ......; if you need to do ...... readings.

2 Use an example to explain how results can be accurate, but not precise.

3 Briefly describe how you would go about setting up a fair test in a laboratory investigation. Give your answer as general advice.

KEY POINTS

1 Care must be taken to ensure fair testing – as far as is possible.
2 You can use a trial run to make sure that you choose the best values for your variables.
3 Careful use of the correct equipment can improve accuracy.
4 If you repeat your results carefully they are likely to become more reliable.

H5   Making measurements

Figure 1 Mark testing how fast a trolley goes down a ramp

Using instruments

Do not panic! You cannot expect perfect results.

Try timing one swing of a pendulum using a stop watch that measures to 0.01 s. Do you always get the same time? Probably not. So can we say that any measurement is absolutely correct?

In any experiment there will be doubts about actual measurements.

a) Look at Figure 1. Suppose, like this student, you tested the time it takes for one type of trolley to run down the track. It is unlikely that you would get two readings exactly the same. Discuss all the possible reasons why.

When you choose an instrument you need to know that it will give you the accuracy that you want. That is, it will give you a true reading.

Perhaps you have used a simple force meter in school for measuring force. How confident were you that you had measured the true force? You could use a very expensive force meter to calibrate yours. The expensive force meter is more likely to show the true reading that is accurate – but are you really sure?

You also need to be able to use an instrument properly.

b) In Figure 1 the student is measuring the time it takes for the car to reach the finish line. Why is he unlikely to get a true measurement?

When you choose an instrument you need to decide how accurate you need it to be. Instruments that measure the same quantity can have different sensitivities. The instrument with the greatest **sensitivity** is the one that can detect the smallest change in the quantity being measured

Choosing the wrong scale can cause you to miss important data or make silly conclusions, for example 'The amount of gold was the same in the two rings – they both weighed 5 grams.'

c) Match the following timers to their best use:

Used to measure	Sensitivity of timer
Time taken to sail around the world	0.1 seconds
Timing a car rolling down a slope	1.0 seconds
Timing ten oscillations of a pendulum	1 minute
Timing a pizza to cook	1 hour

Errors

Even when an instrument is used correctly, the results can still show differences.

Results might differ due to a **random error**. This is most likely to be due to a poor measurement being made. It could be due to not carrying out the method consistently.

The error might be **systematic**. This means that the method was carried out consistently but an error was being repeated.

Check out these two sets of data that were taken from the investigation that Mark did. He tested five different trolleys. The third line is the time expected from calculations:

Type of trolley used	a	b	c	d	e
Time taken for trolley to run down ramp (seconds)	12.6	23.1	24.8	31.3	38.2
	12.1	15.2	24.3	32.1	37.6
Calculated time (seconds)	10.1	13.1	22.1	30.1	35.3

d) Discuss whether there is any evidence for random error in these results.
e) Discuss whether there is any evidence for systematic error in these results.

Anomalies

Anomalous results are clearly out of line. They are not those that are due to the natural variation you get from any measurement. These should be looked at carefully. There might be a very interesting reason why they are so different. If they are simply due to a random error, then they should be discarded (rejected).

If anomalies can be identified while you are doing an investigation, then it is best to repeat that part of the investigation.

If you find anomalies after you have finished collecting data for an investigation, then they must be discarded.

KEY POINTS

1 Results will nearly always vary.
2 Better instruments give more accurate results.
3 Sensitivity of an instrument refers to the smallest change that it can detect.
4 Human error can produce random and systematic errors.
5 We examine anomalies; they might give us some interesting ideas. If they are due to a random error, we repeat the measurements. If there is no time to repeat them, we discard them.

SUMMARY QUESTIONS

1 Copy and complete using the words below:

accurate   discarded   random   sensitivity   systematic   use   variation

There will always be some …… in results. You should always choose the best instruments that you can to get the most …… results. You must know how to …… the instrument properly. The …… of an instrument refers to the smallest change that can be detected. There are two types of error – …… and ……. Anomalies due to random error should be …….

2 Which of the following will lead to a systematic error and which to a random error?
a) Using a weighing machine, which has something stuck to the pan on the top.
b) Forgetting to re-zero the weighing machine.

H6

Presenting data

LEARNING OBJECTIVES

1 What do we mean by the 'range' and the 'mean' of the data?
2 How do you use tables of results?
3 How do you display your data?

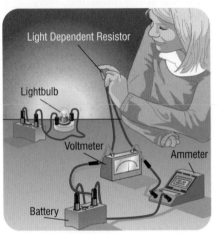

Figure 1 Student using an LDR with a light bulb

For this section you will be working with data from this investigation:

Mel shone a lamp onto a light dependent resistor (LDR). She measured how quickly energy was transferred to the lamp and the resistance of the LDR.

The room was kept as dark as possible while she made the readings.

Tables

Tables are really good for getting your results down quickly and clearly. You should design your table **before** you start your investigation.

Your table should be constructed to fit in all the data to be collected. It should be fully labelled, including units.

In some investigations, particularly fieldwork, it is useful to have an extra column for any notes you might want to make as you work.

While filling in your table of results you should be constantly looking for anomalies.

● Check to see if a repeat is sufficiently close to the first reading.
● Check to see if the pattern you are getting as you change the independent variable is what you expected.

Remember a result that looks anomalous should be checked out to see if it really is a poor reading or if it might suggest a different hypothesis.

Planning your table

Mel knew the values for her independent variable. We always put these in the first column of a table. The dependent variable goes in the second column. Mel will find its values as she carries out the investigation.

Rate of energy transferred to the lamp (W)	Resistance of LDR (Ω)
0.5	
1.4	
2.6	
4.8	
8.4	

So she could plan a table like this:

Or like this:

Rate of energy transferred to the lamp (W)	0.5	1.4	2.6	4.8	8.4
Resistance of LDR (Ω)					

All she had to do in the investigation was to write the correct numbers in the second column to complete the top table.

Mel's results are shown in the alternative format in the table below:

Rate of energy transferred to the lamp (W)	0.5	1.4	2.6	4.8	8.4
Resistance of LDR (Ω)	4000	3000	1000	350	150

The range of the data

Pick out the maximum and the minimum values and you have the range. You should always quote these two numbers when asked for a range. For example, the range is between ……… (the lowest value) and ……… (the highest value) – and don't forget to include the units!

a) What is the range for the dependent variable in Mel's set of data?

The mean of the data

Often you have to find the mean of each repeated set of measurements.

You add up the measurements in the set and divide by how many there are. Miss out any anomalies you find.

The repeat values and mean can be recorded as shown below:

Rate of energy transferred to the lamp (W)	Resistance of LDR (Ω)			
	1st test	2nd test	3rd test	Mean

Displaying your results

Bar charts

If you have a categoric or an ordered independent variable and a continuous dependent variable then you should use a bar chart.

Line graphs

If you have a continuous independent and a continuous dependent variable then a line graph should be used.

Scatter graphs or scattergrams

Scatter graphs are used in much the same way as line graphs, but you might not expect to be able to draw such a clear line of best fit. For example, if you wanted to see if lung capacity was related to how long you could hold your breath, you would draw a scatter graph with your results.

KEY POINTS

1 The range states the maximum and the minimum values.
2 The mean is the sum of the values divided by how many values there are.
3 Tables are best used during an investigation to record results.
4 Bar charts are used when you have a categoric or an ordered independent variable and a continuous dependent variable.
5 Line graphs are used to display data that are continuous.

SUMMARY QUESTIONS

1 Copy and complete using the words below:

categoric   continuous   mean   range

The maximum and minimum values show the …… of the data. The sum of all the values divided by the total number of the values gives the ……. . Bar charts are used when you have a …… independent variable and a continuous dependent variable.
Line graphs are used when you have …… independent and dependent variables.

2 Draw a graph of Mel's results from the bottom of page 12.

H7 Using data to draw conclusions

Identifying patterns and relationships

Now that you have a bar chart or a graph of your results you can begin to look for patterns. You must have an open mind at this point.

Firstly, there could still be some anomalous results. You might not have picked these out earlier. How do you spot an anomaly? It must be a significant distance away from the pattern, not just within normal variation.

A line of best fit will help to identify any anomalies at this stage. Ask yourself – do the anomalies represent something important or were they just a mistake?

Secondly, remember a line of best fit can be a straight line or it can be a curve – you have to decide from your results.

The line of best fit will also lead you into thinking what the relationship is between your two variables. You need to consider whether your graph shows a **linear** relationship. This simply means can you be confident about drawing a straight line of best fit on your graph? If the answer is yes – then is this line positive or negative?

a) Say whether graphs (i) and (ii) in Figure 1 show a positive or a negative linear relationship.

Look at the graph in Figure 2. It shows a positive linear relationship. It also goes through the origin (0,0). We call this a **directly proportional** relationship.

Your results might also show a curved line of best fit. These can be predictable, complex or very complex! Look at Figure 3 below.

(i)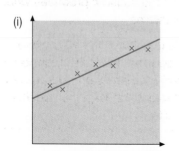

(ii)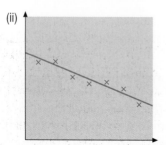

Figure 1 Graphs showing linear relationships

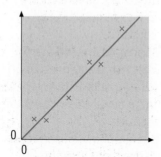

Figure 2 Graph showing a directly proportional relationship

a)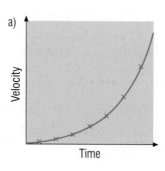

b)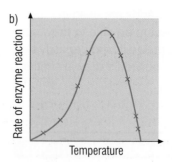

c)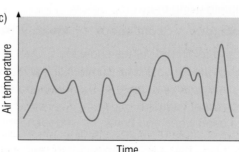

Figure 3 a) Graph showing predictable results. b) Graph showing complex results. c) Graph showing very complex results.

Drawing conclusions

Your graphs are designed to show the relationship between your two chosen variables. You need to consider what that relationship means for your conclusion.

There are three possible links between variables. (See page 5.) They can be:

- causal,
- due to association, or
- due to chance.

You must decide which is the most likely. Remember a positive relationship does not always mean a causal link between the two variables.

Poor science can often happen if a wrong decision is made here. Newspapers have said that living near electricity sub-stations can cause cancer. All that scientists would say is that there is possibly an association. Getting the correct conclusion is very important.

You will have made a prediction. This could be supported by your results. It might not be supported or it could be partly supported. Your results might suggest some other hypothesis to you.

Your conclusion must go no further than the evidence that you have. For example, tests that show an electricity sub-station produces a magnetic field that can be detected up to 5 metres away cannot be used to say the magnetic field is present further away.

Evaluation

If you are still uncertain about a conclusion, it might be down to the reliability and the validity of the results. You could check these by:

- looking for other similar work on the Internet or from others in your class,
- getting somebody else to re-do your investigation, or
- trying an alternative method to see if you get the same results.

NEXT TIME YOU...

... read scientific claims, think carefully about the evidence that should be there to back up the claim.

DID YOU KNOW?

Pythagoras of Samos declared that 'Everything is number'. He believed that everything in the Universe can be explained by simple mathematical relationships. He went on to discover the relationship between the length of a string and the sound it produces when it vibrates.

He developed this idea into a theory that the Sun, the Moon and the planets produced a sort of music that kept them in their orbits!

SUMMARY QUESTIONS

1 Copy and complete using the words below:

anomalous   complex   directly   negative   positive

Lines of best fit can be used to identify ...... results. Linear relationships can be ...... or .... If a graph goes through the origin then the relationship could be ...... proportional. Often a line of best fit is a curve which can be predictable or ....

2 Nasma knew about the possible link between cancer and living near to electricity sub-stations. She found a quote from a National Grid Company survey of sub-stations:

'Measurements of the magnetic field were taken at 0.5 metre above ground level within 1 metre of fences and revealed 1.9 microteslas. After 5 metres this dropped to the normal levels measured in any house.'

Discuss the type of experiment and the data you would expect to see to support a conclusion that it is safe to build houses over 5 metres from an electricity sub-station.

KEY POINTS

1 Drawing lines of best fit help us to study the relationship between variables.
2 The possible relationships are linear, positive and negative; directly proportional; predictable and complex curves.
3 Conclusions must go no further than the data available.
4 The reliability and validity of data can be checked by looking at other similar work done by others, perhaps on the Internet. It can also be checked by using a different method or by others checking your method.

H8 Scientific evidence and society

Now you have reached a conclusion about a piece of scientific research. So what is next? If it is pure research then your fellow scientists will want to look at it very carefully. If it affects the lives of ordinary people then society will also want to examine it closely.

You can help your cause by giving a balanced account of what you have found out. It is much the same as any argument you might have. If you make ridiculous claims then nobody will believe anything you have to say.

Be open and honest. If you only tell part of the story then someone will want to know why! Equally, if somebody is only telling you part of the truth, you cannot be confident with anything they say.

a) 'X-rays are safe, but should be limited' is the headline in an American newspaper. What information is missing? Is it important?

You must be on the lookout for people who might be biased when representing scientific evidence. Some scientists are paid by companies to do research. When you are told that a certain product is harmless, just check out who is telling you.

MOBILE PHONE TUMOUR RISK?

Swedish researchers found that the risk of developing an ear tumour increased if you used a mobile phone. The study was of 750 people. This type of tumour affects one in 100,000 people and the risk increased four times if you used the phone for more than 10 years.

b) Suppose you wanted to know about safe levels of noise at work. Would you ask the scientist who helped to develop the machinery or a scientist working in the local university? What questions would you ask, so that you could make a valid judgement?

We also have to be very careful in reaching judgements according to who is presenting scientific evidence to us. For example, if the evidence might provoke public or political problems, then it might be played down.

Equally others might want to exaggerate the findings. They might make more of the results than the evidence suggests. Take as an example the siting of mobile phone masts. Local people may well present the same data in a totally different way from those with a wider view of the need for mobile phones.

c) Check out some web sites on mobile phone masts. Get the opinions of people who think they are dangerous and those who believe they are safe. Try to identify any political bias there might be in their opinions.

The status of the experimenter may place more weight on evidence. Suppose an electricity company wants to convince an inquiry that it is perfectly reasonable to site a wind turbine in remote moorland in the UK. The company will choose the most eminent scientist in that field who is likely to support them. The small local community might not be able to afford an eminent scientist. The inquiry needs to be carried out very carefully to make a balanced judgement.

VILLAGERS PROTEST AGAINST WIND FARM

There was considerable local opposition from local villagers to building a wind farm near the A14 road in Cambridgeshire. Planners turned down the application after seven months of protests by local residents. Some described it as being like 16 football pitches rotating in the sky. Others were concerned at the effect on the value of their houses. Friends of the Earth were, in principle, in favour. The wind farm company said that it would provide energy for 20,000 homes.

SUMMARY QUESTIONS

1 Copy and complete using the words below:

status   balanced   bias   political

Evidence from scientific investigations should be given in a …… way. It must be checked for any …… from the experimenter.
Evidence can be given too little or too much weight if it is of …… significance.
The …… of the experimenter is likely to influence people in their judgement of the evidence.

2 Collect some newspaper articles to show how scientific evidence is used. Discuss in groups whether these articles are honest and fair representations of the science. Consider whether they carry any bias.

3 Extract from BBC web site about Sizewell nuclear power station:

'A radioactive leak can have devastating results but one small pill could protect you. "Inside out" reveals how for the first time these life-saving pills will be available to families living close to the Sizewell nuclear power station.'

Suppose you were living near Sizewell power station. Who would you trust to tell you whether these pills would protect you from radiation? Who wouldn't you trust?

KEY POINTS
1 Scientific evidence must be presented in a balanced way that points out clearly how reliable and valid the evidence is.
2 The evidence must not contain any bias from the experimenter.
3 The evidence must be checked to appreciate whether there has been any political influence.
4 The status of the experimenter can influence the weight placed on the evidence.

How is science used for everybody's benefit?

LEARNING OBJECTIVES

1 How does science link to technology?
2 How is science used and abused?
3 How are decisions made about science?
4 What are the limitations of science?

Figure 1 Marie Curie and her husband Pierre Curie

In 1896, Henri Becquerel worked in a laboratory in Paris. He noticed that a packet of uranium salts had left a mark on a photographic plate, even though the plate was wrapped in paper. It looked as though light had got in – but that wasn't possible.

He told a young student, Marie Curie, to investigate. She called the effect 'radioactivity'. Becquerel, Marie and her husband Pierre were awarded the 1903 Nobel Prize for Physics for the work they did on radioactivity.

Ernest Rutherford worked on these radioactive materials and discovered that immense amounts of energy could be released from very small amounts of matter. He also noticed that it always took the same amount of time for a particular substance to lose half of its radioactivity. He realised that they could be used to date materials. He investigated radioactivity and demonstrated the principles that led to the development of radioactive tracers and devices such as the modern smoke detector.

Marie Curie continued with her investigations. Because of the reputation of radioactivity, it was used to enhance toothpaste and people would bathe in radioactive springs. Marie Curie eventually died of leukaemia.

Rutherford discovered the atomic nucleus by using his knowledge to fire alpha particles at gold foil and deducing that an atom was nearly all empty space with a small dense nucleus. For his discovery of the nucleus, he was awarded the 1909 Nobel Prize (for Chemistry!)

Figure 2 Stamp honouring Ernest Rutherford

Figure 3 Destruction by an atomic bomb

Once the structure of the nucleus had been determined, the scientific knowledge was there for many technologies to be developed. By 1940 scientists could begin development of the atomic bomb which was exploded over Japan in 1945.

Some people argue that by using these bombs it shortened the Second World War and fewer people were killed. Others argue that using science in such a destructive way is ethically wrong.

Nuclear power stations now deliver 11% of the world's energy needs. They do not produce carbon dioxide, but they do produce radioactive waste. This waste is likely to be potentially dangerous for many thousands of years.

Radioactive materials are used extensively in hospitals for diagnosis of illness and for curing diseases such as cancer.

There is still a great deal to learn about the atom and radioactivity. There are cosmic sources of gamma rays in space which are being explored by satellites. They were first discovered in the Cold War by US satellites. They thought the enemy were testing nuclear bombs in space. More observations led to the conclusion that the sources are massive explosions in distant galaxies. Who knows what will be found?

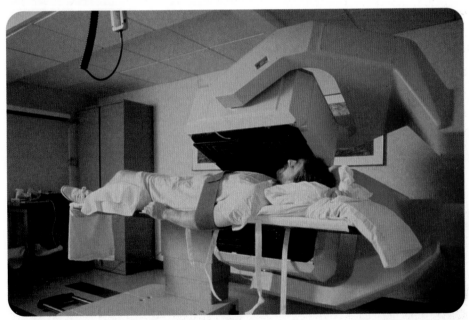

Figure 4 Radioactive tracers emit gamma rays which can be detected by special cameras

DID YOU KNOW?

If you could release all of the energy you have in the atoms that make up your body, you could explode with the force of thirty atom bombs! Don't ever claim that you do not have enough energy.

SUMMARY QUESTIONS

Use the account of the development of radioactivity technology to answer these questions.

1 What early scientific work enabled the smoke detector to be developed?

2 Describe some of the many different ways in which radioactive materials have been used.

3 a) Identify some of these issues raised by the use of radioactive materials: i) ethical, ii) social, iii) economic, iv) environmental.
   b) Which of these issues are decided by individuals and which by society?

KEY POINTS

1 Scientific knowledge can be used to develop technologies.
2 People can exploit scientific and technological developments to suit their own purposes.
3 The uses of science and technology can raise ethical, social, economic and environmental issues.
4 These issues are decided upon by individuals and by society.
5 There are many questions left for science to answer. But science cannot answer questions that start with 'Should we .... ?'

SUMMARY QUESTIONS

1 a) Fit these words into order. They should be in the order that you might use them in an investigation.

design; prediction; conclusion; method; repeat; controls; graph; results; table; improve; safety

2 a) How would you tell the difference between an opinion that was scientific and a prejudiced opinion?

b) Suppose you were investigating the loss of heat from a beaker of hot water. Would you choose to investigate a categoric, continuous or ordered variable? Explain why.

c) Explain the difference between a causal link between two variables and one which is due to association.

3 a) You might have noticed that different items of electrical equipment in the house use different diameters of wire. You ask the question why? You use some accepted theory to try to answer the question.

Explain what you understand by a hypothesis.

Different diameters of wire in a household

b) The diameter of the wire can affect the resistance of the wire. This is a hypothesis. Develop this into a prediction.

c) Explain why a prediction is more useful than a hypothesis.

d) Suppose you have tested your prediction and have some data. What might this do for your hypothesis?

e) Suppose the data does not support the hypothesis. What should you do to the theory that gave you the hypothesis?

4 a) What do you understand by a fair test?

b) Suppose you were carrying out an investigation into how changing the current in an electromagnet affects the magnetic field. You would need to carry out a trial. Describe what a trial would tell you about how to plan your method.

c) How could you decide if your results showed precision?

d) It is possible to calculate the theoretical magnetic field around a coil. How could you use this to check on the accuracy of your results?

5 Suppose you were watching a friend carry out an investigation using the equipment shown opposite. You have to mark your friend on how accurately he is making his measurements. Make a list of points that you would be looking for.

Student using an electromagnet to pick up iron filings

6 a) How do you decide on the range of a set of data?

b) How do you calculate the mean?

c) When should you use a bar chart?

d) When should you use a line graph?

7 a) What should happen to anomalous results?

b) What does a line of best fit allow you to do?

c) When making a conclusion, what must you take into consideration?

d) How can you check on the reliability of your results?

8 a) Why is it important when reporting science to 'tell the truth, the whole truth and nothing but the truth'?

b) Why might some people be tempted not to be completely fair when reporting their opinions on scientific data?

9 a) 'Science can advance technology and technology can advance science.'
What do you think is meant by this statement?

b) Who answers the questions that start with 'Should we . . . '?

10 Wind turbines are an increasingly popular way of generating electricity. It is very important that they are sited in the best place to maximise energy output. Clearly they need to be where there is plenty of wind. Energy companies have to be confident that they get value for money. Therefore they must consider the most economic height to build them. Put them too high and they might not get enough extra energy to justify the extra cost of the turbine. Before deciding finally on a site they will carry out an investigation to decide the best height.

The prediction is that increasing the height will increase the power output of the wind turbine.
A test platform was erected and the turbine placed on it. The lowest height that would allow the turbines to move was 32 metres. The correct weather conditions were waited for and the turbine began turning and the power output was measured in kilowatts.

The results are in the table.

Height of turbine (m)	Power output 1 (kW)	Power output 2 (kW)
32	162	139
40	192	195
50	223	219
60	248	245
70	278	270
80	302	304
85	315	312

a) What was the prediction for this test?

b) What was the independent variable?

c) What was the dependent variable?

d) What is the range of the heights for the turbine?

e) Suggest a control variable that should have been used.

f) This is a fieldwork investigation. Is it possible to control all of the variables? If not, say what you think the scientist should have done to produce more accurate results.

g) Is there any evidence for a random error in this investigation?

h) Was the sensitivity of the power output measurement satisfactory? Provide some evidence for your answer from the data in the table.

i) Draw a graph of the results for the second test.

j) Draw a line of best fit.

k) Describe the pattern in these results.

l) What conclusion can you make?

m) How might this data be of use to people who might want to stop a wind farm being built?

n) Who should carry out these tests for those who might object?

P1a | Energy and energy resources

Figure 1 North sea oil – our reserves of fossil fuels are running out

Figure 2 Renewable energy?

What you already know

Here is a quick reminder of previous work that you will find useful in this unit:

- Fuels store energy from the Sun.
  Coal, oil and natural gas are examples of **fossil fuels**. These fuels were formed over millions of years from dead plants and marine animals.

- We generate most of our electricity in power stations that burn fossil fuels. The Earth's reserves of fossil fuels will run out sooner or later.

- We can use renewable energy sources, such as wind, waves and running water, to generate electricity. Renewable energy sources never run out because they do not burn fuel.

Heat energy is transferred from high to low temperatures. Heat transfer takes place in three different ways:

1 **Conduction** happens in solids, liquids and gases.
   - Metals are good conductors of heat.
   - Gases and most other non-metals are poor conductors.
   - Poor conductors, such as glass, are called thermal insulators.

2 **Convection** only happens in liquids and gases.
   - The flow of the liquid or gas due to convection is called a **convection current**.
   - Convection is more important than conduction in liquids and gases.

3 *Radiation* is energy carried by waves.
   - The Sun radiates energy into space.
   - The Earth absorbs only a tiny fraction of the energy radiated by the Sun.
   - Plants need sunlight for photosynthesis.

RECAP QUESTIONS

1 a) Which fuels listed below are fossil fuels?

   coal   natural gas   hay   oil   wood

   b) List two renewable sources of energy that do not need water.

2 a) Which one of the following renewable energy resources does not depend on energy from the Sun?

   solar heating   tidal power
   wind power   wave power

   b) Which of the above renewable energy resources is most reliable? Explain your answer.

3 Complete the sentences below.

   a) Heat transfer in a solid is due to ....
   b) Heat transfer in a liquid is due to ...... and ....
   c) Heat transfer through a vacuum is due to ....

4 a) Why is natural gas not a renewable source of energy?
   b) Why is natural gas not suitable as a source of energy for road vehicles?
   c) Give two reasons why natural gas is a very suitable fuel for cooking?

Making connections

Energy for everyone

Life is great if you can get energy at the flick of a switch. Sadly, there are many people in poor countries who can't get energy as easily as we can. Better fuel supplies and electricity would improve their lives. Yet people like us in rich countries are using up the world's reserves of fuel. Will there be enough energy for everyone in the future? This module will give you some of the answers but will also raise more questions. Can everyone live like we do?

I like to have a good time with my friends. We like the bright lights and the buzz when we go out to town.

We're trying to develop cheaper and better solar cells. We could use these to supply electricity to people in remote areas.

I can't do without my car. I hate these petrol queues every time there's a petrol shortage. I blame the government.

I'm tired and hungry. I've had to walk miles to gather this wood. I need to get home because my family need it for cooking our meals. I wish we had electricity.

We need lots of renewable energy resources like wind to reduce global warming.

ACTIVITY

Working as a small group, put together a two-minute radio slot to make people think about the issues raised above. Choose someone to be the host of the programme and someone for each person in the pictures above. Give everyone the same amount of time to speak.

Chapters in this unit

○ Heat transfer   ○ Using energy   ○ Electrical energy   ○ Generating electricity

P1a 1.1   Thermal radiation

LEARNING OBJECTIVES

1 What is thermal radiation?
2 Do all objects give off thermal radiation?
3 How does it depend on the temperature of an object?

Figure 1 Keeping watch in darkness

Seeing in the dark

We can use special TV cameras to 'see' animals and people in the dark. These cameras detect thermal radiation. Every object gives out (emits) thermal radiation. The hotter an object is, the more thermal radiation it emits.

Look at the photo in Figure 1. The rhino is hotter than the ground.

a) Why is the water darker than the rhino?
b) Why is there an image of the rhino?

PRACTICAL

Detecting thermal radiation

You can use a thermometer with a blackened bulb to detect thermal radiation. Figure 2 shows how to do this.

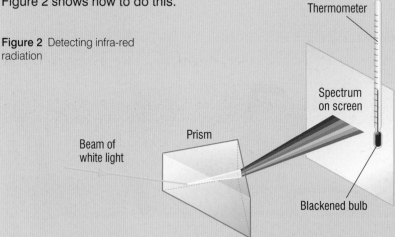

Figure 2 Detecting infra-red radiation

- The glass prism splits a narrow beam of light into the colours of the spectrum.
- The thermometer reading rises when it is placed just beyond the red part of the spectrum. Some of the thermal radiation in the beam goes there. Our eyes cannot detect it but the thermometer can.
- Thermal radiation is also called **infra-red radiation**. This is because it is beyond the red part of the visible spectrum.

● What would happen to the thermometer reading if the thermometer were moved away?

The electromagnetic spectrum

Radio waves, microwaves, infra-red radiation and visible light are part of the electromagnetic spectrum. So too are ultraviolet rays and X-rays. Electromagnetic waves are electric and magnetic waves that travel through space. You will learn more about electromagnetic waves on page 78.

Energy from the Sun

The Sun emits radiation in all parts of the electromagnetic spectrum. Fortunately for us, the Earth's atmosphere blocks most of the radiation, such as ultraviolet rays, that would harm us. But it doesn't block thermal radiation from the Sun.

Figure 3 shows a solar furnace. This is a giant reflector that focuses sunlight.

The temperature at the focus can reach thousands of degrees. That's almost as hot as the surface of the Sun, which is at 5500°C.

Figure 3 A solar furnace in the Eastern Pyrenees, France

The greenhouse effect

The Earth's atmosphere acts like a greenhouse made of glass. In a greenhouse, shorter wavelength radiation from the Sun can pass through the glass. However, longer wavelength thermal radiation is trapped inside by the glass. So the greenhouse stays warm.

Gases in the atmosphere, such as water vapour, methane and carbon dioxide, act like the glass. They trap the thermal radiation given off from the Earth. These gases make the Earth warmer than it would be if it had no atmosphere.

But the Earth is becoming too warm. If the polar ice caps melt, it will cause sea levels to rise. Cutting back our use of fossil fuels will help to reduce 'greenhouse gases'.

SUMMARY QUESTIONS

1 Complete the table to show if the object emits infra-red radiation or light or both.

Object	Infra-red	Light
A hot iron		
A light bulb		
A TV screen		
The Sun		

2 How can you tell if an electric iron is hot without touching it?

3 a) Explain why penguins huddle together to keep warm.
   b) Design an investigation to model the effect of penguins huddling together. You could use beakers of hot water to represent the penguins.

KEY POINTS

1 Thermal radiation is energy transfer by electromagnetic waves.
2 All objects emit thermal radiation.
3 The hotter an object is, the more thermal radiation it emits.

P1a 1.2   Surfaces and radiation

Figure 1 A thermal blanket in use

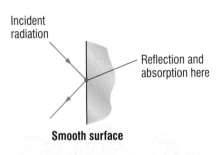

Smooth surface

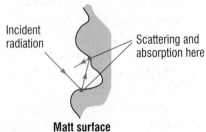

Matt surface

Figure 3 Absorbing infra-red radiation

Which surfaces are the best emitters of radiation?

Rescue teams use thermal blankets to keep accident survivors warm. A thermal blanket has a light, shiny outer surface. This emits much less radiation than a dark, matt surface. The colour and smoothness of a surface affects how much radiation it emits.

Dark, matt surfaces emit more radiation than light, shiny surfaces.

PRACTICAL

Testing different surfaces

To compare the radiation from two different surfaces, you can measure how fast two beakers (or cans) of hot water cool. One beaker needs to be wrapped with shiny metal foil and the other with matt black paper. Figure 2 shows the idea. At the start, the volume and temperature of the water in each beaker need to be the same.

- Why should the volume and temperature of the water be the same at the start?
- Which one will cool faster?

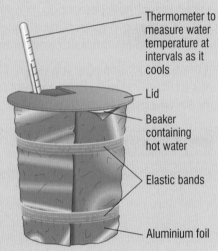

Thermometer to measure water temperature at intervals as it cools

Lid

Beaker containing hot water

Elastic bands

Aluminium foil

Figure 2 Testing different surfaces

Which surfaces are the best absorbers of radiation?

When you use a photocopier, why are the copies warm? This is because thermal radiation from a lamp dries the ink on the paper. Otherwise, the copies will be smudged. The black ink absorbs thermal radiation more easily than the white paper.

- A dark surface absorbs radiation better than a light surface.
- A matt surface absorbs radiation better than a shiny surface because it has lots of cavities. Look at Figure 3. It shows why these cavities trap and absorb the radiation.

Dark, matt surfaces absorb radiation better than light, shiny surfaces.

a) Why does ice on a road melt faster in sunshine if sand is sprinkled on it?
b) Why are solar panels painted matt black?

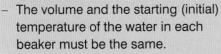

PRACTICAL

Absorption tests

To compare absorption by different surfaces, you can use identical beakers with cold water in. The beakers need to be coated with paint of different colours and different textures.

Figure 4 Testing absorbers

– The volume and the starting (initial) temperature of the water in each beaker must be the same.
– Place the beakers in a sunlit room in the sunlight.
– Use a thermometer to see which beaker warms up fastest.

● Why is it important to use the same volume of water in each beaker?
● Which beaker in Figure 4 do you think would warm up fastest? Give a reason for your answer.

SUMMARY QUESTIONS

1 Explain the following:

   a) Houses in hot countries are usually painted white.
   b) Solar heating panels are painted black.

2 A metal cube filled with hot water was used to compare the heat radiated from its four vertical faces, A, B, C and D.

   An infra-red sensor was placed opposite each face at the same distance, as shown in Figure 5. The sensors were connected to a computer. The results of the test are shown in the graph below.

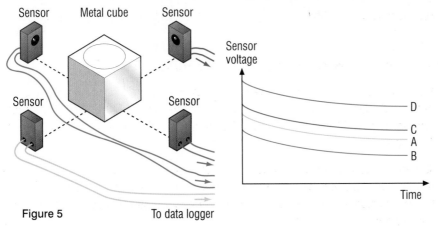

Figure 5   To data logger

   a) Why was it important for the distance from each sensor to the face to be the same?
   b) One face was silvery and shiny, one was silvery and matt, one was black and shiny and one was matt black.
      Which face A, B, C or D was i) silvery and shiny, ii) matt and black?
   c) Which face radiated i) most heat, ii) least heat?
   d) What are the advantages of using data logging equipment to collect the data in this investigation?

3 Explain any advantages and disadvantages of wearing black clothing in a hot country.

KEY POINTS

1 Dark matt surfaces are better emitters of thermal radiation than light shiny surfaces.
2 Dark matt surfaces are better absorbers of thermal radiation than light shiny surfaces.

P1a 1.3   Conduction

LEARNING OBJECTIVES

1   What materials make the best conductors and insulators?
2   Why are metals good conductors?
3   Why are non-metals poor conductors?

Figure 1 At a barbecue – the steel cooking utensils have wooden or plastic handles

Conductors and insulators

When you have a barbecue, you need to know which materials are good thermal conductors and which are good insulators. If you can't remember, you are likely to burn your fingers!

Testing rods of different materials as conductors

The rods need to be the same width and length for a fair test. Each rod is coated with a thin layer of wax near one end. The uncoated ends are then heated together.

Look at Figure 2.

The wax melts fastest on the rod that conducts heat best.

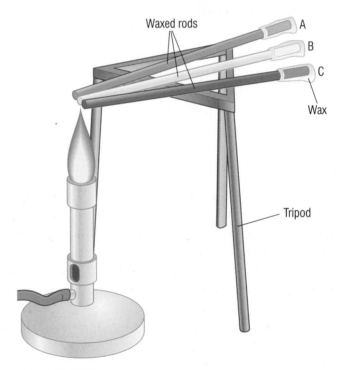

Figure 2 Comparing conductors

- Metals conduct heat better than non-metals.
- Copper is a better conductor of heat than steel.
- Wood conducts heat better than glass.

a) Why do steel pans have handles made of plastic or wood?
b) Name the independent and the dependent variables investigated in Figure 2. (See page 7.)

Testing sheets of materials as insulators

Use different materials to insulate identical cans (or beakers) of hot water. The volume of water and its temperature at the start should be the same. Use a thermometer to measure the water temperature after the same time. The results should tell you which insulator was best.

The table gives the results of comparing two different materials using the method above.

c) Which material, felt or paper, was the best thermal insulator?
d) Which variable shown in the table was controlled to make this a fair test?

Material	Starting temperature (°C)	Temperature after 300 s (°C)
paper	40	32
felt	40	36

Conduction in metals

Metals contain lots of **free electrons**. These electrons move about at random inside the metal and hold the positive ions together. They collide with each other and with the positive ions. (Ions are charged particles.)

(+) Ion
○ Electron
⚪ Atom

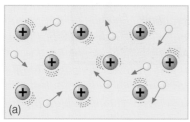
(a)

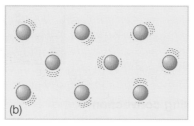
(b)

Figure 4 Energy transfer a) in a metal, b) in a non-metal

When a metal rod is heated at one end, the free electrons at the hot end gain kinetic energy and move faster.

● These electrons **diffuse** (i.e. spread out) and collide with other free electrons and ions in the cooler parts of the metal.
● As a result, they transfer kinetic energy to these electrons and ions.

So energy is transferred from the hot end of the rod to the colder end.

In a non-metallic solid, all the electrons are held in the atoms. Energy transfer only takes place because the atoms vibrate and shake each other. This is much less effective than energy transfer by free electrons. This is why metals are much better conductors than non-metals.

SUMMARY QUESTIONS

1 Choose the best insulator or conductor from the list for a), b) and c).

fibreglass   plastic   steel   wood

a) ...... is used to insulate a house loft.
b) The handle of a frying pan is made of ...... or ....
c) A radiator in a central heating system is made from ....

2 a) Choose a material you would use to line a pair of winter boots? Explain your choice of material.
b) How could you carry out a test on 3 different lining materials?

3 Explain why metals are good conductors of heat.

Materials like wool and fibreglass are good thermal insulators. This is because they contain air trapped between the fibres. Trapped air is a good insulator. We use insulators like fibreglass for loft insulation and for lagging water pipes.

Figure 3 Insulating a loft. The air trapped between fibres make fibreglass a good thermal insulator.

1 Conduction in a metal is due mainly to free electrons transferring energy inside the metal.
2 Non-metals are poor conductors because they do not contain free electrons.
3 Materials such as fibreglass are good insulators because they contain pockets of trapped air.

P1a 1.4   Convection

1 Where is convection important?
2 How does convection occur?
3 Why doesn't convection happen in solids?

Figure 1 A natural glider – birds use convection currents to soar high above the ground

Gliders and birds know how to use convection to stay in the air. Convection currents of warm air can keep them high above the ground for hours.

Convection happens whenever we heat **fluids**. A fluid is a gas or a liquid.

Look at the diagram in Figure 2. It shows a simple demonstration of convection.

The hot gases from the burning candle go straight up the chimney above the candle. Cold air is drawn down the other chimney to replace the air leaving the box.

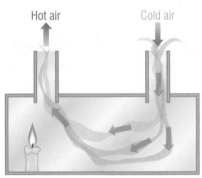

Hot air   Cold air

Figure 2 Convection

Using convection

(1) Hot water at home

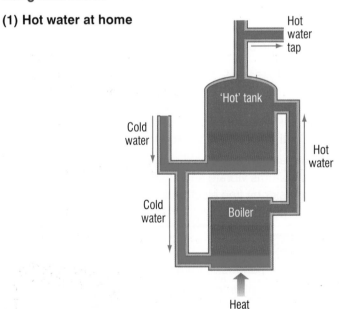

Hot water tap

'Hot' tank

Cold water

Hot water

Cold water

Boiler

Heat

Figure 3 Hot water at home

Most homes have a hot water tank. Hot water from the boiler rises and flows into the tank where it rises to the top. Figure 3 shows the system. When you use a hot water tap at home, you draw off hot water from the top of the tank.

a) What would happen if we connected the hot taps to the bottom of the tank?

(2) Sea breezes

Sea breezes keep you cool at the seaside. On a sunny day, the ground heats up faster than the sea. So the air above the ground warms up and rises. Cooler air from the sea flows in as a 'sea breeze' to take the place of the warm air.

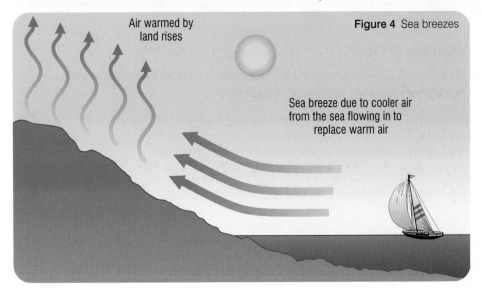

Air warmed by land rises

Figure 4 Sea breezes

Sea breeze due to cooler air from the sea flowing in to replace warm air

How convection works

Convection takes place:

- only in liquids and gases (i.e. fluids)
- due to circulation (convection) currents within the fluid.

The circulation currents are caused because fluids rise where they are heated (as heating makes them less dense). Then they fall where they cool down (as cooling makes them more dense). Convection currents transfer thermal energy from the hotter parts to the cooler parts.

So why do fluids rise when heated?

Most fluids expand when heated. This is because the particles move about more, taking up more space. Therefore the density decreases because the same mass of fluid occupies a bigger volume. So heating part of a fluid makes it less dense and it therefore rises.

GET IT RIGHT!

When you explain convection, remember it is the hot fluid that rises, NOT 'heat'.

SUMMARY QUESTIONS

1 Use each word from the list **once** only to complete the following sentences.

        cools   falls   mixes   rises

When a fluid is heated, it ...... and ...... with the rest of the fluid. The fluid circulates and ...... then it ....

2 Figure 5 shows a convector heater. It has an electric heating element inside and a metal grille on top.

  a) What does the heater do to the air inside the heater?

  b) Why is there a metal grille on top of the heater?

  c) Where does air flow into the heater?

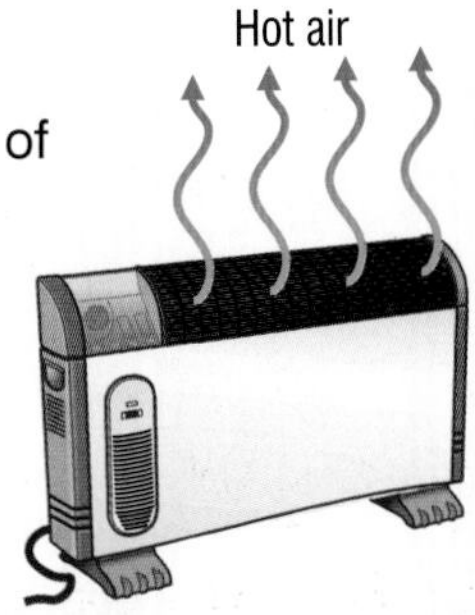

Hot air

Figure 5
A convector heater

3 Describe how you could demonstrate convection currents in water using a strongly coloured crystal. Explain in detail what you would see.

KEY POINTS

1 Convection takes place only in liquids and gases (fluids).
2 Heating a liquid or a gas makes it less dense.
3 Convection is due to a hot liquid or gas rising.

P1a 1.5 Heat transfer by design

LEARNING OBJECTIVES

1 What factors affect the rate of heat transfer from a hot object?
2 What can we do to keep things hot?
3 What can we do to cut down heat losses from a house?

Figure 1 A car radiator helps to transfer heat from the engine

PRACTICAL

Investigating heat transfer

Carry out investigations to find out:

- how the starting temperature of a hot object affects its rate of cooling
- how the size of a hot object affects how quickly it cools.

● Name the independent variable in each investigation. (See page 7.)
● What are your conclusions in each case?

Cooling by design

Lots of things can go wrong if we don't control heat transfer. For example, a car engine that overheats can go up in flames.

The cooling system of a car engine transfers thermal energy from the engine to a radiator. The radiator is flat so it has a large surface area. This increases heat loss through convection in the air and through radiation.

Most cars also have a cooling fan that switches on when the engine is too hot. This increases the flow of air over the surface of the radiator.

a) Why are car radiators painted black?
b) What happens to the rate of heat transfer when the cooling fan switches on?

The vacuum flask

If you are outdoors in cold weather, a hot drink from a vacuum flask keeps you warm. In the summer the same vacuum flask is great for keeping your drinks cold.

The liquid is in the double-walled glass container.

● The vacuum between the two walls of the container cuts out heat transfer by conduction and convection between the walls.
● Glass is a poor conductor so there is little heat conduction through the glass.
● The glass surfaces are silvery to reduce radiation from the outer wall.

c) List the other parts of the flask that are good insulators. What would happen if they weren't good insulators?

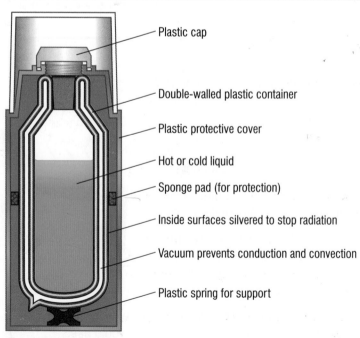

Plastic cap

Double-walled plastic container

Plastic protective cover

Hot or cold liquid

Sponge pad (for protection)

Inside surfaces silvered to stop radiation

Vacuum prevents conduction and convection

Plastic spring for support

Figure 2 A vacuum flask

Reducing heat losses at home

Home heating bills can be expensive. Figure 4 shows how we can reduce heat losses at home and cut our home heating bills.

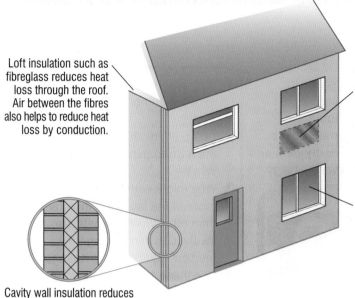

Loft insulation such as fibreglass reduces heat loss through the roof. Air between the fibres also helps to reduce heat loss by conduction.

Aluminium foil between a radiator panel and the wall reflects heat radiation away from the wall.

A double glazed window has two glass panes with dry air or a vacuum between the panes. Dry air is a good insulator so it cuts down heat conduction. A vacuum cuts out heat transfer by convection as well.

Cavity wall insulation reduces heat loss through the walls. We place insulation between the two layers of brick that make up the walls of a house.

Figure 4 Saving money

d) Why is cavity wall insulation better than air in the cavity between the walls of a house?

SUMMARY QUESTIONS

1 Hot water is pumped through a radiator like the one in Figure 5.

Complete the sentences below about the radiator.

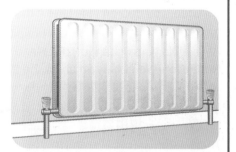

Figure 5 A central heating radiator

a) Heat transfer through the walls of the radiator is due to ....
b) Hot air in contact with the radiator causes heat transfer to the room by ....
c) Heat transfer to the room takes place directly due to ....

2 Some double-glazed windows have a plastic frame and a vacuum between the panes.

a) Why is a plastic frame better than a metal frame?
b) Why is a vacuum between the panes better than air?
c) Design a test to show that double glazing is more effective at preventing heat loss than single glazing.

3 Describe, in detail, how the design of a vacuum flask reduces the rate of thermal energy transfer.

KEY POINTS

1 A radiator has a large surface area so it can lose heat easily.
2 Small objects lose heat more easily than large objects.
3 Heat loss from a building can be reduced using:
   ● aluminium foil behind radiators.
   ● cavity wall insulation.
   ● double glazing.
   ● loft insulation.

P1a 1.6   Hot issues

Pay back time!

Cut your fuel bill!

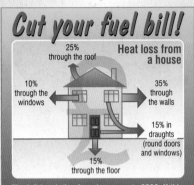

Heat loss from a house

25% through the roof

10% through the windows

35% through the walls

15% in draughts (round doors and windows)

15% through the floor

- The loft insulation for a house costs £200. If this saves £100 per year on the fuel bill, it would pay for itself after 2 years (**the pay-back time**).
- The cavity wall insulation for a house costs £600. If this saves £200 per year on the fuel bill, it would pay for itself after 3 years.

Figure 1 Heat loss from a house

ACTIVITIES

a) i) Figure 1 shows the heat losses from a house. Choose the two best ways to cut heat losses from this house.

ii) A double-glazed window costs £200. It saves £10 per year on the fuel bill. How long is the pay-back time?

b) Produce a poster to encourage people to save energy in the home.

c) What proportion of the cost of energy-saving measures should be paid by householders and by the government. Should grants be made available? Who should receive them? Discuss these issues in a small group and come up with a few suggestions for MPs to consider.

Thermal imaging

We use thermal scanners in hospitals to spot tumours just below the skin. Tumours are warmer than the normal tissue. So they warm the nearby skin and cause it to radiate more energy.

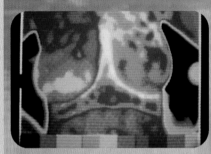

Figure 2 A thermal scan

QUESTIONS

1 Why are thermal scanners unable to detect tumours deep inside the body?

2 Do you think 'high-tech' devices are a good thing in hospitals? Why?

3 Why might some hospitals have more of the latest technology than others? What costs are involved in introducing new medical equipment to hospitals?

4 Use these questions to write a two-minute script for a slot for a weekly TV programme on medical issues.

Colourful chemicals

Imagine if objects changed colour when their temperature changed. A room could be a cool pale blue in summer and a warm shade of red in winter.

Engineers have developed **heat-smart paint** to show if a component gets too hot. The paint changes colour if its temperature goes above a certain level and stays that colour when it cools down. The change is not reversible. If it were, you couldn't tell later if the painted object got too hot.

We use **temperature strips** in hospitals, in industry and in food packaging. Reversible strips change colour and show the corresponding temperature. Non-reversible strips can show the highest or the lowest temperature.

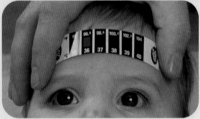

What about reversible heat-smart paints? Scientists in China have invented a reversible heat-smart paint that changes colour and helps to keep buildings warmer in winter and cooler in summer.

Figure 3 Temperature strips

QUESTIONS

5 What would be the best colour for the outside of a building
   a) in summer,   **b)** in winter?

6 What type of temperature strip, reversible or non-reversible, would you use:
   a) in a freezer at home,
   b) on an oven door to tell you if the oven is too hot?

Who am I?
A life-saving invention

I was already a famous scientist when I invented my lamp in 1813. My invention saved the lives of countless coal miners. Before my lamp, coal miners used candles to see underground. The candle flames often caused fatal accidents. They ignited pockets of methane gas, causing explosions in the mine.

As professor of chemistry at the Royal Institution in London, I made important discoveries about gases. I investigated flames and discovered that wire gauze could stop a flame spreading. The wire conducted heat away from the flame and lowered its temperature so the flame couldn't go through it.

QUESTIONS

7 a) What would happen if the gauze had a hole in it?

b) Why was it important to inspect a lamp before it was taken down a mine?

c) What replaced this lamp?

8 Do some research to find out more about the life of the above scientist. Present the main events as a series of bullet-pointed statements. Colour code those connected to his personal life and those connected to his work in science.

Sir Humphry Davy

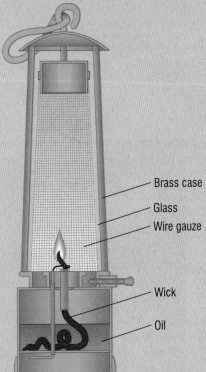

Figure 4 My lamp

Labels: Brass case, Glass, Wire gauze, Wick, Oil

Science and safety

TRAGEDY ON CAMPUS!

Two students were found dead in their flat yesterday. Police said they had been overcome by fumes from a poorly ventilated gas fire. A spokesman for the gas supplier warned anyone with a gas fire at home to make sure that the room is well-ventilated and that the gas fire is serviced regularly.

Gas heaters and boilers need good ventilation. Figure 5 shows how a gas heater works. Hot air and gases produced by the flames rise and escape to the outside through a ventilation duct. Colder air is drawn in at the bottom.

If the ventilation is poor, carbon monoxide gas is produced. As this is lethal to inhale, people can die as a result of poor ventilation. Gas heaters and boilers need servicing regularly.

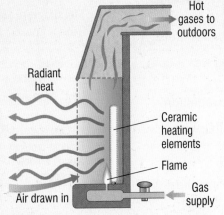

Figure 5 A gas heater

Labels: Hot gases to outdoors, Radiant heat, Ceramic heating elements, Flame, Gas supply, Air drawn in

ACTIVITY

Produce a leaflet to make people aware of the dangers of poorly-ventilated gas heaters and boilers. Make sure you include scientific information, explained so that most people will understand.

SUMMARY QUESTIONS

1 a) Why does a matt surface in sunshine get hotter than a shiny surface?

b) What type of surface is better for a flat roof – a matt dark surface or a smooth shiny surface? Explain your answer.

c) A solar heating panel is used to heat water. Why is its top surface painted matt black?

d) Why is a car radiator painted matt black?

2 Choose the correct word from the list for each of the four spaces in the sentences below.

collide   electrons   ions   vibrate

a) Heat transfer in a metal is due to particles called …… moving about freely inside the metal. They transfer energy when they …… with each other.

b) Heat transfer in a non-metallic solid is due to particles called …… inside the non-metal. They transfer energy because they …… .

3 A heat sink is a metal plate or clip fixed to an electronic component to stop it overheating.

a) When the component becomes hot, how does heat transfer from where it is in contact with the plate to the rest of the plate?

b) Why does the plate have a large surface area?

4 Complete each of the sentences using words from the list below.

conduction   convection   radiation

a) …… cannot happen in a solid or through a vacuum.

b) Heat transfer from the Sun is due to …… .

c) When a metal rod is heated at one end, heat transfer due to …… takes place in the rod.

d) …… is energy transfer by electromagnetic waves.

EXAM-STYLE QUESTIONS

1 The transfer of thermal energy through space from the Sun to the Earth is by

A Conduction

B Convection

C Condensation

D Radiation   (1)

2 Infra-red radiation is absorbed, reflected and emitted to different extents by different surfaces.
Which of the following statements best applies to **dark, matt** surfaces?

A They are good emitters of infra-red radiation.

B They are good reflectors of infra-red radiation.

C They are poor absorbers of infra-red radiation.

D They are poor emitters of infra-red radiation.   (1)

3 The diagram shows water being heated in a saucepan on a hotplate.
Match words from the list with the numbers **1** to **4** in the sentences.

A conduction

B convection

C radiation

D insulator

Heat energy is transferred through the base of the saucepan by ……**1**……

Heat energy is transferred through the water in the saucepan by ……**2**……

Some energy is transferred from the hotplate to the air by ……**3**……

The handle of the saucepan is made from wood because wood is a good ……**4**…….   (4)

4 The diagram shows some ways of reducing energy loss from a house.

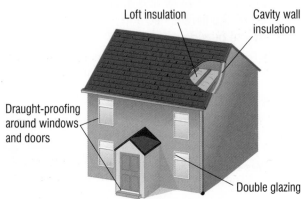

The table shows the cost of fitting, and the annual savings on energy bills, for different methods of reducing energy loss from a house.

Method of reducing energy loss	Cost of fitting	Annual saving
Cavity wall insulation	£800	£100
Double glazing	£4 000	£80
Draught proofing	£60	£60
Loft insulation	£300	£60

(a) Which method pays for itself in the shortest time?

    A cavity wall insulation   **B** double glazing

    C draught proofing   **D** loft insulation   (1)

(b) Which method reduces energy loss by the greatest amount?

    A cavity wall insulation   **B** double glazing

    C draught proofing   **D** loft insulation   (1)

(c) The time it takes for the saving on energy bills to equal the cost of installing the insulation is called the pay-back time. What is the pay-back time for loft insulation?

    A 1 year   **B** 2 years

    C 3 years   **D** 5 years   (1)

(d) Fitting double glazing reduces energy loss by . . .

    A conduction   **B** convection

    C evaporation   **D** radiation   (1)

5 A cook at a barbecue has baked some potatoes. He takes them off the barbecue.

(a) The hot potatoes radiate thermal energy. The amount of thermal energy radiated by a potato depends upon the nature of its surface. Name two other variables that affect the amount of thermal energy radiated by a potato.   (2)

(b) The cook wraps the hot potatoes in clean, shiny foil. Explain why.   (2)

(c) Explain what the difference would be if the cook wrapped the potatoes in black, dull foil.   (2)

(d) Suggest why:

    (i) the outside of the potatoes cooks before the inside.   (2)

    (ii) some cooks put metal skewers through the potatoes before they put them on the barbecue.   (2)

HOW SCIENCE WORKS QUESTIONS

Tamsin was asked to investigate how quickly different metals conducted heat. She was given four metal rods. They were made of brass, steel, iron and copper. She was told to stick pins to the metal rods, using a jelly that easily melted. She thought carefully about how to do the investigation. She decided to stick the pins to the metal rods and then heat the rods with a Bunsen burner. She would time how long it took for the pins to fall off.

Tamsin is going to need some help getting reliable and valid results.

a) How should she arrange these pins on the metal rods? Explain your ideas.   (2)

b) How should the pins be attached to the metal rods?   (1)

c) How should she heat the metal rods? She only has one Bunsen burner.   (1)

d) How could she make the results more accurate? Explain your ideas.   (2)

e) Tamsin will need a table to record her results. Produce a table for Tamsin.   (3)

f) What type of graph should Tamsin use to present her results?   (1)

g) Once Tamsin has had a go at the investigation, she suggests that you try it to see if you get the same results. How might this show the reliability of Tamsin's results?   (1)

h) In another lesson Tamsin investigated which of two materials was the better thermal insulator. She wrapped a copper beaker in each material, A and B, then filled the beaker with hot water. Here are her results:

Material	Temp. of water at start (°C)	Temp. of water after 10 minutes (°C)
A	91.8	72.3
B	79.3	70.8

She concluded that Material B is a better thermal insulator than Material A.

Comment on the validity of her conclusion drawn from this data.   (2)

P1a 2.1

Forms of energy

LEARNING OBJECTIVES

1 What forms of energy are there?
2 How can we describe energy changes?

On the move

Cars, buses, planes and ships all use energy from fuel. They carry their own fuel. Electric trains use energy from fuel in power stations. Electricity transfers energy from the power station to the train.

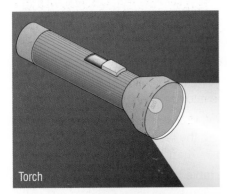
Torch

Skier

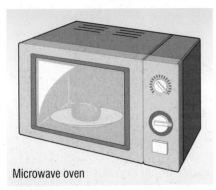
Microwave oven

Figure 2 Energy changes

Figure 1 The French TGV (Train à grande vitesse) electric train can reach speeds of more than 500 km/hour

We describe energy stored or transferred in different ways as *forms of energy*.

Here are some examples of forms of energy:

- *Chemical energy* is energy stored in fuel (including food). This energy is released when chemical reactions take place.
- *Kinetic energy* is the energy of a moving object.
- *Gravitational potential energy* is the energy of an object due to its position.
- *Elastic (or strain) energy* is the energy stored in a springy object when we stretch or squash it.
- *Electrical energy* is energy transferred by an electric current.
- *Thermal (heat) energy* of an object is energy due to its temperature. This is partly because of the random kinetic energy of the particles of the object.

a) What form of energy is supplied to the train in Figure 1?
b) What does TGV mean?

We say that energy is *transformed* when it changes from one form into another.

In the torch in Figure 2, the torch's battery pushes a current through the bulb. This makes the torch bulb emit light and it also gets hot. We can show the energy changes using a flow diagram.

Look at the example below:

chemical energy in the battery → electrical energy → light energy + thermal energy

c) What happens to the thermal energy of the torch bulb?

PRACTICAL

Energy changes

When an object starts to fall freely, it gains kinetic energy because it speeds up as it falls. So its gravitational potential energy changes to kinetic energy as it falls.

Look at Figure 3. It shows a box that hits the floor with a thud. All of its kinetic energy changes to heat and sound energy at the point of impact. The proportion of kinetic energy transformed to sound is much smaller than that changed to heat.

● Draw an energy flow diagram to show the changes in Figure 3.

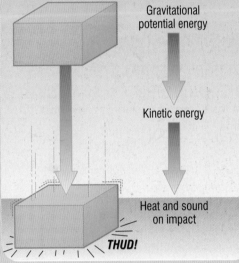

Gravitational potential energy

Kinetic energy

Heat and sound on impact

THUD!

Figure 3 An energetic drop

SCIENCE @ WORK

Tall buildings need firm foundations. Engineers make the foundations using a pile driver to hammer steel girders end-on into the ground. The pile driver lifts a heavy steel block above the top end of the girder. Then it lets the block crash down onto the girder. The engineers keep doing this until the bottom end of the girder reaches solid rock.

Figure 4 A pile driver in action

d) Where does the energy supplied to the hammer come from?

NEXT TIME YOU...

... ride a bike, think about what happens to the chemical energy stored in your body as you ride along. But make sure you watch where you're going!

SUMMARY QUESTIONS

1 Copy and complete a) and b) using the words below:

electric   kinetic   gravitational potential   thermal

a) When a ball falls in air, it loses ...... energy and gains ...... energy.
b) When an electric heater is switched on, it changes ...... energy into ...... energy.

2 a) List two different objects you could use to light a room if you have a power cut. For each object, describe the energy changes that happen when it produces light.
   b) Which of the two objects in a) is:
      i) easier to obtain energy from,
      ii) easier to use?

3 Read the 'Science @ Work' box at the top of this page.
   Explain the energy changes involved in using a pile driver.

KEY POINTS

1 Energy exists in different forms.
2 Energy can change (transform) from one form into another form.

P1a 2.2   Conservation of energy

LEARNING OBJECTIVES

1 What energy changes happen on a roller coaster ride?
2 What do we mean by 'conservation of energy'?
3 Why is conservation of energy a very important idea?

At the fun-fair

Fun-fairs are very exciting places because lots of energy changes happen quickly. A roller coaster gains gravitational potential energy when it climbs. Then it loses gravitational potential energy when it races downwards.

As it descends:

its gravitational potential energy $\rightarrow$ kinetic energy + sound + thermal energy due to air resistance and friction

a) When a roller coaster gets to the bottom of a descent, what energy transformations happen if:
   i) we apply the brakes to stop it?
   ii) it goes up and over a second 'hill'?

Figure 1 On a roller coaster – having fun with energy transformations!

PRACTICAL

Investigating energy changes

When energy changes happen, does the total amount of energy stay the same? We can investigate this question with a simple pendulum.

Figure 2 shows a pendulum bob swinging from side to side.

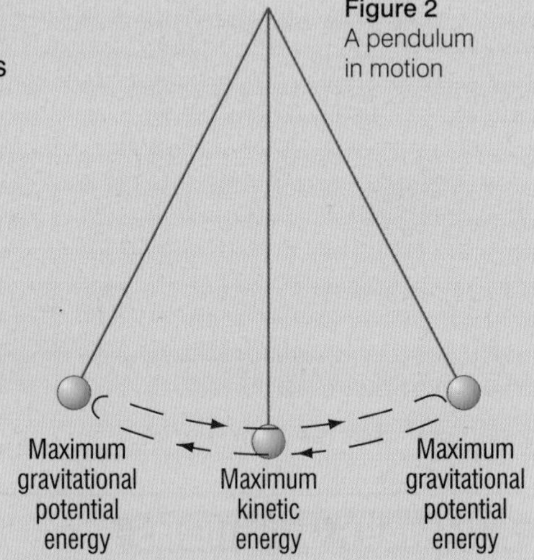

Figure 2
A pendulum in motion

Maximum gravitational potential energy | Maximum kinetic energy | Maximum gravitational potential energy

- As it moves towards the middle, its gravitational potential energy changes to kinetic energy.
- As it moves away from the middle, its kinetic energy changes back to gravitational potential energy. You should find that the bob reaches the same height on each side.
- What does this tell you about the energy of the bob at its maximum height on each side?
- Why is it difficult to mark the exact height the pendulum bob rises to? How could you make your judgement more accurate?

Conservation of energy

Scientists have done lots of tests to find out if the total energy after a change is the same as the energy before the change. All the tests so far show it is the same.

This important result is known as the **conservation of energy**.

It tells us that **energy cannot be created or destroyed.**

Bungee jumping

What energy changes happen to a bungee jumper after jumping off the platform?

- Some of the gravitational potential energy of the bungee jumper changes to kinetic energy as the jumper falls with the rope slack.
- Once the slack in the rope has been used up, the rope slows the bungee jumper's fall. Most of the gravitational potential energy and kinetic energy of the jumper is changed into elastic (strain) energy.
- After reaching the bottom, the rope pulls the jumper back up. As the jumper rises, most of the elastic (strain) energy of the rope changes back to gravitational potential energy and kinetic energy of the jumper.

The bungee jumper doesn't return to the same height as at the start. This is because some of the initial gravitational potential energy has been changed to heat energy as the rope stretched then shortened again.

Figure 3 Bungee jumping

b) What happens to the gravitational potential energy lost by the bungee jumper?
c) Draw a flow diagram to show the energy changes.

PRACTICAL

Bungee jumping

You can try out the ideas about bungee jumping using the experiment shown in Figure 4.

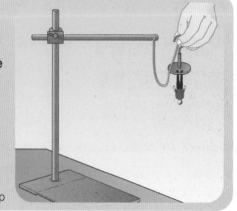

Figure 4 Testing a bungee jump

SUMMARY QUESTIONS

1 a) Complete the sentences below using the words below (one option is used twice):

   electrical   gravitational potential   thermal

   A person going up in a lift gains …… energy. The lift is driven by electric motors. Some of the …… energy supplied to the motors is changed to …… energy instead of …… energy.

2 a) A ball dropped onto a trampoline returns to the same height after it bounces. Describe the energy change of the ball from the point of release to the top of its bounce.
   b) What can you say about the energy of the ball at the point of release compared with at the top of its bounce?
   c) You could use the test above to see which of three trampolines was the bounciest.
      i) Name the independent variable in this test. (See page 7.)
      ii) Is this variable categoric, discrete or continuous? (See page 4.)

3 One exciting fairground ride acts like a giant catapult. The capsule, in which you are strapped, is fired high into the sky by rubber straps. Explain the energy changes taking place in the ride.

KEY POINTS

1 Energy can be transformed from one form to another or transferred from one place to another.
2 Energy cannot be created or destroyed.

P1a 2.3   Useful energy

LEARNING OBJECTIVES

1 What do we mean by 'useful' energy?
2 What causes some energy to be 'wasted'?
3 What eventually happens to wasted energy?

Figure 1 Using energy

Energy for a purpose

Where would we be without machines? We use washing machines at home. We use machines in factories to make the goods we buy. We use them in the gym to keep fit and we use them to get us from place to place.

a) What happens to all the energy you use in a gym?

A machine transfers energy for a purpose. Friction between the moving parts of a machine causes the parts to warm up. So not all of the energy supplied to a machine is usefully transferred. Some energy is wasted.

- **Useful energy** is energy transferred to where it is wanted in the form it is wanted.
- **Wasted energy** is energy that is not usefully transferred or transformed.

b) What happens to the kinetic energy of a machine when it stops?

PRACTICAL

Investigating friction

Friction in machines always causes energy to be wasted. Figure 2 shows two examples of friction in action. Try one of them out.

- In **A**, friction acts between the drill bit and the wood. The bit becomes hot as it bores into the wood. Some of the electrical energy supplied to the bit changes into thermal energy of the drill bit (and the wood).
- In **B**, when the brakes are applied, friction acts between the brake blocks and the wheel. This slows the bicycle and the cyclist down. Some of the kinetic energy of the bicycle and the cyclist changes into thermal energy of the brake blocks (and the bicycle wheel).

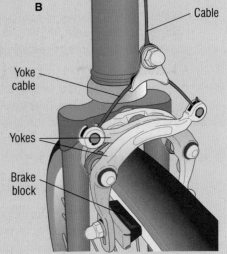

Figure 2 Friction in action. A) Using a drill, B) braking.

Figure 3 Disc brakes

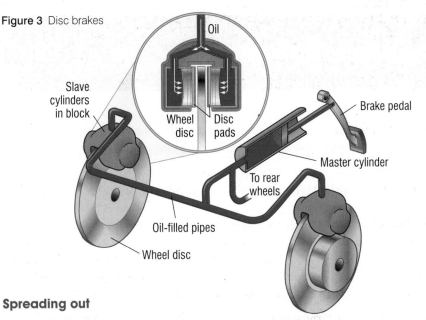

NEXT TIME YOU...

... are in a car slowing down at traffic lights, think about what is making the car stop. Figure 3 shows how the disc brakes of a car work. When the brakes are applied, the pads are pushed onto the disc in each wheel. Friction between the pads and each disc slows the wheel down. Some of the kinetic energy of the car changes into thermal energy of the disc pads and the discs.

Spreading out

- Wasted energy spreads out to the surroundings.
  For example, the gears of a car get hot when the car is running. So thermal energy transfers from the gear box to the surrounding air.

- Useful energy eventually transfers to the surroundings too.
  For example, the useful energy supplied to the road wheels of a car changes into thermal energy of the tyres, the road and the surrounding air.

- Energy becomes less useful, the more it spreads out.
  For example, the hot water from the cooling system of a CHP (combined heat and power) power station gets used to heat nearby buildings. The thermal energy supplied to the buildings will eventually be lost to the surroundings.

c) The hot water from many power stations flows into rivers or lakes. Why is this wasteful?

Figure 4 Energy spreading out

SUMMARY QUESTIONS

1 Copy and complete the table below. It should show what happens to the energy transferred in each case.

Energy transfer by	Useful energy	Wasted energy
a) an electric heater		
b) a television		
c) an electric kettle		
d) headphones		

2 What would happen to:

   a) a gear box that was insulated so it could not lose thermal energy to the surroundings?
   b) a jogger wearing running shoes, which are well-insulated?
   c) a blunt electric drill if you use it to drill into hard wood?

3 Explain why a swinging pendulum eventually stops.

KEY POINTS

1 Useful energy is energy in the place we want it and in the form we need it.
2 Wasted energy is energy that is not useful energy.
3 Useful energy and wasted energy both end up being transferred to the surroundings, which become warmer.
4 As energy spreads out, it gets more and more difficult to use for further energy transfers.

P1a 2.4   Energy and efficiency

LEARNING OBJECTIVES

1 What do we mean by efficiency?
2 How can we make machines more efficient?

When you lift an object, the useful energy from your muscles goes to the object as gravitational potential energy. This depends on its weight and how high it is raised.

- Weight is measured in **newtons (N)**. The weight of a 1 kilogram object on the Earth's surface is about 10 N.
- Energy is measured in **joules (J)**. The energy needed to lift a weight of 1 N by a height of 1 metre is equal to 1 joule.

Your muscles get warm when you use them so they must waste some energy.

a) You lower a weight. What happens to its gravitational potential energy?

Figure 1 represents the energy transfer through a device. It shows how we can represent any energy transfer where energy is wasted. This type of diagram is called a **Sankey diagram**.

Because energy cannot be created or destroyed,

energy supplied = useful energy delivered + energy wasted

For any device that transfers energy,

$$\text{efficiency} = \frac{\text{useful energy transferred by the device}}{\text{total energy supplied to the device}}$$

For example, a light bulb with an efficiency of 0.15 would radiate 15 J of energy as light for every 100 J of electrical energy we supply to it.

The percentage efficiency of the light bulb is 15% (= 0.15 × 100%).

b) How much energy is wasted for every 100 J of electrical energy supplied?
c) What happens to the wasted energy?

Energy transfer per second INTO machine

MACHINE OR APPLIANCE

Energy wasted per second

Useful energy transfer per second OUT of machine

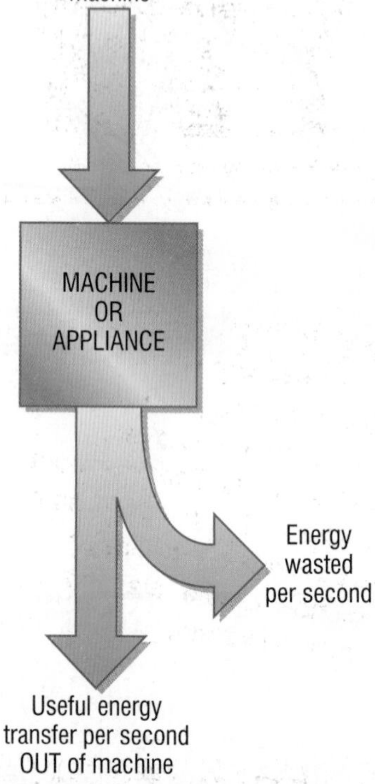

Figure 1 Energy transfer shown on a Sankey diagram

Worked example

An electric motor is used to raise an object. The object gains 60 J of gravitational potential energy when the motor is supplied with 200 J of electrical energy. Calculate the efficiency of the motor.

Solution

Total energy supplied to the device = 200 J

Useful energy transferred by the device = 60 J

$$\text{Efficiency of the motor} = \frac{\text{useful energy transferred by the motor}}{\text{total energy supplied to the motor}}$$

$$= \frac{60 \text{ J}}{200 \text{ J}} = 0.30$$

PRACTICAL

Investigating efficiency

Figure 3 shows how you can use an electric winch to raise a weight. You can use the joulemeter to measure the electrical energy supplied.

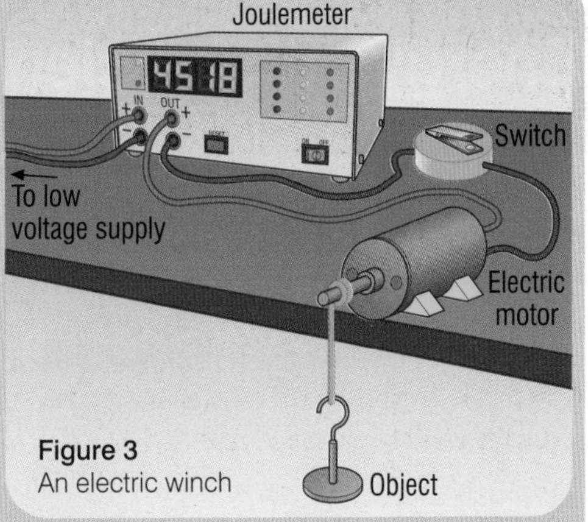

– If you double the weight for the same increase in height, do you need to supply twice as much electrical energy to do this task?

– The gravitational potential energy gained by the weight = weight in newtons × height increase in metres

● Use this equation and the joulemeter measurements to work out the efficiency of the winch.

Figure 3 An electric winch

Joulemeter, Switch, Electric motor, To low voltage supply, Object

Improving efficiency

	Why machines waste energy	How to reduce the problem
1	Friction between the moving parts causes heating.	Lubricate the moving parts to reduce friction.
2	The resistance of a wire causes the wire to get hot when a current passes through it.	Use wires in circuits with as little electrical resistance as possible.
3	Air resistance causes energy transfer to the surroundings.	Streamline the shapes of moving objects to reduce air resistance.
4	Sound created by machinery causes energy transfer to the surroundings.	Cut out noise (e.g. tighten loose parts to reduce vibration).

d) Which of the above solutions would not reduce the energy supplied?

SUMMARY QUESTIONS

1 Complete the sentences below using words from the list.

supplied to   wasted by

a) The useful energy from a machine is always less than the total energy …… it.

b) Friction between the moving parts of a machine causes energy to be …… the machine.

c) Because energy is conserved, the energy …… a machine is the sum of the useful energy from the machine and the energy …… by the machine.

2 An electric motor is used to raise a weight. When you supply 60 J of electrical energy to the motor, the weight gains 24 J of gravitational potential energy.
Work out:
a) the energy wasted by the motor,
b) the efficiency of the motor.

3 A machine is 25% efficient. If the total energy supplied to the machine is 3200 J, how much useful energy can be transferred?

DID YOU KNOW?

No machine can be more than 100% efficient because we can never get more energy from a machine than we put into it. An inventor in 19th century America showed off a machine he said gave out useful energy without any energy being supplied to it. He was found out when an accomplice was discovered pedalling away under the machine!

Figure 2 Energy from nowhere?

GET IT RIGHT!

Efficiency and percentage efficiency are numbers without units. The maximum efficiency is 1 or 100%, so if a calculation produces a number greater than this it must be wrong.

KEY POINTS

1 Energy is measured in joules.

2 The efficiency of a device =
$$\frac{\text{useful energy transferred by the device}}{\text{total energy supplied to the device}}$$

3 Wasted energy causes inefficiency.

P1a 2.5   Energy and efficiency issues

Walk to and from school or 'car share'?

People in poor countries want more energy to raise their standard of living. People like us in rich countries use much more energy than people in poor countries. What can we do to help them?

Switch things off when they are not in use?

Ideas about energy

Recycle materials more?

The bouncy ball test

Release a ball above a hard floor and see if it rebounds to the same height. Repeat your measurements as often as necessary.

If the ball does bounce back to the same height, it hasn't lost any energy.

What if it doesn't? Some of its energy must have changed to sound and heat energy when it hit the floor.

Figure 1 A bouncy test

A BURNING ISSUE!
By Jack Daniels

– row over Council plans causes chaos

Last night's Council meeting had to be abandoned when protestors objected to plans for a local incinerator.

The Council want to use it to burn waste paper and to heat their buildings. Nearby residents claim it will produce smoke and noise 24 hours a day and will ruin their lives.

A Council officer said 'Money will be saved on fuel bills. We can't let protestors tell us what to do.'

MORE ON PAGE 2

QUESTIONS

1 a) Compare the rebound height with the original height.
  b) Use the comparison to work out what fraction of the initial gravitational potential energy is lost in the impact.
2 How could you check the accuracy of your measurements?
3 Comment on the reliability of your measurements. (See page 3.)
4 List the variables that might affect your answer to 1b) in other tests. Label each variable as categoric, discrete or continuous. (See page 4.)
5 Comment on the conclusion drawn in 1b). Is it a powerful generalisation? Or does it have limitations? How would you extend the investigation given time?

James Joule VIP!

The unit of energy is named after James Joule. In 1840, he found he could heat water by making a falling weight turn a paddle in the water.

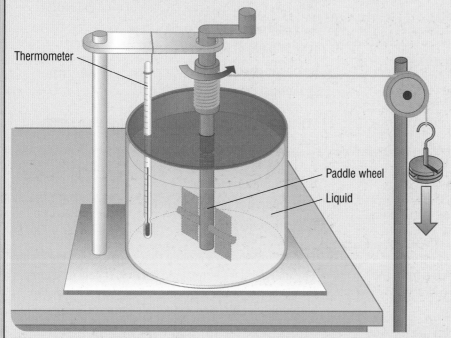

Thermometer

Paddle wheel

Liquid

Figure 2 Heating water

Figure 3
James Joule

The water gains thermal energy and the weight loses gravitational potential energy. Joule showed that the water gained the same amount of energy as the weight lost. He had discovered a very important principle:

Energy cannot be created or destroyed.

He repeated his tests with different weights and liquids and reached the same conclusion in each experiment. He realised that the total amount of energy is unchanged every time.

Hybrid cars

I have a petrol engine and a battery-powered motor. I use less fuel than you and in slow traffic the petrol engine switches off and the motor takes over. When I accelerate, the engine switches on again. Mine is the best car!

But you can't go far without recharging and you're too slow!

My car doesn't use petrol so it doesn't cause fumes. It's also really quiet!

SUMMARY QUESTIONS

1 The devices listed below transfer energy in different ways.

1. Car engine   2. Electric bell
3. Electric light bulb   4. Gas heater

The next list gives the useful form of energy the devices are designed to produce.

Match words A, B, C and D with the devices numbered 1 to 4.

A Heat (thermal energy)   B Light
C Movement (kinetic energy)   D Sound

2 Use words from the list to complete the sentences:

useful   wasted   thermal   light   electrical

When a light bulb is switched on, ... energy is changed into ...... energy and into ...... energy of the surroundings. The energy that radiates from the light bulb is ...... energy. The rest of the energy supplied to the light bulb is ...... energy.

3 You can use an electric motor to raise a load. In a test, you supply the winch with 10 000 J of electrical energy and the load gains 1500 J of gravitational potential energy.

a) Calculate its efficiency.

b) How much energy is wasted?

c) Copy and complete the energy transfer diagram below for the winch.

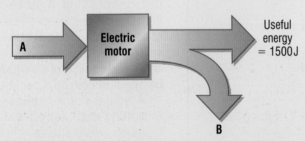

4 A ball gains 4.0 J of gravitational potential energy when it is raised to a height of 2.0 m above the ground. When it is released, it rebounds to a height of 1.5 m.

a) How much kinetic energy did it have just before it hit the ground? Assume air resistance is negligible.

b) How much gravitational potential energy did it have at the top of the rebound?

c) How much energy did it lose in the rebound?

d) What happened to the energy it lost on impact?

EXAM-STYLE QUESTIONS

1 On a building site a machine is used to lift a bag of sand from the ground to the top of a building.
What type of energy has the bag of sand gained?

A elastic potential energy

B gravitational potential energy

C kinetic energy

D thermal energy   (1)

2 What type of energy is stored in a stretched rubber band?

A chemical energy

B elastic strain energy

C gravitational potential energy

D kinetic energy   (1)

3 The picture shows a mobile that hangs over a baby's cot. The mobile plays a tune and rotates. It gets its energy from a battery. The electrical energy supplied by the battery is transformed into other forms of energy.

Match words from the list with the numbers **1** to **4** in the sentences.

A kinetic energy

B light

C sound

D thermal energy

A motor makes the mobile go round. The motor transforms electrical energy mainly into ......**1**....... When the mobile is switched on it becomes warm after a short while. This is because some of the electrical energy is transformed into ......**2**...... Speakers in the mobile transform electrical energy into ......**3**...... There is a 'power on' indicator on the mobile that transforms electrical energy into ......**4**...... .   (4)

4 An electric fan is used to move air around a room.

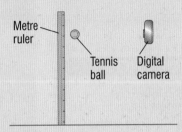

(a) The fan **usefully** transforms electrical energy into

   A elastic energy

   B heat energy

   C kinetic energy

   D sound (1)

(b) Energy that is not usefully transformed by the fan is **wasted** as

   A heat energy and sound

   B heat energy only

   C kinetic energy and sound

   D sound energy only (1)

(c) Which of the following statements about the energy wasted by the fan is **not** true?

   A It makes the surroundings warmer.

   B It can no longer be transformed in useful ways.

   C It becomes very thinly spread out.

   D It makes the surroundings cooler. (1)

(d) A second design of fan transforms useful energy at the same rate but wastes less of the energy supplied to it. This means that the second fan

   A is 100% efficient.   B is less efficient.

   C is more efficient.   D has the same efficiency. (1)

5 A chair lift carries skiers to the top of a mountain.

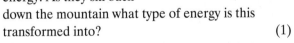

(a) When the skiers get to the top of the mountain they have gained gravitational potential energy. As they ski back down the mountain what type of energy is this transformed into? (1)

(b) The chair lift is powered by an electric motor. What useful energy transformation takes place in the motor? (2)

(c) Some of the electrical energy supplied to the motor is wasted as heat. Why does this happen? (1)

(d) The energy required to lift two skiers to the top of the mountain is 240 000 J. The energy supplied to the motor is 800 000 J. Calculate the efficiency of the motor. (2)

Whilst watching a tennis match I wondered why, when they asked for a new set of balls, they were fetched from a fridge. Could it be that they behave differently when they are hot? I decided to test this idea and set up a controlled investigation.

The tennis balls were heated to different temperatures and then dropped from the same height. I used a digital camera to photograph the bounce so that I could get an accurate reading of how high each ball bounced.

My prediction was that as the temperature increased the ball would bounce higher.

My results, and the manufacturer's results, are in this table.

Temperature (°C)	Height bounced (cm)	
	My results	Manufacturer's
3	11.0	14.0
10	37.3	40.5
19	53.9	57.1
29	64.1	67.0
40	70.2	73.4
51	74.5	77.5
60	74.3	79.3

a) Plot a graph of my results, including a line of best fit. (3)

b) What is the sensitivity of the instrument used to measure the height of the bounce? (1)

c) What is the pattern in the results? (2)

d) What do these results suggest about my prediction? (1)

e) Is there any evidence for a random error in my investigation? Explain your answer. (2)

f) Is there any evidence for a systematic error in my investigation? Explain your answer. (2)

g) What is the importance of these results to the professional tennis player? (1)

P1a 3.1 Electrical devices

LEARNING OBJECTIVES

1 Why are electrical devices so useful?
2 What energy transformations take place in everyday electrical devices?
3 How do we choose an electrical device for a particular job?

DID YOU KNOW?

People without electricity supplies can now listen to radio programmes – thanks to the British inventor Trevor Bayliss. In 1999, he invented the clockwork radio and patented it. When you turn a handle on the radio, you wind up a clockwork spring in the radio. When the spring unwinds, it turns a small electric generator in the radio. It doesn't need batteries or mains electricity. Clockwork radios are now mass-produced and sold all over the world.

Figure 2 A clockwork radio

- What form of energy is stored in the spring of the clockwork radio when you wind it up?
- What happens to this energy when the spring unwinds?

Everyday electrical devices

We use electrical devices every day. They change electrical energy into useful energy at the flick of a switch. Some of the electrical energy we supply to them is wasted.

Figure 1 Electrical devices – how many can you see in this photo?

Device	Useful energy	Energy wasted
Light bulb	Light from the glowing filament.	Heat transfer from the filament to surroundings.
Electric heater	Thermal energy of the surroundings.	Light from the glowing element.
Electric toaster	Thermal energy of bread.	Thermal energy of the toaster case and the air around it.
Electric kettle	Thermal energy of water.	Thermal energy of the kettle itself.
Hairdryer	Kinetic energy of the air driven by the fan. Thermal energy of air flowing past the heater filament.	Sound of fan motor (thermal energy of the motor heats the air going past it, so is not wasted). Thermal energy of the hairdryer itself.
Electric motor	Kinetic energy of object driven by the motor. Potential energy of objects lifted by the motor.	Thermal energy and sound energy of the motor.
Personal stereo	Kinetic energy of the motor. Sound.	Thermal energy of the motor
Computer disc drive	Energy stored in magnetic dots on the disc.	Thermal energy and sound energy of the motor that drives the disc.

PRACTICAL

Energy transformations

Carry out a survey of electrical devices you find at school or at home.

● Record the useful and wasted energy transformations of each device.

a) What energy transformations happen in an electric toothbrush?

Choosing an electrical device

Figure 4 On stage

We use electrical devices for many purposes. For example, suppose you were a rock musician at a concert. You would need devices that change sound energy into electrical energy and then back into sound energy. See if you can spot some of these devices in Figure 4.

b) What electrical device changes
  i) sound energy into electrical energy?
  ii) electrical energy into sound energy?
c) What other electrical device would you need?

SUMMARY QUESTIONS

1 Copy and complete using the words below:

electrical   light   thermal

When a battery is connected to a light bulb, …… energy is transferred from the battery to the light bulb. The filament of the light bulb becomes hot and transfers …… energy to its surroundings as well as …… energy.

2 Match each electrical device in the list below with the energy transfer A, B or C it is designed to bring about.

1. Electric drill   3. Electric oven
2. Food mixer   4. Electric bell

Energy transfer   A   Electrical energy   →   heat
                    B   Electrical energy   →   sound
                    C   Electrical energy   →   movement

KEY POINTS

1 Electrical energy is energy transfer due to an electric current.
2 Uses of electrical devices include heating, lighting, making objects move (using an electric motor) and creating sound and visual images.

P1a 3.2

Electrical power

LEARNING OBJECTIVES

1 What do we mean by power?
2 What are the units of power?
3 How can we calculate the power of a device?

Powerful machines

When you use a lift to go up, a powerful electric motor pulls you and the lift upwards. The lift motor transforms energy from electrical energy to gravitational potential energy when the lift is raised. We also get electrical energy transformed to wasted thermal energy and sound energy.

- The energy we supply per second to the motor is the **power** supplied to it.
- The more powerful the lift motor is, the faster it is able to move a particular load.

Figure 1 A lift motor

In general we can say that:

the more powerful a device, the faster the rate at which it transforms energy.

We measure the power of a device in watts (W) or kilowatts (kW).

For any device,

- its input power is the energy per second supplied to it.
- its output power is the useful energy per second transferred by it.

1 watt is a rate of transfer of energy of 1 joule per second (J/s).

1 kilowatt is equal to 1000 watts.

Power (in watts, W) = rate of transfer of energy

$$= \frac{\text{energy transferred (in joules, J)}}{\text{time taken (in seconds, s)}}$$

Worked example

A motor transfers 10 000 J of energy in 25 s. What is its power?

Solution

Power (in watts, W) $= \dfrac{\text{energy transferred (in joules, J)}}{\text{time taken (in seconds, s)}}$

Power $= \dfrac{10\,000\,\text{J}}{25\,\text{s}} = 400\,\text{W}$

NEXT TIME YOU...

... see the Sun set, think of all you could do with its almost unlimited power!

a) What is the power of a lift motor that transfers 50 000 J of energy from the electricity supply in 10 s?

Power ratings

Here are some typical values of power ratings for different energy transfer 'devices':

Device	Power rating
A torch	1 W
An electric light bulb	100 W
An electric cooker	10 000 W = 10 kW (where 1 kW = 1000 watts)
A railway engine	1 000 000 W = 1 megawatt (MW) = 1 million watts
A Saturn V rocket	100 MW
A very large power station	10 000 MW
World demand for power	10 000 000 MW
The Sun	100 000 000 000 000 000 000 MW

Figure 2 Rocket power

b) How many 100 W electric light bulbs would use the same amount of power as a 10 kW electric cooker?

Muscle power

How powerful is a weight lifter?

A 30 kg dumbell has a weight of 300 N. Raising it by 1 m would give it 300 J of gravitational potential energy. A weight lifter could lift it in about 0.5 seconds. The rate of energy transformation would be 600 J/s (= 300 J/0.5 s). So the weight lifter's power output would be about 600 W in total!

c) An inventor has designed an exercise machine that can also generate 100 W of electrical power. Do you think people would buy this machine in case of a power cut?

Figure 3 Muscle power

SUMMARY QUESTIONS

1 a) Which is more powerful?
     ii) A torch bulb or a mains filament lamp.
     iii) A 3 kW electric kettle or a 10 000 W electric cooker.
   b) There are about 20 million homes in Britain. If a 3 kW electric kettle was switched on in 1 in 10 homes at the same time, how much power would need to be supplied?

2 The input power of a lift motor is 5000 W. In a test, it transforms 12 000 J of electrical energy to gravitational potential energy in 20 seconds.

   a) How much electrical energy is supplied to the motor?
   b) What is its efficiency in the test?

3 Choose one of the energy transfer devices listed at the top of this page. Carry out some research and describe how it works.

4 A machine has a power rating of 100 kW. If the machine runs for 2 minutes, how much energy does it transfer?

KEY POINTS

1 The unit of power is the watt (W), equal to 1 J/s.
2 1 kilowatt (kW) = 1000 watts
3 Power (in watts) =

$$\frac{\text{energy transferred (in joules)}}{\text{time taken (in seconds)}}$$

P1a 3.3 Using electrical energy

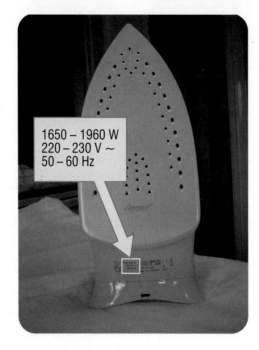

1650 – 1960 W
220 – 230 V ~
50 – 60 Hz

Figure 1 Mains power

GET IT RIGHT!

Remember that a kilowatt-hour (kW h) is a unit of energy.

How much electrical energy is transferred from the mains when you use an electric heater? You can work this out if you know its power and how long you use it for.

A 1 kW heater uses the same amount of electrical energy in 1 hour as a 2 kW heater would use in half-an-hour. For ease, we say that:

the energy supplied to a 1 kW device in 1 hour is **1 kilowatt-hour (kW h)**.

We use the kilowatt-hour as the unit of energy supplied by mains electricity. You can work out the energy, in kilowatt-hours, used by a mains device in a certain time using this equation:

$$\text{Energy transferred (kilowatt-hours, kW h)} = \text{power of device (kilowatts, kW)} \times \text{time in use (hours, h)}$$

For example,

- a 1 kW heater switched on for 1 hour uses 1 kW h of electrical energy (= 1 kW × 1 hour).
- a 1 kW heater switched on for 10 hours uses 10 kW h of electrical energy (= 10 kW × 1 hour).
- a 0.5 kW heater switched on for 6 hours uses 3 kW h of electrical energy (= 0.5 kW × 6 hours).

a) How many kW h are used by a 100 W lamp in 24 hours?

How many joules are there in 1 kilowatt-hour?

One kilowatt-hour is the amount of electrical energy supplied to a 1 kilowatt device in 1 hour. So 1 kilowatt-hour = 1000 joules/second × 60 × 60 s = 3 600 000 J.

Paying for electrical energy

The **electricity meter** in your home measures the amount of electrical energy your family uses. It records the total energy supplied, no matter how many devices you all use. It gives us a reading of the number of kilowatt-hours (kW h) of energy supplied by the mains.

Figure 2 An electricity meter

NELEB

L. Jones
26 Homewood Road
Otwood M51 9YZ

Meter readings present	previous	units	pence per unit	amount	VAT %
31534	30092	1442	5.79	83.49	Zero
Standing charge					07.30
TOTAL NOW DUE					90.79
PERIOD ENDED					31.3.06

Figure 3 Checking your bill

In most houses, somebody reads the meter every three months. Look at the electricity bill in Figure 3.

The difference between the two readings is the number of kilowatt-hours (or units) supplied since the last bill.

b) Check for yourself that 1442 kW h of electrical energy is supplied in the bill shown.

We use the kilowatt-hour to work out the cost of electricity. For example, a cost of 7p per kW h (or 7p per unit) means that each kilowatt-hour of electrical energy costs 7p. Therefore,

total cost = number of kW h used × cost per kW h

c) Work out the cost of 1442 kW h at 7p per kW h.

SUMMARY QUESTIONS

1 Use words from the list to complete the sentences below.

hour   kilowatt   kilowatt-hours

   a) The ...... is a unit of power.
   b) Electricity meters record the mains electrical energy transformed in units of ....
   c) One ...... is the energy transformed by a 1 ......device in 1 ....

2 a) Work out the number of kW h transformed in each case below.
   i) A 3 kilowatt electric kettle is used 6 times for 5 minutes each time.
   ii) A 1000 watt microwave oven is used for 30 minutes.
   iii) A 100 watt electric light is used for 8 hours.
   b) Calculate the total cost of the electricity used in a) if the cost of electricity is 7.0p per kW h.

3 An electric heater is left on for 3 hours.
   During this time it uses 12 kWh of electrical energy. What is the power of the heater?

KEY POINTS

1 Energy transferred (kilowatt-hours, kWh) = power of device (kilowatts, kW) × time in use (hours, h)
2 Total cost = number of kWh used × cost per kWh

P1a 3.4   The National Grid

LEARNING OBJECTIVES

1 Why is there a National Grid for electricity?
2 How does electricity from power stations reach our homes?

SCIENCE @ WORK

The cables of the National Grid system are well-insulated from each other and from the ground. The insulators used on electricity pylons need to be very effective as insulators – or else the electricity would short-circuit to the ground. In winter, ice on the cables can cause them to snap. Teams of electrical engineers are always on standby to deal with sudden emergencies.

Figure 1 Electricity pylons carry the high voltage cables of the National Grid

Your electricity supply at home reaches you through the **National Grid**. This is a network of cables connecting power stations to homes and other buildings. The network also contains transformers. Step-up transformers are used at power stations and step-down transformers are used at sub-stations near homes.

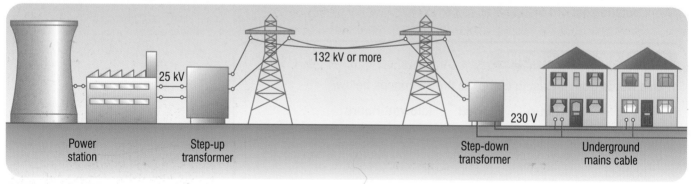

Figure 2 The National Grid

GET IT RIGHT!

Remember that step-up transformers are used at power stations and step-down transformers are used at sub-stations near homes.

The National Grid's voltage is 132 000 volts or more. This is because transmitting electricity at a high voltage reduces power loss, making the system more efficient.

Power stations produce electricity at a voltage of 25 000 volts.

● We use *step-up* transformers to step this voltage up to the grid voltage.
● We use *step-down* transformers at local sub-stations to step the grid voltage down to 230 volts for use in homes and offices.

DEMONSTRATION

Watch a demonstration of the effect of a transformer using this apparatus.

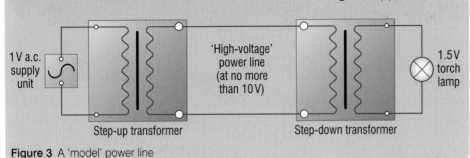

Figure 3 A 'model' power line

Power and the grid voltage

By making the grid voltage as high as possible, the energy losses are reduced to almost zero. This is because less current passes through the cables (for the same power delivered) so its heating effect is less.

a) What difference would it make if we didn't step up the grid voltage?

Underground or overground?

Lots of people object to electricity pylons. They say they spoil the landscape or they affect their health. Electric currents produce electric and magnetic fields that might affect people.

Why don't we bury all cables underground?

Underground cables would be:

- much more expensive,
- much more difficult to repair,
- difficult to bury where they cross canals, rivers and roads.

What's more, overhead cables are high above the ground. Underground cables could affect people more because the cables wouldn't be very deep.

b) Give two reasons why underground cables are more difficult to repair?

SUMMARY QUESTIONS

1 Complete the sentences below using words from the list.

bigger   down   smaller   up

a) Power stations are connected to the National Grid using step- ...... transformers. This type of transformer makes the voltage ....

b) Homes are connected to the National Grid using step- ...... transformers. This type of transformer makes the voltage ....

2 Would you buy a house next to an electricity sub-station? Find out why some people would be worried. What advice would you offer them?

3 a) Why is electrical energy transferred through the National Grid at a much higher voltage than it is generated in a power station?

b) Why are transformers needed to connect local sub-stations to the National Grid?

KEY POINTS

1 The National Grid is a network of cables and transformers.
2 We use step–up transformers to step up power stations' voltages to the grid voltage,
3 We use step-down transformers to step the grid voltage down for use in our homes.
4 A high grid voltage reduces energy loss and makes the system more efficient.

P1a 3.5   Essential electricity issues

On holiday

Before you go on holiday abroad, be sure to find out what the voltage is in the country you are visiting.

- In North America, the mains voltage is 115 V not 230 V. A 230 V hairdryer won't work very well at 115 V. Some devices have a dual-voltage switch to enable it to work at either voltage. But make sure you reset the switch to 230 V when you get home!

- In most EU countries, the mains voltage is 230 V, the same as in the UK. But take an adaptor because the mains sockets are different to those in the UK.

19th November 1878 1d   Cyprus under British Administration - page 2

Floodlit Football – A Brilliant Success!

Successful Trial Of Bright Idea

Supporters of Blackburn Rovers and Accrington Stanley will remember yesterday after being treated to one of the first floodlit football matches in Britain.   Six thousand fans paid to enter the ground and a further twenty thousand watched from Coronation Park.   The players, attired in picturesque costumes, amused the crowds before the match by playing leapfrog and racing.   The leather ball, which was painted white so the players could see it, was kicked off at about a quarter to eight. Although the players' faces could not be distinguished at a distance, the ball could be seen very well and the crowd had no difficulty following the match. Blackburn had a resounding victory – three goals to nil!

Turn to Page 12

Lighting The Way - London Gets Electric Street Lighting!

QUESTION

2 A football ground has 8 towers of floodlights, each using 50 kW of electrical power.

a) How much electrical energy, in kW, is used when the lights are on for 4 hours?

b) How much does the electricity cost at 7 p per kW h?

QUESTION

1 Why would it be very dangerous to use a 115 V device on 230 V?

Bygone times – before electricity

- Many towns used lamp lighters before they had electric street lamps installed. The lamp lighters would go round the streets at dusk and light all the gas lamps. Then they would go round and turn them off at dawn.

- A steam train is a sight to see at a distance but not if you get too close. The ash and smoke from a steam engine are very unpleasant if it blows in your face. Steam trains on the London Underground were replaced by electric trains long ago. Travelling on the Underground would be very unpleasant if the carriages were pulled by steam engines.

QUESTIONS

3 What did people use to wash clothes before the invention of the washing machine?

4 How would your life be different without electricity? Write an account of 'A day in my life without electricity'.

Shop around?

You can get your electricity from any one of a number of different electricity companies. You can even get your gas and electricity from the same company. Companies offer different deals to attract new customers.

	Homepower	Power Co	PowerGreen
First 100 kW h of electricity	9p per kW h	10p per kW h	
Electricity above 100 kW h	7p per kW h	5p per kW h	8p per kW h

Go online now to find a better deal!

QUESTION

5 Look at the table opposite and work out which would be the best deal if

a) you use 100 kW h of electricity per month on average,

b) you use 300 kW h of electricity per month on average.

A not-so brilliant idea!

Nikolai Tesla was a brilliant electrical engineer. He made important inventions and discoveries about electric motors and generators. He even discovered how to supply electricity using radio waves. No cables were needed to supply the electricity. But no supply company would take his idea up. Why? – because anyone could tap into a radio power grid for free – just by putting an aerial up. The company wouldn't know who was using their electricity.

ACTIVITY

Think up an invention that could make you rich using Nikolai's idea.

SUMMARY QUESTIONS

1 a) Name a device that transforms electrical energy into:
  i) light and sound energy,
  ii) kinetic energy.

  b) Complete the sentences below.
  i) In an electric bell, electrical energy is transformed into useful energy in the form of ...... energy and ...... energy.
  ii) In a washing machine, electrical energy is transformed into useful energy in the form of ...... energy and sometimes as ...... energy.

2 a) Which two units in the list below can be used to measure energy?

  joule   kilowatt   kilowatt-hour   watt

  b) Rank the electrical devices below in terms of energy used from highest to lowest,
  A a 0.5 kW heater used for 4 hours,
  B a 100 W lamp left on for 24 hours,
  C a 3 kW electric kettle used 6 times for 10 minutes each time,
  D a 750 W microwave oven used for 10 minutes.

3 a) The readings of an electricity meter at the start and the end of a month are shown below.

0	9	3	7	2		0	9	6	1	5

  i)   Which is the reading at the end of the month?
  ii) How many units of electricity were used during the month?
  iii) How much would this electricity cost at 7p per kWh?

  b) A pay meter in a holiday home supplies electricity at a cost of 10p per kWh.
  i) How many kWh would be supplied for £1.00?
  ii) How long could a 2 kW heater be used for after £1 is put in the meter slot?

4 An escalator in a shopping centre is powered by a 50 kW electric motor. The escalator is in use for a total time of 10 hours every day.

  a) How much electrical energy in kWh is supplied to the motor each day?

  b) The electricity supplied to the motor costs 7p per kWh. What is the daily cost of the electricity supplied to the motor?

  c) How much would be saved each day if the motor was replaced by a more efficient 40 kW motor?

EXAM-STYLE QUESTIONS

1 The devices shown transform electrical energy into other forms of energy.

The list gives the useful form of energy the devices are designed to produce. Match the words in the list with the devices numbered **1** to **4**.

A kinetic energy   **B** light
C sound   **D** thermal energy   (4)

2 A 3 kW electric motor is switched on for 15 minutes. How much energy, in kilowatt hours, does it transfer during this time?

A 0.0075 kWh   **B** 0.075 kWh
C 0.75 kWh   **D** 7.50 kWh   (1)

3 Which of the following does **not** represent a unit of energy?

A J   **B** kJ
C kW   **D** kWh   (1)

4 The diagram shows the readings on a household electricity meter, in kWh, at the beginning and end of one week. Each kWh of electricity costs 8p.

1	8	2	4	2		1	8	5	1	1

At the beginning of the week   At the end of the week

(a) How many kWh of electricity were used during the week?
  A 242   **B** 269
  C 511   **D** 753   (1)

(b) On one day 30 kWh of electricity were used. How much would this electricity cost?
  A 24p   **B** 30p
  C £2.40   **D** £3.00   (1)

(c) During the week a 2 kW iron was used for 2.5 hours. How much energy was transformed by the iron?
  A 0.50 kWh   **B** 0.75 kWh
  C 5.00 kWh   **D** 7.50 kWh   (1)

(d) How much does it cost to use a 9 kW shower for half an hour?

A 3.6p
B 4.5p
C 36p
D 45p (1)

5 A student uses an electric iron.

(a) What useful energy transformation takes place in the iron? (1)

(b) The iron has a power of 1.2 kW. What is meant by 'power'? (1)

(c) Electricity cost 8 p per kWh. How much does it cost the student to use the iron for 30 minutes? (3)

6 Each town in Britain used to have its own power station. Now electricity is supplied by a system called the National Grid.

(a) Why is the National Grid system better than each town having its own supply? (2)

(b) Electricity in power stations is generated at 25 000 volts. Explain why:

(i) it is transmitted across the National Grid system at 132 000 volts.

(ii) it is supplied to homes at 230 volts. (2)

(c) What is the name of the device used to change the potential difference of the mains supply from 25 000 volts to 132 000 volts before transmission across the National Grid? (2)

(d) Suggest why the cables of the National Grid are carried high above the ground rather than being buried underground. (2)

HOW SCIENCE WORKS QUESTIONS

Josh set up an investigation to measure the efficiency of a small electric motor. He set the motor up to lift different masses. By measuring the voltage and the current used, he could calculate the energy used by the motor to lift different masses to the same height.

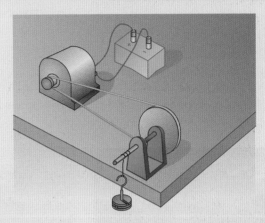

Josh hypothesised that heavier masses would reduce the efficiency of a motor. His prediction was that, if he increased the mass lifted by the motor, it would use much more energy than the energy gained by the masses. He thought this would happen because the motor would require more energy and more heat would be lost. His results are in the table below.

Mass lifted (g)	Efficiency (%)
50	10
100	16
150	24
200	22
250	21
300	19
350	15

a) Plot a graph of these results. (3)

b) Describe the pattern shown by these results. (3)

c) Do these results wholly support, partly support or refute Josh's hypothesis? (1)

d) How could Josh improve the accuracy of these results? (1)

e) Why might these results not be reliable? (1)

f) How could Josh improve the reliability of these results? (1)

P1a 4.1   Fuel for electricity

LEARNING OBJECTIVES

1 How is electricity generated in a power station?
2 What fossil fuels do we burn in power stations?
3 How do we use nuclear fuels in power stations?

Figure 2 Inside a gas-fired power station

SCIENCE @ WORK

When a popular TV programme ends, lots of people decide to put their kettles on. The national demand for electricity leaps as a result. Engineers meet these surges in demand by switching gas turbine engines on in gas-fired power stations.

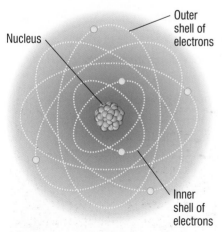

Figure 3 The structure of the atom

In a power station

Almost all the electricity you use is generated in power stations.

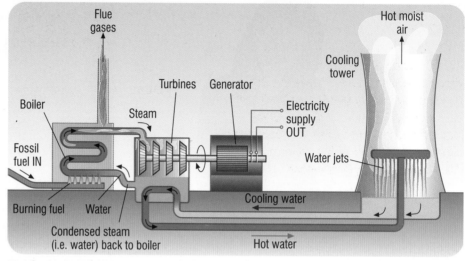

Figure 1 Inside a fossil fuel power station

- In a *coal* or *oil-fired power station*, the burning fuel heats water in a boiler to produce steam. The steam drives a turbine that turns an electricity generator.

a) What happens to the steam after it has been used?
b) What happens to the thermal energy of the steam after it has been used?

- In a *gas-fired power station*, we burn natural gas directly in a gas turbine engine. This produces a powerful jet of hot gases and air that drives the turbine. A gas-fired turbine can be switched on very quickly.

PRACTICAL

Turbines

See how we can use water to drive round the blades of a turbine.

- Why is steam better than water?

Nuclear power

Do you know what's inside an atom? Figure 3 shows you.

- Every atom contains a positively charged nucleus surrounded by electrons.
- The nucleus is composed of two types of particles, neutrons and protons.
- Atoms of the same element can have different numbers of neutrons in the nucleus.

How is electricity obtained from a nuclear power station?

The fuel in a nuclear power station is uranium. The uranium fuel is contained in sealed cans in the core of the reactor. The nucleus of a uranium atom is unstable and can split in two. Energy is released when this happens. We call this process *nuclear fission*. Because there are lots of uranium atoms in the core, it becomes very hot.

The thermal energy of the core is taken away by a fluid (called the 'coolant') that is pumped through the core. The coolant is very hot when it leaves the core. It flows through a pipe to a 'heat exchanger', then back to the reactor core. The thermal energy of the coolant is used to turn water into steam in the heat exchanger. The steam drives turbines which turn electricity generators.

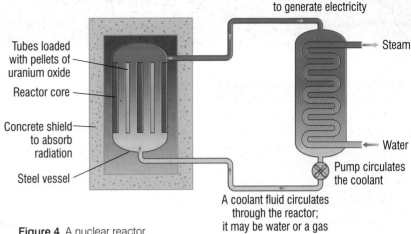

Tubes loaded with pellets of uranium oxide

Reactor core

Concrete shield to absorb radiation

Steel vessel

The heated fluid is used to boil water; the steam produced drives a turbine to generate electricity

Steam

Water

Pump circulates the coolant

A coolant fluid circulates through the reactor; it may be water or a gas

Figure 4 A nuclear reactor

Comparing nuclear power and fossil fuel power

	Nuclear power station	Fossil fuel power station
Fuel	uranium	coal, oil or gas
Energy released per kg of fuel	1 000 000 kW h (= about 10 000 × energy released per kg of fossil fuel)	100 kW h
Waste	radioactive waste that needs to be stored for many years	non-radioactive waste
Greenhouse gases	no – because uranium releases energy without burning	yes – because fossil fuels produce gases like carbon dioxide when they burn

SUMMARY QUESTIONS

1 Complete the sentences below using words from the list.

coal   gas   oil   uranium

a) ...... is not a fossil fuel.
b) Power stations that use ...... as the fuel can be switched on very quickly.
c) Steam is used to make the turbines rotate in a power station that uses coal, ... or...... as fuel.

2 a) State one advantage and one disadvantage of:
   i) an oil-fired power station compared with a nuclear power station,
   ii) a gas-fired power station compared with a coal-fired power station.
b) Look at the table above:
   How many kilograms of fossil fuel would give the same amount of energy as 1 kg of uranium fuel?
c) Some people think that more nuclear power stations are the only way to reduce greenhouse gases significantly. Explain your views on this.

KEY POINTS

1 Electricity generators in power stations are driven by turbines.
2 Much more energy is released per kilogram from uranium than from fossil fuel.

P1a 4.2

Energy from wind and water

LEARNING OBJECTIVES

1 How can we use the wind to generate electricity?
2 What type of power station uses falling water to generate electricity?
3 How can we use waves and tides to generate electricity?

Figure 1 A wind farm – why do some people oppose these developments?

Wind power

A wind turbine is an electricity generator at the top of a narrow tower. The force of the wind drives the turbine's blades around. This turns a generator. The power generated increases as the wind speed increases.

a) What happens if the wind stops blowing?

Wave power

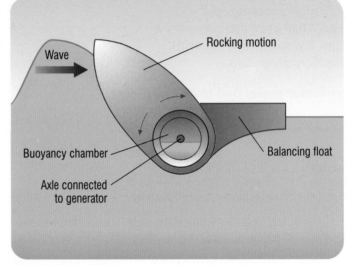

Figure 2 Energy from waves

A wave generator uses the waves to make a floating section move up and down. This motion drives a turbine which turns a generator. A cable between the generator and the shore delivers electricity to the grid system.

Wave generators need to withstand storms and they don't produce a constant supply of electricity. Also, lots of cables (and buildings) would be needed along the coast to connect the wave generators to the electricity grid. This would spoil areas of coastline. In addition, tidal flow patterns might be changed, affecting the habitats of marine life and birds.

b) What could happen if the waves get too high?

PRACTICAL

Pumped storage

When electricity demand is low, we can use wind and wave power to pump water uphill. We can use the energy stored in this way later.

See how we can pump water 'uphill' and then use it to generate electricity.

● What would happen if the upper 'reservoir' is too high?

Hydroelectric power

We can generate hydroelectricity when rainwater collected in a reservoir (or water in a pumped storage scheme) flows downhill. The flowing water drives turbines that turn electricity generators at the foot of the hill.

c) Where does the energy for hydroelectricity come from?

Tidal power

Tidal power stations trap the water from each high tide behind a barrage. We can then release the high tide into the sea through turbines. The turbines drive generators in the barrage. One of the most promising sites in Britain is the Severn estuary. This is because the estuary becomes narrower as you move 'up-river' away from the open sea. So it 'funnels' the incoming tide and makes it higher than elsewhere.

Figure 4 A tidal power station

Figure 3 A hydroelectric scheme

d) Why is tidal power more reliable than wind power?

SUMMARY QUESTIONS

1 Complete the following sentences below using words from the list.

hydroelectric   tidal   wave   wind

a) ...... power does not need water.
b) ...... power does not need energy from the Sun.
c) ...... power is obtained from water running downhill.
d) ...... power is obtained from water moving up and down.

2 a) Use the table below for this question.
   i) How many wind turbines would give the same total output as a tidal power station?
   ii) How many kilometres of wave generators would give the same total output as a hydroelectric power station?
   b) Use the words below to fill in the location column in the table.

coastline   estuaries   hilly or coastal areas   mountain areas

	Output	Location
Hydroelectric power station	500 MW per station	
Tidal power station	2000 MW per station	
Wave power generators	20 MW per kilometre of coastline	
Wind turbines	2 MW per wind turbine	

c) Imagine you are a government adviser on alternative energy sources. Put the four methods in the table into an order to prioritise government spending. Explain your choices.

P1a 4.3   Power from the Sun and the Earth

Figure 1 Energy from the Sun

Figure 3 A solar-powered vehicle. Think of some advantages and disadvantages of this car.

Solar power

Solar radiation transfers energy to you from the Sun – sometimes more than you want if you get sunburnt. But we can use the Sun's energy to generate electricity using **solar cells**. We can also use it to heat water directly in **solar heating panels**.

a) Which generates electricity – a solar cell or a solar heating panel?

PRACTICAL

Solar cells

Use a solar cell to drive a small motor.

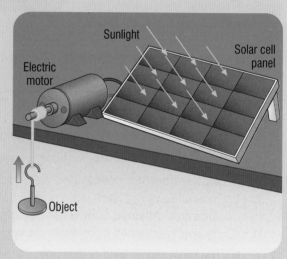

Figure 2 Solar cells at work

● What happens if you cover the solar cells with your hand?

(1) **Solar cells** in use now convert less than 10% of the solar energy they absorb into electrical energy. We connect them together to make solar cell panels.

● They are useful where we only need small amounts of electricity (e.g. in watches and calculators) or in remote places (e.g. on small islands in the middle of an ocean).
● They are very expensive to buy even though they cost nothing to run.
● We need lots of them to generate enough power to be useful – and plenty of sunshine!

(2) A **solar heating panel** heats water that flows through it. Even on a cloudy day in Britain, a solar heating panel on a house roof can supply plenty of hot water.

b) If the water stopped flowing through a solar heating panel, what would happen?

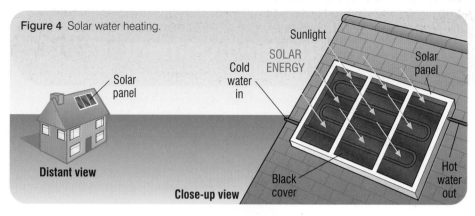

Figure 4 Solar water heating.

Distant view

Close-up view

Sunlight

SOLAR ENERGY

Solar panel

Cold water in

Solar panel

Black cover

Hot water out

Geothermal energy

Geothermal energy comes from energy released by radioactive substances, deep within the Earth.

- The energy released by these radioactive substances heats the surrounding rock.
- As a result, heat is transferred towards the Earth's surface.

We can build geothermal power stations in volcanic areas or where there are hot rocks deep below the surface. Water gets pumped down to these rocks to produce steam. Then the steam produced drives electricity turbines at ground level.

GET IT RIGHT!

- Make sure you know the difference between a solar cell panel (in which sunlight is used to make electricity) and a solar heating panel (in which sunlight is used to heat water).
- The heat flow from below the ground (geothermal energy) comes from energy released by radioactive substances deep inside the Earth.

Figure 5 A geothermal power station and how it works.

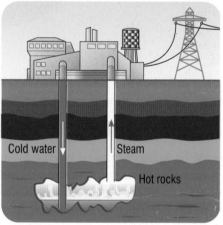

Cold water

Steam

Hot rocks

c) Why don't geothermal power stations need energy from the Sun?

SUMMARY QUESTIONS

1 Match words from the list below with the spaces in the sentences.

   geothermal energy   solar energy   radiation   radioactivity

   a) The best energy resource to use in a calculator is …… .
   b) …… inside the Earth releases …… energy.
   c) …… from the Sun generates electricity in a solar cell.

2 A satellite in space uses a solar cell panel for electricity. The panel generates 300 W of electrical power and has an area of 10 m².

   a) Each cell generates 0.2 W. How many cells are in the panel?
   b) The satellite carries batteries that are charged by electricity from the solar cell panels. Why are batteries carried as well as solar cell panels?

3 Discuss the advantages and disadvantages of using solar and geothermal energy to generate electricity.

KEY POINTS

1 We can convert solar energy into electricity using solar cells or use it to heat water directly in solar heating panels.

2 Geothermal energy comes from the energy released by radioactive substances deep inside the Earth.

P1a 4.4

Energy and the environment

Can we get energy without creating any problems? Look at the chart in Figure 1.

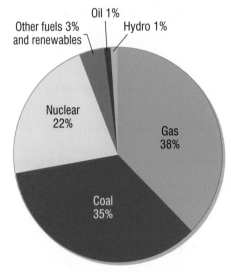

Figure 1 Energy sources for electricity

It shows the energy sources we use at present to generate electricity. What effect does each one have on our environment?

Fossil fuel problems

- When we burn coal, oil or gas, the chemical reaction makes 'greenhouse gases' such as carbon dioxide. These gases cause global warming. We only get a small percentage of our electricity from oil-fired power stations. We use much more oil to produce fuels for transport.
- Burning fossil fuels can also produce sulfur dioxide. This gas causes acid rain in the atmosphere. We can remove the sulfur from a fuel before burning it to stop acid rain. For example, natural gas has its sulfur impurities removed before we use it.
- Fossil fuels are not renewable. Sooner or later, we will have used up the Earth's reserves of fossil fuels. We will then have to find alternative sources of energy. But how soon? Oil and gas reserves could be used up within the next 50 years.

a) Which gas given off when we burn fossil fuels contributes towards:
   i) global warming?
   ii) acid rain?

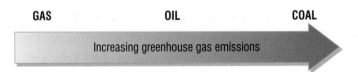

Figure 2 Greenhouse gases from fossil fuels

Nuclear v renewable

We need to cut back on fossil fuels to stop global warming. Should we rely on nuclear power or on renewable energy in future?

(1) Nuclear power
Advantages
- No greenhouse gases (unlike fossil fuel).
- Much more energy from each kilogram of uranium fuel than from fossil fuel.

Disadvantages
- Used fuel rods contain radioactive waste, which has to be stored safely for centuries.
- Nuclear reactors are safe in normal operation. However, an explosion at one could release radioactive material over a wide area. This would affect these areas for many years.

b) Why is nuclear fuel non-renewable?

(2) Renewable energy sources and the environment
Advantages
Renewable energy resources

- never run out,
- do not produce greenhouse gases or acid rain,
- do not create radioactive waste products.

Disadvantages
- Wind turbines are unsightly and create a whining noise that can upset people nearby.
- Tidal barrages affect river estuaries and the habitats of creatures and plants there.
- Hydroelectric schemes need large reservoirs of water, which can affect nearby plant and animal life. Habitats are often flooded to create dams.
- Solar cells would need to cover large areas to generate large amounts of power.

c) Do wind turbines affect plant and animal life?

Figure 3 Chernobyl, the site of the world's most serious accident at a nuclear power station

Figure 4 The effects of acid rain

KEY POINTS

1 Fossil fuels produce greenhouse gases.
2 Nuclear fuels produce radioactive waste.
3 Renewable energy resources can affect plant and animal life.

SUMMARY QUESTIONS

1 Choose words from the list to complete each of the sentences in a), b) and c).

    acid rain fossil fuels greenhouse gas
     plant and animal life radioactive waste

  a) Most of Britain's electricity is produced by power stations that burn ....
  b) A gas-fired power station does not produce ...... or much ....
  c) A tidal power station does not produce ...... like a nuclear power station does but it does affect ...... locally.

2 Match each energy source with a problem it causes.

  Problem: A Acid rain, B Noise, C Radioactive waste, D Takes up land
  Energy source: i) Coal, ii) Hydroelectricity, iii) Uranium, iv) Wind power

3 Make a leaflet for the general public explaining the issues involved in generating electricity using nuclear power.

P1a 4.5   Big energy issues

Nuclear or not?

Figure 1 A nuclear power station

FOR—
About a quarter of Britain's electricity comes from nuclear power stations. Many of these stations are due to close by 2020. A new nuclear power station takes several years to build. So the Uk government must build new nuclear power stations.

AGAINST—
We don't want new nuclear power stations. We can get our electricity from renewable devices like wind turbines. We believe that renewable energy devices can provide enough electricity. We don't need new nuclear power stations.

ACTIVITY

Who is right? Find out what your friends think. Then read on before forming your opinion.

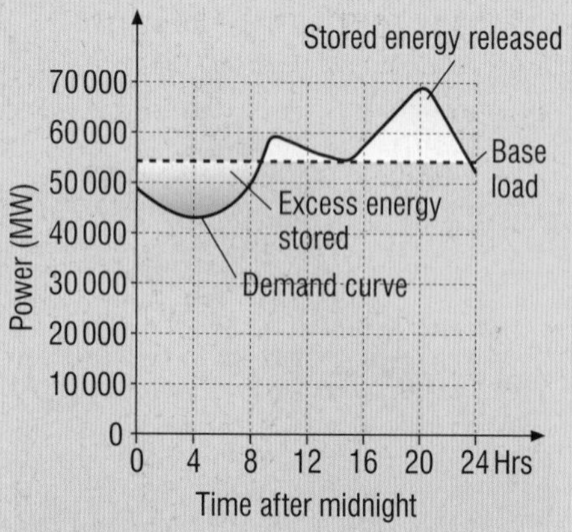

Supply and demand

The demand for electricity varies during each day. It is also higher in winter than in summer. Our electricity generators need to match these changes in demand.

- Power stations can't just 'start up' instantly. The 'start up' time depends on the type of power station:

| natural gas | oil | coal | nuclear |

shortest start-up time ⟶ ⟶ longest start-up time

- Renewable energy resources are unreliable. The amount of electricity they generate depends on the conditions:

Hydroelectric	Upland reservoir could run dry.
Wind, waves	Wind and waves too weak on very calm days.
Tidal	Height of tide varies both on a monthly and yearly cycle.
Solar	No solar energy at night and variable during the day.

The variable demand for electricity is met by:

- using nuclear, coal and oil-fired power stations to provide a constant amount of electricity (the *base load* demand),
- using gas-fired power stations and pumped-storage schemes to meet daily variations in demand and extra demand in winter,
- using renewable energy sources when demand is high and renewables are in operation (e.g. use of wind turbines in winter when wind speeds are suitable),
- using renewable energy sources when demand is low to store energy in pumped storage schemes.

Figure 2 Electricity demand

QUESTION

1 We need to cut back on fossil fuels to reduce greenhouse gases. What would happen if we went over completely to:

a) renewable energy?

b) nuclear power?

Fusion power

Energy from the Sun is produced by a process called **fusion**. Deep inside the Sun, the enormous pressure forces small nuclei to fuse together. These nuclei merge and form heavier nuclei. Energy is released in the process. Scientists have successfully built experimental fusion reactors that release energy – but not for long!

Research is continuing to find out how to turn small experimental reactors into a reactor that can supply large amounts of power. The benefits would be fantastic because we can get the fuel – hydrogen – from sea water. Even better, the reaction products, such as helium, are not radioactive!

Figure 3 Testing fusion

QUESTION

2 Explain why fusion reactors offer the promise of limitless fuel supplies and no pollution.

Nothing is free

Fossil fuels

Removing the sulfur from coal and oil is expensive.

Stopping greenhouse gases escaping, if it could be done, would be even more expensive.

Energy saving

Most home owners are unlikely to buy energy-saving improvements until energy bills go up even more.

Nuclear power

The cost of building and running a nuclear power station is very high.

So is the cost of decommissioning it (i.e. taking it out of use).

Also, radioactive waste products are expensive to store.

Renewables

There are no fuel costs for renewables but capital costs of setting up are high.

This is because lots of expensive equipment is needed to 'collect' large quantities of renewable energy.

ACTIVITY

Who pays? Should we pay through higher taxes or through higher energy bills?
Take a vote!

The big energy debate

Is it possible to generate enough electricity for everyone and to cut back on greenhouse gases? Here are some suggestions:

1. Develop renewable energy resources on a much larger scale.

2. Use energy more efficiently.

Build more nuclear power stations.

Continue to use fossil fuels but remove the greenhouse gases produced.

ACTIVITY

Add your own suggestions. Work in a group and narrow them down to the two most popular ones. Then use your scientific knowledge to debate which one is best!

SUMMARY QUESTIONS

1 Use the list of fuels below to answer a) to e).

coal   natural gas   oil   uranium   wood

a) Which fuels from the list below are fossil fuels?

b) Which fuels from the list cause acid rain?

c) Which fuels release chemical energy when they are used?

d) Which fuel releases the most energy per kilogram?

e) Which fuel produces radioactive waste?

2 a) Complete the following sentences using words from the list.

hydroelectric   tidal   wave   wind

i) ...... power stations trap sea water.

ii) ...... power stations trap rain water.

iii) ...... generators must be located along the coast line.

iv) ...... turbines can be located on hills or off-shore.

b) Which renewable energy resource transforms

i) the kinetic energy of moving air into electrical energy?

ii) the gravitational potential energy of water running downhill into electrical energy?

iii) the kinetic energy of water moving up and down into electrical energy?

3 a) Complete the sentences below using words from the list.

**coal-fired   geothermal
hydroelectric   nuclear**

i) A ...... power station does not produce greenhouse gases and uses energy which is from inside the Earth.

ii) A ...... power station uses running water and does not produce greenhouse gases.

iii) A ...... power station releases greenhouse gases.

iv) A ...... power station does not release greenhouse gases but does produce waste products that need to be stored for many years.

b) Wood can be used as a fuel. State whether it is
i) renewable or non-renewable,
ii) a fossil fuel or a non-fossil fuel.

EXAM-STYLE QUESTIONS

A hydroelectric power station uses two lakes.

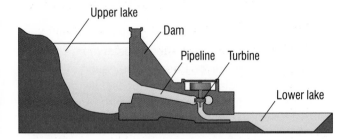

1 As water flows from the top to the bottom lake it turns a turbine coupled to a generator that produces electricity. What is the energy transformation that takes place as the water flows?

A Electrical energy to kinetic energy.

B Gravitational potential energy to kinetic energy.

C Kinetic energy to gravitational potential energy.

D Kinetic energy to heat energy.   (1)

2 Where does geothermal energy come from?

A Radioactive processes in nuclear power stations.

B Radioactive processes within the Earth.

C The decay of organic material.

D The movement of the tides.   (1)

3 Renewable energy sources can be used to generate electricity. However these sources are not always available.

Match words from the list with the numbers **1** to **4** in the table.

A hydroelectric scheme

B solar cells

C tidal barrage

D wind farm

Renewable energy source	Source is available to generate electricity ...
1	only during the daylight
2	only when the weather is suitable
3	only during certain periods of the day and night
4	usually whenever it is needed

(4)

4 Wind energy, waves, tides, falling water and solar energy can all be used as energy sources to generate electricity.

(a) What do all these energy sources have in common?

  A They are available at any time of the day or night.

  B They are renewable energy sources.

  C They do not affect wildlife.

  D They do not cause any sort of pollution. (1)

(b) Which of these energy sources is most appropriate to generate electricity to run a well in a remote African village?

  A falling water   B solar energy

  C tides   D waves   (1)

(c) Which of these energy sources is most likely to produce noise pollution when used to generate electricity?

  A solar energy   B tides

  C waves   D wind energy   (1)

(d) Which of these energy sources is **least** likely to be associated with damaging wildlife or the habitat of wildlife when used to generate electricity?

  A falling water   B tides

  C waves   D wind energy   (1)

5 In coal, gas and oil-fired power stations fuels are burnt to produce heat.

(a) How is heat produced in a nuclear power station? (1)

(b) How is the heat used to produce electricity? (4)

(c) Apart from the cost of the electricity what are the advantages and disadvantages of using a nuclear power station to produce electricity? (5)

6 In the UK there are three different fossil fuels burnt in power stations.

(a) Name the three fossil fuels. (3)

(b) During burning all fossil fuels release carbon dioxide into the atmosphere. Some also release sulfur dioxide.

  (i) Why does the release of carbon dioxide into the atmosphere produce a problem for the environment? (3)

  (ii) Why is the release of sulfur dioxide a problem for the environment? (2)

HOW SCIENCE WORKS QUESTIONS

Tamara was interested in solar cells. She had been given a solar cell panel in a physics kit and set out to find how surface area affected the voltage that the panel could produce. Her solar cell panel was 10 cm × 3 cm. She set up a circuit with a voltmeter and the solar cell panel.

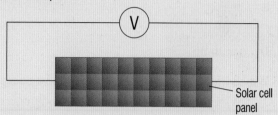

Solar cell panel

She took the circuit into the garden and covered different parts of the panel with black paper. Her preliminary work showed that it did not matter which part of the solar cell panel was covered, just how much was covered.

a) What do you think Tamara did in her preliminary work? (2)

Her final results are in this table.

Part of panel covered	Test 1 (V)	Test 2 (V)	Average (V)
None	0.3	0.4	0.35
A bit	0.3	0.3	0.3
A bit more	0.2	0.3	0.25
Most	0.1	0.1	0.1
All	0.1	0.1	0.1

b) Tamara was pleased that her results showed what she had expected.
What do you think these results show? (1)

c) Farzana said that Tamara's independent variable was not good enough.
What did Farzana mean by this? (1)

d) How could Tamara have improved her independent variable? (1)

e) Farzana looked at the voltage readings and suggested to Tamara that they were not very useful.
Why do you think Farzana thought that the readings were not very useful? (1)

f) Farzana suggested that she used a better voltmeter.
What type of voltmeter do you think Farzana suggested? (1)

g) Is there any evidence of a zero error in Tamara's results? (1)

h) What could Tamara do about this? (1)

EXAMINATION-STYLE QUESTIONS

Physics A

1   In a nuclear power station the process that produces heat is called

   A   fission

   B   fusion

   C   radiation

   D   uranium   *(1 mark)*

See page 63

2   Which of these devices will transfer most energy?

   A   A 2 kW kettle used for 3 hours.

   B   A 3 kW heater used for 2 hours.

   C   A 4 kW motor used for 2 hours.

   D   A 7 kW shower used for 1 hour.   *(1 mark)*

See page 54

GET IT RIGHT!

The device with the biggest power rating may not transfer the most energy.

3   Which of these statements about solar cells is correct?

   A   In a solar cell, water is heated which produces steam and drives a turbine.

   B   Solar cells can produce electricity directly from the Sun's radiation.

   C   Solar cells produce electricity even in the dark.

   D   Solar cells transform geothermal energy into electrical energy   *(1 mark)*

See pages 66–7

4   Thermal energy can be transferred in different ways.
   Match the words in the list with the numbers **1** to **4** in the sentences.

   A   electrons   **B**   liquids

   C   particles   **D**   solids

   Conduction occurs mainly in ......**1**...... All metals are good conductors because they have a lot of free ......**2**....... Convection occurs in gases and ......**3**...... Radiation does not involve ......**4**......   *(4 marks)*

See pages 24–31

GET IT RIGHT!

Read through all of the sentences first and make sure that they all make sense with your choice of words before you select your answers in.

5   Electrical devices transform energy from electrical energy to other forms.
   Match the words in the list with the numbers **1** to **4** in the sentences.

   A   kilowatt-hours   **B**   power

   C   joules   **D**   time

   The ......**1**...... of a device is the rate at which it transforms energy. Energy is normally measured in ......**2**...... The amount of electrical energy a device transforms depends on the rate at which the device transforms energy and the ......**3**...... for which it used. The amount of electrical energy transferred from the mains is measured in ......**4**......   *(4 marks)*

See pages 52–4

6   A student is doing an experiment on the rate of heat transfer from a beaker of hot water. Which of the following is true?

   A   The darker the colour of the beaker the slower the rate of heat transfer.

   B   The hotter the water the faster the rate of heat transfer.

   C   The shape of the beaker does not affect the rate of heat transfer.

   D   The temperature of the water does not affect the rate of heat transfer.   *(1 mark)*

See pages 26, 32–3

Physics B

1   The chart shows the energy resources used to produce electricity in Britain.

See pages 62–9

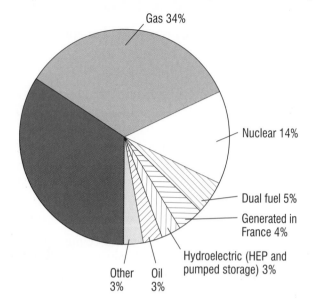

Gas 34%

Nuclear 14%

Dual fuel 5%

Generated in
France 4%

Hydroelectric (HEP and
pumped storage) 3%

Other
3%

Oil
3%

(a)   What percentage of the electricity is produced from coal?   *(1 mark)*

(b)   Give one advantage and one disadvantage, other than cost, of producing
      electricity from coal.   *(2 marks)*

(c)   In one power station, for every 1000 J of energy obtained from coal 300 J is
      wasted as heat. Use the following equation to work out the efficiency of the
      power station. Show clearly how you work out your answer.

See page 44

$$\text{Efficiency} = \frac{\text{Useful energy transferred by the device}}{\text{Total energy transferred to the device}}$$ *(3 marks)*

GET IT RIGHT!

When calculating efficiency
make sure that you have
correctly identified the
useful energy transferred
by the device and the total
energy supplied **to** the
device.

(d)   In Britain 3% of the electricity is produced from *other* resources. One *other*
      resource is to use energy from the tides.
      Discuss the advantages and disadvantages, other than cost, of producing
      electricity from tidal energy.   *(3 marks)*

(e)   Name one *other* resource, apart from the tides, not already given in the
      chart that is used to produce electricity.   *(1 mark)*

2   A thermos flask is used to keep hot things hot and cold things cold. It does this
    by minimising heat transfer.
    Explain how each of the following minimises heat transfer:

See page 32

(a)   the tight fitting plastic stopper.   *(2 marks)*

(b)   the silver coating on the surfaces of the glass walls.   *(2 marks)*

(c)   the vacuum between the glass walls.   *(2 marks)*

P1b | Radiation and the Universe

What you already know

Here is a quick reminder of previous work that you will find useful in this unit:

The Solar System
- The Moon orbits the Earth. The Earth and the other planets orbit the Sun.
- The Solar System consists of the Sun, the planets and their moons. The nearest star to the Sun is far beyond the Solar System.
- The Sun is a star. All stars give out their own light. They appear as pinpoints of light in the night sky because they are so far away.
- The Moon and the planets reflect sunlight. They do not give out their own light. We see them because they reflect sunlight to us.

Light
- We can use a prism to split sunlight into the colours of the spectrum (red, orange, yellow, green, blue, indigo and violet).
- Light that contains all the colours of the spectrum is called white light.
- We represent the path of light by light rays. Light travels in straight lines and is reflected by a mirror.

Gravity
- Gravity is a force of attraction between any two objects.
- The force of gravity between two objects depends on their masses and their distance apart.
- An orbiting object is kept in its orbit about a larger object by the force of gravity between it and the larger object. For example,
  - the Moon orbits the Earth,
  - satellites orbit the Earth,
  - the planets orbit the Sun.

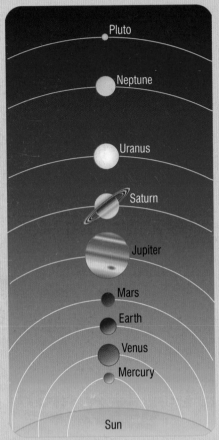

Figure 1 The Solar System showing the planets. The distances are not to scale.

Labels: Pluto, Neptune, Uranus, Saturn, Jupiter, Mars, Earth, Venus, Mercury, Sun

---

RECAP QUESTIONS

1 a) Put the objects listed below in order of increasing size:

   the Earth   the Moon   the Sun

   b) Which is nearer to the Earth – the Sun or the Moon?

2 Complete the sentences below using words from the list.

   planet   satellite   star   Sun

   a) The Sun is a ....
   b) The Moon is a natural ...... of the Earth.
   c) The Earth is a ....
   d) Planets reflect light from the ....

3 The letters ROYGBIV represent the colours of the spectrum. What colour does each letter stand for?

4 a) What happens when a light ray strikes a mirror?
   b) An image of an object seen in a mirror always has the same colour as the object. What does this tell you about light and mirrors?
   c) How do we show the direction of a light ray?

5 a) What is the name for the force that keeps us on the Earth?
   b) What keeps the planets in their orbits round the Sun?
   c) What stops a rocket from leaving the Earth?

Making connections

Figure 2 A GPS receiver uses radio waves to tell you where you are

Radiation all around us

We use radiation in many different ways. Here are some different ways in which we use radiation.

On the move

If you want to know where you are or where you are heading, a GPS (Global Position Satellite) receiver will tell you. Satellites above you send out signals all the time. The signals are short-wave radio waves. You can pick them up with a hand-held receiver wherever you are.

Fixing a fracture

Have you or someone you know ever broken a limb? Doctors need to X-ray a broken bone before they reset it in plaster. X-rays are high-energy electromagnetic waves. The X-ray picture tells them exactly where it is broken and how badly it is broken. If it isn't reset correctly, the bones will re-grow crooked. Then they may need to be reset – and that can be very painful!

The Hubble Space Telescope

For almost twenty years, the Hubble Space Telescope has been orbiting the Earth. It's like a giant eye in space. Its pictures are beamed to the ground using radio waves.

It has sent us thousands of amazing images of objects in space. They range from nearby planets to distant galaxies at the edge of the Universe. In all this time, astronauts have only ever had to go once into space to repair it.

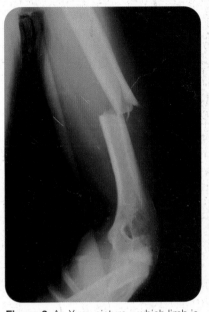

Figure 3 An X-ray picture – which limb is broken?

Figure 4 The Hubble Space Telescope sends us fantastic images using radio waves

ACTIVITY

The people in the village of Downdale want a mobile phone mast because they can't get a signal when they use their mobile phones. But where should the mast go?

Discuss with your friends the question of how they should decide where it should go.

Figure 5 No to mobile phone masts!

A mobile phone revolt!

Where would you be without your mobile phone? But what would you say if a mobile phone company wanted to put a mobile phone mast outside your house? Many people would object. They say that mobile phone radiation could be a risk to health. They don't want masts near their homes. But they won't give up their mobiles.

Chapters in this unit

○ Electromagnetic waves
●───────── Radioactivity
●───────── The origins of the Universe

P1b 5.1 The electromagnetic spectrum

Figure 1 Notice the spectrum is continuous. The frequencies/wavelengths at the boundaries are approximate as the different parts of the spectrum are not precisely defined.

We all use waves from different parts of the electromagnetic spectrum. Figure 1 shows the spectrum and some of its uses.

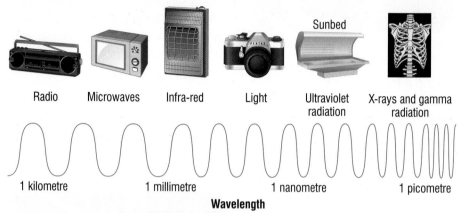

| Radio | Microwaves | Infra-red | Light | Ultraviolet radiation | X-rays and gamma radiation |

| 1 kilometre | 1 millimetre | 1 nanometre | 1 picometre |

Wavelength
(1 nanometre = 0.000 001 millimetres, 1 picometre = 0.001 nanometres)

Electromagnetic waves are electric and magnetic disturbances that transfer energy from one place to another.

Wavelength

Electromagnetic waves do not transfer matter. The energy they transfer depends on the **wavelength** of the waves. This is why waves of different wavelengths have different effects.

a) Which part of the electromagnetic spectrum causes sunburn?

The wavelength is the distance from one wave peak to the next wave peak along the waves.

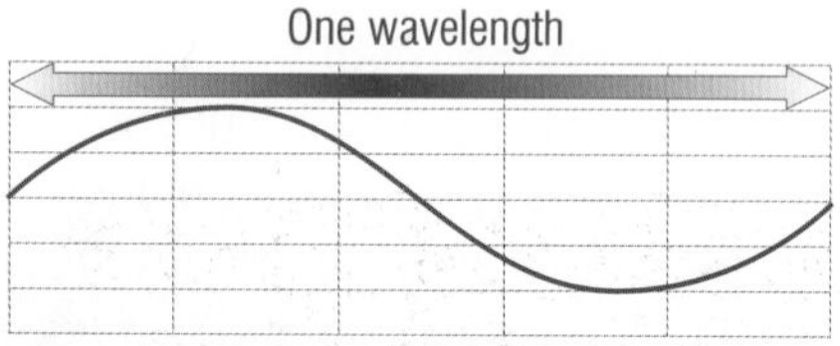

Waves from different parts of the electromagnetic spectrum have different wavelengths.

- Long-wave radio waves have wavelengths of more than 1000 m.
- X-rays and gamma rays have wavelengths of less than a millionth of a millionth of a metre (= 0.000 000 000 001 m).

b) Where in the electromagnetic spectrum would you find waves of wavelength 0.01 m?

Frequency

The **frequency** of electromagnetic waves of a certain wavelength is the number of complete waves passing a point each second.

The unit of frequency is the hertz (Hz), where:

- 1 hertz (Hz) = 1 complete wave per second,
- 1 kilohertz (kHz) = 1000 Hz (= 1 thousand hertz),
- 1 megahertz (MHz) = 1 000 000 Hz (= 1 million hertz).

One wavelength

Figure 2 Wavelength – take care **not** to measure the distance between a peak and a trough. Measure the distance between neighbouring peaks (or troughs).

The speed of electromagnetic waves

All electromagnetic waves travel at a speed of 300 million m/s through space or in a vacuum. This is the distance the waves travel each second.

We can link the speed of the waves to their frequency and wavelength using this equation:

$$\text{wave speed} = \text{frequency} \times \text{wavelength}$$
$$\text{(metre/second, m/s)} \quad \text{(hertz, Hz)} \quad \text{(metre, m)}$$

1 We can work out the wavelength if we know the frequency and the wave speed. To do this, we rearrange the equation into:

$$\text{wavelength (in metres)} = \frac{\text{wave speed (in m/s)}}{\text{frequency (in Hz)}}$$

> **Worked example**
>
> A mobile phone gives out electromagnetic waves of frequency 900 million Hz. Calculate the wavelength of these waves.
>
> The speed of electromagnetic waves in air = 300 million m/s.
>
> **Solution**
>
> $$\text{wavelength (in metres)} = \frac{\text{wave speed (in m/s)}}{\text{frequency (in Hz)}} = \frac{300\,000\,000 \text{ m/s}}{900\,000\,000 \text{ Hz}} = 0.33 \text{ m}$$

c) Work out the wavelength of electromagnetic waves of frequency 102 million Hz.

2 We can work out the frequency if we know the wavelength and the wave speed. To do this, we rearrange the equation into:

$$\text{frequency (in Hz)} = \frac{\text{wave speed (in m/s)}}{\text{wavelength (in metres)}}$$

d) Work out the frequency of electromagnetic waves of wavelength 1500 m.

> ### SUMMARY QUESTIONS
>
> 1 Choose words from the list to complete each sentence in a), b) and c).
>
> > **greater than**   **smaller than**   **the same as**
>
>   a) The wavelength of light waves is …… the wavelength of radio waves.
>   b) The speed of radio waves in a vacuum is …… the speed of gamma rays.
>   c) The frequency of X-rays is …… the frequency of infra-red radiation.
>
> 2 a) Fill in the missing parts of the electromagnetic spectrum in the list below.
>
> > **radio**   ……   **infra-red**   **visible**   ……   **X-rays**   ……
>
>   b) Work out:
>   i) the wavelength of radio waves of frequency 600 million Hz,
>   ii) the frequency of microwaves of wavelength 0.30 m.

> ### DID YOU KNOW?
>
> Do you know the frequency of your favourite radio station? For example, a local radio station on 102 MHz sends out radio waves at a frequency of 102 MHz (= 102 000 000 Hz). Every radio station has its own frequency channel.

> ### KEY POINTS
>
> 1 The electromagnetic spectrum (in order of increasing wavelength) is:
>
> > gamma and X-rays
> > ultraviolet
> > visible
> > infra-red
> > microwaves
> > radio.
>
> 2 All electromagnetic waves travel through space at a speed of 300 million m/s.
> 3 Wave speed = wavelength × frequency.

P1b 5.2

Gamma rays and X-rays

X-rays

Have you ever broken an arm or a leg? If you have, you will have gone to your local hospital for an X-ray photograph.

X-rays pass through soft tissue but they are absorbed by bones and thick metal plates. To make a **radiograph** or X-ray picture, X-rays from an X-ray tube are directed at the patient. A light-proof cassette containing a photographic film is placed on the other side of the patient.

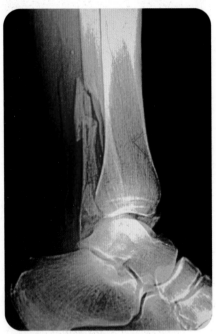

Figure 2 Spot the break

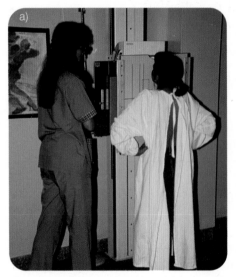

Figure 1 a) Taking a chest X-ray. b) A chest X-ray.

- When the X-ray tube is switched on, X-rays from the tube pass through the patient's body. They leave a 'shadow' image on the film showing the bones.
- When the film is developed, the parts exposed to X-rays are darker than the other parts. So the bones appear lighter than the surrounding tissue which appears dark. The developed film shows a 'negative image' of the bones.

a) Why is a crack in a bone visible on a radiograph (X-ray image)?

Gamma radiation

Gamma radiation is electromagnetic radiation from radioactive substances. Gamma rays and X-rays have similar wavelengths so they have similar properties. For example, a lead plate will stop gamma radiation or X-rays if it is several centimetres thick.

Gamma radiation is used:

- to kill harmful bacteria in food,
- to sterilise surgical instruments,
- to kill cancer cells.

b) Will gamma radiation pass through thin plastic wrappers?

FOUL FACTS

We lose about 20% of the world's food through spoilage. One of the major causes is bacteria. The bacteria produce waste products that cause food poisoning. Exposing food to gamma radiation kills 99% of disease-carrying organisms, including *Salmonella* (found in poultry) and *Clostridium* (the cause of botulism).

Using gamma radiation

Doctors and medical physicists use gamma therapy to destroy cancerous tumours. A narrow beam of gamma radiation is directed at the tumour. The beam is aimed at it from different directions in order to kill the tumour but not the surrounding tissue. The cobalt-60 source, which produces the gamma radiation, is in a thick lead container. When it is not in use, it is rotated away from the exit channel.

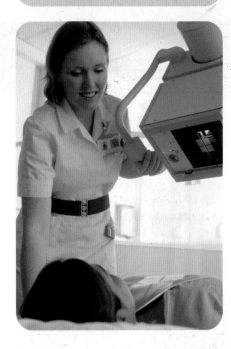

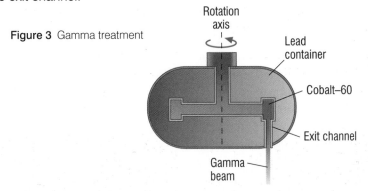

Figure 3 Gamma treatment

c) Why does the gamma beam need to be narrow?

Safety matters

Too much X-radiation or gamma radiation is dangerous and causes cancer. High doses kill living cells. Low doses cause cell mutation and cancerous growth. There is no evidence of a lower limit below which living cells would not be damaged.

Some people use equipment or substances that produce X-radiation or gamma radiation (or alpha or beta radiation) at work. (See page 97.) These workers must wear a film badge. If the badge is over-exposed to such radiation, its wearer is not allowed to continue working with the equipment.

d) Why does a film badge have a plastic case, and not a metal case?

Figure 4 A film badge tells you how much ionising radiation the wearer has received. Who might wear these?

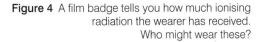

SUMMARY QUESTIONS

1 Choose the correct words from the list to complete each sentence below.

absorb   damage   penetrate

a) X-rays and gamma rays …… thin metal sheets.
b) Thick lead plates will …… X-rays and gamma rays.
c) X-rays and gamma rays …… living tissue.

2 When an X-ray photograph is taken, why is it necessary:

a) to place the patient between the X-ray tube and the film cassette?
b) to have the film in a light-proof cassette?
c) to shield those parts of the patient not under investigation from X-rays? Explain what would happen to healthy cells.

KEY POINTS

1 X-rays and gamma radiation are absorbed by dense materials such as bone and metal.
2 X-rays and gamma radiation damage living tissue when they pass through it.
3 X-rays are used in hospitals to take radiographs.
4 Gamma rays are used to kill harmful bacteria in food, to sterilise surgical equipment and to kill cancer cells.

P1b 5.3 Light and ultraviolet radiation

Light from ordinary lamps and from the Sun is called *white light*. This is because it has all the colours of the visible spectrum in it. You see the colours of the spectrum when you look at a rainbow. You can also see them if you use a glass prism to split a beam of white light. But the human eye can't detect the ultraviolet radiation beyond the violet part of the spectrum or the infra-red radiation beyond the red part of the spectrum. (See page 24.)

- Coloured filters can be used to filter out colours from a beam of white light. For example, a red filter absorbs all colours except red from the light beam. So the beam is red when it comes out of the filter.
- Each colour of the visible spectrum has a different wavelength. The wavelength increases across the spectrum as you go from violet to red.
- Ultraviolet radiation is electromagnetic radiation between violet light and X-rays in wavelength.

a) Is the wavelength of ultraviolet radiation longer or shorter than the wavelength of light ?

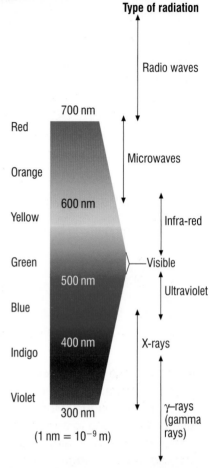

Figure 1 The electromagnetic spectrum with an expanded view of the visible range

Ultraviolet radiation

Ultraviolet radiation makes some chemicals emit light. Posters and ink that glow in ultraviolet light contain these chemicals. The chemicals absorb ultraviolet radiation and emit light as a result.

Ultraviolet radiation is harmful to human eyes and can cause blindness. Ultraviolet (UV) wavelengths are smaller than light wavelengths. UV rays carry more energy than light rays. Too much UV radiation causes sunburn and can cause skin cancer.

- If you stay outdoors in summer, use skin creams to block UV radiation and prevent it reaching the skin.
- If you use a sunbed to get a suntan, don't exceed the recommended time. You should also wear special 'goggles' to protect your eyes.

b) How does invisible ink work?

Electromagnetic waves and substances

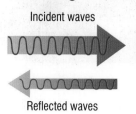
Incident waves

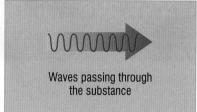
Waves passing through the substance

Transmitted waves

Reflected waves

Figure 2 Electromagnetic waves and substances

When electromagnetic waves are directed at a substance:

- some or all of the waves may be **reflected** at the surface. The type of surface and the wavelength of the waves determine if the waves are totally or partly reflected or not reflected at all. For example,
  - light directed at ordinary glass is partly reflected,
  - X-rays directed at plastic are not reflected at all.
- some or all of the waves that go into a substance may be **absorbed** by it. The substance would become hotter due to the energy it gains from the absorbed radiation. Also, the radiation itself may create an alternating current at the same frequency as itself.
- The waves that are not absorbed by the substance are **transmitted** by it. The substance and the wavelength of the waves determine if the waves pass through it. For example:
  - ultraviolet radiation is mostly but not completely absorbed by glass,
  - X-rays mostly pass through human tissue and are mainly absorbed by bone.

c) Is the light from invisible ink due to ultraviolet light being reflected or absorbed or transmitted by the ink?

DEMONSTRATION

Ultraviolet radiation

Watch your teacher place different coloured clothes under an ultraviolet lamp. The lamp must point downwards so you can't look directly at the glow from it. Observe what happens.

- What do white clothes look like under a UV lamp?

d) How does a 'security' marker pen work?

Figure 3 Using an ultraviolet lamp to detect biological stains. The stain absorbs ultraviolet radiation from the lamp and gives out visible light as a result. The background red lighting makes the light from the stain more visible.

SUMMARY QUESTIONS

1 Choose words from the list for each of the spaces in the sentences below. Each option can only be used once.

> **red light**   **blue light**   **ultraviolet radiation**   **white light**

   a) …… has a longer wavelength than …… .
   b) …… from the Sun is absorbed by the ozone layer.
   c) …… includes all the colours of the spectrum.

2 a) Why is ultraviolet radiation harmful?
   b) i) How does the Earth's ozone layer help to protect us from ultraviolet radiation from the Sun?
      ii) Why do people outdoors in summer need suncream?

3 Explain what happens to the energy carried by electromagnetic waves when they are reflected, transmitted or absorbed.

KEY POINTS

1 Ultraviolet radiation is in the electromagnetic spectrum between violet light and X-radiation.
2 Ultraviolet radiation has a shorter wavelength than light.
3 Ultraviolet radiation harms the skin and the eyes.

P1b 5.4

Infra-red, microwaves and radio waves

LEARNING OBJECTIVES

1 What do we use infra-red radiation for?
2 Why are microwaves used for heating?
3 When do we use infra-red radiation, microwaves and radio waves for communications?

Figure 1 Infra-red devices

Infra-red radiation

All objects emit infra-red radiation.

● The hotter an object is, the more infra-red radiation it emits. (See page 24 for more about the properties of infra-red radiation.)
● Infra-red radiation is absorbed by the skin. It damages or kills skin cells because it heats up the cells.

a) Can you remember where infra-red radiation lies in the electromagnetic spectrum? (Look back to page 78 if necessary.)

Infra-red devices

● *Heaters* in grills, toasters, and electric heaters all emit infra-red radiation to heat objects.
● *Infra-red scanners* are used in medicine to detect 'hot spots' on the body surface, which can mean the underlying tissue is unhealthy. You can use *infra-red cameras* to see people and animals in darkness.
● *Optical fibres* in communications systems use infra-red radiation instead of light. This is because infra-red radiation is absorbed less than light in the glass fibres.
● *Remote control handsets* for TV and video equipment transmit signals carried by infra-red radiation. When you press a button on the handset, it sends out a sequence of infra-red pulses.

PRACTICAL

Testing infra-red radiation

Can infra-red radiation pass through paper?

You can use a remote handset to find out.

● What happens?

Microwaves

Microwaves lie between radio waves and infra-red radiation in the electromagnetic spectrum. They are called '*micro*waves' because they are shorter in wavelength than radio waves.

We use microwaves for:

● *communications*, because they can pass through the atmosphere and reach satellites orbiting the Earth. We use them to 'beam' signals from one place to another, because they don't spread out as much as radio waves;
● *heating food in microwave ovens*. These heat the food from the inside as well as from the outside. Unlike infra-red radiation, microwaves penetrate substances like food.

b) i) Can microwaves pass through plastic?
   ii) Why is it dangerous to put metal objects in a microwave oven?

Figure 2 A microwave oven heats food from the inside as well as from the outside

Radio waves

Radio wave frequencies range from about 300 000 Hz to 3000 million Hz (where microwave frequencies start). Radio waves are longer in wavelength and lower in frequency than microwaves.

We use radio waves to carry radio, TV and mobile phone signals.

- Radio waves are emitted from an aerial when we apply an alternating voltage to the aerial. The frequency of the radio waves produced is the same as the frequency of the alternating voltage.
- When the radio waves pass across a receiver aerial, they cause a tiny alternating voltage in the aerial. The frequency of the alternating voltage is the same as the frequency of the radio waves received.

Figure 3 A radio transmitter

PRACTICAL

Testing microwaves

Look at the demonstration shown.

- What does this show?

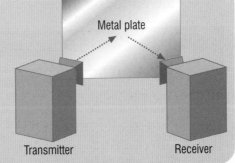

Figure 4 Testing microwaves   Transmitter   Receiver

KEY POINTS

	Frequency	Wavelength	Applications
Infra-red	↑		heaters, communications (remote handsets, optical fibres)
Microwaves			microwave oven, communications
Radio waves		↓	communications

SUMMARY QUESTIONS

1 Use words from the list to complete the sentences below:

   infra-red radiation   light   microwaves   radio waves

   a) In a TV set, the aerial detects …… and the screen emits ……. .
   b) In a microwave oven, food absorbs ……, heats up and emits ……. .

2 Complete the table below showing the type of electromagnetic radiation produced by each device a) to d).

Device	Infra-red	Microwave	Radio
a) Electric toaster			
b) Microwave oven			
c) TV broadcast transmitter			
d) Remote handset			

3 Describe how a radio transmitter produces radio waves and what happens to the radio waves at a receiver aerial.

DID YOU KNOW?

The sinking of the *Titanic* in 1912 claimed over 1500 lives. There weren't enough lifeboats for everyone. A few years earlier, two ships collided and everyone was saved – because an SOS radio message was sent out. Nearby ships got there in good time. Ship owners decided they didn't need lifeboats for everyone. After the *Titanic* disaster, they were made to put all the lifeboats back!

P1b 5.5   Communications

Radio communications

The radio and microwave spectrum is divided into *frequency bands*. How we use each band depends on its frequency range. This is because the higher the frequency of the waves:

- the more information they can carry,
- the shorter their range (due to increasing absorption by the atmosphere),
- the less they spread out (because they diffract less).

Figure 1 Using a car radio

Wavebands

Waveband	Frequency range	Uses
Microwaves	greater than 3000 MHz	Satellite links (e.g. phone and TV) Mobile phones
UHF (ultra-high frequency)	300–3000 MHz	Terrestrial TV Mobile phones
VHF (very high frequency)	30–300 MHz	Local radio (FM), Emergency services Digital radio
HF (high frequency)	3–30 MHz	Amateur radio, CB
MF (medium frequency – also called 'medium wave' or MW)	300 kHz – 3 MHz	National radio (analogue)
LF (low frequency – also called 'long wave' or LW)	less than 300 kHz	International radio (analogue)
(M = mega = million)		

a) What is the difference between satellite TV and terrestrial TV?

Radio waves and the ionosphere

The ionosphere is a layer of gas in the upper atmosphere. It reflects radio waves that have frequencies less than about 30 MHz. So it reflects HF, MF and LF wavebands.

The ionosphere is stronger in summer than in winter. This is why you can listen to distant radio stations in summer but not in winter. Radio waves from these stations bounce back and forth between the ionosphere and the ground.

b) Why can't you listen to distant MF and HF radio stations in winter?

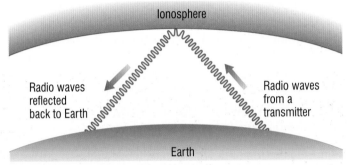

Figure 2 LF, MF and HF radio waves are reflected by the ionosphere. So they can be sent very long distances despite the curvature of the Earth.

c) Why can't you watch TV stations that are below the horizon?

Optical fibre communications

Optical fibres are very thin glass fibres. We use them to transmit signals carried by light or infra-red radiation. The light rays can't escape from the fibre. When they reach the surface of the fibre, they are reflected back into the fibre.

In comparison with radio waves and microwaves:

● optical fibres can carry much more information – this is because the frequency of light and infra-red radiation is much higher,
● optical fibres are more secure because the signals stay in the fibre.

d) Why can't we use optical fibres for satellite communications?

Satellite TV

Satellite TV signals are carried by microwaves. We can detect them on the ground because they pass through the ionosphere. But you can't watch distant TV stations because the signals go straight through the ionosphere into space – they are not reflected back.

PRACTICAL

Optical fibres

Observe light shone into an optical fibre.

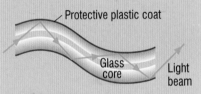

Figure 3 Optical fibres

● How are optical fibres used in hospitals?

SUMMARY QUESTIONS

1 Choose the correct word from the list to fill in each of the spaces in the sentences below.

microwaves   radio waves

a) TV signals are carried by ....
b) Satellite TV signals are carried by ....
c) A beam of ...... can travel from the ground to a satellite but a beam of ...... waves cannot if its frequency is below 30 MHz.

2 a) Why is it not possible to tune your radio in to American local radio stations?
b) Why are signals in optical fibres more secure than radio signals?

3 Explain why we use microwaves for satellite communications.

KEY POINTS

1 The use we make of radio waves depends on the frequency of the waves.
2 Visible light and infra-red radiation are used to carry signals in optical fibres.

P1b 5.6   Analogue and digital signals

LEARNING OBJECTIVES

1 How do digital and analogue signals differ?
2 What are the advantages of digital signals?

In the next ten years, we will all have to change our TV sets or adapt them. At present, TV stations transmit *analogue* signals and *digital* signals. But after the 'Big Switchover', they will only send out digital signals.

- **A digital signal** is a sequence of pulses. The voltage level of each pulse is either high (a '1') or low (a '0') with no in-between levels. Each '0' or '1' is called a **bit**. Mobile phone signals and signals from computers are digital.
- **An analogue signal** is a wave that varies continuously in amplitude or frequency between zero and a maximum value. For example, a microphone generates electrical waves when it detects sound waves.

a) A 'digibox' changes an analogue signal to a digital signal. Why is a digibox needed to receive digital TV at present?

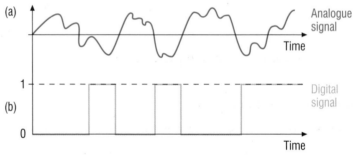

Figure 1 a) An analogue signal, b) a digital signal.

Sending signals

The waves we use to carry a signal are called **carrier waves**. They could be radio waves, microwaves, infra-red radiation or light.

- To send a digital signal, the pulses are used to switch the carrier waves on and off repeatedly. Digital radio transmitters, scanners and fax machines all convert analogue signals into digital signals which are then sent.

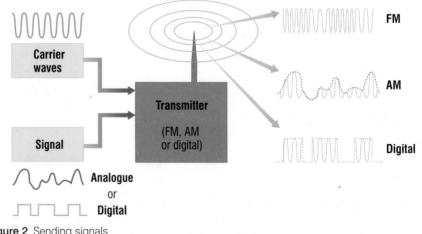

Figure 2 Sending signals

- To send an analogue signal, the signal waves are used to vary or **modulate** the carrier waves. The amplitude (amplitude modulation AM) or the frequency (frequency modulation FM) of the carrier waves is modulated in this process.

b) Is an e-mail message analogue or digital?

Why digital is better than analogue

- Digital signals suffer **less interference** than analogue signals. Interference causes a hissing noise when you listen to analogue radio. It doesn't happen with digital signals because regenerator circuits are used to clean 'noisy' pulses. So a digital signal has a higher quality than an analogue signal.

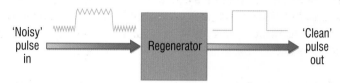

'Noisy' pulse in → Regenerator → 'Clean' pulse out

Figure 3 Cleaning a noisy pulse

- **Much more information** can be sent using digital signals instead of analogue signals. Digital pulses can be made very short so more pulses can be carried each second.

c) Do video phones use analogue or digital signals?

SUMMARY QUESTIONS

1 Choose a word from the list to complete the sentences below.

   analogue   carrier   digital

   a) AM and FM are forms of …… signals in which the signal modulates a …… wave.
   b) …… signals have a higher quality than …… signals.
   c) …… signals consist of pulses.

2 Look at the diagram below. It shows a communication system.

   Match the boxes labelled **A–D** with the words from the list below.

   carrier wave   receiver   signal   transmitter

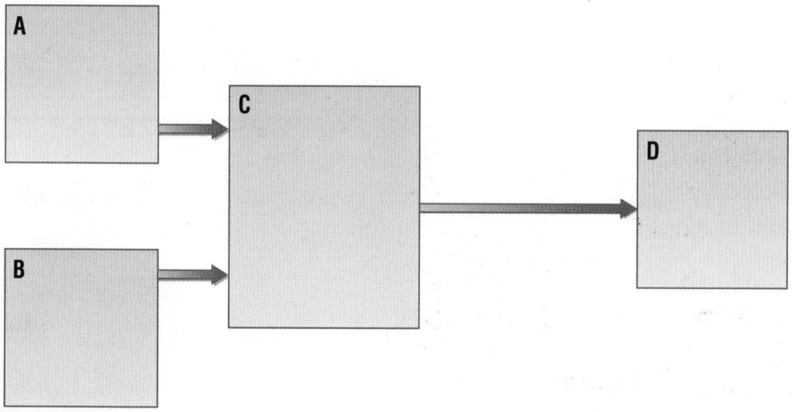

   A
   C
   D
   B

3 Describe how analogue and digital signals can be changed from one to the other.

KEY POINTS

1 Analogue signals vary continuously in amplitude.
2 Digital signals are either high ('1') or low ('0').
3 Digital transmission, when compared with analogue transmission, is free of noise and distortion. It can also carry much more information.

P1b 5.7   Microwave issues

A key scientific invention

The Battle of the Atlantic was one of the most important battles in the Second World War. Enemy U-boat submarines almost stopped supplies from North America reaching Britain by sinking so many British cargo ships. But the submarine menace was defeated as a result of an invention in 1940 by the British scientists, John Randall and Henry Boot.

They invented the high-power magnetron. It was the first high-power microwave transmitter. It replaced the low-power microwave transmitters used until then in radar sets. The new high-power radar sets were fitted into aircraft and warships to find submarines when they surfaced.

Randall and Boot's invention was invaluable. Now we use it in microwave ovens as well as in radar systems.

QUESTION

1   A high-power radar set has a longer range than a low-power set. Why was this important in the Battle of the Atlantic?

The Big Switchover

Digital TV is in a different waveband to analogue TV. Viewers have a greater choice of TV channels on digital. When analogue TV ends, its waveband will be sold off to mobile phone companies. They will get their money back from the charges their customers pay. But the Big Switchover could be costly for TV viewers because they will have to replace their TV set or buy a digibox to adapt it.

ACTIVITY

Either
Imagine you are a journalist on your local newspaper and the date for the Big Switchover has been set. Write a short article about it for your newspaper.
Or
Discuss this viewer's opinion on the 'Big Switchover':

I'm perfectly happy with my old TV. Why should I have to spend good money to switch from analogue to digital? It's just not right!

Using your mobile phone

When you use a mobile phone to talk to a friend, the handset sends out a radio signal. This is detected by the nearest receiver mast. The receiver is linked to a telephone exchange so your call is then routed to your friend's phone. The local mast sends out radio waves carrying the return signal from your friend.

Mobile phone mast (serves users in the cell)

Mobile phone cell

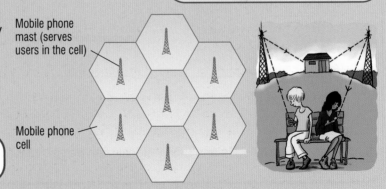

ACTIVITY

Compare mobile phone costs from two different companies and say which is best for you.

Selling the radio spectrum

How can you sell radio waves? Mobile phone companies are only allowed to use a narrow band of frequencies in the UHF waveband. Mobile phone companies have to pay the Government to use these frequencies.

Who decides what each frequency band can be used for? Imagine the chaos if air traffic controllers and taxi drivers used the same frequency bands. Engineers advise the Government on the best use of each frequency band. Users are then required by law to keep to the band chosen for them.

ACTIVITY

Imagine a taxi firm uses an 'ambulance' radio channel by mistake. Write a short story about a 'mix-up' that happened when the taxi firm used the 'ambulance' radio channel.

Mobile phone hazards 12:00

Microwaves and short wave radio waves penetrate living tissues and heat the water inside living cells. This can damage or even kill the cells. Microwave ovens have safety switches that turn the microwaves off when the door is open. Also, the metal casing acts as a shield to stop microwaves from escaping.

Mobile phones send out radio waves when they are used. The waves are very low-power waves.

Is the radiation from a mobile phone hazardous? At the present time, there is no conclusive scientific evidence one way or the other. Some people believe that mobile phones can cause brain tumours. The government recommends caution, particularly for young people, until scientists and doctors can find out more.

Are mobile phones intrusive? People can get upset when mobile phone users share their views with everyone within hearing range. A videophone user who points the phone camera at someone else can be prosecuted. Mobile phone technology is here to stay but users should not upset other people or use mobile phones illegally.

Menu   Contacts

QUESTION

2 **a)** Why might young people be more affected by mobile phone radiation than older people?

   b) How would scientists see if there were a link (correlation) between the use of mobile phones and brain tumours?

   c) How might scientists show that mobile phones cause brain tumours?

   d) Mobile phones can be dangerous in other ways as well.
   Why is driving and talking on your mobile phone dangerous?
   You might step off the pavement at the wrong moment if you are talking to someone on your mobile at the same time. Design a poster to warn people about the dangers of using a mobile phone.

ACTIVITY

A mobile phone company wants to put a mobile phone mast on the roof of your school. The teachers and the students don't want it. The school governors say the company will pay rent to the school and the money can be used for more computers.

Discuss your opinions on this proposal with your friends.

How would you advise your student council to respond to the proposal?

SUMMARY QUESTIONS

1 a) Place the four different types of electromagnetic waves listed below in order of increasing wavelength.

A Infra-red waves   **B** Microwaves
C Radio waves   **D** Gamma rays

b) The radio waves from a local radio station have a wavelength of 3.3 metres in air and a frequency of 91 million hertz.
  i) Write down the equation that links frequency, wavelength and wave speed.
  ii) Calculate the speed of the radio waves in air.

2 At the top of page 282 you will find the typical wavelengths of electromagnetic waves.

Match each of **A**, **B**, **C** and **D** below with **1** to **4** in the second list.

A 0.0005 mm   **B** 1 millionth of 1 mm
C 10 cm   **D** 1000 m

  1 X-rays   **2** light   **3** microwaves   **4** radio

3 a) Complete the following sentences using words from the list below.

  **gamma radiation   infra-red radiation
  light   ultraviolet radiation**

  i)   The Earth's ozone layer absorbs ....
  ii) An ordinary lamp gives out ...... and ....
  iii) ...... passes through a metal object.

b) Which type of radiation listed above damages the following parts of the human body?
  i)   the internal organs,
  ii) the eyes but not the internal organs,
  iii) the skin but not the eyes or the internal organs.

4 a) Complete each of the sentences below using words from the list.

  **microwave   mobile phone
  radio waves   TV**

  i) A ...... beam can travel from a ground transmitter to a satellite, but a beam of ...... cannot if its frequency is below 30 MHz.
  ii) ...... signals and ...... signals always come from a local transmitter.

b) i) Explain the difference between a digital signal and an analogue signal.
  ii) State and explain two advantages of digital transmission compared with analogue transmission.

EXAM-STYLE QUESTIONS

1 Electromagnetic waves can be grouped according to their wavelength and frequency.
Match the words in the list with the spaces **1** to **4** in the diagram.
A gamma rays   **B** microwaves
C ultraviolet rays   **D** visible light

Increasing wavelength, decreasing frequency

| 1 | X-rays | 2 | 3 | Infra red rays | 4 | Radio waves |

(4)

2 The number of waves passing a point each second is the . . .
A amplitude   **B** frequency
C speed   **D** wavelength   (1)

3 Which of the following statements about the waves of the electromagnetic spectrum is true?
A They all have the same frequency.
B They all have the same wavelength.
C They all travel at the same speed through space.
D They cannot travel through a vacuum.   (1)

4 The uses of the radiations in different parts of the electromagnetic spectrum depend on their wavelength and frequency.

(a) Shadow pictures of the bones can be produced using . . .
A microwaves.   **B** ultraviolet rays.
C visible light.   **D** X-rays.   (1)

(b) Which type of electromagnetic radiation is used to send signals from a TV remote control?
A infra-red rays.   **B** microwaves.
C radio waves.   **D** ultraviolet rays.   (1)

(c) Which type of electromagnetic radiation is used to sterilise surgical instruments?
A gamma rays   **B** microwaves
C ultraviolet rays   **D** visible light   (1)

(d) What is the equation that relates the speed, wavelength and frequency of the waves of the electromagnetic spectrum?
A Speed = frequency × wavelength
B Speed = frequency ÷ wavelength
C Speed = wavelength ÷ frequency
D Speed = wavelength + frequency   (1)

5 (a) Information can be transmitted through optical fibres.
Name two types of electromagnetic wave used to carry information through an optical fibre. (2)

(b) Information can be sent as a digital signal or an analogue signal. What is the difference between a digital and an analogue signal? (2)

(c) A signal gets weaker as it travels and needs to be amplified. Explain why an amplified analogue signal will have deteriorated compared with the original signal. (3)

6 Astronauts in space wear special suits designed to prevent dangerous radiation from the Sun reaching their bodies.

Explain how each of these types of electromagnetic radiation can harm the body:

(a) gamma rays (2)

(b) ultraviolet rays (3)

(c) microwaves. (2)

HOW SCIENCE WORKS QUESTIONS

Your teacher has set up a demonstration of light radiation. She used a slide projector to shine light onto a prism. The prism split the light into the colours of the rainbow – a spectrum. Then a thermistor was placed into the spectrum of light.

Thermistors can be used to measure heat. When put into a circuit, the hotter the thermistor the greater the voltage, measured by a voltmeter.

You can get a better idea of what she did from this diagram.

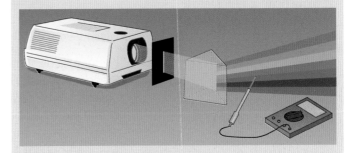

The thermistor was gradually moved through the spectrum from the violet end to the red end and beyond. The voltage was taken every 10 seconds and the colour of light was also recorded.

Here are the results.

Time (seconds)	Voltage (mV)	Colour
0	745	none
10	750	violet
20	760	indigo
30	770	blue
40	780	green
50	790	yellow
60	800	orange
70	810	red
80	990	none

a) What is the pattern in these results? Complete the sentence:
The longer the wavelength of light ...... (1)

b) Which result could be an anomaly? (1)

c) What should be done with this anomaly? (2)

d) If you wanted to draw a graph showing how the voltage varied with time, explain what type of graph you would use. (2)

P1b 6.1

Observing nuclear radiation

LEARNING OBJECTIVES

1 How can we observe radioactivity?
2 When does a radioactive source give out radiation (radioactivity)?
3 Why does a radioactive source give out radiation (radioactivity)?

A key discovery

Figure 1 Becquerel's key

If your photos showed a mysterious image, what would you think? In 1896, the French physicist, *Henri Becquerel*, discovered the image of a key on a film he developed. He remembered the film had been in a drawer under a key. On top of that there had been a packet of uranium salts. The uranium salts must have sent out some form of radiation that passed through paper (e.g. the film wrapper) but not through metal (e.g. the key).

Becquerel asked a young research worker, *Marie Curie*, to investigate. She found that the salts gave out radiation all the time. It happened no matter what was done to them. She used the word *radioactivity* to describe this strange new property of uranium.

She and her husband, Pierre, did more research into this new branch of science. They discovered new radioactive elements. They named one of the elements *polonium*, after Marie's native country, Poland.

a) You can stop a lamp giving out light by switching it off. Is it possible to stop uranium giving out radiation?

Marie Curie 1867-1934

Becquerel and the Curies were awarded the Nobel prize for the discovery of radioactivity. Pierre died in a road accident. Marie went on with their work. She was awarded a second Nobel prize in 1911 for the discovery of polonium and radium. She died in 1934 in middle-age from leukaemia. This is a disease of the blood cells and was caused by the radioactive materials she worked with.

Figure 2 Marie Curie 1867–1934

PRACTICAL

Investigating radioactivity

We can use a *Geiger counter* to detect radioactivity. Look at Figure 3. The counter clicks each time a particle of radiation from a radioactive substance enters the Geiger tube.

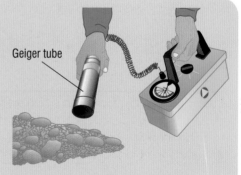

Figure 3 Using a Geiger counter

What stops the radiation? Ernest Rutherford carried out tests to answer this question about a century ago. He put different materials between the radioactive substance and a 'detector'.

He discovered two types of radiation:

- One type (**alpha radiation**, symbol α) was stopped by paper.
- The other type (**beta radiation**, symbol β) went through it.

Scientists later discovered a third type, **gamma radiation** (symbol γ), even more penetrating than beta radiation.

b) Can gamma radiation go through paper?

A radioactive puzzle

Why are some substances radioactive? Every atom has a nucleus made up of protons and neutrons. Electrons move about in the space surrounding the nucleus.

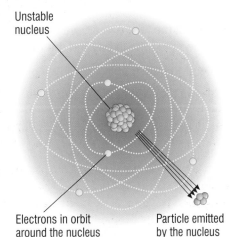

Unstable nucleus

Electrons in orbit around the nucleus

Particle emitted by the nucleus

Figure 4 Radioactive decay

Most atoms each have a stable nucleus that doesn't change. But the atoms of a radioactive substance each have a nucleus that is unstable. An unstable nucleus becomes stable by emitting alpha, beta or gamma radiation. We say an unstable nucleus *decays* when it emits radiation.

We can't tell when an unstable nucleus will decay. It is a **random** event that happens without anything being done to the nucleus.

c) Why is the radiation from a radioactive substance sometimes called nuclear radiation?

SUMMARY QUESTIONS

1 Complete the sentences below, using words from the list.

   proton   neutron   nucleus   radiation

   a) The ...... of an atom is made up of ...... and ....
   b) When an unstable ...... decays, it emits ....

2 a) The radiation from a radioactive source is stopped by paper. What type of radiation does the source emit?
   b) The radiation from a different source goes through paper. What can you say about this radiation?

3 Explain why some substances are radioactive.

KEY POINTS

1 A radioactive substance contains unstable nuclei.
2 An unstable nucleus becomes stable by emitting radiation.
3 There are 3 types of radiation from radioactive substances – alpha, beta and gamma radiation.
4 Radioactive decay is a random event – we cannot predict or influence when it will happen.

P1b 6.2 Alpha, beta and gamma radiation

LEARNING OBJECTIVES

1 How far can each type of radiation travel in air and what stops it?
2 What is alpha, beta and gamma radiation?
3 Why is alpha, beta and gamma radiation dangerous?

Penetrating power

Alpha radiation can't penetrate paper.

But what stops beta and gamma radiation? And how far can each type of radiation travel through air? We can use a Geiger counter to find out.

- To test different materials, we need to place each material between the tube and the radioactive source. Then we can add more layers of material until the radiation is stopped.
- To test the range in air, we need to move the tube away from the source. When the tube is beyond the range of the radiation, it can't detect it.

Look at the table below:

It shows the results of the two tests.

Type of radiation	Absorber materials	Range in air
alpha (α)	paper	about 10 cm
beta (β)	aluminium sheet (1 cm thick) lead sheet (2–3 mm thick)	about 1 m
gamma (γ)	thick lead sheet (several cm thick) concrete (more than 1 m thick)	unlimited

Gamma radiation spreads out in air without being absorbed. It does get weaker as it spreads out.

a) Why is a radioactive source stored in a lead-lined box?

FOUL FACTS

Radium is an element. It is so radioactive that it glows with light on its own. Many years ago, the workers in a US factory used radium paint on clocks and aircraft dials. They often licked the brushes to make a fine point to paint very accurately on the dials. Many of them later died from cancer.

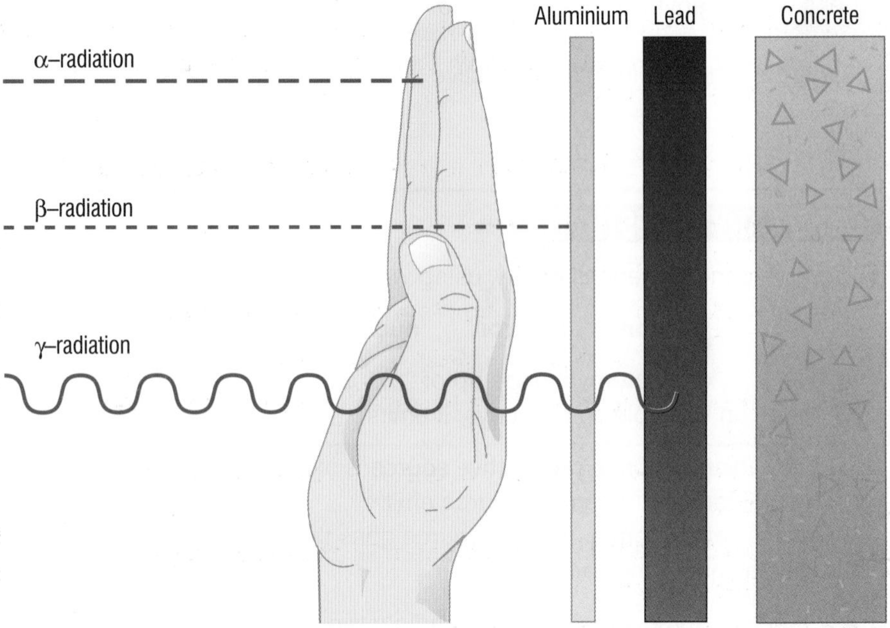

Figure 1 The penetrating powers of α, β and γ radiation

The nature of alpha, beta and gamma radiation

What are these mysterious radiations? They can be separated using a magnetic field. Look at Figure 2.

We use magnetic fields to deflect electron beams in a TV tube. The beams create the picture as they scan across the inside of the tube.

- β-radiation is easily deflected, in the same way as electrons. So it has a negative charge. In fact, a β-particle is a fast-moving electron. It is emitted by an unstable nucleus containing too many neutrons when it decays.
- α-radiation is deflected in the opposite direction to β-radiation because an α-particle has a positive charge. α-radiation is harder to deflect than β-radiation. This is because an α-particle is a lot heavier than a β-particle. It has a much greater mass. In fact, an alpha particle is two protons and two neutrons stuck together, the same as a helium nucleus.
- γ-radiation is not deflected by a magnetic field or an electric field. This is because gamma radiation is electromagnetic radiation so is uncharged.

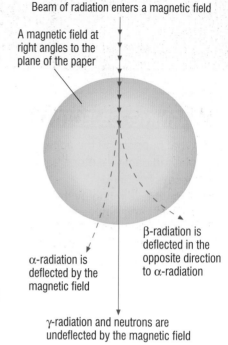

Beam of radiation enters a magnetic field

A magnetic field at right angles to the plane of the paper

β-radiation is deflected in the opposite direction to α-radiation

α-radiation is deflected by the magnetic field

γ-radiation and neutrons are undeflected by the magnetic field

Figure 2 Radiation in a magnetic field

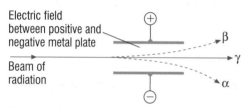

Electric field between positive and negative metal plate

Beam of radiation

Figure 3 Radiation passing through an electric field

Note that α and β-particles passing through an electric field are deflected in opposite directions.

b) How do we know that gamma radiation is not made up of charged particles?

Radioactivity dangers

The radiation from a radioactive substance can knock electrons out of atoms. The atoms become charged because they lose electrons. The process is called **ionisation**.

X-rays also cause ionisation. Ionisation in a living cell can damage or kill the cell. Damage to the genes in a cell can be passed on if the cell generates more cells. Strict rules must always be followed when radioactive substances are used.

Alpha radiation has a greater ionising effect than beta or gamma radiation. This makes it is more dangerous in the body than beta or gamma radiation. See page 81 for more information.

Figure 4 Radioactive warning

c) Why should long-handled tongs be used to move a radioactive source?

SUMMARY QUESTIONS

1 Choose words from the list to complete the sentences below:

alpha   beta   gamma

a) Electromagnetic radiation from a radioactive substance is called ...... radiation.

b) A thick metal plate will stop ...... and ...... radiation but not ...... radiation.

2 Which type of radiation is: a) uncharged? b) positively charged? c) negatively charged?

3 Explain why ionising radiation is dangerous.

KEY POINTS

1 **α-radiation** is stopped by paper or a few centimetres of air.

2 **β-radiation** is stopped by thin metal or about a metre of air.

3 **γ-radiation** is stopped by thick lead and has an unlimited range in air.

P1b 6.3   Half-life

LEARNING OBJECTIVES

1 What happens to the activity of a radioactive isotope as it decays?
2 What do we mean by the 'half-life' of a radioactive source?

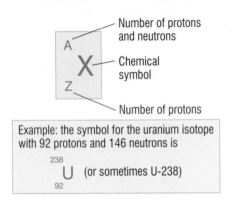

Example: the symbol for the uranium isotope with 92 protons and 146 neutrons is

$$^{238}_{92}U$$ (or sometimes U-238)

Figure 1 The symbol for an isotope

Every atom of an element always has the same number of protons in its nucleus. However, the number of neutrons in the nucleus can differ. Each type of atom is called an **isotope**. (So isotopes of an element contain the same number of protons but different numbers of neutrons.)

The **activity** of a radioactive substance is the number of atoms that decay per second. Each unstable atom (the 'parent' atom) forms an atom of a different isotope (the 'daughter' atom) when its nucleus decays. Because the number of parent atoms goes down, the activity of the sample decreases.

We can use a Geiger counter to monitor the activity of a radioactive sample. We need to measure the *count rate* due to the sample. This is the number of counts per second (or per minute). The graph below shows how the count rate of a sample decreases.

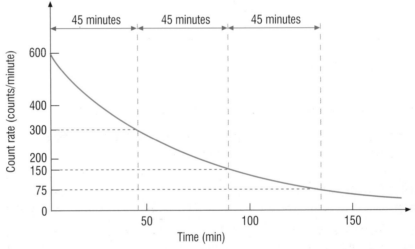

Figure 2 Radioactive decay: a graph of count rate against time

The graph shows that the count rate decreases with time. The count rate falls from:

- 600 counts per minute (c.p.m.) to 300 c.p.m. in the first 45 minutes,
- 300 counts per minute (c.p.m.) to 150 c.p.m. in the next 45 minutes.

The time taken for the count rate (and therefore the number of parent atoms) to fall by half is always the same. This time is called the **half-life**. The half-life shown on the graph is 45 minutes.

a) What will the count rate be after 135 minutes from the start?

The half-life of a radioactive isotope is the time it takes:

- **for the number of nuclei of the isotope in a sample (and therefore the mass of parent atoms) to halve,**
- **for the count rate due to the isotope in a sample to fall to half its initial value.**

The random nature of radioactive decay

We can't predict **when** an individual atom will suddenly decay. But we **can** predict how many atoms will decay in a certain time – because there are so many of them. This is a bit like throwing dice. You can't predict what number you will get with a single throw. But if you threw 1000 dice, you would expect one-sixth to come up with a particular number.

Suppose we start with 1000 unstable atoms. Look at the graph below:

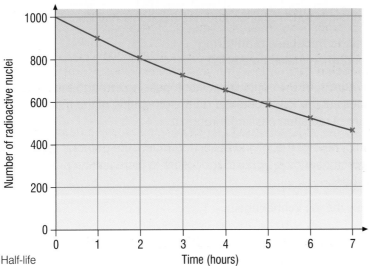

Figure 3 Half-life

If 10% disintegrate every hour,

100 atoms will decay in the first hour, leaving 900.
90 atoms (= 10% of 900) will decay in the second hour, leaving 810.

The table below shows what you get if you continue the calculations.
The results are plotted as a graph in Figure 3.

Time from start (hours)	0	1	2	3	4	5	6	7
No. of unstable atoms present	1000	900	810	729	656	590	530	477
No. of unstable atoms that decay in the next hour	100	90	81	73	66	59	53	48

b) Use the graph in Figure 3 to work out the half-life of this radioactive isotope.

NEXT TIME YOU...

. . . help someone choose numbers for the lottery, think about whether this is something you can predict. The balls come out of the machine at random; is there any way of predicting what they will be?

SUMMARY QUESTIONS

1 Complete the following sentences using words from the list below.

half-life   stable   unstable

a) In a radioactive substance, …… atoms decay and become ……. .
b) The …… of a radioactive isotope is the time taken for the number of …… atoms to decrease to half.

2 A radioactive isotope has a half-life of 15 hours. A sealed tube contains 8 milligrams of the substance.

What mass of the substance is in the tube:

a) 15 hours later?
b) 45 hours later?

KEY POINTS

1 The **half-life** of a radioactive isotope is the time it takes for the number of nuclei of the isotope in a sample to halve.
2 The number of unstable atoms and the activity decreases to half in one half-life.

P1b 6.4   Radioactivity at work

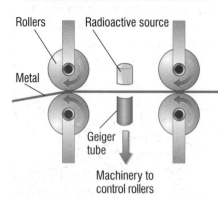

Figure 1 Thickness monitoring using a radioactive source

Uses of radioactivity

Radioactivity has many uses. For each use, we need a radioactive isotope that emits a certain type of radiation and has a suitable half life.

(1) Automatic thickness monitoring
This is used when making metal foil.

Look at Figure 1. The amount of radiation passing through the foil depends on the thickness of the foil. A detector on the other side of the metal foil measures the amount of radiation passing through it.

- If the thickness of the foil increases too much, the detector reading drops.
- The detector sends a signal to the rollers to increase the pressure on the metal sheet.

This makes the foil thinner again.

a) What happens if the thickness of the foil decreases too much?
b) Why is beta radiation, not alpha or gamma radiation, used here?

(2) Radioactive tracers
These are used to trace the flow of a substance through a system. For example, doctors use radioactive iodine to find out if a patient's kidney is blocked.

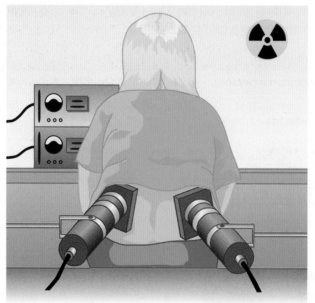

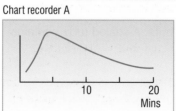

Figure 2 Using a tracer to monitor a patient's kidneys

Before the test, the patient drinks water containing a tiny amount of the radioactive substance. A detector is then placed against each kidney. Each detector is connected to a chart recorder.

- The radioactive substance flows in and out of a normal kidney. So the detector reading goes up then down.
- For a blocked kidney, the reading goes up and stays up. This is because the radioactive substance goes into the kidney but doesn't flow out again.

Radioactive iodine is used for this test because:

- its half life is 8 days, so it lasts long enough for the test to be done but decays almost completely after a few weeks,
- it emits gamma radiation, so it can be detected outside the body,
- it decays into a stable product.

c) In Figure 2, which kidney is blocked, A or B? How can you tell?

(3) Radioactive dating

This is used to find how old ancient material is, i.e. its age.

- *Carbon dating* is used to find the age of ancient wood.
  Living wood contains a tiny proportion of radioactive carbon. This has a half-life of 5600 years. When a tree dies, it no longer absorbs any carbon. So the amount of radioactive carbon in it decreases.
  To find the age of a sample, we need to measure the count rate from the wood. This is compared with the count rate from the same mass of living wood. For example, suppose the count rate in a sample of wood is half the count rate of an equal mass of living wood. Then the sample must be 5600 years old.

- *Uranium dating* is used to find the age of igneous rocks.
  These rocks contain radioactive uranium, which has a half-life of 4500 million years. Each uranium atom decays into an atom of lead. We can work out the age of a sample by measuring the number of atoms of uranium and lead. For example, if a sample contains 1 atom of lead for every atom of the uranium, the age of the sample must be 4500 million years. This is because there must have **originally** been 2 atoms of uranium for each atom of uranium now present.

d) What could you say about an igneous rock with uranium but no lead in it?

SUMMARY QUESTIONS

1 Choose the correct word from the list to complete each of the following sentences:

   alpha   beta   gamma

   a) In the continuous production of thin metal sheets, a source of ...... radiation should be used to monitor the thickness of the sheets.
   b) A radioactive tracer given to a hospital patient needs to emit ...... or ...... radiation.
   c) The radioactive source used to trace a leak in an underground pipeline should be a source of ...... radiation.

2 a) What are the ideal properties of a radioactive isotope used as a medical tracer?
   b) A sample of old wood was carbon dated and found to have 25% of the count rate measured in an equal mass of living wood. The half-life of the radioactive carbon is 5600 years. How old is the sample of wood?

KEY POINTS

1 The use we can make of a radioactive substance depends on:
   a) its half-life, and
   b) the type of radiation it gives out.

P1b 6.5   Radioactivity issues

Nuclear waste

The fuel rods in nuclear power stations are radioactive. Used fuel rods are very hot and are still very radioactive when they are removed from a nuclear reactor. They contain many radioactive isotopes that are formed when the uranium nuclei split.

Figure 1 Storage of nuclear waste

- After removal from a reactor, used fuel rods are stored in large tanks of water for up to a year. The water cools down the rods.
- Remote-control machines are then used to open the fuel rods. The machines remove unused uranium. This is stored in sealed containers so it can be used again.
- The remaining material contains many radioactive substances with long half lives. This radioactive waste must be stored in secure conditions for many years.

ACTIVITY

a) Why does radioactive waste need to be stored:
   i) securely?
   ii) for many years?
b) Some people say that nuclear power stations are better for the environment than power stations that burn fossil fuels. Discuss this issue.

Chernobyl

When the nuclear reactors in Ukraine exploded in 1986, emergency workers and scientists struggled for days to contain the fire. More than 100 000 people were evacuated from Chernobyl and the surrounding area. Over thirty people died in the accident. Many more have developed leukaemia or cancer. It was, and remains (up to now), the world's worst nuclear accident.

Could it happen again?

- Most nuclear reactors are of a different design.
- The Chernobyl accident did not have a high-speed shutdown system like most reactors have.
- The operators at Chernobyl ignored safety instructions.

Figure 2 Chernobyl

There are thousands of nuclear reactors in the world. They have been working for many years. Countries such as Sweden wanted to 'phase' them out after Chernobyl. Now they are planning new ones because they need electricity.

ACTIVITY

Should the UK government replace our existing nuclear reactors with new ones? Debate this question with your friends and take a vote on it.

Radioactivity all around us

When we use a Geiger counter, it clicks even without a radioactive source near it. This is due to **background radioactivity**. Radioactive substances are found naturally all around us.

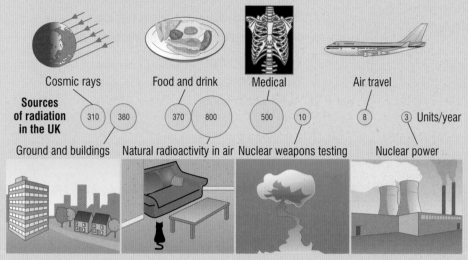

Figure 3 Sources of background radiation in the UK

Figure 3 shows the sources of background radioactivity. The numbers tell you how much radiation each person gets on average in a year from each source.

Radioactive risks

The effect on living cells of radiation from radioactive substances depends on:

- the type and the amount of radiation received (the dose), and
- whether the source of the radiation is inside or outside the body.

	Alpha radiation	Beta radiation	Gamma radiation
Source inside the body	**very dangerous!!!** – affects all the surrounding tissue	**dangerous!!** – reaches cells throughout the body	
Source outside the body	some **danger!** – absorbed by the skin; damages skin cells		

- The larger the dose of radiation someone gets, the greater the risk of cancer. High doses kill living cells.
- The smaller the dose, the less the risk – but the dose is never zero. So there is a very low level of risk to every one of us because of background radioactivity.

Radioactivity on the move

A nuclear power company needs to move radioactive waste from its nuclear power stations around the country to a specially designed storage site.

They intend to move the waste in strong metal containers which can withstand high-speed crashes. They plan to move the containers by train on main lines passing through towns and cities.

Lots of people are protesting about these plans. They want the waste moved by sea on ships. The company thinks that would be unsafe, as a ship might sink.

SUMMARY QUESTIONS

1 Which type of radiation, alpha, beta or gamma,

a) can pass through lead?

b) travels no further than about 10 cm in air?

c) is stopped by an aluminium metal plate but not by paper?

d) consists of electrons?

e) consists of helium nuclei?

f) is uncharged?

2 The table gives information about four radioactive isotopes **A**, **B**, **C** and **D**. Match each statement 1 to 4 with **A**, **B**, **C** or **D**.

1 The isotope which gives off radiation with an unlimited range.

2 The isotope which has the longest half-life.

3 The isotope which decays the fastest.

4 The isotope with the smallest mass.

Isotope	Type of radiation emitted	Half-life
A californium-241	alpha	4 minutes
B cobalt-60	gamma	5 years
C hydrogen-3	beta	12 years
D strontium-90	beta	28 years

3 The following measurements were made of the count rate due to a radioactive source.

Time (hours)	0	0.5	1.0	1.5	2.0	2.5
Count rate due to the source (counts per minute)	510	414	337	276	227	188

a) Plot a graph of the count rate (on the vertical axis) against time.

b) Use your graph to find the half-life of the source.

4 In a carbon dating experiment of ancient wood, a sample of the wood gave a count rate of 0.4 counts per minute. The same mass of living wood gave a count rate of 1.6 counts per minute.

a) How many half-lives did the count rate take to decrease from 1.6 to 0.4 counts per minute?

b) The half-life of the radioactive carbon in the wood is 5600 years. What is the age of the sample?

EXAM-STYLE QUESTIONS

1 Some people working in hospitals may be exposed to different types of nuclear radiation. Which of the following statements describes what they can do to reduce their exposure to nuclear radiation?

A Wear a badge containing photographic film.

B Wear a lead-lined apron.

C Wear a sterile gown.

D Wear rubber boots (1)

2 The diagram shows an atom of carbon.
Match the words in the list with the numbers **1** to **4** in the sentences.

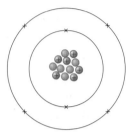

A Electrons   B Neutrons

C Nucleus   D Positive

Particles shown by the symbol × in the diagram are called ......**1**...... They orbit the ......**2**...... of an atom. This is made up of protons and ......**3**...... Protons have a ......**4**...... charge. (4)

3 Which of the following statements about radioactive decay is true?

A High pressures increase the rate of radioactive decay.

B High temperatures increase the rate of radioactive decay.

C Low temperatures increase the rate of radioactive decay.

D Radioactive decay is unaffected by external conditions. (1)

4 The three main types of nuclear radiation are alpha particles, beta particles and gamma radiation.

(a) Which types of nuclear radiation will **not** go through a sheet of paper?

A Alpha particles only.

B Beta particles only.

C Both alpha particles and beta particles.

D Both beta particles and gamma rays. (1)

(b) Which types of nuclear radiation can travel through a sheet of aluminium several centimetres thick?

A Alpha particles only.

B Beta particles only.

C Gamma rays only.

D Both beta particles and gamma rays. (1)

(c) Smoke detectors used in houses often contain a source of alpha radiation. This radiation will not harm people in the house because . . .

A Alpha particles are not very ionising.

B Alpha particles are very ionising.

C Alpha particles do not damage human cells.

D Alpha particles travel only a few centimetres in air. (1)

(d) Alpha particles and beta particles are deflected by magnetic fields, but gamma rays are not. This is because gamma rays

A are too heavy.

B have no charge.

C move too quickly.

D move too slowly. (1)

5 The graph shows how the number of radioactive atoms in a sample of a radioactive gas changes with time.

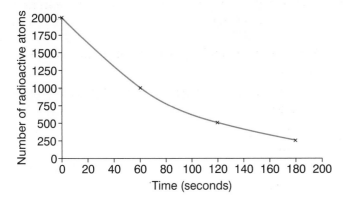

(a) (i) Use the graph to find the half-life of the radioactive gas. (2)

(ii) Explain what will happen to the half-life as the sample of gas gets older. (1)

(b) A radioactive source is to be used as a medical tracer injected into the body. The table shows four sources that are available.

Radioactive source	Half-life	Radiation emitted
A	4 days	Alpha
B	6 hours	Gamma
C	10 years	Beta
D	10 years	Gamma

(i) Which source would be the most suitable to use? (1)

(ii) Explain your choice. (1)

HOW SCIENCE WORKS QUESTIONS

How do you know who to believe?

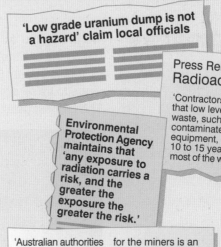

'Low grade uranium dump is not a hazard' claim local officials

Press Release: Radioactive Waste

'Contractors have stated that low level radioactive waste, such as contaminated medical equipment, can be left for 10 to 15 years allowing most of the waste to decay.'

Environmental Protection Agency maintains that 'any exposure to radiation carries a risk, and the greater the exposure the greater the risk.'

'Australian authorities consider that a safe threshold level for radiation has not been decided scientifically. For safety at uranium mines they say that a level for the public is 1mSv per year and for the miners is an average of 20mSv per year over a three year period.'

'The Food Standards Agency maintains that of the 175 samples of water tested, none broke the legal safety limits for radioactive pollution.'

'World Heath Organisation guidelines for drinking water recommend less that 0.1mSv per year in drinking water.'

a) These press releases come from several different sources. Make a list of the sources and next to each source score them 1 to 5 as to whether you would trust them.
1 = no trust and 5 = total trust.
Explain your reasoning. (6)

b) What are the ethical, social, economic and environmental issues involved in making decisions about safe levels of radiation? You should use information from the press releases to help you in your answer. (4)

P1b 7.1

The expanding Universe

LEARNING OBJECTIVES

1 How big is the Universe and is its size changing?
2 What is a red shift?

We live on the third rock out from a middle-aged star on the outskirts of a big galaxy we call the Milky Way. The galaxy contains about 100 000 million stars. Its size is about 100 000 light years across. This means that light takes 100 000 years to travel across it. But it's just one of billions of galaxies in the Universe. The furthest galaxies are about 13 000 million light years away!

Figure 1 Galaxies

a) Why do stars appear as points of light?

NEXT TIME YOU...

... go out on a clear night, look up at the stars. Even on a very clear night, you can only see a few hundred nearby stars unless you use binoculars or a telescope.

Red shift

We can find out lots of things about stars and galaxies by studying the light from them. We can use a prism to split the light into a spectrum. The wavelength of light increases across the spectrum from blue to red. We can tell from the spectrum if a star or galaxy is moving towards us or away from us. This is because:

● the light waves are stretched out if the star or galaxy is moving away from us. We call this a **red shift** because the spectrum of light is shifted towards the red part of the spectrum.
● the light waves are squashed together if the star or galaxy is moving towards us. We call this a *blue shift* because the spectrum of light is shifted towards the blue part of the spectrum.

Also, the faster a star or galaxy is moving towards or away from us, the bigger the shift is.

Red shifts and blue shifts are examples of the **Doppler effect**. This is the change in the observed wavelengths (and frequency) of waves due to the motion of the source towards or away from the observer. Christian Doppler discovered the effect in 1842 using sound waves. He demonstrated it by sending an open railway carriage filled with trumpeters speeding past a line of trained listeners.

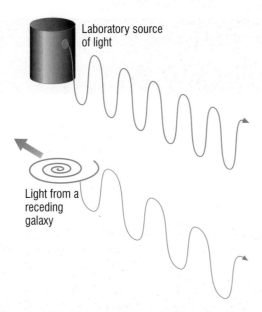

Laboratory source of light

Light from a receding galaxy

Figure 2 Red shift

b) What do you think happens to the light from a star that is moving towards us?

In 1929, Edwin Hubble discovered that the light from distant galaxies was '*red-shifted*'. He found that the further a galaxy is from us, the bigger its red shift is. He concluded that:

- the distant galaxies are moving away from us (i.e. receding),
- the speed (of recession) of a distant galaxy is proportional to its distance from us.

Why should the distant galaxies be moving away from us? We have no special place in the Universe. So all the distant galaxies must be moving away from each other. In other words, *the whole Universe is expanding*.

c) Galaxy X is 2000 million light years away. Galaxy Y is 4000 million light years away. Which galaxy, X or Y, has the bigger red shift?

SUMMARY QUESTIONS

1 Complete the sentences below using words from the list.

    approaching   expanding   orbiting   receding

a) The Earth is …… the Sun.
b) The Universe is …… .
c) The distant galaxies are …… .
d) A blue shift in the light from a star would tell us it is …… .

2 a) Put these objects in order of increasing size:

    Andromeda galaxy   Earth   Sun   Universe

b) Complete the sentences below using words from the list.

    galaxy   star   red shift   planet

  i) The Earth is a …… in orbit round a …… called the Sun.
  ii) There is a …… in the light from a distant …… .

KEY POINTS

1 Light from a distant galaxy is red-shifted to longer wavelengths.
2 The most distant galaxies are about 13 000 million light years away.
3 The Universe is expanding.

P1b 7.2   The Big Bang

LEARNING OBJECTIVES

1 Why is the Universe expanding?
2 What is the Big Bang theory of the Universe?

The Universe is expanding, but what is making it expand? The **Big Bang theory** was put forward to explain the expansion. This states that:

- the Universe is expanding after exploding suddenly in a Big Bang from a very small initial point,
- space, time and matter were created in the Big Bang

Many scientists disagreed with the Big Bang theory. They put forward an alternative theory, the Steady State theory. The scientists said that the galaxies are being pushed apart. They thought that this is caused by matter entering the Universe through 'white holes' (the opposite of black holes).

Figure 1 The Big Bang

Which theory is weirder – everything starting from a Big Bang or matter leaking into the Universe from outside? Until 1965, most people backed the Steady State theory.

It was in 1965 that scientists first detected microwaves coming from every direction in space. The existence of this **background microwave radiation** can only be explained by the Big Bang theory.

a) Scientists think the Big Bang happened about 13 000 million years ago. What was before the Big Bang?

Background microwave radiation

- It was created as high-energy gamma radiation just after the Big Bang.
- It has been travelling through space since then.
- As the Universe has expanded, it stretched out to longer and longer wavelengths and is now microwave radiation.
- It has been mapped out using microwave detectors on the ground and on satellites.

b) What will happen to background microwave radiation as the Universe expands?

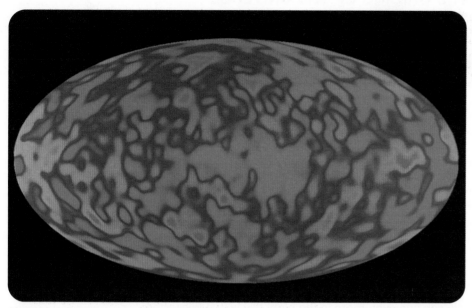

Figure 2 A microwave image of the Universe from COBE, the Cosmic Background Explorer satellite

The future of the Universe

Will the Universe expand forever? Or will the force of gravity between the distant galaxies stop them from moving away from each other? The answer to this question depends on their total mass and how much space they take up – in other words, the density of the Universe.

- If the density of the Universe is less than a certain amount, it will expand forever. The stars will die out. So will everything else as the Universe heads for a Big Yawn!
- If the density of the Universe is more than a certain amount, it will stop expanding and go into reverse. Everything will head for a Big Crunch!

Recent observations by astronomers suggest that the distant galaxies are accelerating away from each other. It looks like we're in for a Big Ride followed by a Big Yawn.

c) What could you say about the future of the Universe if the galaxies were slowing down?

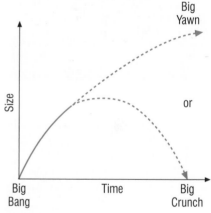

Figure 3 The future of the Universe

SUMMARY QUESTIONS

1 Complete the sentences below using words from the list.

   created   detected   expanded   stretched

   a) The Universe was …… in an explosion called the Big Bang.
   b) The Universe …… suddenly in and after the Big Bang.
   c) Microwave radiation from space can be …… in all directions.
   d) Radiation created just after the Big Bang has been …… by the expansion of the Universe and is now microwave radiation.

2 What will happen to the Universe:

   a) if its density is less than a certain value?
   b) if its density is greater than a certain value?

KEY POINTS

1 The Universe started with the Big Bang, a massive explosion from a very small point.
2 Background microwave radiation is radiation created just after the Big Bang.

P1b 7.3   Looking into space

When we look at the night sky, we sometimes see unexpected objects in the sky, as well as planets and stars. Such objects include:

● shooting stars which are small objects from space that burn up when they enter the Earth's atmosphere,
● comets which are frozen rocks that orbit the Sun – we only see them when they get near the Sun because then they get so hot that they emit light,
● stars that explode (supernova) or flare up then fade (nova).

a) Which is nearer to us, a comet bright enough to see, or a shooting star?

We can see even more in the night sky with a telescope.

● A telescope makes stars appear much brighter. Because it is much wider than your eye, it collects much more light than your eye can. All the light it collects is channelled into your eye. So you can see stars too faint to see without a telescope.
● A telescope makes the Moon and the planets appear bigger. A telescope with magnification ×20 would make Venus appear 20 times wider. As well as that, you can see more detail. For example, you can see the Great Red Spot on the surface of Jupiter. This was first observed by Galileo almost 400 years ago.

b) Why can you see more stars by using a telescope?

The Earth's atmosphere affects telescopes on the ground. It scatters the light from space objects and makes their images fuzzy.

c) Why doesn't the Earth's atmosphere affect the Hubble Space Telescope?

Figure 1 A comet

Figure 2 Jupiter's Great Red Spot

Figure 3 Colliding galaxies – an image from Hubble Space Telescope. The Hubble Space Telescope (HST) is in orbit around the Earth. It gives us amazing images of objects in space. Compared with telescopes on the ground, HST enables us to see objects in much more detail. We can also see things that are much further away.

PRACTICAL

Telescopes

You can make a simple astronomical telescope with two lenses.

Look at Figure 4. The objective lens forms an image of a distant object in front of the eyepiece. You see a magnified picture of this image when you look through the eyepiece.

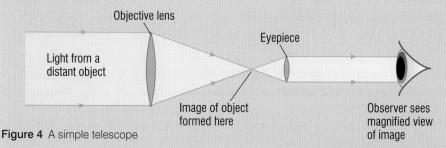

Figure 4 A simple telescope

Make and test a simple telescope to look at a distant object. What difference would it make if you looked at an object through the wrong end of a telescope?

Never use binoculars or a telescope to look at the Sun. You would be blinded permanently because far too much light would be channelled into your eyes.

Beyond the visible spectrum

(1) *Radio telescopes* are used to map out sources of radio waves, such as distant galaxies. Radio waves, as well as light (and some ultraviolet radiation), can reach the ground. The bigger a radio telescope is, the more detail it can map out and the further away it can detect radio sources.

(2) *Satellites* are used to carry detectors of electromagnetic waves that can't penetrate the Earth's atmosphere. Specially designed detectors are used for each type of radiation. Using these detectors, astronomers have discovered many unusual space objects such as:

- massive stars that suddenly explode and emit bursts of gamma rays,
- planets beyond the Solar System that give off infra-red radiation as they orbit nearby stars,
- black holes that destroy stars at the centre of galaxies.

d) Why can't we detect infra-red radiation from space using ground-based detectors?

SUMMARY QUESTIONS

1 Complete the following sentences using words from the list below.

gamma rays   infra-red radiation   light   radio waves

a) ...... and ...... can reach the ground from space.
b) ...... and ...... from space are absorbed by the Earth's atmosphere.

2 a) Why do we get much better images from the Hubble Space Telescope than from telescopes on the ground?
b) Why do gamma ray detectors need to be on satellites to detect gamma rays from space whereas radio telescopes are based on Earth?
c) Which objects in space produce i) gamma rays ii) infra-red radiation.

Figure 5 Jodrell Bank Radio Telescope

KEY POINTS

1 The Earth's atmosphere absorbs all electromagnetic waves (except visible light, radio waves and some ultraviolet radiation).
2 Satellite detectors are used to make observations outside the visible and the radio spectrum.
3 We also get clearer images from telescopes on satellites detecting visible light.

P1b 7.4   Looking into the unknown

A short history of the Universe

Light we can see from the most distant galaxies has been travelling through space for thousands of millions of years. Big telescopes looking at these galaxies are looking back in time.

- In the first moments after the Big Bang, matter formed from the radiation given out in the Big Bang.
- After the first few seconds, protons and neutrons started to clump together to form nuclei. At this stage, the Universe was opaque, very hot and about the size of the Solar System.
- After about 100 000 years, as it expanded further, it cooled and atoms formed. This was when it became clear. The background microwave radiation we now detect was released.
- After a thousand million years or so, the Universe turned lumpy as galaxies formed. Stars formed in the galaxies and lit them up.

ACTIVITY

Make a time line on a poster to illustrate the history of the Universe.

Galileo (1564–1642)

Galileo was already a well-known scientist in 1609 when he found out about the newly-invented telescope. Within a short time, he had made his own. He used it to observe the Moon, the stars and the planets.

He discovered:

- the Moon's surface is covered with craters,
- moons orbiting the planet Jupiter,
- many more stars too faint to be seen with the unaided eye.

He published his observations in support of the Copernican model of the Solar System. This was the theory that the Earth and the planets orbit the Sun. The theory went against the teaching of the Church which said the Earth is at the centre of the Universe.

ACTIVITY

Imagine what Galileo's trial would have been like.
Write a short play about it and act it out with your friends.

Galileo was reprimanded by the Church in 1613 but he continued to teach the Copernican model. He published his work in 1630. In 1632, he was summoned to the Inquisition in Rome and forced to say his work was wrong. He was placed under house arrest for the rest of his life. But his discoveries and his teaching were taken up by other scientists in Britain and Northern Europe.

ACTIVITY

Imagine you're an astronaut on Mars. Write a weblog about a day in your life. Include some background music and photos.

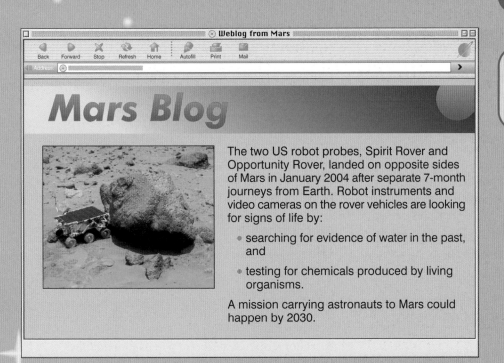

Mars Blog

The two US robot probes, Spirit Rover and Opportunity Rover, landed on opposite sides of Mars in January 2004 after separate 7-month journeys from Earth. Robot instruments and video cameras on the rover vehicles are looking for signs of life by:

- searching for evidence of water in the past, and
- testing for chemicals produced by living organisms.

A mission carrying astronauts to Mars could happen by 2030.

Space invaders!

Asteroids are massive chunks of rock orbiting the Sun. They are found mostly between Mars and Jupiter. Sometimes, an asteroid gets pulled toward the Sun and crosses the Earth's orbit. In 1992, an asteroid narrowly missed the Earth. On a scale where the Sun is 1 metre away, it came within just 3 cm of the Earth! If it had hit the Earth, the impact could have killed millions of people.

ACTIVITY

Make a poster to convince people that the Government should pay for an asteroid 'early warning' system.

The search for extra-terrestrial intelligence (SETI)

The search for extra-terrestrial intelligence has gone on for more than 40 years. We can use radio telescopes to detect signals in a band of wavelengths. Such signals would indicate the existence of living beings. They would be at least as advanced as we are, perhaps on a planet in a distant solar system. Radio astronomers have searched without success for such radio signals. However, just one SETI signal would change our outlook for ever!

ACTIVITY

Imagine SETI signals have been detected from Andromeda. It is in all the newspapers, on radio and on TV. You do a survey of 100 people to see how people have reacted to this news. The results are in the table below.

Question	Yes	No
1. Have you heard about the discovery of signals from space aliens?	55	45
2. Should we send peaceful signals back?	70	30
3. Do you think the signals are from a more advanced civilisation than us?	30	70

a) Make a bar chart to display these findings.
b) Discuss with your friends what you would put into a 5-minute return signal. It could include video and audio, as well as text.

SUMMARY QUESTIONS

1 a) Put the objects listed below in order of increasing size.

A the Milky Way galaxy   B Jupiter
C the Moon   D the Sun

b) Complete the following sentences.
   i) Light from a distant ...... is shifted to the red part of the spectrum. This is because it has been stretched to longer ....
   ii) The distant galaxies are moving ...... from each other because the ...... is expanding.

2 Light from a distant galaxy has a change of wavelength due to the motion of the galaxy.

   a) Is this change of wavelength an increase or a decrease?

   b) What is the name for this change of wavelength?

   c) Which way is the galaxy moving?

   d) What would happen to the light it gives out if it were moving in the opposite direction?

3 a) Galaxy A is further from us than galaxy B.
   i) Which galaxy, A or B, produces light with a greater red shift?
   ii) Galaxy C gives a bigger red shift than galaxy A. What can we say about the distance to galaxy C compared with galaxy A?

   b) All the distant galaxies are moving away from each other.
   i) What does this tell us about the Universe?
   ii) What does it tell us about our place in the Universe?

4 a) Complete the following sentences.
   i) The Universe was created in a massive explosion called ....
   ii) The expansion of the Universe is making the distant galaxies move ....
   iii) The Universe was created about thirteen ...... years ago.

   b) i) What is background microwave radiation?
   ii) What did the discovery of background microwave radiation prove?

5 a) An astronomical observatory has two big telescopes, X and Y.
   X is bigger than Y. Which one can see furthest into space?

   b) The Hubble Space Telescope gives better images than any telescope on the ground. Why?

EXAM-STYLE QUESTIONS

1 Optical telescopes should never be used to look directly at the Sun because

   A this would permanently damage the eyesight of the observer.

   B this would make the telescope catch fire.

   C there is nothing to see on the Sun.

   D the image would always appear blurred.   (1)

2 Astronomers believe that the Universe

   A has always been the same size.

   B is getting bigger.

   C is getting smaller.

   D was getting bigger but will now stay the same size.   (1)

3 Astronomers study different bodies found in the Universe.
   Match the words in the list with the numbers **1** to **4** in the table.

   Galaxies   Solar systems   Sun   Planets   (4)

Body	Description
1	Main source of energy for the Earth
2	Give light that gives evidence about the origin of the Universe
3	Consist of a central star orbited by planets
4	Reflect light from the Sun

4 Observations of bodies in space are made with telescopes. Some telescopes are positioned on the ground and some are in orbit around the Earth.

   (a) Which of these devices could **not** be used to make observations of the night sky?

      A Binoculars   B Camera

      C Cloud chamber   D Naked eye   (1)

   (b) Which of the following are **not** detected by telescopes?

      A Radio waves   B Sound waves

      C Visible light   D X-rays   (1)

   (c) One advantage of a telescope in orbit is that it produces clearer images.
      This is because . . .

      A it is closer to the stars being observed.

      B it is warmer in space.

      C it is easier to move the telescope around.

      D light is not scattered by the atmosphere.   (1)

(d) Which of the following statements is **not** true when applied to a large optical telescope in orbit?

    A It is easier to maintain than one on the ground.

    B The large mirrors are effectively weightless.

    C The mirrors do not suffer atmospheric corrosion.

    D Weather does not affect its performance. (1)

5 The Big Bang theory is one theory of the origin of the Universe.

(a) What are the main ideas of the Big Bang theory? (2)

(b) One piece of evidence for this theory is red-shift.

    (i) What is red-shift? (2)

    (ii) What does red-shift tell us about distant galaxies? (1)

    (iii) Explain how red-shift is evidence for the Big Bang theory. (2)

6 The following table gives some data about the planets in the Solar System.

Planet	Diameter (km)	Distance from the Sun (million km)
Mercury	4640	58
Venus	12230	108
Earth	12683	150
Mars	6720	228
Jupiter	141920	778
Saturn	120160	1431
Uranus	46880	2886
Neptune	49920	4529
Pluto	2284	5936

Use the information given in the table to help you answer the questions.

Some planets can be observed with the naked eye, but others can only be seen with a telescope. The ancient Greeks did not have telescopes.

(a) Suggest a reason why the ancient Greeks were able to observe:

    (i) Venus and Mars

    (ii) Jupiter and Saturn (2)

(b) Uranus and Neptune are much bigger than Mars but were unknown to the Greeks. Suggest why. (2)

(c) Why was Pluto discovered much later than Uranus and Neptune? (1)

HOW SCIENCE WORKS QUESTIONS

The Big Bang

Fred Hoyle, who studied physics at school in Yorkshire then at Cambridge University, first used the term the 'Big Bang', although he was a life-long opponent of the theory. Other opponents were the Soviet Union, who imprisoned scientists who supported the Big Bang theory. Pope Pius XII embraced the idea, but the church changed its mind later, before finally accepting it after the discovery of background microwave radiation in 1965.

One of the difficulties with the theory was that the universe seemed to be younger than the stars in it! So the theory produced a hypothesis that the universe must be much older than had been calculated. This produced a prediction that the distance to the galaxies must be greater than previously calculated.

Investigations were designed to find the true age of the universe, so that the theory could be supported . . . or not!

Technology was lacking to do these measurements. Bigger and better telescopes were built. Finally they gave the answer that the Big Bang supporters had wanted. The universe was at least twice as old as was previously measured and it fell to Fred Hoyle to record the discovery for the meeting of astronomers!

Fred Hoyle (1915–2001)

Use this account to give one example of each of the following:

a) a hypothesis (1)

b) a theory (1)

c) a prediction (1)

d) political influence (1)

e) the importance of technology to scientific progress. (1)

EXAMINATION-STYLE QUESTIONS

Physics A

1 The light coming to us from distant galaxies shows a change in wavelength. This change is called . . .

See pages 106–7

   A   Blue shift.

   B   Radio shift.

   C   Red shift.

   D   Star shift.   *(1 mark)*

2 What type of signal is shown on the diagram below?

See page 88

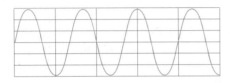

   A   Analogue

   B   Binary

   C   Digital

   D   Frequency   *(1 mark)*

3 Match the words in the list below with the numbers **1** to **4** in the sentences.

See page 110

   A   atmosphere

   B   solar system

   C   space

   D   universe

Observations of the ......**1**...... and the galaxies in the ......**2**...... can be carried out by telescopes on the Earth or in ......**3**...... Telescopes outside the Earth's ......**4**......are not affected by the weather.   *(4 marks)*

4 The half-life of the radioactive element americium is 500 years. A sample of americium contains 8 000 atoms. After how many years will the sample contain 1 000 atoms.

See page 101

   A   500 years

   B   1 000 years

   C   1 500 years

   D   2 000 years   *(1 mark)*

GET IT RIGHT!

Make sure you know what is meant by 'half-life' and how to use it in calculations.

Physics B

1 Electromagnetic radiation can be used for many different purposes.

See pages 78–85

(a) Which electromagnetic radiation is used:

(i) to take shadow pictures of bones?

(ii) in sun beds?

(iii) to sterilise surgical instruments? *(3 marks)*

GET IT RIGHT!

Make sure you know at least one use of each type of electromagnetic radiation.

(b) Electromagnetic radiation can be hazardous as well as useful.

Explain why the skin should be protected from ultraviolet radiation.
(2 marks)

(c) Microwaves can be used to cook food in a microwave oven.

(i) Explain how microwaves cook food. *(2 marks)*

(ii) Explain how the microwaves could harm you if they escaped from the oven. *(2 marks)*

(d) Some microwaves have a wavelength of 0.02 metres and a frequency of 15 000 million hertz.
Use the equation speed = frequency $\times$ wavelength to calculate the speed of these microwaves. *(2 marks)*

GET IT RIGHT!

This calculation involves a very large number. In setting out your working be careful not to lose or gain any zeros.

2 Some substances give out radiation from the nuclei of their atoms all the time. These substances are said to be radioactive.

(a) Describe the basic structure of an atom. *(4 marks)*

See page 95

(b) A teacher has two radioactive sources, one emits only alpha particles and the other emits only beta particles.
The sources are unlabelled. Describe a simple test he can do to determine which is which. *(3 marks)*

See pages 96–7

P2 | Additional physics

Figure 1 Spot the units!

Increasing wavelength

Radio waves
Microwaves
Infra-red radiation
Light
Ultraviolet radiation
X and γ radiation

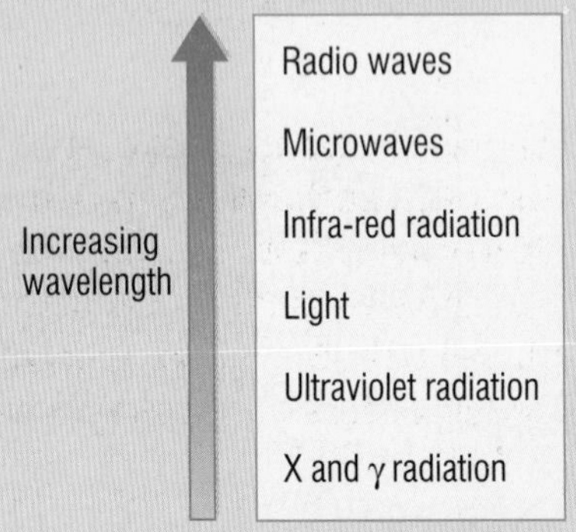

Figure 2 The electromagnetic spectrum

What you already know

Here is a quick reminder of previous work that you will find useful in this unit:

Electricity

* In an electric circuit, energy is transferred from a voltage supply to the other parts of the circuit.
* Current passes round an electric circuit if the circuit is complete.
* Insulators do not conduct electricity.

Force

* If the forces acting on an object are not balanced, they will change the motion of the object.
* Weight is caused by the force of gravity on a mass.
* Friction acts between two surfaces in contact with each other when they slide or try to slide past each other.

Energy

* Energy cannot be created or destroyed. It can only be transformed from one form to another form.
* Power is the rate of transfer of energy.

Radiation

* Radioactive substances decay because the nuclei of some atoms are unstable. An unstable nucleus emits α, β or γ radiation when it decays.
* X-rays and α, β and γ radiation ionise substances they pass through.

RECAP QUESTIONS

1. a) Sort the materials below into two lists – electrical conductors and insulators.

   air   brass   copper   plastic   wood

   b) A student replaces a battery in an electric torch but the torch still doesn't work. Suggest two possible reasons why it doesn't work.

2. a) List the forces acting on you at this moment, assuming you are sitting still.

   b) i) When you are sitting still, what can you say about the forces acting on you?

   ii) If the force your seat exerts on you suddenly decreased, what would happen to you?

3. a) Which has the longer wavelength, γ radiation or microwaves?

   b) Which electromagnetic waves can pass through the body?

4. a) i) What is an ion?

   ii) List four different types of ionising radiation.

   b) i) Which is most easily absorbed, α, β or γ radiation?

   ii) Where in the atom does α, β or γ radiation come from?

5. What are the units in the cartoon at the top of this page used to measure?

Making connections

Taking off!

To fly high, you need to take off first. The first powered flight was by the Wright brothers in 1903. Now planes can carry hundreds of people for thousands of miles in a few hours. We can send space probes far into space. Where will people have got to by the end of this century? Read on to find out where the physics in this unit can take you.

Jets and rockets

The first jet engine was invented by a British engineer, Frank Whittle. He worked out how to create a jet of hot gases by burning aviation fuel. He used his scientific knowledge of materials, energy and forces to design and test the first jet engine.

On the launch pad

Space is only a few miles above your head but gravity stops you going there – unless you are in a rocket. A rocket is a jet engine with its own oxygen supply. Jet planes don't need to carry oxygen to burn aviation fuel in their engines because they use oxygen in the atmosphere. But a single-stage rocket can't get far enough into space to escape from the Earth. The Russian physicist, Konstanin Tsiolovsky predicted in 1895 that space rockets would need to be multistage.

Keeping in touch

Space travel would be impossible without electronic circuits for control and communications. A radio signal from a space probe is weaker than the light from a torch lamp on the Moon. The communication circuits in a space probe detect and process very weak signals. On-board cameras and sensors collect and send information back to Earth. Control circuits operate on-board rockets to change the path of a space probe. The electronic circuits in a space probe need to be totally reliable.

Interstellar travel

Voyager 2 was launched in 1975. Now it is on its way out of the Solar System after sending back amazing pictures of the outer planets and their moons. Space probes and satellites need power supplies that last for many years.

Space travel by astronauts far from the Sun would need powerful electricity generators powered by nuclear reactors. Nuclear submarines carry small nuclear reactors for their electricity. New types of nuclear reactors such as fusion reactors would be better. The probes and the reactors would probably need to be built on the Moon, using local materials.

ACTIVITY

Discuss:

What things do you think people will be able to do in the year 2099 that we can't do today? What breakthroughs in science will these rely on?

Chapters in this unit

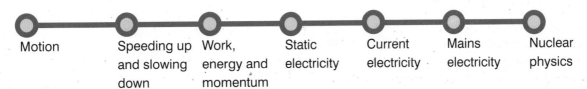

Motion | Speeding up and slowing down | Work, energy and momentum | Static electricity | Current electricity | Mains electricity | Nuclear physics

P2 1.1   Distance–time graphs

1 How can we tell from a distance–time graph if an object is stationary?
2 How can we tell from a distance–time graph if an object is moving at constant speed?
3 How do we calculate the speed of a body?

Figure 1 Capturing the land speed record

DID YOU KNOW?

- A top sprinter can travel a distance of about 10 metres every second.
- A cheetah is faster than any other animal. It can run about 30 metres every second – but only for about 20 seconds!
- A vehicle travelling at the speed limit of 70 miles per hour (mph) on a UK motorway travels a distance of 31 metres every second.
- The land speed record at present is 763 mph, which is more than Mach 1, the speed of sound.
- The air speed record was broken in November 2004 by X-43A, an experimental scram-jet plane. It reached 6600 mph or Mach 9.6! Whoosh . . .

Some motorways have marker posts every kilometre. If you are a passenger in a car on a motorway, you can use these posts to check the speed of the car. You need to time the car as it passes each post. The table below shows some measurements made on a car journey:

Distance (metres, m)	0	1000	2000	3000	4000	5000	6000
Time (seconds, s)	0	40	80	120	160	200	240

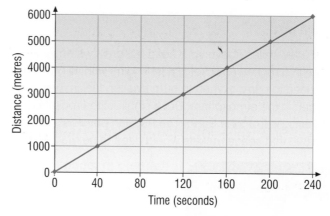

Figure 2 A distance–time graph

Look at the readings plotted on a graph of distance against time in Figure 2.

The graph shows that:

- the car took 40 s to go from each marker post to the next. So its speed was **constant**.
- the car went a distance of 25 metres every second (= 1000 metres ÷ 40 seconds). So its speed was 25 metres per second.

If the car had travelled faster, it would have gone further than 1000 metres every 40 seconds. So the line on the graph would have been **steeper**.

The slope on a distance–time graph represents speed.

a) What can you say about the steepness of the line if the car had travelled slower than 25 metres per second?

Speed

For an object moving at constant speed, we can calculate its speed using the equation:

$$\text{speed (metre/second, m/s)} = \frac{\text{distance travelled (metre, m)}}{\text{time taken (second, s)}}$$

The scientific unit of speed is the metre per second, usually written as metre/second or m/s.

Speed in action

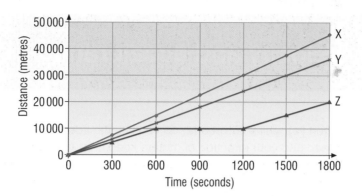

Figure 3 Comparing distance–time graphs

Long-distance vehicles are fitted with recorders that can check that their drivers don't drive for too long. The information from a recorder may be used to plot a distance–time graph.

Look at the distance–time graph above for three lorries, X , Y and Z, on the same motorway.

- X went fastest because it travelled furthest in the same time.
- Y travelled more slowly than X. From the graph, you can see it travelled 30 000 metres in 1500 seconds. So its speed was 20 m/s (= 30 000 m ÷ 1500 s).

b) Calculate the speed of X.

- Z stopped for some of the time. Its speed was zero in this time.

c) How long did Z stop for?
d) Calculate the **average** speed of Z.

PRACTICAL

Be a distance recorder!

Take the measurements needed to plot distance–time graphs for a person:

- walking,
- running, and
- riding a bike.

Remember that you must always label the graph axes, which includes units.

- Compare the slopes of the lines and work out average speeds.

SUMMARY QUESTIONS

1 Choose the correct word from the list to complete a) to c) below.

distance   speed   time

a) The unit of …… is the metre/second.
b) An object moving at steady …… travels the same …… every second.
c) The steeper the line on a distance–time graph of a moving object, the greater its …… is.

2 A vehicle on a motorway travels 1800 m in 60 seconds. Calculate:

a) the speed of the vehicle in m/s.
b) how far it would travel at this speed in 300 seconds.

KEY POINTS

1 The steeper the line on a distance–time graph, the greater the speed it represents.
2 Speed (metre/second, m/s) =

$$\frac{\text{distance travelled (metre, m)}}{\text{time taken (second, s)}}$$

P2 1.2

Velocity and acceleration

When you visit a fairground, do you like the rides that throw you round? Your speed and your direction of motion keep changing. We use the word **velocity** for speed in a given direction. An exciting ride would be one that changes your velocity often and unexpectedly!

Velocity is speed in a given direction.

- An object moving steadily round in a circle has a constant speed. Its direction of motion changes as it goes round so its velocity is not constant.

- Two moving objects can have the same speed but different velocities. For example, a car travelling north at 30 m/s on a motorway has the same speed as a car travelling south at 30 m/s. But their velocities are not the same because they are moving in opposite directions.

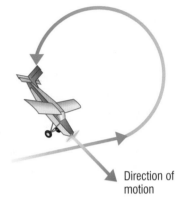

Direction of motion

Figure 2 Speed and velocity

a) How far apart are the two cars 10 seconds after they pass each other?

Figure 1 You experience plenty of changes in velocity on a corkscrew ride!

Acceleration

Figure 3 On a test circuit

A car maker claims their new car 'accelerates more quickly than any other new car'. A rival car maker is not pleased by this claim and issues a challenge. Each car in turn is tested on a straight track with a velocity recorder fitted.

The results are shown in the table:

Time from a standing start (seconds, s)	0	2	4	6	8	10
Velocity of car X (metre/second, m/s)	0	5	10	15	20	25
Velocity of car Y (metre/second, m/s)	0	6	12	18	18	18

Which car accelerates more? The results are plotted on the velocity–time graph in Figure 4. You can see the velocity of Y goes up from zero faster than the velocity of X does. So Y accelerates more in the first 6 seconds.

NEXT TIME YOU...

... go 'skateboarding', go round in a circle and think about how your velocity is changing.

Figure 4 Velocity–time graphs

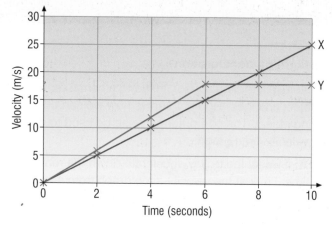

The acceleration of an object is its change of velocity per second. The unit of acceleration is the metre per second squared, abbreviated to m/s².

Any object with a changing velocity is accelerating. We can work out its acceleration using the equation:

$$\text{Acceleration (metre/second squared, m/s}^2) = \frac{\text{change in velocity (metre/second, m/s)}}{\text{time taken for the change (second, s)}}$$

Worked example

In Figure 4, the velocity of Y increases from zero to 18 m/s in 6 seconds. Calculate its acceleration.

Solution

Change of velocity = 18 m/s – 0 m/s = 18 m/s

Time taken = 6.0 s

$$\text{Acceleration} = \frac{\text{change in velocity (metre/second, m/s)}}{\text{time taken for the change (second, s)}} = \frac{18\,\text{m/s}}{6.0\,\text{s}} = 3.0\,\text{m/s}^2$$

b) Calculate the acceleration of X in Figure 4.

Deceleration

A car decelerates when the driver brakes. We use the term **deceleration** or *negative acceleration* for any situation where an object slows down.

SUMMARY QUESTIONS

1 Complete a) to c) using the words below:

   acceleration   speed   velocity

   a) An object moving steadily round in a circle has a constant ....
   b) If the velocity of an object increases by the same amount every second, its ...... is constant.
   c) Deceleration is when the ...... of an object decreases.

2 The velocity of a car increased from 8 m/s to 28 m/s in 8 s without change of direction. Calculate:

   a) its change of velocity,   b) its acceleration.

KEY POINTS

1 Velocity is speed in a given direction.
2 Acceleration is change of velocity per second.
3 A body travelling at a steady speed is accelerating if its direction is changing.

P2 1.3

More about velocity–time graphs

1 How can we tell from a velocity–time graph if an object is accelerating or decelerating?
2 What does the area under a velocity–time graph represent?

Figure 2 Measuring motion using a computer

Investigating acceleration

We can use a motion sensor linked to a computer to record how the velocity of an object changes. Figure 1 shows how we can do this, using a trolley as the moving object. The computer can also be used to display the measurements as a velocity–time graph.

Test A: If we let the trolley accelerate down the runway, its velocity increases with time. Look at the velocity–time graph from a test run in Figure 2.

Figure 1 A velocity–time graph on a computer

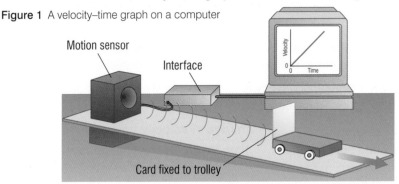

Motion sensor

Interface

Card fixed to trolley

● The line goes up because the velocity increases with time. So it shows the trolley was accelerating as it ran down the runway.
● The line is straight which tells us that the increase in velocity was the same every second. In other words, the acceleration of the trolley was constant (or uniform).

Test B: If we make the runway steeper, the trolley accelerates faster. This would make the line on the graph in Figure 2 steeper than for test A. So the acceleration in test B is greater.

The slope on a graph is a measure of its steepness. The tests shows that:

the slope of the line on a velocity–time graph represents acceleration.

a) If you made the runway less steep than in test A, would the line on the graph be steeper or less steep than in A?

PRACTICAL

Investigating acceleration

Use a motion sensor and a computer to find out how the slope of a runway affects a trolley's acceleration.

● Name i) the independent variable, and ii) the dependent variable in this investigation. (See page 7.)
● What relationship do you find between the variables? (See page 14.)

Braking

Braking reduces the velocity of a vehicle. Look at the graph in Figure 3. It is the velocity–time graph for a vehicle that brakes to a standstill at a set of traffic lights. The velocity is constant until the driver applies the brakes.

Using the slope of the line:

- The section of the graph for constant velocity is flat. The line's slope is zero so the acceleration in this section is zero.
- When the brakes are applied, the velocity decreases to zero and the vehicle decelerates. The slope of the line is negative in this section.

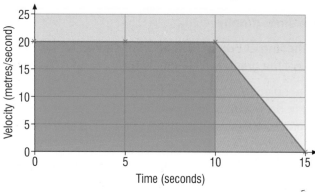

Figure 3 Braking

b) How would the slope of the line differ if the deceleration had taken longer?

Look at the graph in Figure 3 again.

Using the area under the line:

- Before the brakes are applied, the vehicle moves at a velocity of 20 m/s for 10 s. It therefore travels 200 m in this time ($= 20$ m/s $\times 10$ s). This distance is represented on the graph by the area under the line from 0 s to 10 s. This is the shaded rectangle on the graph.
- When the vehicle decelerates in Figure 3, its velocity drops from 20 m/s to zero in 5 s. We can work out the distance travelled in this time from the area of the purple triangle in Figure 3. This area is $\frac{1}{2} \times$ the height $\times$ the base of the triangle. So the vehicle must have travelled a distance of 50 m when it was decelerating.

The area under the line on a velocity–time graph represents distance travelled.

c) Would the total distance travelled be greater or smaller if the deceleration had taken longer?

SUMMARY QUESTIONS

1 Match each of the following descriptions to one of the lines, labelled A, B, C and D, on the velocity–time graph.

 1 Accelerated motion throughout
 2 Zero acceleration
 3 Accelerated motion, then decelerated motion
 4 Deceleration

 A   C
 B   D

2 Look at the graph in question 1.
 Which line represents the object that travelled:

 a) the furthest distance?   b) the least distance?

KEY POINTS

1 The slope of the line on a velocity–time graph represents acceleration.
2 The area under the line on a velocity–time graph represents distance travelled.

P2 1.4   Using graphs

LEARNING OBJECTIVES

1 How can we calculate speed from a distance–time graph?
2 How can we calculate distance from a velocity–time graph?
3 How can we calculate acceleration from a velocity–time graph?

Using distance–time graphs

For an object moving at constant speed, we saw at the start of this chapter that the distance–time graph is a straight line.

The speed of the object is represented by the slope of the line. To find the slope, we need to draw a triangle under the line, as shown in Figure 1. The height of the triangle represents the distance travelled and the base represents the time taken. So

$$\text{the slope of the line} = \frac{\text{the height of the triangle}}{\text{the base of the triangle}}$$

and this represents the object's speed.

a) Find the speed of the object in the graph in Figure 1.

For a moving object with a changing speed, the distance–time graph is not a straight line. The graphs in Figure 2 show two examples.

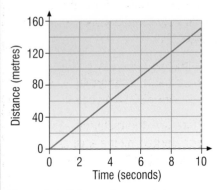

Figure 1 A distance–time graph for constant speed

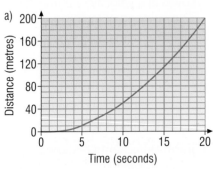

Figure 2 Distance–time graphs for changing speed

In Figure 2a, the slope of the graph increases gradually, so the object's speed must have increased gradually.

b) What can you say about the speed in Figure 2b?

Using velocity–time graphs

Look at the graph in Figure 3. It shows the velocity–time graph of an object X moving with a constant acceleration. Its velocity increases at a steady rate. So the graph shows a straight line which has a constant slope.

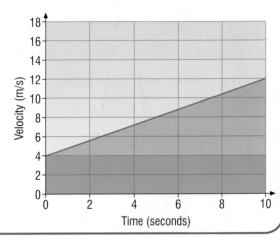

Figure 3 A velocity–time graph for constant acceleration

To find the acceleration from the graph, remember the slope of the line on a velocity–time graph represents the acceleration.

In Figure 3, the slope is given by the height divided by the base of the triangle under the graph.

The height of the triangle represents the change of velocity and the base of the triangle represents the time taken.

Therefore, the slope represents the acceleration, because:

$$\text{acceleration} = \frac{\text{change of velocity}}{\text{time taken}}$$

Worked example

Use the graph in Figure 3 to find the acceleration of object X.

Solution

The height of the triangle represents an increase of velocity of 8 m/s ($= 12\,\text{m/s} - 4\,\text{m/s}$).

The base of the triangle represents a time of 10 s.

$$\text{Therefore, the acceleration} = \frac{\text{change of velocity}}{\text{time taken}} = \frac{8\,\text{m/s}}{10\,\text{s}} = 0.8\,\text{m/s}^2$$

To find the distance travelled from the graph, remember the area under a velocity–time graph represents the distance travelled. The shape under the graph in Figure 3 is a triangle on top of a rectangle. So the distance travelled is represented by the area of the triangle plus the area of the rectangle under it.

Look at the worked example opposite:

Worked example

Use the graph in Figure 3 to calculate the distance moved by object X.

Solution

The area of the triangle $= \frac{1}{2} \times$ its height $\times$ its base.

Therefore, the distance represented by the area of triangle $= \frac{1}{2} \times 8\,\text{m/s} \times 10\,\text{s}$
$= 40\,\text{m}$

The area of the rectangle under the triangle $=$ its height $\times$ its base

Therefore, the distance represented by the area of the rectangle $= 4\,\text{m/s} \times 10\,\text{s}$
$= 40\,\text{m}$

So the distance travelled by X $= 40\,\text{m} + 40\,\text{m} = 80\,\text{m}$

SUMMARY QUESTIONS

1 The graph shows how the velocity of a cyclist on a straight road changes with time.

a) Describe the motion of the cyclist.
b) Use the graph to work out
   i) the initial acceleration of the cyclist,
   ii) the distance travelled by the cyclist in the first 40 s.

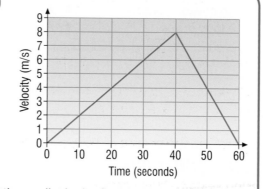

2 In a motor cycle test, the speed from rest was recorded at intervals.

Time (seconds, s)	0	5	10	15	20	25	30
Velocity (metre/second, m/s)	0	10	20	30	40	40	40

a) Plot a velocity–time graph of these results.
b) What was the initial acceleration?
c) How far did it move in:
   i) the first 20 seconds?
   ii) the next 10 s?

KEY POINTS

To carry out calculations involving:
1 The slope on a distance–time graph represents speed.
2 The slope on a velocity–time graph represents acceleration.
3 The area under the line on a velocity–time graph represents the distance travelled.

P2 1.5 · Transport issues

The Big Fuel protest

In 2001, lorry drivers in Britain decided their fuel costs were too high so they blockaded fuel depots. They were angry at the government because most of the cost of the fuel is tax (which raises money for the government).

Garages ran out of petrol and drivers had to queue for hours to fill up. Car drivers were a lot more careful about using their precious fuel.

Car journeys in built-up areas use more fuel per kilometre than 'out of town' journeys at the same average speed. This is because cars slow down and speed up more often in built-up areas. More fuel is used by a car that keeps stopping and starting than one driven at constant speed.

On a motorway journey the faster the speed of a car, the more fuel it uses. Air resistance at high speed is much greater than at low speed, so more fuel is used.

QUESTION

The table shows some information about fuel usage by a petrol-engine car.

| | Distance travelled per litre of fuel (km) | |
	at 48 kilometres per hour (30 mph)	at 100 kilometres per hour (63 mph)
Driving in town	12	–
On the 'open road'	15	10

1 A driver on the 'open road' would use 6 litres of fuel to drive 60 kilometres at 100 km/h.
   a) How much fuel would the driver use to drive 60 km at 48 km/h:
      i) in town?   **ii)** on the open road?
   b) The driver pays 85 p per litre for petrol. How much would be saved on a motorway journey of 60 km by driving at 48 km/h instead of 100 km/h?

ACTIVITY

Discuss the issues below in a small group.

What are your views on the different ways that people might protest against the cost of fuel? Would you agree with the protesters? Think about the arguments that might be used by:

- An environmentalist
- A lorry driver
- An oil company
- A government official

Epic journeys

Journey 1: Christopher Columbus and his three ships left the Canary Islands on 8th September 1492. He reached the Bahama Islands on 12th October after a 5500 km journey across the Atlantic Ocean.

Journey 2: Neil Armstrong and Buzz Aldrin were the first astronauts to land on the Moon. They spent 22 hours on the Moon. The 380 000 km journey to the Moon took four days.

Journey 3: If a space rocket accelerated for a year at 2 m/s² (about the same as a car starting from rest), the rocket would reach a speed of 60 000 km/s – about a fifth of the speed of light.

QUESTION

2 Work out the speed, in kilometres per hour, of journeys 1 and 2.

Speed cameras

Speed cameras are very effective in stopping motorists speeding. A speeding motorist caught by a speed camera is fined and can lose his or her driving licence. In some areas, residents are supplied with 'mobile' speed cameras to catch speeding motorists. Some motorists think this is going too far. Lots of motorists say speed cameras are being used by councils to increase their income.

A report from one police force said that where speed cameras had been introduced:

- average speeds fell by 17%,
- deaths and serious injuries had fallen by 55%.

Another police force reported that, in their area, as a result of installing more speed cameras in 2003:

- there were no child deaths in road accidents for the first time since 1927,
- 420 fewer children were involved in road accidents compared with the previous year.

ACTIVITY

Discuss with your friends:

a) Do the bullet-pointed statements opposite prove the argument that speed cameras save lives.

b) In what sort of areas do you think speed cameras should be used?

ACTIVITY

Should more residents be supplied with mobile speed cameras? Write a letter to your local newspaper to argue your case.

Congestion charges

ACTIVITY

Do you think congestion charges are a good solution to traffic problems in our cities? Discuss the issue with your friends and take a vote on the question.

Green travel

Travelling to and from school or work can take ages unless you live nearby. Everybody seems to want to travel at the same time. Traffic accidents and rail cancellations in the rush hour cause hours of chaos. Traffic fumes cause pollution and burning fuel produces greenhouse gases.

Green travel means changing the way we travel to improve the environment.

Here are some suggestions about a green travel plan for your school:

- School buses; use school buses instead of cars.
- Car sharing; encourage drivers to share their cars with other drivers.
- Flexitime; finish the school day at different times for each year group.
- Everybody should walk or cycle to school.

ACTIVITY

With the help of your friends, conduct a survey to find out

a) if people in your school and parents think a green travel plan is a good idea,

b) what they think of the suggestions above,

c) if they have any better suggestions.

Write a short report to tell your headteacher about your survey and your findings.

Was your sample large enough to draw any firm conclusions? Explain your answer.

Travelling across London by road was quicker a hundred years ago than it is today – even though modern cars can travel ten times faster than the horse-drawn carriages that were used then. Congestion charges were introduced in London in 2003 to improve traffic flow. If motorists enter the congestion zone without paying the daily charge, they are likely to be fined heavily.

People in Edinburgh in 2004 voted against proposals for congestion charges. But many people in other cities want to introduce them. However, lots of people who need to travel into cities think they are unfair.

SUMMARY QUESTIONS

1 A train travels at a constant speed of 35 m/s. Calculate:

   a) how far it travels in 20 s,

   b) how long it takes to travel a distance of 1400 m.

2 The figure shows the distance–time graph for a car on a motorway.

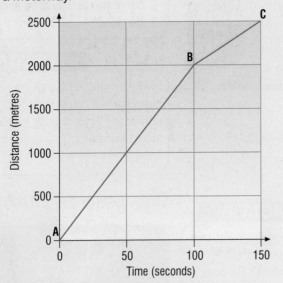

   a) Which part of the journey was faster, A to B or B to C?

   b) i) How far did the car travel from A to B and how long did it take?

      ii) Calculate the speed of the car between A and B?

3 a) A car took 8 s to increase its velocity from 8 m/s to 28 m/s. Calculate

      i) its change of velocity,

      ii) its acceleration.

   b) A vehicle travelling at a velocity of 24 m/s slowed down and stopped in 20 s. Calculate its deceleration.

4 The figure shows the velocity–time graph of a passenger jet before it took off.

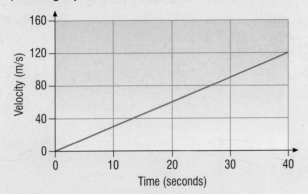

   a) Calculate the acceleration of the jet.

   b) Calculate the distance it travelled before it took off.

                                                    [Higher]

EXAM-STYLE QUESTIONS

1 The graph shows how far a marathon runner travels during a race.

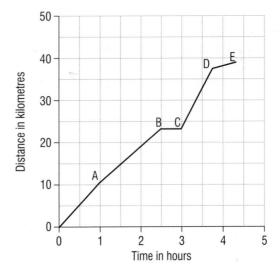

   (a) What was the distance of the race?   (1)

   (b) How long did it take the runner to complete the race?   (1)

   (c) What distance did the runner travel during the first 2 hours of the race?   (1)

   (d) For how long did the runner rest during the race? (1)

   (e) Ignoring the time for which the runner was resting, between which two points was the runner moving the slowest?
       Give a reason for your answer   (2)

2 The table gives values of distance and time for a cyclist travelling along a straight road.

Distance in metres	0	20	40	60	80	100
Time in seconds	0	2	4	6	8	10

   (a) Draw a graph of distance against time. Two of the points have been plotted for you.   (3)

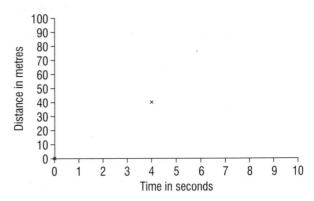

(b) Use your graph to find the distance travelled in 5 seconds. (1)

(c) Use your graph to find the time at which the distance is 30 metres. (1)

(d) Describe the motion of the cyclist. (1)

3 A van travels on a straight 'test-track' road. The graph shows how the speed of the van changes with time.

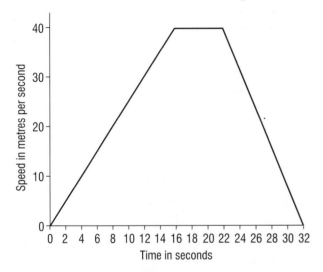

(a) (i) Name the independent variable shown on the graph. (1)

(ii) Would you describe this variable as categoric, discrete or continuous? (1)

(b) (i) A manufacturer of vans makes four different types of van. How should they display the data so that potential buyers can best compare the top speed of the vans carrying the same load? (1)

(ii) The data in (b) (i) is given for the same load each time. Would the load best be described as an independent, a dependent or a control variable? (1)

(c) Calculate the acceleration of the van during the first 16 seconds. Give a unit with your answer. (4)

(d) Calculate the distance travelled in metres between 22 and 32 seconds. (3)

[Higher]

Read the article below, then answer the questions that follow:

PARENTS DEMAND ROAD BUMPS

Parents protested yesterday at the speed of cars travelling through the Brooklands estate. They claimed that walking their young children to school was getting very dangerous. Mrs Nifty said that she often had to run across the road to miss the traffic. Mr Sloe claimed that the cars always travelled faster than the speed limit, and nothing was done about it. Mrs Divert said that it had got much worse since they put traffic calming measures, such as 'speed bumps', into the nearby Brands estate. The police sergeant attending the protest said that he understood their concerns and would investigate.

a) What do you think Mr Sloe's comments were based on? (1)

b) What evidence should have been gathered to show a link between the traffic calming measures in the Brands estate and the speed of traffic in the Brooklands estate? (1)

On hearing about the protests a science teacher decided to carry out an investigation with his students. He decided to investigate the speed of the traffic outside Brooklands School.

c) Describe a method for measuring the speed of passing cars which includes using a stopwatch. (2)

d) What time of day should this survey be carried out? Why? (2)

e) Suggest how many cars should be surveyed. (1)

f) Should the drivers know they are being surveyed? Explain your answer. (2)

P2 2.1 Forces between objects

LEARNING OBJECTIVES

1 When two objects interact, what can we say about the forces acting?
2 What is the unit of force?

Equal and opposite forces

Whenever two objects push or pull on each other, they exert equal and opposite forces on one another. The unit of force is the newton (abbreviated N).

- A boxer who punches an opponent with a force of 100 N experiences a reverse force of 100 N from his opponent.
- Two roller skaters pull on opposite ends of a rope. The skaters move towards each other. This is because they pull on each other with equal and opposite forces. Two newtonmeters could be used to show this.

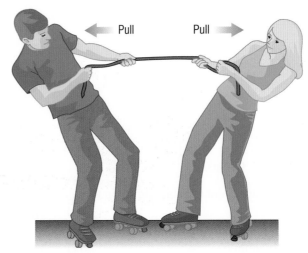

Figure 1 Equal and opposite forces

FOUL FACTS

Quicksand victims sink because they can't get enough support from the sand. The force of gravity on the victim (acting downwards) is greater than the upwards force of the sand on the victim. Sometimes the incoming tide drowns the victim!

PRACTICAL

Action and reaction

Test this with a friend if you can, using roller skates and two newtonmeters. Don't forget to wear protective head gear!

- What did you find out?
- Comment on the accuracy of your readings.

a) A hammer hits a nail with a downward force of 50 N. What is the size and direction of the force of the nail on the hammer?

In the mud

A car stuck in mud can be difficult to shift. A tractor can be very useful here. Figure 2 shows the idea. At any stage, the force of the rope on the car is equal and opposite to the force of the car on the rope.

To pull the car out of the mud, the force of the ground on the tractor needs to be greater than the force of the mud on the car. These two forces aren't necessarily equal to one another because the objects are not the same.

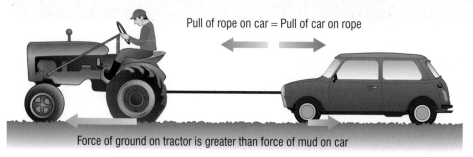

Pull of rope on car = Pull of car on rope

Force of ground on tractor is greater than force of mud on car

Figure 2 In the mud

b) A lorry tows a broken-down car. When the force of the lorry on the tow rope is 200 N, what is the force of the tow rope on the lorry?

Friction in action

The motive force on a car is the force that makes it move. This force is due to friction between the ground and the tyre of each drive wheel. Friction acts where the tyre is in contact with the ground.

Figure 3 Motive force

Direction of car

Force of tyre   Force of road
on road   on tyre

When the car moves forwards:

- the force of friction of the ground on the tyre is in the forward direction,
- the force of friction of the tyre on the ground is in the reverse direction.

The two forces are equal and opposite to one another.

c) What happens if there isn't enough friction between the tyre and the ground?

SUMMARY QUESTIONS

1 Complete the sentences below using words from the list.

  downwards   equal   opposite   upwards

  a) The force on a ladder resting against a wall is …… and …… to the force of the wall on the ladder.
  b) A book is at rest on a table. The force of the book on the table is ……. . The force of the table on the book is ……. .

2 When a student is standing at rest on bathroom scales, the scales read 500 N.

  a) What is the size and direction of the force of the student on the scales?
  b) What is the size and direction of the force of the scales on the student?

KEY POINTS

1 When two objects interact, they always exert equal and opposite forces on each other.
2 The unit of force is the newton.

P2 2.2 Resultant force

LEARNING OBJECTIVES

1 What is a resultant force?
2 What happens if the resultant force on an object is zero?
3 What happens if the resultant force on an object is not zero?

Most objects around you are acted on by more than one force. We can work out the effect of the forces on an object by replacing them with a single force, the **resultant force**. This is a single force that has the same effect as all the forces acting on the object.

When the resultant force on an object is zero, the object:
- remains stationary if it was at rest, or
- continues to move at the same speed and in the same direction if it was already moving.

PRACTICAL

Investigating forces

Make and test a model hovercraft floating on a cushion of air from a balloon, and/or
Use a glider on an air track to investigate the relationship between force and acceleration.

- What relationship do you find between force and acceleration?
  (See page 14.)

1 **A glider on a linear air track** floats on a cushion of air. Provided the track is level, the glider moves at constant velocity (i.e. with no change of speed or direction) along the track because friction is absent. The resultant force on the glider is zero.

Figure 1 The linear air track

a) What happens to the glider if the air track blower is switched off, and why?

2 **When a heavy crate is pushed across a rough floor**, the crate moves at constant velocity across the floor. The push force on the crate is equal and opposite to the force of friction of the floor on the crate. The resultant force on the crate is therefore zero.

b) What difference would it make if the floor were smooth?

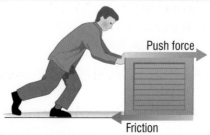

Push force

Friction

Figure 2 Overcoming friction

When the resultant force on an object is not zero, the movement of the object depends on the size and direction of the resultant force.

1 **When a jet plane is taking off,** the thrust force of its engines is greater than the force of air resistance on it. The resultant force on it is the difference between the thrust force and the force of air resistance on it. The resultant force is therefore non-zero. The greater the resultant force, the quicker the take-off is.

Figure 3 A passenger jet on take-off

Drag force   Engine force

c) What can you say about the thrust force and the force of air resistance when the plane is moving at constant velocity at constant height?

2 **When a car driver applies the brakes,** the braking force is the resultant force on the car. It acts in the opposite direction to that in which the car is moving, so it slows the car down.

d) What can you say about the resultant force if the brakes had been applied harder?

NEXT TIME YOU...

. . . are in a plane, think about the forces that are operating when you are taking off. What happens when a plane is taking off into a strong head wind?

Braking force

Figure 4 Braking

KEY POINTS

	Object at the start	Resultant force	Effect on the object
1	at rest	zero	stays at rest
2	moving	zero	velocity stays the same
3	moving	non-zero in the same direction as the direction of motion of the object	accelerates
4	moving	non-zero in the opposite direction to the direction of motion of the object	decelerates

SUMMARY QUESTIONS

1 Complete the following sentences using words from the list.

greater than   less than   equal to

A car starts from rest and accelerates along a straight flat road.

a) The force of air resistance on it is ...... the motive force of its engine.
b) The resultant force is ...... zero.
c) The downward force of the car on the road is ...... the support force of the road on the car.

2 A jet plane lands on a runway and stops.

a) What can you say about the direction of the resultant force on the plane as it lands?
b) What can you say about the resultant force on the plane when it has stopped?

GET IT RIGHT!

Remember that if a body is accelerating it can be speeding up, slowing down or changing direction. If a body is accelerating there must be a resultant force acting on it.

P2 2.3   Force and acceleration

LEARNING OBJECTIVES

1 How does the acceleration of an object depend on the size of the resultant force?
2 What effect does the mass of the object have on its acceleration?

PRACTICAL

Investigating force and acceleration

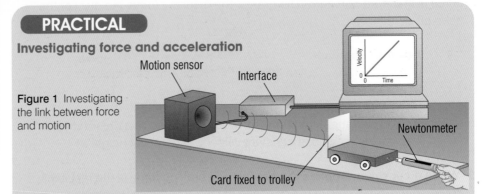

Figure 1 Investigating the link between force and motion

We can use the apparatus above to accelerate a trolley with a constant force.

Use the newtonmeter to pull the trolley along with a constant force.

You can double or treble the total moving mass by using double-deck and triple-deck trolleys.

A motion sensor and a computer record the velocity of the trolley as it accelerates.

● What are the advantages of using a data logger and computer in this investigation?

You can display the results as a velocity–time graph on the computer screen.

Figure 2 shows velocity–time graphs for different masses. You can work out the acceleration from the gradient of the line, as explained on page 127.

Look at some typical results in the table below:

Resultant force (newtons)	0.5	1.0	1.5	2.0	4.0	6.0
Mass (kilograms)	1.0	1.0	1.0	2.0	2.0	2.0
Acceleration (m/s²)	0.5	1.0	1.5	1.0	2.0	3.0
Mass × acceleration (kg m/s²)	0.5	1.0	1.5	2.0	4.0	6.0

The results show that the resultant force, the mass and the acceleration are linked by the equation

resultant force = mass × acceleration
(newtons, N)   (kilograms) (metres/second²)

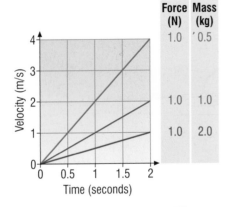

Force (N)	Mass (kg)
1.0	0.5
1.0	1.0
1.0	2.0

Figure 2 Velocity–time graph for different combinations of force and mass

Worked example
Calculate the resultant force on an object of mass 6.0 kg when it has an acceleration of 3.0 m/s².

Solution
Resultant force = mass × acceleration = 6.0 kg × 3.0 m/s² = 18.0 N

a) Calculate the resultant force on a sprinter of mass 50 kg who accelerates at 8 m/s².

Maths notes

We can write the word equation on the previous page as:

Resultant force, $F = ma$,

where m = mass and a = acceleration.

Rearranging this equation gives $\quad a = \dfrac{F}{m} \quad$ or $\quad m = \dfrac{F}{a}$

Worked example

Calculate the acceleration of an object of mass 5.0 kg acted on by a resultant force of 40 N.

Solution

Rearranging $F = ma$ gives $a = \dfrac{F}{m} = \dfrac{40\,\text{N}}{5.0\,\text{kg}} = 8.0\,\text{m/s}^2$

---

b) Calculate the acceleration of a car of mass 800 kg acted on by a resultant force of 3200 N.

Speeding up or slowing down

If the velocity of an object changes, it must be acted on by a resultant force. Its acceleration is always in the same direction as the resultant force.

- The velocity of the object increases if the resultant force is in the **same** direction as the velocity. We say its acceleration is positive because it is in the same direction as its velocity.
- The velocity of the object decreases (i.e. it decelerates) if the resultant force is **opposite** in direction. We say its acceleration is negative because it is opposite in direction to its velocity.

KEY POINT

$$\begin{array}{c} \text{Resultant force} \\ \text{(newtons, N)} \end{array} = \begin{array}{c} \text{mass} \\ \text{(kilograms)} \end{array} \times \begin{array}{c} \text{acceleration} \\ \text{(metres/second}^2\text{)} \end{array}$$

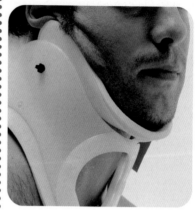

SUMMARY QUESTIONS

1 Complete a) to c) using the words below:

acceleration   resultant force   mass   velocity

   a) A moving object decelerates when a ...... acts on it in the opposite direction to its ....

   b) The greater the ...... of an object, the less its acceleration when a ...... acts on it.

   c) The ...... of a moving object increases when a ...... acts on it in the same direction as it is moving in.

2 Copy and complete the following table:

	a)	b)	c)	d)	e)
Force (newtons, N)	?	200	840	?	5000
Mass (kilograms, kg)	20	?	70	0.40	?
Acceleration (metre/second squared, m/s²)	0.80	5.0	?	6.0	0.20

GET IT RIGHT!

If an object is accelerating there must be a resultant force acting on it.

P2 2.4   On the road

Forces on the road

For any car travelling at constant velocity, the resultant force on it is zero. This is because the motive force of its engine is balanced by the resistive forces (i.e. friction and air resistance) on it.

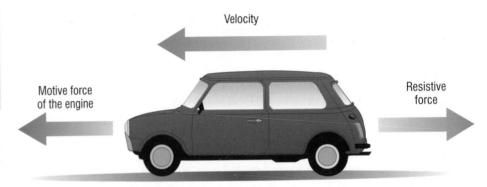

Figure 1 Constant velocity

A car driver uses the accelerator pedal (also called the gas pedal) to vary the motive force of the engine.

a) What do you think happens if the driver presses harder on the accelerator?

The braking force needed to stop a vehicle in a certain distance depends on:

● the velocity of the vehicle when the brakes are first applied
● the mass of the vehicle.

We can see this using the equation 'resultant force = mass × acceleration', in which the braking force is the resultant force.

1 The greater the velocity, the greater the deceleration needed to stop it in a certain distance. So the braking force must be greater than at low velocity.
2 The greater the mass, the greater the braking force needed for a given deceleration.

Stopping distances

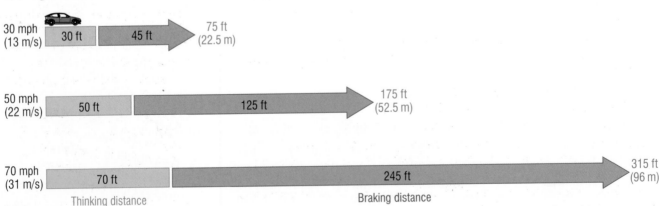

Figure 2 Stopping distances

Driving tests always ask about stopping distances. This is the shortest distance a vehicle can safely stop in, and is in two parts:

- **The thinking distance:** the distance travelled by the vehicle in the time it takes the driver to react (i.e. during the driver's reaction time).
- **The braking distance:** the distance travelled by the vehicle during the time the braking force acts.

The stopping distance = the thinking distance + the braking distance.

Figure 2 shows the stopping distance for a vehicle on a dry flat road travelling at different speeds. Check for yourself that the stopping distance at 31 m/s (70 miles per hour) is 96 m.

> b) What are the thinking distance, the braking distance and the stopping distance at 13 m/s (30 mph)?

Factors affecting stopping distances

1 **Tiredness, alcohol and drugs** all increase reaction times. So they increase the thinking distance (because thinking distance = speed × reaction time). Therefore, the stopping distance is greater.
2 **The faster a vehicle is travelling,** the further it travels before it stops. This is because the thinking distance and the braking distance both increase with increased speed.
3 **In adverse road conditions,** for example on wet or icy roads, drivers have to brake with less force to avoid skidding. Stopping distances are therefore greater in poor road conditions.
4 **Poorly maintained vehicles,** for example with worn brakes or tyres, take longer to stop because the brakes and tyres are less effective.

Figure 3 Stopping distances are further than you might think!

> c) Why are stopping distances greater in poor visibility?

PRACTICAL

Reaction times

Use an electronic stopwatch to test your own reaction time under different conditions in an investigation. Ask a friend to start the stopwatch when you are looking at it with your finger on the stop button. The read-out from the watch will give your reaction time.

- How can you make your data as reliable as possible?
- What conclusions can you draw?

SUMMARY QUESTIONS

1 Each of the following factors affects the thinking distance or the braking distance of a vehicle. Which of these two distances is affected in each case below?

a) The road surface condition affects the …… distance.
b) The tiredness of a driver increases his or her …… distance.
c) Poorly maintained brakes affects the …… distance.

2 a) Use the chart in Figure 2 to work out, in metres, the increase in i) the thinking distance, ii) the braking distance, iii) the stopping distance from 13 m/s (30 mph) to 22 m/s (50 mph). (1 foot = 0.30 m.)
b) A driver has a reaction time of 0.8 s. Calculate her thinking distance at a speed of i) 15 m/s, ii) 30 m/s.

KEY POINTS

1 The **thinking distance** is the distance travelled by the vehicle in the time it takes the driver to react.
2 The **braking distance** is the distance the vehicle travels under the braking force.
3 The **stopping distance** = the **thinking distance** + the **braking distance**.

P2 2.5   Falling objects

LEARNING OBJECTIVES

1 What is the difference between mass and weight?
2 What is terminal velocity?

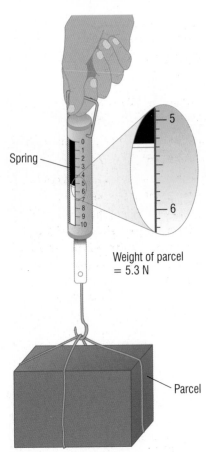

Spring

Weight of parcel = 5.3 N

Parcel

Figure 1 Using a newtonmeter to weigh an object

How to reduce your weight

Your weight is due to the gravitational force of attraction between you and the Earth. This force is very slightly weaker at the equator than at the poles. This is because the equator is slightly further from the centre of the Earth than the poles are.

So if you want to reduce your weight, go to the equator. However, your mass will be the same no matter where you are.

● The **weight** of an object is the force of gravity on it.
● The **mass** of an object is the quantity of matter in it.

We can measure the weight of an object using a newtonmeter.

The weight of an object:

● of mass 1 kg is 10 N,
● of mass 5 kg is 50 N

The force of gravity on a 1 kg object is the **gravitational field strength** at the place where the object is. The unit of gravitational field strength is the newton per kilogram (N/kg). The value of the Earth's gravitational field strength at its surface is about 10 N/kg.

If we know the mass of an object, we can calculate the force of gravity on it (i.e. its weight) using the equation

$$\underset{\text{(newtons, N)}}{\text{weight}} = \underset{\text{(kilograms, kg)}}{\text{mass}} \times \underset{\text{(newtons/kilogram, N/kg)}}{\textbf{gravitational field strength}}$$

Worked example
Calculate the weight in newtons of a person of mass 55 kg.

Solution
Weight = mass × gravitational field strength = 55 kg × 10 N/kg = 550 N

a) Calculate the weight of a steel bar of mass 20 kg.

The forces on falling objects

If we release an object above the ground, it falls because of its weight (i.e. the force of gravity on it).

If the object falls freely, no other forces act on it. So the resultant force on it is its weight. It accelerates downwards at a constant acceleration of 10 m/s², called the acceleration due to gravity. For example, if we release a 1 kg object above the ground,

● the force of gravity on it is 10 N, and
● its acceleration (= force/mass = 10 N/1 kg) = 10 m/s².

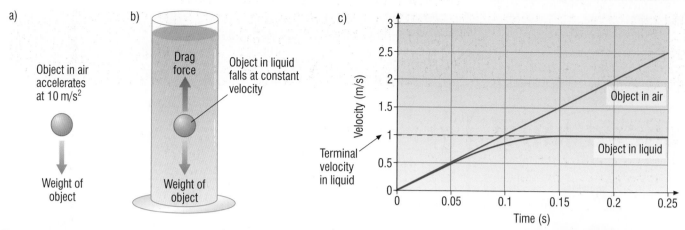

Figure 2 Falling objects. a) Falling in air, b) falling in a liquid, c) velocity–time graph for a) and b).

If the object falls in a fluid, the fluid drags on the object. The **drag force** increases with speed. At any instant, the resultant force on the object is its weight minus the drag force on it. When an object moves through the air (i.e. the fluid is air) the drag force is called air resistance.

- The acceleration of the object decreases as it falls. This is because the drag force increases as it speeds up. So the resultant force on it decreases.
- The object reaches a constant velocity when the drag force on it is equal and opposite to its weight. We call this velocity its **terminal velocity**. The resultant force is then zero, so its acceleration is zero.

b) Why does an object released in water eventually reach a constant velocity?

FOUL FACTS

If a parachute **fails** to open, the parachutist could reach a terminal velocity of more than 60 m/s (about 140 miles per hour). The drag force is then equal to his or her weight. The force of the impact on the ground would be equal to **many** times the weight, resulting in almost certain death.

SUMMARY QUESTIONS

1 Complete a) to c) using the words below:

equal to   greater than   less than

When an object is released in a fluid:

a) the drag force on it is …… its weight before it reaches its terminal velocity.

b) its acceleration is …… zero after it reaches its terminal velocity.

c) the resultant force on it is initially …… its weight.

2 A parachutist of mass 70 kg supported by a parachute of mass 20 kg reaches a constant speed.

a) Explain why the parachutist reaches a constant speed.
b) Calculate:
   i) the total weight of the parachutist and the parachute,
   ii) the size and direction of the force of air resistance on the parachute when the parachutist falls at constant speed.

PRACTICAL

Investigating the motion of a parachutist

Release an object with and without a parachute.

Make suitable measurements to compare the two situations.

- Why does the object fall at constant speed when the parachute is open?
- Evaluate the reliability of the data you collected. How could you improve the quality of your data?

Figure 3 Using a parachute

KEY POINTS

1 The weight of an object is the force of gravity on it.
2 An object falling freely accelerates at about 10 m/s².
3 An object falling in a fluid reaches a terminal velocity.

P2 2.6   Speed limits

Speed kills!

At 35mph you are twice as likely to kill someone as you are at 30mph.

Kill your speed

- At 20 mph, the stopping distance is 12 metres.
- At 40 mph, the stopping distance is 36 metres.
- At 60 mph, the stopping distance is 72 metres.

ACTIVITY

A local radio station wants your help to make a 30-second road safety 'slot' aimed at car drivers. The idea is to repeat the slot every hour. With the help of your friends, decide what message to put across, then plan and record it. You could put the message across as a 'newsflash' or a catchy jingle.

GALILEO, THE FIRST SCIENTIST OF THE SCIENTIFIC AGE

Galileo was one of the first scientists to test scientific ideas by doing experiments. He realised that if reliable observations don't support a theory, the theory has to be changed. He investigated accelerated motion by timing a ball as it rolled down a slope. He put marks down the slope at equal distances. He lived before the invention of mechanical clocks and watches. So he devised a 'water clock' to time the ball each time it passed a mark.

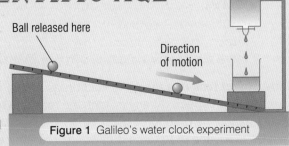

Figure 1 Galileo's water clock experiment

Figure 1 shows the arrangement. The clock was a dripping water vessel. He collected the water from when the ball was released to when it passed each mark. He used the mass of water collected as a measure of time. He repeated the test for each mark in turn. If possible, try this experiment yourself.

QUESTION

1 The table shows some results from Galileo's water clock experiment.

Mark	Start	1	2	3	4	5
Mass of water collected (grams)	0	28	39	48	56	63

a) What can you say about the time taken to pass from one mark to the next as the ball rolled down the slope?

b) Explain why the results show that the ball accelerated as it moved down the slope.

ACTIVITY

Sign Tests

Some road safety campaigners reckon there are too many road signs in some places. Drivers can't read them all as they approach them.

Look at these signs for a second and then write down from memory what the signs were. You and your friends could do a survey to see how the results from females and males compare.

2 Athletes are tested routinely to make sure they do not use drugs that boost performance.

a) Why are these tests important?

b) Why do athletes need to be careful about what they eat and drink in the days before a race?

c) Find out how scientific instruments help to fight the battle against drugs in sport.

d) Predict what the men's 100 m record will be in 2050.

SPEED RECORDS

In athletics, the 100 m race is a dramatic event. Electronic timers are used to time it and cameras are used to record the finish in case there is a 'dead heat'. The world record for the time has become shorter and shorter over successive years.

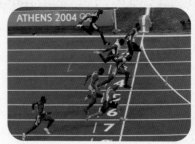
ATHENS 2004

● Jesse Owens	1936	10.2 s
● Jim Hines	1968	9.95 s
● Maurice Green	1999	9.79 s
● Tim Montgomery	2002	9.78 s
● Assafa Powell	2005	9.77 s

Anti-skid surfaces

Have you noticed that road surfaces near road junctions and traffic lights are often different from normal road surfaces?

● The surface is rougher than normal. This gives increased friction between the surface and a vehicle tyre. So it reduces the chance of skidding when a driver brakes.

● The surface is lighter in colour so it is marked out clearly from a normal road surface.

Skidding happens when the brakes are applied too harshly. The wheels lock and the tyres slide on the road as a result. Increased friction between the tyres and the road allows more force to be applied without skidding happening. So the stopping distance is reduced.

Discuss the following issues with your friends:

● Should drivers involved in accidents also be tested for tiredness and drugs?

● Would tiredness tests be reliable? Would drivers on medical drugs be caught unfairly?

● Should drivers be pulled over for 'on the spot' tests?

Campaigners in the village of Greystoke want the council to resurface the main road at the traffic lights in the village. A child was killed crossing the road at the traffic lights earlier in the year. The council estimates it would cost £45 000. They say they can't afford it. Campaigners have found some more data to support their case.

● There are about 50 000 road accidents each year in the UK.

● The cost of road accidents is over £3000 million per year.

● Anti-skid surfaces have cut accidents by about 5%.

a) Estimate how much each road accident costs.

b) Imagine you are one of the campaigners. Write a letter to your local newspaper to counter the council's response that they can't afford it.

SUMMARY QUESTIONS

1 A student is pushing a box across a rough floor. Friction acts between the box and the floor.

a) Complete the sentences below using words from the list.

in the same direction as
in the opposite direction to

  i) The force of friction of the box on the floor is …… the force of friction of the floor on the box.

  ii) The force of the student on the box is …… the force of friction of the box on the floor.

b) The student is pushing the box towards a door. Which direction, towards the door or away from the door, is

  i) the force of the box on the student? *away*

  ii) the force of friction of the student on the floor? *towards?*

2 a) The weight of an object of mass 100 kg on the Moon is 160 N. *1000*

  i) Calculate the gravitational field strength on the Moon. *160 N*

  ii) Calculate the weight of the object on the Earth's surface.

  The gravitational field strength near the Earth's surface is 10 N/kg.

b) Calculate the acceleration and the resultant force in each of the following situations.

  i) A sprinter of mass 80 kg accelerates from rest to a speed of 9.6 m/s in 1.2 s.

  ii) A train of mass 70 000 kg decelerates from a velocity of 16 m/s to a standstill in 40 s without change of direction.

3 The figure shows the velocity–time graphs for a metal object X dropped in air and a similar object Y dropped in a tank of water.

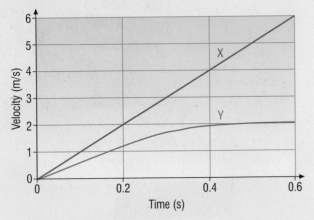

a) What does the graph for X tell you about its acceleration?

b) In terms of the forces acting on Y, explain why it reached a constant velocity.

EXAM-STYLE QUESTIONS

1

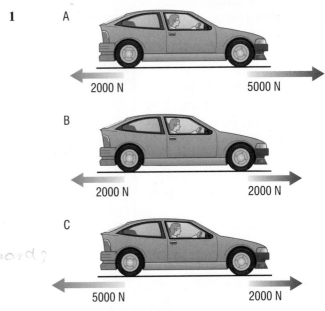

A

2000 N   5000 N

B

2000 N   2000 N

C

5000 N   2000 N

A car travels on a straight, level road.
The diagrams show the car at three stages, **A**, **B** and **C** of its journey. The arrows show the forward and backwards forces acting on the car.

(a) What is happening to the car at:

  (i) Stage A? *accel*

  (ii) Stage B? *constant*

  (iii) Stage C? *decel*   (3)

(b) The driver of the car sees some traffic lights ahead change to red. He applies the brakes. Between seeing the lights change and applying the brakes, there is a time delay called the reaction time.

  (i) Suggest two things that would increase the reaction time of the driver.

  (ii) Suggest two things that would increase the braking distance of the car.   (4)

(c) The manufacturer of the car makes the same model but with three different engine sizes. The designers wanted to test which model had the highest top speed. They used light gates (sensors) and data loggers to take their measurements. Why didn't they use stopwatches to collect their data?   (1)

2 The diagram shows a sky-diver. Two forces, **X** and **Y** act on the sky-diver.

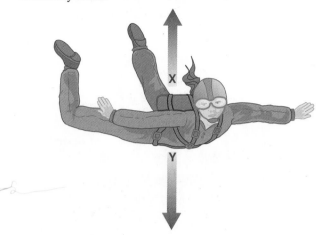

Force **Y** is the weight of the sky-diver.

(a) Write down the equation which links weight, gravitational field strength and mass. (1)

(b) What causes force **X**? (1)

(c) As the sky-diver falls, the size of force **X** increases. What happens to the size of force **Y**? (1)

(d) Describe the motion of the sky-diver when:

(i) force **X** is smaller than force **Y**.

(ii) force **X** is equal to force **Y**. (3)

3 The graph shows how the velocity of a parachutist changes with time during a parachute jump.

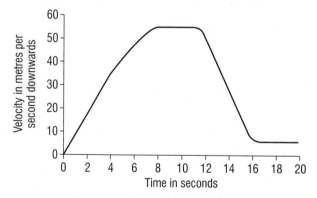

(a) Describe the motion of the parachutist during the first 4 seconds of the jump. (1)

(b) (i) What is the terminal velocity of the parachutist before her parachute opens? (1)

(ii) Explain in terms of the forces acting on the parachutist why she reaches terminal velocity. (3)

(c) Explain why the data shown above can be presented as a line graph. (2)

HOW SCIENCE WORKS QUESTIONS

Weighty problems

Weight is something we are all familiar with and take very much for granted. You now understand that it is about the force of gravity acting on a mass. In the past this realisation had a big impact on science. Sir Isaac Newton attempted to explain why the Earth didn't fall apart as it spun on its own axis. Many people thought the Earth can't be spinning because it would fall apart if it was. Newton worked out that the force of gravity was easily strong enough to stop the Earth falling apart. Newton suggested a way the Earth's spinning motion could be tested: dropping an object from the top of a very tall tower.

The commonly accepted theory was that the object would fall to Earth behind the tower. Newton said that as the top of the tower was travelling much faster than the surface of the Earth, it would fall in front of the tower. Unfortunately there was not a tower tall enough to test the prediction!

Newton even worked out that gravity would eventually take the object to the centre of the Earth if it were able to go through the Earth. Robert Hooke pointed out an error in Newton's thinking and suggested it would follow an ellipse around the centre of the Earth.

Newton worked on this idea and many years later Edmund Halley used Newton's calculations to work out when a comet would return to be seen from the Earth. Halley died aged 85, some 16 years before his prediction about the comet was proved to be correct.

Use this passage to help you to answer these questions.

a) The observation that the Earth did not fall apart as it rotated produced which hypothesis from Newton? (1)

b) What was the prediction that was made from this hypothesis? (1)

c) What was the unscientific expectation for the object falling from the tower? (1)

d) What was the technology that was missing to test this prediction? (1)

Theories are there to be tested. Newton's theories about motion needed to be tested.

e) What was Halley's prediction that had been based on Newton's theories? (1)

f) Did Halley's prediction support Newton's theory? How do you know? (1)

P2 3.1   Energy and work

Working out

Figure 1 Working out

In a fitness centre or a gym, you have to work hard to keep fit. Raising weights and pedalling on an exercise bike are just two ways to keep fit. Whichever way you choose to keep fit, you have to apply a force to move something. So the work you do causes transfer of energy.

a) When you pedal on an exercise bike, where does the energy transferred go to?

When an object is moved by a force, we say **work** is done on the object by the force. The force transfers energy to the object. So we say the work done by the object is the energy transferred. For example, if you raise an object and increase its gravitational potential energy by 20 J, the work you do on the object is 20 J.

Work done = energy transferred

The work done by a force depends on the force and the distance moved. We use the following equation to calculate the work done by a force when it moves an object:

work done   =   force   ×   distance moved in the direction of the force
(joules, J)   (newtons, N)   (metres, m)

Note
Change of gravitational potential energy (in J) =

  weight × change of height
  (in N)   (in m)

Worked example
A 20 N weight is raised through a height of 0.4 m. Calculate i) the work done, ii) the gain of gravitational potential energy of the object.

Solution
i) The force needed to lift the weight = 20 N

   Work done = force × distance moved in the direction of the force = 20 N × 0.4 m
        = 8.0 J

ii) Gain of gravitational potential energy = work done = 8.0 J

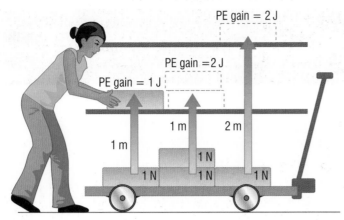

Figure 2 Using joules

b) A weightlifter raises a 200 N metal bar through a height of 1.5 m. Calculate the gain of gravitational potential energy.

NEXT TIME YOU...

. . . step on a box, calculate your increase of gravitational potential energy. Your muscles push you up with a force equal and opposite to your weight. So your gain of gravitational potential energy is equal to your weight × the height of the step.

Figure 3 Steps

PRACTICAL

Doing work

Carry out a series of experiments to calculate the work done in performing some simple tasks.

- Comment on the accuracy of your measurements. How sensitive are your measuring instruments? How accurately can you read them in your experiments?

Friction at work

Work done to overcome friction is mainly transformed into heat energy.

1 If you rub your hands together vigorously, they become warm. Your muscles do work to overcome the friction between your hands. The work you do is transformed into heat energy.

2 Brake pads become hot if the brakes are applied for too long. Friction between the brake pads and the wheel discs opposes the motion of the wheel. The kinetic energy of the vehicle is transformed into heat energy. A small proportion of the energy may be transformed into sound if the brakes 'squeal'.

SUMMARY QUESTIONS

1 Calculate the work done when:

   a) a force of 20 N makes an object move 4.8 m in the direction of the force,
   b) an object of weight 80 N is raised through a height of 1.2 m.

2 a) A student of weight 450 N steps on a box of height 0.20 m.
      i) Calculate the gain of gravitational potential energy of the student.
      ii) Calculate the work done by the student if she steps on and off the box fifty times.
   b) The student steps off the floor onto a platform and gains 270 J of gravitational potential energy. Calculate the height of the platform.

KEY POINTS

1 Work done = energy transferred.
2 Work done (joules) = force (newtons) × distance moved in the direction of the force (metres).

P2 3.2 Kinetic energy

LEARNING OBJECTIVES

1 What are kinetic energy and elastic potential energy?
2 How does the kinetic energy of an object depend on its speed?
3 How can we calculate kinetic energy? [Higher]

PRACTICAL

Investigating kinetic energy

The kinetic energy of an object is the energy it has due to its motion. It depends on: • its mass, • its speed.

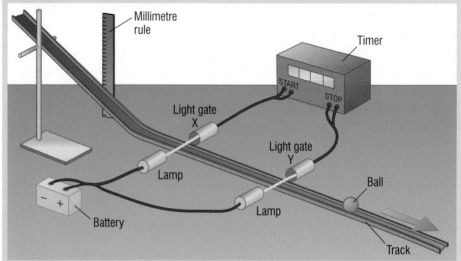

Figure 1 Investigating kinetic energy

Figure 1 shows how we can investigate how the kinetic energy of a ball depends on its speed.

1 The ball is released on a slope from a measured height above the foot of the slope. We can calculate the gravitational potential energy it loses from its weight × its drop of height. The kinetic energy it gains is equal to its loss of gravitational potential energy.

2 The ball is timed, using light gates, over a measured distance between X and Y after the slope.

• Why do light gates improve the quality of the data you can collect in this investigation?

Some sample measurements for a ball of mass 0.5 kg are shown in the table.

Height drop to foot of slope (metres, m)	0.05	0.10	0.16	0.20
Initial kinetic energy of ball (joules, J)	0.25	0.50	0.80	1.00
Time to travel 1.0 m from X to Y (seconds, s)	0.98	0.72	0.57	0.50
Speed (metres/second, m/s)	1.02	?	?	2.00

Work out the speed in each case. The first and last values have been worked out for you. *Can you see a link between speed and height?* If the height drop is increased by four times then the speed doubles. The height drop is proportional to the (speed)².

a) Check the other measurements to see if they fit this rule.

The exact link between the kinetic energy of an object and its speed is given by the equation

kinetic energy = ½ ×   **mass**   ×   **speed²**
(joules, J)   (kilograms, kg)   (metre/second)², (m/s)²)

Worked example

Calculate the kinetic energy of a vehicle of mass 500 kg moving at a speed of 12 m/s.

Solution

Kinetic energy = ½ × mass × speed² = 0.5 × 500 kg × (12 m/s)² = 36 000 J.

Elastic potential energy

When you stretch a rubber band or a bowstring, the work you do is stored in it as **elastic potential energy**. Figure 2 shows one way you can transform elastic potential energy into kinetic energy.

An object is **elastic** if it regains its shape after being stretched or squashed. A rubber band is an example of an elastic object.

Elastic potential energy is the energy stored in an elastic object when work is done on it to change its shape.

Figure 2 Using elastic potential energy

SCIENCE @ WORK

Sports scientists design running shoes:
- to reduce the force of each impact when the runner's foot hits the ground,
- to return as much kinetic energy as possible to each foot in each impact.

Figure 3 A sports shoe

b) Some of the kinetic energy of the foot is wasted in each impact. What is this energy transformed into?

SUMMARY QUESTIONS

1 a) A catapult is used to fire an object into the air. Describe the energy transformations when the catapult is i) stretched, ii) released.
   b) An object of weight 2.0 N fired vertically upwards from a catapult reaches a maximum height of 5.0 m. Calculate:
      i) the gain of gravitational potential energy of the object,
      ii) the kinetic energy of the object when it left the catapult.

2 A car moving at a constant speed has 360 000 J of kinetic energy. When the driver applies the brakes, the car stops in a distance of 95 m.

   a) Calculate the force that stops the vehicle.
   b) What happens to the kinetic energy of the car?
   c) The speed of the car was 30 m/s when its kinetic energy was 360 000 J. Calculate its mass. [Higher]

KEY POINTS

1 **Elastic potential energy** is the energy stored in an elastic object when work is done on the object.

2 The **kinetic energy** of a moving object depends on its mass and its speed.

3 Kinetic energy (J) =

   ½ × **mass** × **speed²**
      (kg)   (m/s)²

   [Higher]

P2 3.3 Momentum

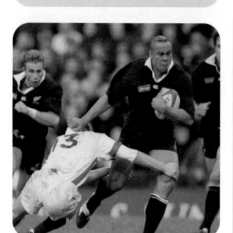

Figure 1 A contact sport

LEARNING OBJECTIVES

1 How can we calculate momentum?
2 What is its unit?
3 What happens to the total momentum of two objects when they collide?

Momentum is important to anyone who plays a contact sport. In a game of rugby, a player with a lot of momentum is very difficult to stop.

The momentum of a moving object = its mass × its velocity.

The unit of momentum is the kilogram metre/second (kg m/s).

a) Calculate the momentum of a 40 kg person running at 6 m/s.

PRACTICAL

Investigating collisions

When two objects collide, the momentum of each object changes. Figure 2 shows how to use a computer and a motion sensor to investigate a collision between two trolleys.

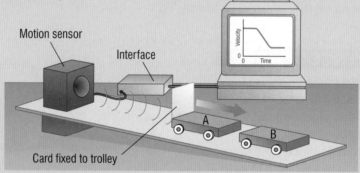

Figure 2 Investigating collisions

Trolley A is given a push so it collides with a stationary trolley B. The two trolleys stick together after the collision. The computer gives the velocity of A before the collision and the velocity of both trolleys afterwards.

● What does each section of the velocity–time graph show?

1 **For two trolleys of the same mass**, the velocity of trolley A is halved by the impact. The combined mass after the collision is twice the moving mass before the collision. So the momentum (= mass × velocity) after the collision is the same as before the collision.

2 **For a single trolley pushed into a double trolley**, the velocity of A is reduced to one-third. The combined mass after the collision is three times the initial mass. So once again, the momentum after the collision is the same as the momentum before the collision.

In both tests, the total momentum is unchanged (i.e. is conserved) by the collision. We can use this rule to predict what happens whenever objects collide or push each other apart in an 'explosion'.

Momentum is conserved in any collision or explosion provided no external forces act on the objects that collide or explode.

If a vehicle crashes into the back of a line of cars, each car in turn is 'shunted' into the one in front. Momentum is transferred along the line of cars to the one at the front.

Figure 3 A 'shunt' collision

Worked example

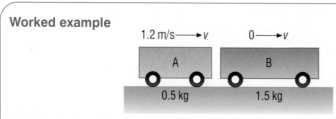

A 0.5 kg trolley A is pushed at a velocity of 1.2 m/s into a stationary trolley B of mass 1.5 kg. The two trolleys stick to each other after the impact.

Calculate:
a) the momentum of the 0.5 kg trolley before the collision,
b) the velocity of the two trolleys straight after the impact.

Solution
a) Momentum = mass × velocity = 0.5 kg × 1.2 m/s = 0.6 kg m/s.
b) The momentum after the impact = the momentum before the impact = 0.6 kg m/s
    (1.5 kg + 0.5 kg) × velocity after the impact = 0.6 kg m/s

    the velocity after the impact = $\dfrac{0.6 \text{ kg m/s}}{2 \text{ kg}}$ = 0.3 m/s

b) Calculate the speed after the collision if trolley A had a mass of 1.0 kg.

SUMMARY QUESTIONS

1 Complete a) and b) using the words below:

        force   mass   momentum   velocity

    a) The momentum of a moving object is its ...... × its ....
    b) ...... is conserved when objects collide, provided no external ......
        acts.

2 A 1000 kg rail wagon moving at a velocity of 5.0 m/s on a level track
    collides with a stationary 1500 kg wagon. The two wagons move
    together after the collision.

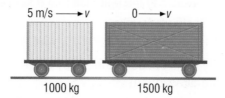

    a) Calculate the momentum of the 1000 kg wagon before the collision.
    b) Show that the two wagons move at a velocity of 2.0 m/s after the
        collision.

KEY POINTS

1 Momentum (kg m/s) =
    mass (kg) × velocity (m/s).
2 Momentum is conserved
    whenever objects interact,
    provided no external forces
    act on them.

P2 3.4 More on collisions and explosions

LEARNING OBJECTIVES

1 Why does momentum have a direction as well as size?
2 When two objects fly apart, why is their total momentum zero?

PRACTICAL

Investigating a controlled explosion

When a bomb explodes, fragments of metal fly off in all directions. The fragments fly off with enormous momentum in different directions. Figure 1 shows a more controlled explosion using trolleys. When the trigger rod is tapped, a bolt springs out and the trolleys recoil from each other.

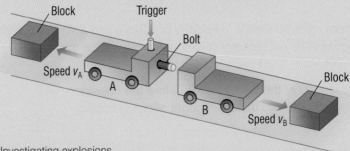

Figure 1 Investigating explosions

Using trial and error, we can place blocks on the runway so the trolleys reach them at the same time. This allows us to compare the speeds of the trolleys. Some results are shown in Figure 2.

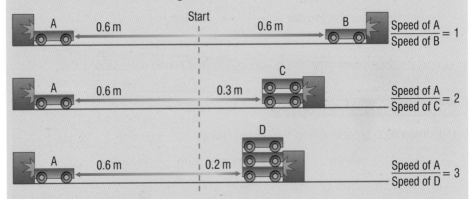

Figure 2 Using different masses

● Did your results agree exactly with the ones above? If not, try to explain why.

● Two single trolleys travel equal distances in the same time. This shows that they recoil at equal speeds.
● A double trolley only travels half the distance that a single trolley does. Its speed is half that of the single trolley.

In each test,

1 the mass of the trolley × the speed of the trolley is the same, and
2 they recoil in opposite directions.

So momentum has size and direction. The results show that the trolleys recoil with equal and opposite momentum.

a) Why does a stationary rowing boat recoil when someone jumps off it?

DID YOU KNOW?

Crash tests with dummies in cars are used to test car safety features such as seat belts. In a 'head-on' crash test between two cars, if the cars have equal and opposite momentum before the collision, they have no momentum afterwards. All their kinetic energy is transformed into heat, sound and work done deforming the cars.

Conservation of momentum in an explosion

In the trolley examples:

- momentum of A after the explosion = (mass of A × velocity of A)
- momentum of B after the explosion = (mass of B × velocity of B)
- total momentum before the explosion = 0 (because both trolleys were at rest).

Using conservation of momentum gives:

(mass of A × velocity of A) + (mass of B × velocity of B) = 0

Therefore

(mass of A × velocity of A) = −(mass of B × velocity of B)

This tells us that A and B move apart with equal and opposite amounts of momentum.

Momentum in action

When a shell is fired from an artillery gun, the gun barrel recoils backwards. The recoil of the gun barrel is slowed down by a spring. This lessens the backwards motion of the gun.

Figure 3 An artillery gun in action

Worked example

An artillery gun of mass 2000 kg fires a shell of mass 20 kg at a velocity of 120 m/s. Calculate the recoil velocity of the gun.

Solution

Applying the conservation of momentum gives:

mass of gun × recoil velocity of gun = −(mass of shell × velocity of shell)

If we let V represent the recoil velocity of the gun,

$$2000 \text{ kg} \times V = -(20 \text{ kg} \times 120 \text{ m/s})$$

$$V = \frac{-2400 \text{ kg m/s}}{2000 \text{ kg}} = -1.2 \text{ m/s}$$

---

b) A 600 kg cannon recoils at a speed of 0.5 m/s when a 12 kg cannon ball is fired from it.
Calculate the velocity of the cannon ball when it leaves the cannon.

SUMMARY QUESTIONS

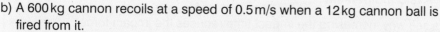

1 A 30 kg skater and a 40 kg skater standing in the middle of an ice rink push each other away. Complete the following sentences using words from the list.

force   momentum   velocity

40 kg   30 kg

a) They move apart with equal and opposite ....
b) The 30 kg skater moves away with a bigger ...... than the other skater.
c) They push each other with equal and opposite ....

2 In question 1, the 30 kg skater moves away at 2.0 m/s. Calculate:

a) her momentum,
b) the velocity of the other skater.

KEY POINTS

1 Momentum has size and direction.
2 When two objects push each other apart, they move apart with equal and opposite momentum.

P2 3.5   Changing momentum

1 What does a force do to the momentum of an object?
2 How can we calculate the change in momentum caused by a force? [Higher]

Figure 1 A crash test

Crumple zones at the front end and rear end of a car are designed to lessen the force of an impact. The force changes the momentum of the car.

● In a front-end impact, the momentum of the car is reduced.
● In a rear-end impact, the momentum of the car is increased.

In both cases the effect of a crumple zone is to increase the impact time and so lessen the impact force.

Car makers test the design of a crumple zone by driving a remote control car into a brick wall.

PRACTICAL

Investigating impacts

We can test an impact using a trolley and a brick, as shown in Figure 2. When the trolley hits the brick, the Plasticine flattens on impact, making the impact time longer. This is the key factor that reduces the impact force.

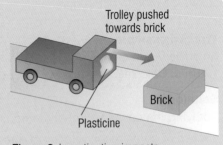

Trolley pushed towards brick

Brick

Plasticine

Figure 2 Investigating impacts

a) Why is rubber matting under a child's swing a good idea?

HIGHER

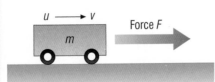

Figure 3 Force and momentum

Force and momentum

Let's see why increasing the impact time reduces the impact force.

Suppose the force acts on the trolley for a time t and causes the velocity to change from u to v.

● The deceleration due to the impact $= \dfrac{\text{change of velocity}}{\text{time taken}} = \dfrac{v - u}{t}$

● Using force = mass × acceleration:

$$\text{the force on the trolley, } F = \frac{m(v - u)}{t} = \frac{mv - mu}{t}$$

where m is the mass of the trolley

● The initial momentum of the trolley $= mu$, and the final momentum of the trolley $= mv$

So the force,

$$F = \frac{\text{final momentum} - \text{initial momentum}}{\text{time taken}} = \frac{\text{change of momentum}}{\text{time taken}}$$

$$\text{force, } F = \frac{\text{change of momentum}}{\text{time taken}}$$

The equation shows that:

1 Making the time longer (increasing the value of *t*) makes the force smaller. Crumple zones in cars are designed to make impact times longer so impact forces are reduced.

b) What difference does it make if the impact time is made shorter instead of longer?

2 When a resultant force acts on a moving object, a change of momentum takes place.

In general, the force needed to cause a change of momentum is given by:

$$\text{force (newtons, N)} = \frac{\textbf{change of momentum (kilogram metre/second, kg m/s)}}{\textbf{time taken (seconds, s)}}$$

> **Worked example**
>
> A bullet of mass 0.004 kg moving at a speed of 90 m/s is stopped by a bullet-proof vest in 0.0003 s.
>
> Calculate the impact force.
>
> **Solution**
>
> Initial momentum of bullet = mass × velocity = 0.004 kg × 90 m/s
> = 0.36 kg m/s
>
> Final momentum of bullet = 0
>
> $$\text{Impact force} = \frac{\text{change of momentum}}{\text{time taken}} = \frac{0.36 \text{ kg m/s}}{0.0003 \text{ s}} = 1200 \text{ N}$$

c) Calculate the impact force if the impact time had been 0.0002 s.

SCIENCE @ WORK

Scientists at Oxford University have developed new lightweight material for bullet-proof vests. The material is so strong and elastic that bullets bounce off it.

KEY POINTS

1 The more time an impact takes, the less the force exerted.

2 $\text{Force (newtons)} = \dfrac{\text{change of momentum (kilogram metre/second)}}{\text{time taken (seconds)}}$

[Higher]

SUMMARY QUESTIONS

1 Copy and complete each of the following sentences using a word or words from the list.

decreases   increases   is zero   stays the same

a) The momentum of a moving object ...... if no forces act on it.
b) In an impact in which a moving object is speeded up, its momentum ....
c) When an object is thrown into the air, the force of gravity on it ...... its momentum as it goes up.

2 a) Calculate the initial momentum of an 800 kg car travelling at 30 m/s.
b) What force is required to stop the car in i) 12 s, ii) 30 s? [Higher]

P2 3.6   Forces for safety

Motor News

CLUNK CLICK!

When seat belts were first introduced, some car users claimed that they should not be forced by law to wear them. A very successful campaign was launched to convince car users to 'belt up'. It included the catchy phrase 'Clunk click every trip'. As a result, deaths and injuries in road accidents fell significantly. A seat belt stops its wearer from continuing forwards when the car stops suddenly. Someone without a seat belt would hit the windscreen in a 'short sharp' impact and suffer major injury.

- The time taken to stop someone in a car is longer with a seat belt than without it. So the decelerating force is reduced by wearing a seat belt.
- The seat belt acts across the chest so it spreads the force out. Without the seat belt, the force would act on the head when it hits the windscreen.

ACTIVITY

'Clunk click every trip' is a positive message. Sometimes a negative message has bigger effect. Come up with your own short message to remind parents to check that children in cars must always wear seat belts.

NEWS

Air bags

An airbag in action

A crazy motorist was sent to prison for three years yesterday at Newtown County Court. He drove for twenty miles at top speed down the wrong side of a motorway. He was stopped when he drove into a police car blocking his route. One of the police officers said, 'We braced ourselves for the impact when he didn't stop. The airbags in our car inflated and took the force of the impact.' The bravery of the police officers was commended by the judge.

QUESTION

1 Explain why an inflated air bag in front of a car user reduces the force on a user of a 'head-on' crash.

G-FORCES

We sometimes express the effect of an impact on an object or person as a force-to-weight ratio. We call this the 'g-force'. For example, a g-force of 2g means the force on an object is twice its weight. You would experience a g-force of

- about 3–4 g on a fairground ride that whirls you round,
- about 10 g in a low-speed car crash,
- more than 50 g in a high-speed car crash-force. You would be lucky to survive though!

Analysing a road crash

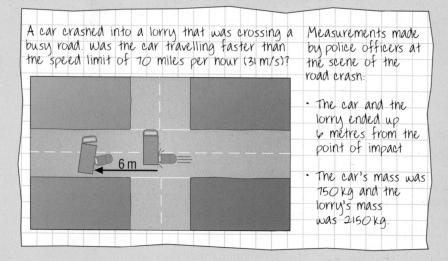

A car crashed into a lorry that was crossing a busy road. Was the car travelling faster than the speed limit of 70 miles per hour (31 m/s)?

6 m

Measurements made by police officers at the scene of the road crash:

- The car and the lorry ended up 6 metres from the point of impact

- The car's mass was 750 kg and the lorry's mass was 2150 kg.

QUESTION

2 The speed of a vehicle for a braking distance of 6 m is 9 m/s.
   a) Use this speed to calculate the momentum of the car and the lorry immediately after the impact.
   b) Use conservation of momentum to calculate the velocity of the car immediately before the collision.
   c) Was the car travelling over the speed limit before the crash?

Safety costs

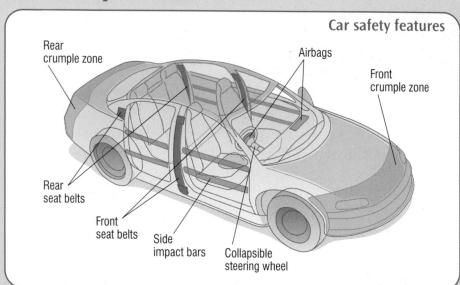

Car safety features

Rear crumple zone

Airbags

Front crumple zone

Rear seat belts

Front seat belts

Side impact bars

Collapsible steering wheel

ACTIVITY

a) With the help of your friends, find out what safety features are in some other new cars. Find out if they are compulsory or optional. List the price (including tax) of each car.
b) Use your information to say if cheaper cars have fewer safety features than more expensive cars.
c) What do you think could be done to make more cars safer?

Car makers need to sell cars. If their cars are too expensive, people won't buy them. Safety features add to the cost of a new car. Some safety features (e.g. seat belts) are required by law and some (e.g. side impact bars) are optional. The table shows the main safety features in a new car.

Car make and price **Nippy, £6500**		
Front seat belts	✔
Rear seat belts	✔
Airbags	
Front crumple zone	✔
Rear crumple zone	
Side impact bars	
Collapsible steering wheel	✔

ACTIVITY

Do you think all cars should have the best safety features money can buy? Or should owners choose these as options? What are the points for and against these views?

Which do you support?

SUMMARY QUESTIONS

1 a) Copy and complete the following sentences using words from the list.

equal to   greater than   less than

When a braking force acts on a vehicle and slows it down,

i) the work done by the force is …… the energy transferred from the object,

ii) the kinetic energy after the brakes have been applied is …… the kinetic energy before they were applied.

b) A student pushes a trolley of weight 150 N up a slope of length 20 m. The slope is 1.2 m high.

11 N

20 m   1.2 m

i) Calculate the gravitational potential energy gained by the trolley.

ii) The student pushed the trolley up the slope with a force of 11 N. Show that the work done by the student was 220 J.

iii) Give one reason why all the work done by the student was not transferred to the trolley as gravitational potential energy.

2 A 700 kg car moving at 20 m/s is stopped in a distance of 80 m when the brakes are applied.

a) Show that the kinetic energy of the car at 20 m/s is 140 000 J.

b) Calculate the braking force on the car.   [Higher]

3 A student of mass 40 kg standing at rest on a skateboard of mass 2.0 kg jumps off the skateboard at a speed of 0.30 m/s. Calculate:

a) i) the momentum of the student,
   ii) the recoil velocity of the skateboard,

b) the kinetic energy of i) the student, ii) the skateboard, after they move apart.   [b] – Higher]

4 A car bumper is designed not to bend in impacts at less than 4 m/s. It was fitted to a car of mass 900 kg and tested by driving the car into a wall at 4 m/s. The time of impact was measured and found to be 1.8 s. Work out the impact force.   [Higher]

EXAM-STYLE QUESTIONS

1 The picture shows a catapult.

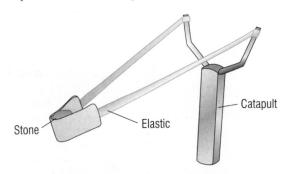

Stone   Elastic   Catapult

(a) When a force is applied to the stone, work is done in stretching the elastic and the stone moves backwards.

   (i) Write down the equation you could use to calculate the work done.   (1)

   (ii) The average force applied to the stone is 20 N. This moves it backwards 0.15 m. Calculate the work done and give its unit.   (3)

(b) The work done is stored as energy.

   (i) What type of energy is stored in the stretched elastic?   (1)

   (ii) What type of energy does the stone have when it is released?   (1)

2 (a) The diagram shows three cars, **A**, **B** and **C**, travelling along a straight, level road at 25 m/s.

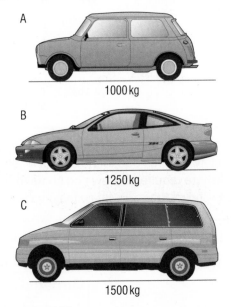

A

1000 kg

B

1250 kg

C

1500 kg

   (i) Explain which vehicle, **A**, **B** or **C** has the greatest momentum.   (2)

   (ii) Would you need a more sensitive weighing device to be more certain of your answer to part (i)? Give your reasoning.   (2)

(b) The diagram shows three identical cars, **D**, **E** and **F**, all of mass 1500 kg, travelling along a straight, level road at different speeds.

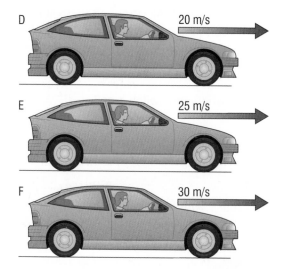

D 20 m/s

E 25 m/s

F 30 m/s

Explain which vehicle, **D**, **E** or **F** has the greatest momentum. (2)

(c) Calculate the momentum of car **E**, include the unit with your answer. (4)

3 A student is doing an investigation of the conservation of momentum with a horizontal air track and two 'gliders'.

(a) Explain what is meant by conservation of momentum. (2)

(b) Apart from collisions, give another type of event in which conservation of momentum applies. (1)

(c) The diagram shows the air track and the two 'gliders', **X** and **Y**.

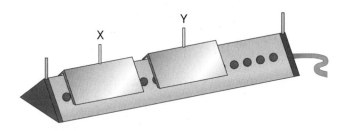

X Y

The mass of **X** is 0.2 kg and its velocity is 1.5 m/s to the right.

The mass of **Y** is 0.3 kg and it is stationary. When 'glider' **X** collides with trolley **Y** they move off together.

Calculate the velocity of the 'gliders' after the collision and give their direction. (4)

HOW SCIENCE WORKS QUESTIONS

Claire was interested in how ancient catapults were used to fire rocks at the enemy. She designed a catapult that was similar to one she found in a history book. She couldn't work out the angle at which to fire the catapult, so she used 'stoppers' to test three different positions. Her catapult looked like this:

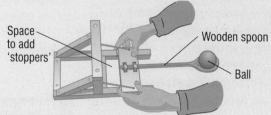

Space to add 'stoppers'

Wooden spoon

Ball

As the ball was fired the spoon was pulled by the force of the elastic bands. The spoon hit the wooden support and the ball was fired into the distance. The three positions in which the wooden spoon was stopped are shown in the diagram opposite.

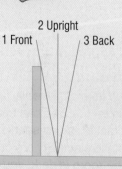

2 Upright

1 Front

3 Back

Here are Claire's results:

	Distance travelled (cm)		
	Front	Upright	Back
1st go	110	114	110
2nd go	117	116	112
3rd go	109	121	108
Mean	112	117	110

a) Claire made a prediction that the backward position would make the ball travel the furthest. Do the results support her prediction? Explain your answer. (1)

b) If you had to have a new prediction, what might it be? (1)

c) Do the results show precision? Explain your answer. (1)

d) What is the independent variable in Claire's investigation? (1)

e) Would you describe this as a discrete, categoric or ordered variable? (1)

f) How could it be changed into a continuous variable? (1)

g) What would be the advantage of using a continuous independent variable? (3)

P2 4.1

Electrical charges

LEARNING OBJECTIVES

1 What happens when insulating materials are rubbed together?
2 What is transferred when objects become charged?
3 What happens when charges are brought together?

Have you ever stuck a balloon on a ceiling? All you need to do is to rub the balloon on your clothing before you touch it on the ceiling. The rubbing action charges the balloon with **static electricity**. The charge on the balloon attracts it to the ceiling.

a) Why does a TV screen crackle when you switch it on?

DEMONSTRATION

The Van de Graaff generator

A Van de Graaff generator can make your hair stand on end. The dome charges up when the generator is switched on. Massive sparks are produced if the charge on the dome builds up too much.

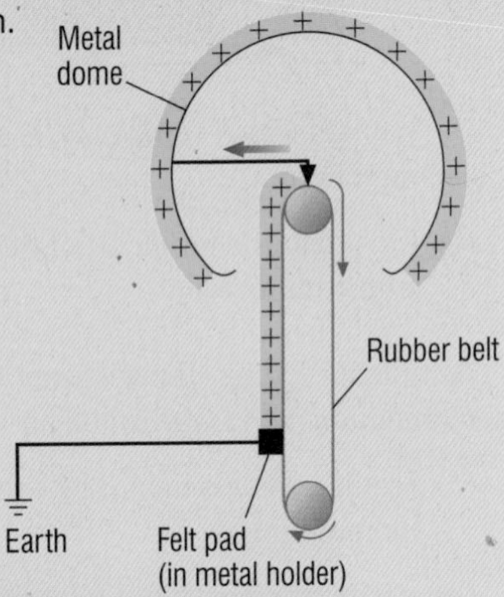

Figure 1 The Van de Graaff generator

The Van de Graaff generator charges up because:

– the belt rubs against a felt pad and becomes charged,
– the belt carries the charge onto an insulated metal dome,
– sparks are produced when the dome can no longer hold any more charge.

● Why should you keep away from a Van de Graaff generator?

NEXT TIME YOU...

... take off a woolly jumper, listen out! You can hear it crackle as tiny sparks from static electricity are created. If the room is dark, you can even see the sparks.

DID YOU KNOW?

You can get charged up just by sitting in a plastic chair. If this happens, you may feel a slight shock from static electricity when you stand up.

Inside the atom

The protons and neutrons make up the nucleus of the atom. Electrons move about in the space round the nucleus.

● A proton has a positive charge.
● An electron has an equal negative charge.
● A neutron is uncharged.

An uncharged atom has equal numbers of electrons and protons. Only electrons can be transferred to or from an atom.

1 Adding electrons to an uncharged atom makes it negative (because the atom then has more electrons than protons).

2 Removing electrons from an uncharged atom makes it positive (because the atom has fewer electrons than protons).

○ Electron
● Proton
○ Neutron

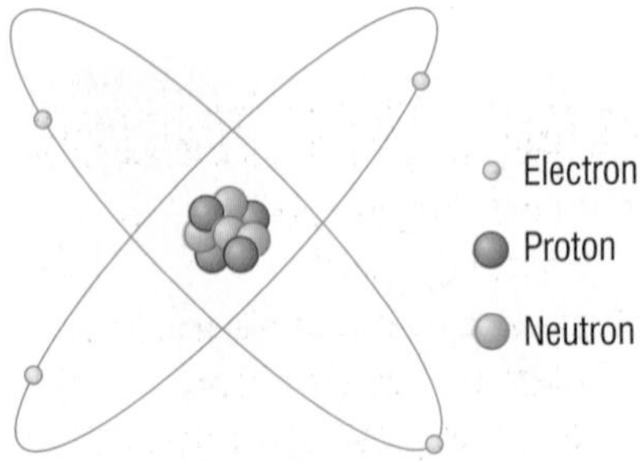

Figure 2 Inside an atom

Charging by friction

Some insulators become charged by rubbing them with a dry cloth.

- Rubbing a polythene rod with a dry cloth transfers electrons to the surface atoms of the rod from the cloth. So the polythene rod becomes negatively charged.
- Rubbing a perspex rod with a dry cloth transfers electrons from the surface atoms of the rod onto the cloth. So the perspex rod becomes positively charged.

b) Glass is charged positively when it is rubbed with a cloth.
   Does glass gain or lose electrons when it is charged?

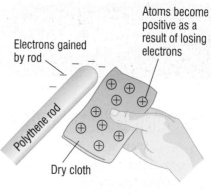

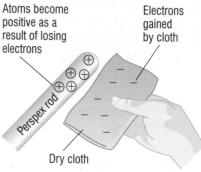

Figure 3 Charging by friction

PRACTICAL

The force between two charged objects

Two charged objects exert a force on each other. Figure 4 shows how you can investigate this force.

- What happens?

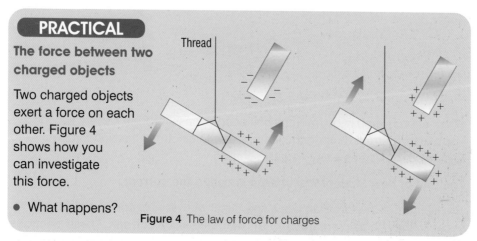

Figure 4 The law of force for charges

Your results in the experiment above should show that:

- two objects with the same type of charge (i.e. like charges) repel each other.
- two objects with opposite types of charge (i.e. unlike charges) attract each other.

Like charges repel. Unlike charges attract.

c) What force keeps the electrons inside an atom?

SUMMARY QUESTIONS

1 Choose words from the list to complete a) and b) below:

   to   from   loses   gains

   a) When a polythene rod is charged using a dry cloth, it becomes negative because it …… electrons that transfer …… it …… the cloth.
   b) When a perspex rod is charged using a dry cloth, it becomes positive because it …… electrons that transfer …… it …… the cloth.

2 When rubbed with a dry cloth, perspex becomes positively charged. Polythene and ebonite become negatively charged. State whether or not attraction or repulsion takes place when:

   a) a perspex rod is held near a polythene rod,
   b) a perspex rod is held near an ebonite rod,
   c) a polythene rod is held near an ebonite rod.

KEY POINTS

1 Like charges repel; unlike charges attract.
2 Insulating materials that lose electrons when rubbed become positively charged.
3 Insulating materials that gain electrons when rubbed become negatively charged.

P2 4.2

Charge on the move

LEARNING OBJECTIVES

1 Why can't we charge metals by rubbing them?
2 How is charge transferred through conducting materials?
3 What happens when a charged conductor is connected to Earth?
4 Why do charged objects sometimes produce sparks. [Higher]

Charge and current

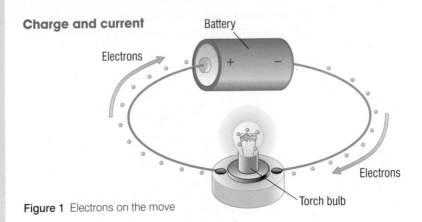

Figure 1 Electrons on the move

When a torch lamp is on, millions of electrons pass through it every second. The electric current through the lamp is due to electrons passing through it. Each electron carries a tiny negative charge.

The rate of flow of electrical charge is called the *current*.

The filament of the torch lamp is a fine metal wire. Metals conduct electricity because they contain **conduction (or delocalised) electrons**. These electrons move about freely inside the metal. They are not confined to a single atom. When the torch is switched on, the battery pushes electrons through the filament.

Insulators can't conduct electricity because all the electrons are held in atoms.

a) When electrons pass through a wire in a circuit, do they move towards the positive or the negative end of the wire?

Charging a conductor

A conductor can only hold charge if it is insulated from the ground. If it isn't insulated, it won't hold any charge because electrons transfer between the conductor and the ground.

To charge an insulated conductor, it needs to be brought into contact with a charged object.

- If the object is positively charged, electrons transfer from the conductor to the object. So the conductor becomes positive because it loses electrons.

- If the object is negatively charged, electrons transfer to the conductor from the object. So the conductor becomes negative because it gains electrons.

b) A negatively charged rod is touched against a metal can on the ground. Why *doesn't* the can become negatively charged?

PRACTICAL

Using an electroscope

Figure 2 shows an electroscope, a device that detects charge, being charged. The charged rod makes direct contact with the cap. The leaf of the electroscope is repelled by the metal plate when the electroscope is charged. This happens because they both gain the same type of charge.

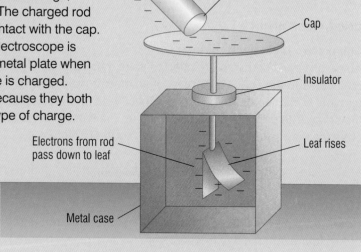

Figure 2 Charging a conductor

- Charged polythene rod
- Cap
- Insulator
- Electrons from rod pass down to leaf
- Leaf rises
- Metal case

● What happens to the leaf if you repeat the test with a positively charged rod?

Discharging

To discharge a charged conductor safely, a conducting path (e.g. a wire) needs to be provided between the object and the ground. The conducting path allows electrons to transfer between the object and the ground. Then we say that the object is **earthed**. (See Figure 3.)

c) A positively charged metal can is discharged by earthing it. Does the can gain or lose electrons?

HIGHER

Sparks and strikes

If we supply a conductor with more and more charge, its **electric potential energy** increases. The **potential difference** (i.e. voltage) between the conductor and the ground increases.

If the potential difference becomes high enough, a *spark* may jump between the conductor and any nearby earthed object. A lightning strike is a dramatic example of what happens when a charged thundercloud can hold no more charge. (See Figure 4.)

SUMMARY QUESTIONS

1 Complete the following sentences:
  a) An electric current is ....
  b) A metal is a conductor because it contains ....
  c) A ...... metal object loses electrons when it is connected to the ground.

2 a) Why can't we charge a metal object if it is earthed?
  b) A drawing pin is fixed to the dome of a Van de Graaff machine with its point in the air. Explain why this stops the dome charging up when the machine is switched on. [Higher]

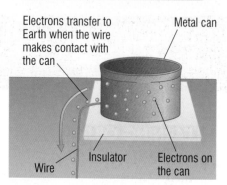

Electrons transfer to Earth when the wire makes contact with the can

Metal can

Wire

Insulator

Electrons on the can

Figure 3 Earthing a negatively charged conductor

DID YOU KNOW?

A lightning strike is a massive flow of charge between a thundercloud and the ground. A lightning conductor on a tall building prevents lightning strikes by allowing the thundercloud to discharge gradually. The conductor is joined to the ground by a thick copper strip. This allows charge to flow safely between the conductor tip and the ground.

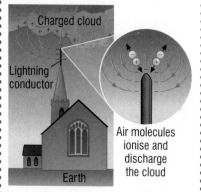

Charged cloud

Lightning conductor

Air molecules ionise and discharge the cloud

Earth

Figure 4 A lightning conductor

KEY POINTS

1 Electrical current is the rate of flow of charge.
2 A metal object can only hold charge if it is isolated from the ground.
3 A metal object is earthed by connecting it to the ground.
4 If a metal object gains too much charge, it will produce sparks. [Higher]

P2 4.3 Uses and dangers of static electricity

LEARNING OBJECTIVES

1 In what ways is static electricity useful?
2 In what ways is static electricity dangerous?
3 How can we get rid of static electricity where it is dangerous?

Using electrostatics

The electrostatic paint sprayer

Automatic paint sprayers are used to paint metal panels. The spray nozzle is connected to the positive terminal of an electrostatic generator. The negative terminal is connected to the metal panel. The panel attracts paint droplets from the spray. The droplets of paint all pick up the same charge and repel each other, so they spread out to form a fine cloud of paint.

a) Why are the spray nozzle and the panel oppositely charged?

The electrostatic precipitator

Coal-fired power stations produce vast quantities of ash and dust. Electrostatic precipitators remove this material from the flue gases before they get into the atmosphere.

The particles of ash and dust pass through a grid of wires in the precipitator. Look at Figure 2. The grid wires are negative so the particles become negatively charged when they touch it. The charged particles are attracted onto the positively charged metal plates. The plates are shaken at intervals so the ash and dust that build up on them drop to the floor of the precipitator. They are then removed.

b) What difference would it make if the grid was not charged?

Figure 1 An electrostatic paint sprayer

Ash and dust collect on plates

Grid of charged wires

Metal plates charged oppositely to the grid wires

Waste gases carrying ash and dust

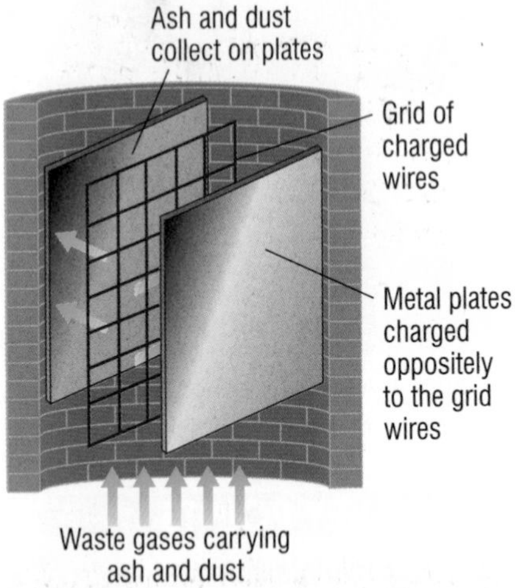

Figure 2 An electrostatic precipitator

The photocopier

The key part of a photocopier is a charged drum or plate. This loses charge from the parts of its surface exposed to light. Figure 3 shows how a photocopier works.

1 Photocopiers with a photoconducting drum – drum positively charged until light falls on it.

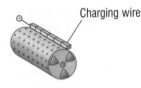

Charging wire

2 Light reflected off the paper onto the drum. The areas of black do not reflect so the drum keeps its charge in these areas.

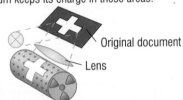

Original document

Lens

3 The black toner sticks to the drum where it is still charged and is pressed onto paper.

Toner

4 The paper is finally heated to stick the toner to it permanently.

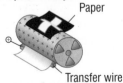

Paper

Transfer wire

Figure 3 Inside a photocopier

c) Why are photocopies sometimes charged when they come out of the photocopier?

Electrostatics hazards

Pipe problems

When a road tanker pumps oil or petrol into a storage tank, the connecting pipe must be earthed. If it isn't, the pipe could become charged. A build-up of charge would cause a spark. This could cause an explosion as the fuel vapour reacts with oxygen in the air.

Static electricity is also generated when grains of powder are pumped through pipes. Friction between the grains and the pipe charges them. An explosion could happen due to a spark igniting the powder.

d) Why is the rubber hose of a petrol pump made of special conducting rubber?

Antistatic floors

In a hospital, doctors use anaesthetic gases during operations. Some of these gases are explosive. If the gas escapes into the air, a tiny spark could make it explode. To eliminate static charge in operating theatres, an **antistatic material** is used for the floor surface. This material is a poor electrical insulator so it conducts charge to Earth.

e) Why do the doctors and nurses wear antistatic clothes in an operating theatre?

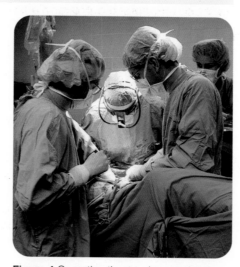

Figure 4 Operating theatres have antistatic floors

PRACTICAL

Getting rid of the charge

Charge up an electroscope.

- How do you discharge it? Explain what happens.

GET IT RIGHT!

Remember that electrostatic charge has its uses as well as its dangers.

SUMMARY QUESTIONS

1 Complete a) and b) using the words below:

> **attracted** **gain** **lose** **repelled**

a) Positively charged paint droplets from a paint spray are …… by the spray nozzle. The droplets …… electrons when they reach the negatively charged metal panel.

b) Dust particles in an electrostatic precipitator touch a positively charged wire. The particles …… electrons to the wire and are then …… by a negatively charged metal plate.

2 a) The delivery pipe between the road tanker and the storage tank must be earthed before any petrol is pumped from the tanker. Why is this an important safety measure?

b) Why does an operating theatre in a hospital have antistatic floor covering?

KEY POINTS

1 A spark from a charged object can make powder grains or certain gases explode.

2 To eliminate static electricity,
a) use antistatic materials, and
b) earth metal pipes and objects.

P2 4.4   Static issues

An electric discovery

What does the word 'charge' mean? Someone who runs at top speed 'charges along' filled with adrenalin. An electrically charged object is filled with static electricity. The term 'electric charge' was first used over 300 years ago when scientists discovered that certain materials such as ebonite, glass and resin attracted bits of paper when they are rubbed. They knew this effect had been discovered by the ancient Greeks using amber, a naturally occurring fossil resin. So they used the word 'electric', from the Greek word for 'amber', to describe the attractive power of these materials. The action of rubbing a suitable material was said to **charge** it with electricity.

Further experiments showed that:

● identical charged materials always repel each other,
● ebonite and glass attract,
● ebonite and resin repel,
● glass and resin attract.

More tests showed that there are two types of charge and they cancel each other out. So the two types of charge were called 'positive' and 'negative'.

QUESTION

1 a) Why did scientists conclude from these results that there are only two types of charge?

b) In terms of electrons, explain why equal and opposite amounts of charge cancel each other out.

Powder tests

The diagram shows how to test the charging of powder grains. The powder is poured through a pipe into a metal can on an electroscope.

If the powder is charged, the metal plate of the electroscope and the gold leaf attached to it both become charged. As a result, the leaf is repelled by the plate.

To find out if the powder charge is positive or negative, a negatively charged rod (e.g. polythene) held near the can will make the leaf rise further if the charge on the electroscope is negative.

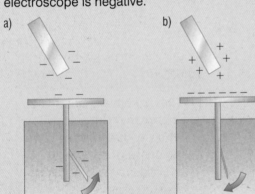

An electroscope test. a) The leaf rises when a negative rod is brought near. b) The leaf falls when a positive rod is brought near.

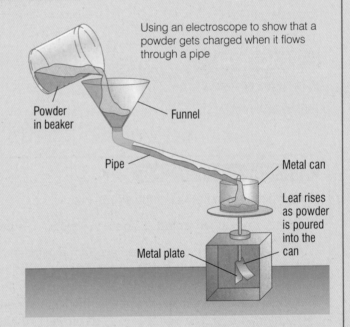

Using an electroscope to show that a powder gets charged when it flows through a pipe

Powder in beaker

Funnel

Pipe

Metal can

Leaf rises as powder is poured into the can

Metal plate

QUESTION

2 An electroscope is charged negatively by touching the cap with a negatively charged rod. Explain, in terms of electrons, why this makes the leaf go up and stay up.

The ink jet printer

An ink jet printer has an 'ink gun' inside that directs a jet of charged ink droplets at the paper. The ink droplets pass between two metal 'deflecting' plates before reaching the paper.

- By making one plate positive and the other negative, the droplets can be deflected as they pass between the plates. This happens because the droplets are attracted to the oppositely charged plate.
- The plates are made positive and negative by applying a potential difference to them. The potential difference is controlled by signals from the computer. The computer is programmed to make the inkjet print characters and graphics on the paper at high speed.

An ink jet printer

QUESTION

3 What do you think would happen if the ink droplets are too big?

A chip problem

Computer chips can be damaged by static electricity. Most microcomputers contain *CMOS* chips. Tiny amounts of charge on the pins of a CMOS chip can destroy its electrical properties. To prevent chips being damaged by static electricity, manufacturers insert them into antistatic foam sheets before packaging them.

Special tools are available to transfer chips to and from circuits to prevent them becoming charged in the transfer. Touching the chip briefly when a charged object is nearby would cause it to become charged. The figure shows how this can happen.

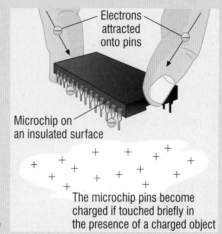

Electrons attracted onto pins

Microchip on an insulated surface

The microchip pins become charged if touched briefly in the presence of a charged object

Microchip damage

ACTIVITY

A company that makes computers has found that some of its chips don't work. The supplier says the company must be more careful when the chips are used. Imagine you work in the company. You think the problem is at the supplier. Send an e-mail to the supplier to find out.

Global junk

Computers sooner or later become out of date. But what happens to them then? At the present time, thousands of old or damaged computers are shipped out every year to junkyards in poor countries. People survive there by taking valuable material out of these computers and selling it. However, this is often dangerous work and chemicals from the junk get into local water supplies. Most of the junk is not biodegradable. It's mounting up all the time.

Computer junk

ACTIVITY

What can we do to stop this problem?

a) Discuss ways to tackle the problem.
b) Present a five-minute radio slot to raise awareness of the issue and to suggest some solutions.

SUMMARY QUESTIONS

1 a) Helen has just had a shock. She got up from a plastic chair to open the door and got an electric shock when she touched the door handle.
   i) How did she become charged?
   ii) Why did she feel a shock when she touched the door handle?

b) An object was charged by rubbing it with a dry cloth. When it was held near a negatively charged rod, it repelled the rod.
   i) State if the object was charged positively or negatively.
   ii) Would the object attract or repel a positively charged rod?

2 Complete the sentences below using words from the list.

from   on   to

a) A polythene rod is charged negatively by rubbing it with a cloth.
   i) Electrons transfer ...... the cloth ...... the rod.
   ii) The electrons ...... the rod cannot move about freely.

b) A positively charged rod is touched on an insulated metal object.
   i) Electrons transfer ...... the metal object ...... the rod.
   ii) If the metal object is then 'earthed', electrons transfer ...... it ...... the ground.

3 A paint sprayer in a car factory is used to paint a metal panel. The spray nozzle is connected to the negative terminal of a voltage supply unit. The metal panel is connected to the positive terminal of the voltage supply unit.

a) What type of charge is gained by the paint droplets when they leave the spray nozzle?

b) Why is the metal panel made positive?

c) Why is there an electric current along the wires joining the metal panel and the paint spray nozzle to the voltage supply unit?

4 a) i) In an ink jet printer, what difference would it make if the droplets were not charged?
   ii) In an electrostatic precipitator, how are the dust particles charged?

b) When an airplane is being refuelled, explain why a wire is connected between the aircraft and the fuel tanker?

EXAM-STYLE QUESTIONS

1 A plastic rod is rubbed with a dry cloth.

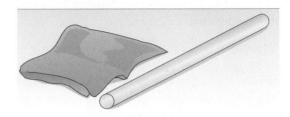

(a) The rod becomes negatively charged. Explain how this happens. (3)

(b) What charge is left on the cloth? (1)

(c) What happens if the negatively charged rod is brought close to another negatively charged rod. (1)

2 The picture shows an electrostatic paint spray being used to apply paint to a sheet of metal.

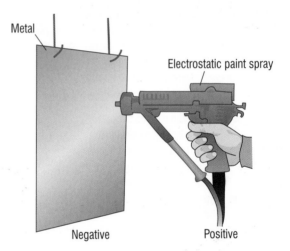

(a) The paint droplets are given a positive charge as they leave the nozzle. Explain why. (2)

(b) The sheet of metal is given a negative charge. Explain why. (3)

(c) (i) A painter wanted to find out the best distance between the nozzle of the paint spray and the sheet of metal to be painted. What could the painter use to measure the independent variable in this investigation? (1)

(ii) Why would it be a good idea for the painter to carry out some trials before deciding upon the range of the independent variable? (2)

3 The picture shows an electrostatic smoke precipitator. This is used to separate smoke particles from waste gases in a chimney.

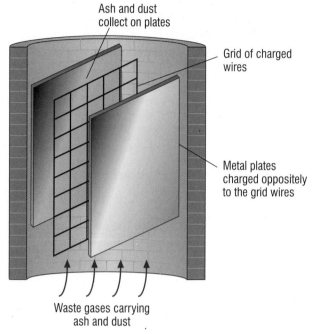

Ash and dust collect on plates

Grid of charged wires

Metal plates charged oppositely to the grid wires

Waste gases carrying ash and dust

Explain how the smoke precipitator works. (6)

4 A photocopier uses static electricity to make photocopies.

The following sentences describe how the photocopier works.
The sentences are in the wrong order.

A Black ink powder is attracted to the charged parts of the plate.

B The paper is heated so the powder melts and sticks to the paper.

C The copying plate is given a charge.

D This is now a photocopy of the original page.

E Where light hits the plate the charge leaks away, leaving a pattern of the page.

F Black ink powder is transferred onto a piece of paper.

G An image of the page to be copied is projected onto the charged copying plate.

Arrange the sentences in the right order. Start with sentence **C** and finish with sentence **D**.

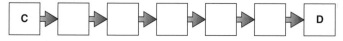

(4)

HOW SCIENCE WORKS QUESTIONS

Lightning conductors are very important in protecting buildings from lightning strikes. New designs must be thoroughly tested. They must work first time and every time. They have to be tested in a standard way. This method is described in the diagram below.

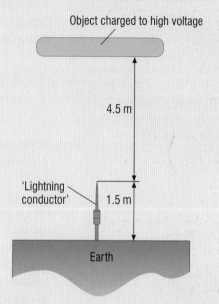

Object charged to high voltage

4.5 m

'Lightning conductor'

1.5 m

Earth

The conditions must be followed strictly. This includes the temperature of the room and the humidity. The charge is built up on the object above the lightning conductor and photographs are taken of the 'lightning' as it forms. This allows accurate measurements to be made of the time taken for the lightning conductor to respond. The measurements are made in microseconds.

a) Explain why it is important that the testing is carried out in exactly the same way each time. (1)

b) To find the correct temperature for these tests, the scientists carried out surveys.
Suggest when they carried out the surveys. (1)

c) What do you think they were measuring? (1)

d) How many sets of data do you think they collected? (1)

e) What is the sensitivity of the equipment used to time the response of the lightning conductor? (1)

f) Explain why repeat tests on the same lightning conductor might give different results. (1)

g) Should this testing be carried out by the company manufacturing the lightning conductors or by an independent company? Explain your answer. (1)

P2 5.1 Electric circuits

LEARNING OBJECTIVES

1 Why are electric circuits represented by circuit diagrams?
2 What are the circuit symbols for a cell, a switch and other common components?

An electric torch can be very useful in a power cut at night. But it needs to be checked to make sure it works. Figure 1 shows what is inside a torch. The circuit in Figure 1 shows us how the torch is connected to the switch and the two cells.

Figure 1 An electric torch

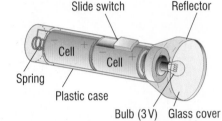

a) Why does the switch have to be closed to turn the lamp on?

A circuit diagram is a very helpful way of showing how the components in a circuit are connected together. Each component has its own symbol. Figure 2 shows the symbols for some of the components you will meet in this course. The function of each component is also described in Figure 2. You need to recognise these symbols and remember what each component is used for – otherwise you'll get mixed up in your exams. More importantly, you could get a big shock if you mix them up!

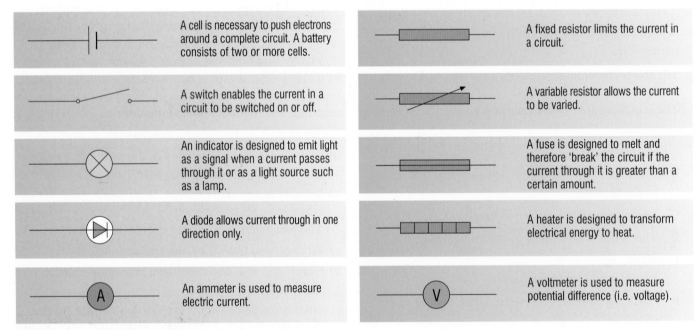

A cell is necessary to push electrons around a complete circuit. A battery consists of two or more cells.	A fixed resistor limits the current in a circuit.
A switch enables the current in a circuit to be switched on or off.	A variable resistor allows the current to be varied.
An indicator is designed to emit light as a signal when a current passes through it or as a light source such as a lamp.	A fuse is designed to melt and therefore 'break' the circuit if the current through it is greater than a certain amount.
A diode allows current through in one direction only.	A heater is designed to transform electrical energy to heat.
An ammeter is used to measure electric current.	A voltmeter is used to measure potential difference (i.e. voltage).

Figure 2 Components and symbols

NEXT TIME YOU...

... switch a light bulb on, remember it's part of a very long circuit that goes all the way back to a transformer at a local sub-station.

b) What components are in the circuit diagram in Figure 3?

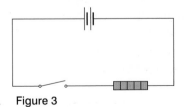

Figure 3

PRACTICAL

Circuit tests

Connect a variable resistor in series with the torch lamp and a battery, as shown in Figure 4. Adjusting the slider of the variable resistor alters the amount of current flowing through the bulb and therefore affects its brightness.

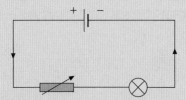

Figure 4 Using a variable resistor

- In Figure 4, the torch lamp goes dim when the slider is moved one way. What happens if the slider is moved back again?
- What happens if you include a diode in the circuit?

DID YOU KNOW...

You would damage a portable radio if you put the batteries in the wrong way round unless a diode is in series with the battery. The diode only allows current through when it is connected as shown in Figure 5. If the battery is reversed in the circuit, the diode stops electrons passing round the circuit.

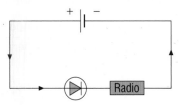

Figure 5 Using a diode

c) Would the radio in Figure 5 work if the diode was 'turned round' in the circuit?

SUMMARY QUESTIONS

1 Name the numbered components in the circuit diagram.

2 a) Redraw the circuit diagram in question 1 with a diode in place of the switch so it allows current through.
   b) What further component would you need in this circuit to alter the current in it?

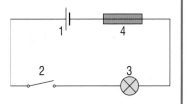

KEY POINTS

1 Every component has its own agreed symbol.
2 A circuit diagram shows how components are connected together.
3 A battery consists of two or more cells connected together.

P2 5.2 Resistance

LEARNING OBJECTIVES

1 Where should you put an ammeter and a voltmeter in a circuit?
2 What is resistance and what is its unit?
3 What is Ohm's law?
4 What happens if you reverse the current in a resistor?

Ammeters and voltmeters

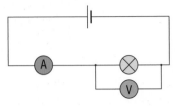

Figure 1 Using an ammeter and a voltmeter

Look at the ammeter and the voltmeter in the circuit in Figure 1.

- The ammeter measures the current through the torch lamp. It is connected in **series** with the lamp so the current through them is the same. The ammeter reading gives the current in amperes (A) (or milliamperes, (mA) for small currents, where 1 mA = 0.001 A).
- The voltmeter measures the potential difference (p.d.) across the torch lamp. It is connected in **parallel** with the torch lamp so it measures the pd across it. The voltmeter reading gives the p.d. in volts (V).

Electrons passing through a torch lamp have to push their way through lots of vibrating atoms. The atoms resist the passage of electrons through the torch lamp.

We define the **resistance** of an electrical component as:

$$\text{Resistance (ohms)} = \frac{\textbf{potential difference (volts)}}{\textbf{current (amperes)}}$$

The unit of resistance is the **ohm**. The symbol for the ohm is the Greek letter Ω.

We can write the definition above as:

$$R = \frac{V}{I}$$

where V = potential difference (volts)
I = current (amperes)
R = resistance (ohms).

Worked example

The current through a wire is 2.0 A when the potential difference across it is 12 V.

Calculate the resistance of the wire.

Solution

$$R = \frac{12\,V}{2.0\,A} = 6.0\,\Omega$$

GET IT RIGHT!

Ammeters are always connected in series and voltmeters are always connected in parallel.

a) The current through a wire is 0.5 A when the current through it is 4.0 V. Calculate the resistance of the wire.

PRACTICAL

Investigating the resistance of a wire

Does the resistance of a wire change when the current through it is changed? Figure 2 shows how we can use a variable resistor to change the current through a wire. Make your own measurements and use them to plot a current–potential difference graph like the one in Figure 2.

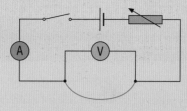

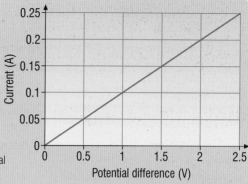

Figure 2 Investigating the resistance of a wire. (a) Circuit diagram. (b) A current–potential difference graph for a wire.

- Discuss how your measurements compare with the ones from the table used to plot the graph in Figure 2.
- Calculate the resistance of the wire you tested.

Current (A)	0.05	0.10	0.15	0.20	0.25
Potential difference (V)	0.50	1.00	1.50	2.00	2.50

b) Calculate the resistance of the wire that gave the results in the table.

Current–potential difference graphs

The graph in Figure 2 and your own graph should show:

- a straight line through the origin,
- that the current is directly proportional to the potential difference.

Reversing the potential difference makes no difference to the shape of the line. The resistance is the same whichever direction the current is in.

The graph shows that the resistance (= potential difference/current) is constant. This was first discovered for a wire at constant temperature by Georg Ohm and is known as **Ohm's law**:

The current through a resistor at constant temperature is directly proportional to the potential difference across the resistor.

We say a wire is an **ohmic conductor** because its resistance is constant.

SUMMARY QUESTIONS

1. a) Draw a circuit diagram to show how you would use an ammeter and a voltmeter to measure the current and potential difference across a wire.
   b) The potential difference across a resistor was 3.0 V when the current through it was 0.5 A. Calculate the resistance of the resistor.

2. Rearranging the equation $R = \dfrac{V}{I}$ gives $V = IR$ or $I = \dfrac{V}{R}$

   Use these equations to calculate the missing values in each line of the table.

Resistor	Current (A)	Potential difference (V)	Resistance (Ω)
W	2.0	12.0	?
X	4.0	?	20
Y	?	6.0	3.0
Z	0.5	12.0	?

KEY POINTS

1. Resistance (ohms) =
$$\frac{\text{potential difference (volts)}}{\text{current (amperes)}}$$

2. The current through a resistor at constant temperature is directly proportional to the potential difference across the resistor.

P2 5.3

More current–potential difference graphs

Have you ever switched a light bulb on only to hear it 'pop' and fail? Electrical appliances can fail at very inconvenient times. Most electrical failures are because too much current passes through a component in the appliance.

PRACTICAL

Investigating different components

The current through a component in a circuit depends on its resistance. We can use the circuit in Figure 2 on the previous page to find out what affects the resistance of a component. We can also see if reversing the component in the circuit has any effect.

Make your own measurements using a filament lamp and a diode.

Plot your measurements on a current–potential difference graph.

● Why can you use a line graph to display your data? (See page 13.)

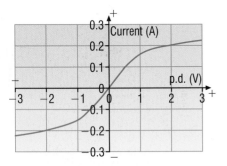

Figure 1 A current–potential difference graph for a filament lamp

Using current–potential difference graphs

A filament lamp

Figure 1 shows the current–potential difference graph for a torch lamp (i.e. a low-voltage filament lamp). The 'reverse' measurements are plotted on the negative sections of each axis.

● The line **curves** away from the current axis. So the current is **not** directly proportional to the potential difference. The filament lamp is a non-ohmic conductor.
● The resistance (= potential difference/current) increases as the current increases. So the resistance of a filament lamp increases as the filament temperature increases.
● Reversing the potential difference makes no difference to the shape of the curve. The resistance is the same for the same current, regardless of its direction.

a) Calculate the resistance of the lamp at i) 0.1 A, ii) 0.2 A.

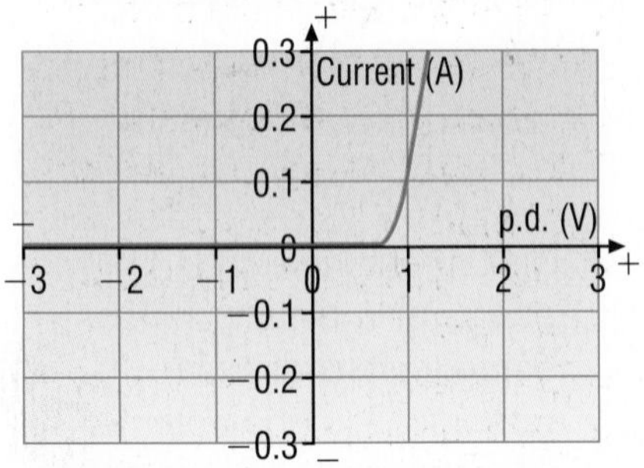

The diode

Look at Figure 2 for a diode:
● In the 'forward' direction, the line curves towards the current axis. So the current is not directly proportional to the potential difference. A diode is not an ohmic conductor.
● In the reverse direction, the current is negligible. So its resistance in the reverse direction is much higher than in the forward direction.

Figure 2 A current–potential difference graph for a diode

b) What can we say about the forward resistance as the current increases?

PRACTICAL

Thermistors and light-dependent resistors (LDRs)

We use thermistors and LDRs in sensor circuits. A thermistor is a temperature-dependent resistor. The resistance of an LDR depends on how much light is on it.

Test a thermistor and then an LDR in series with a battery and an ammeter.

● What did you find out about each component tested?

a)   b)

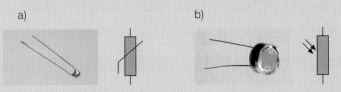

Figure 3 a) A thermistor and its circuit symbol, b) an LDR and its circuit symbol

Current–potential difference graphs for a thermistor and an LDR

For a thermistor, Figure 4 shows the current–potential difference graph at two different temperatures.

● At constant temperature, the line is straight so its resistance is constant.
● If the temperature is increased, its resistance decreases.

For a light dependent resistor, Figure 5 shows the current–potential difference graph in bright light and in dim light.

c) What does the graph tell us about an LDR's resistance if the light intensity is constant?
d) If the light intensity is increased, what happens to the resistance of the LDR?

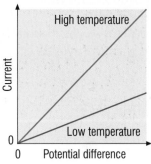

Figure 4 Thermistor graphs

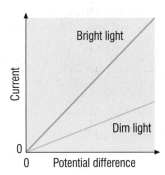

Figure 5 LDR graphs

SUMMARY QUESTIONS

1 Complete a) to d) using the words below:

diode   filament lamp   resistor   thermistor

a) The resistance of a ...... decreases as its temperature increases.
b) The resistance of a ...... depends on which way round it is connected in a circuit.
c) The resistance of a ...... increases as the current through it increases.
d) The resistance of a ...... does not depend on the current through it.

2 A thermistor is connected in series with an ammeter and a 3.0 V battery, as shown.

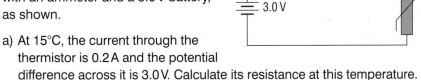

a) At 15°C, the current through the thermistor is 0.2 A and the potential difference across it is 3.0 V. Calculate its resistance at this temperature.
b) State and explain what happens to the ammeter reading if the thermistor's temperature is increased.

KEY POINTS

1 *Filament lamp:* resistance increases with increase of the filament temperature.
2 *Diode:* 'forward' resistance low; 'reverse' resistance high.
3 *Thermistor:* resistance decreases if its temperature increases.
4 *LDR:* resistance decreases if the light intensity on it increases.

P2 5.4   Series circuits

LEARNING OBJECTIVES

1 What can we say about the current and potential difference for components in a series circuit?
2 Why do we often connect cells in series?
3 How can we find the total resistance of a series circuit?

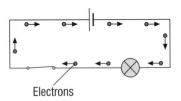

Electrons

Figure 1 A torch lamp circuit

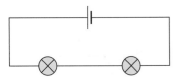

Figure 2 Lamps in series

Circuit rules

In the torch circuit in Figure 1, the lamp, the cell and the switch are connected in series with each other. The same number of electrons pass through each component every second. So the same current passes through each component.

The same current passes through components in series with each other.

a) If the current through the lamp is 0.12 A, what is the current through the cell?

In Figure 2, each electron from the cell passes through two lamps. Each electron is pushed through each lamp by the cell. The potential difference (or *voltage*) of the cell is a measure of the energy transferred from the cell by each electron that passes through it. Since each electron in the circuit in Figure 2 goes through both lamps, the potential difference of the cell is shared between the lamps. This rule applies to any series circuit.

The total potential difference of the voltage supply in a series circuit is shared between the components.

b) In Figure 2, if the potential difference of the cell is 1.2 V and the potential difference across one lamp is 0.8 V, what is the potential difference across the other lamp?

Cells in series

What happens if we use two or more cells in series in a circuit. Provided we connect the cells so they act in the 'same direction', each electron gets a push from each cell. So an electron would get the same push from a battery of three 1.5 V cells in series as it would from a single 4.5 V cell.

In other words:

The total potential difference of cells in series is the sum of the potential difference of each cell.

PRACTICAL

Investigating potential differences in a series circuit

Figure 3 shows how to test the potential difference rule for a series circuit. The circuit consists of a filament lamp in series with a variable resistor and a cell. We can use the variable resistor to see how the voltmeter readings change when we alter the current. Make your own measurements.

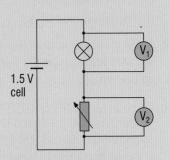

Figure 3 Voltage tests

● How do they compare with the data in the table on the next page?

Filament lamp	Voltmeter V_1 (volts)	Voltmeter V_2 (volts)
normal	1.5	0.0
dim	0.9	0.6
very dim	0.5	1.0

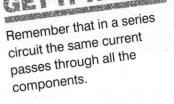

The measurements in the table show that the voltmeter readings for each setting add up to 1.5 V. This is the potential difference of the cell. The share of the cell's potential difference across each component depends on the setting of the variable resistor.

c) What would voltmeter V_2 read if voltmeter V_1 showed 0.4 V?

The resistance rule for components in series

In Figure 3, suppose the current through the lamp is 0.1 A when the lamp is dim.

Using data from the table above:

- The resistance of the lamp would then be 9 Ω (= 0.9 V/0.1 A).
- The resistance of the variable resistor at this setting would be 6 Ω (= 0.6 V/0.1 A).

If we replaced these two components by a single resistor, what should its resistance be for the same current of 0.1 A? We can calculate this because we know the potential difference across it would be 1.5 V (from the cell). So the resistance would need to be 15 Ω (= 1.5 V/0.1 A). This is the sum of the resistance of the two components. The rule applies to any series circuit.

The total resistance of components in series is equal to the sum of their separate resistances.

d) What is the total resistance of a 2 Ω resistor in series with a 3 Ω resistor?

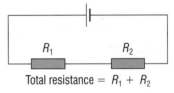

Total resistance = $R_1 + R_2$

Figure 4 Resistors in series

SUMMARY QUESTIONS

1 Complete a) and b) using the list below:

**greater than   less than
the same as**

For the circuit in the diagram,

Two 1.5 V cells

P 2 Ω   Q 10 Ω

a) the current through the battery is …… the current through resistor P.
b) the potential difference across resistor Q is …… the potential difference across the battery.

2 For the circuit in question 1, each cell has a potential difference of 1.5 V.

a) Calculate: i) the total resistance of the two resistors,
             ii) the total potential difference of the two cells.
b) Show that the current through the battery is 0.25 A.
c) Calculate the potential difference across each resistor.

P2 5.5 Parallel circuits

PRACTICAL

Investigating parallel circuits

Figure 1 shows how you can investigate the current through two lamps in parallel with each other. You can use ammeters in series with the lamps and the cell to measure the current through the lamp.

Set up your own circuit and collect your data.

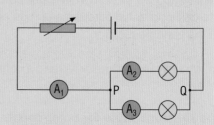

Figure 1 At a junction

- How do your measurements compare with the ones in the table for different settings of the variable resistor shown below?
- Discuss if your own measurements show the same pattern.

Look at the sample data below:

Ammeter A_1 (A)	Ammeter A_2 (A)	Ammeter A_3 (A)
0.50	0.30	0.20
0.30	0.20	0.10
0.18	0.12	0.06

In each case, the reading of ammeter A_1 is equal to the sum of the readings of ammeters A_2 and A_3.

This shows that the current from the cell is equal to sum of the currents through the two lamps. This rule applies wherever components are in parallel.

a) If ammeter A_1 reads 0.40 A and A_2 reads 0.1 A, what would A_3 read?

The total current through the whole circuit is the sum of the currents through the separate components.

Potential difference in a parallel circuit

Figure 2 shows two resistors X and Y in parallel with each other. A voltmeter is connected across each resistor. The voltmeter across resistor X shows the same reading as the voltmeter across resistor Y. This is because each electron from the cell either passes through X or through Y. So it delivers the same amount of energy from the cell, whichever resistor it goes through. In other words:

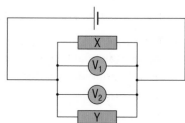

Figure 2 Components in parallel

For components in parallel, the potential difference across each component is the same.

Calculations on parallel circuits

Components in parallel have the same potential difference across them. The current through each component depends on the resistance of the component.

- The bigger the resistance of the component, the smaller the current through it. The resistor which has the largest resistance passes the smallest current.
- We can calculate the current using the equation:

$$\text{current (amperes)} = \frac{\text{potential difference (volts)}}{\text{resistance (ohms)}}$$

b) A $3\,\Omega$ resistor and a $6\,\Omega$ resistor are connected in parallel in a circuit. Which resistor passes the most current?

Worked example

The circuit diagram shows three resistors $R_1 = 1\,\Omega$, $R_2 = 2\,\Omega$ and $R_3 = 6\,\Omega$ connected in parallel to a 6 V battery.

Calculate:

i) the current through each resistor,
ii) the current through the battery.

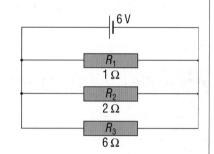

Solution

i) $I_1 = \dfrac{V_1}{R_1} = \dfrac{6}{1} = 6\,\text{A}$

$I_2 = \dfrac{V_2}{R_2} = \dfrac{6}{2} = 3\,\text{A}$

$I_3 = \dfrac{V_3}{R_3} = \dfrac{6}{6} = 1\,\text{A}$

ii) The total current from the battery $= I_1 + I_2 + I_3 = 6\,\text{A} + 3\,\text{A} + 1\,\text{A} = 10\,\text{A}$

SUMMARY QUESTIONS

1 Choose words from the list to complete a) and b):

current   potential difference

a) Components in parallel with each other have the same ....
b) For components in parallel, each component has a different ....

2 The circuit diagram shows three resistors $R_1 = 2\,\Omega$, $R_2 = 3\,\Omega$ and $R_3 = 6\,\Omega$ connected to each other in parallel and to a 6 V battery.

Calculate:

a) the current through each resistor,
b) the current through the battery.

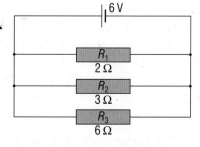

KEY POINTS

1 For components in parallel,
   a) the potential difference is the same across each component,
   b) the total current is the sum of the currents through each component,
   c) the bigger the resistance of a component, the smaller its current is.

P2 5.6   Circuits in control

A magic eye

When you go shopping, doors often open automatically in front of you. An automatic door has a sensor that detects anyone who approaches it. Children think there's a magic eye. But Figure 1 shows you it's no more than an electric circuit.

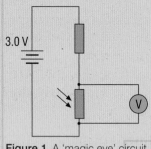

3.0 V

Figure 1 A 'magic eye' circuit

The 'light beam' sensor in Figure 1 is a light-dependent resistor (LDR) in series with a resistor and a battery. A voltmeter is connected across the LDR to show what happens when the LDR is covered. If you make and test this circuit, you should find the voltmeter reading goes up when the LDR is covered. This can be used to switch an electric motor or an alarm circuit on.

The development of microelectronics

- The first amplifier, the electronic valve, was invented in the 1920s.
- The first electronic switch, the transistor, was invented in the 1940s.
- The microchip was invented in the 1970s.
- The World Wide Web was invented in the 1990s.

The latest computers contain microchips which each contain millions of tiny electronic switches. We measure the capacity of a chip in **bytes**, where a byte is a sequence of bits of data (0's and 1's).

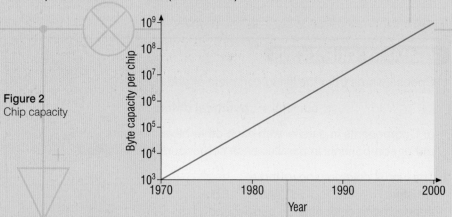

Figure 2
Chip capacity

Figure 2 shows the growth in the capacity of chips since the first one was invented. As chip capacity has increased, electronic devices have become smaller and smaller, as well as more and more sophisticated. They have also become cheaper and cheaper. If cars had changed in the same way, everyone in the world could have a car for less than £1 that would travel 10 000 kilometres on a litre of petrol.

News Flash

No more school!

The Government today announced that children will not have to go to school for lessons any more. Instead, each child will sit in front of a home computer every day. Children who do not go on-line for their lessons will be sent to 'boot camps' to learn. The schools will reopen as amusement arcades with entertainers instead of teachers.

ACTIVITY

Do you think this government policy is a good or a bad idea?

Either: Write a poem about it

or hold a discussion about the issue.

Robots in charge

ACTIVITY

Science fiction writers often write far-fetched stories about robots.

a) Robots are only automated machines programmed to do certain tasks. So why does the word 'robot' catch everyone's attention?

b) Use a science-fiction story to discuss the boundary between science fiction and science.

Robots took over the world in the last century — but only in a play by the Czech writer, Karel Čapek. He used the word 'robot' for machine 'slaves'. Real robots were not invented until many years later. Now we use robotic machines for:

- routine jobs, such as on assembly lines in factories,
- dangerous jobs, such as bomb disposal,
- space exploration, such as the two Rover robots which landed on Mars in 2004.

Electronic logic

We use logic circuits in lots of electronic devices, including computers. A logic circuit has an output that depends on the inputs. Figure 3 shows the symbols for two simple logic circuits, an AND gate and an OR gate. Figure 3 shows an AND gate with a temperature sensor and a light sensor connected to its inputs. If the temperature AND the light intensity are too high, the output of the AND gate is high and it switches an alarm circuit on.

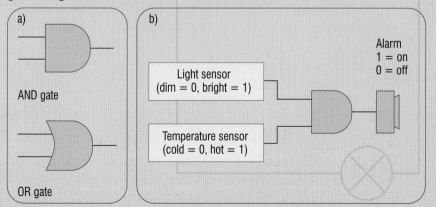

Figure 3 Logic gates. a) Symbols for an AND gate and an OR gate. b) An alarming circuit.

QUESTIONS

1 What could you use the circuit for in Figure 3b)?

2 If the AND gate was replaced by an OR gate, the alarm would switch on if the temperature OR the light intensity is too high. What could you use this circuit for?

SUMMARY QUESTIONS

1 Sketch a circuit diagram to show:

a) a torch bulb, a cell and a diode connected in series so that the torch bulb is on,

b) a variable resistor, two cells in series and a torch bulb whose brightness can be varied by adjusting the variable resistor.

2 Match each component in the list to each statement a) to d) that describes it.

diode   filament lamp   resistor   thermistor

a) Its resistance increases if the current through it increases.

b) The current through it is proportional to the potential difference across it.

c) Its resistance decreases if its temperature is increased.

d) Its resistance depends on which way round it is connected in a circuit.

3 a) Sketch a circuit diagram to show two resistors P and Q connected in series to a battery of two cells in series with each other.

b) In the circuit in a), resistor P has a resistance of 4 Ω, resistor Q has a resistance of 2 Ω and each cell has a potential difference of 1.5 V. Calculate
i) the total potential difference of the two cells,
ii) the total resistance of the two resistors,
iii) the current in the circuit,
iv) the potential difference across each resistor.

4 a) Sketch a circuit diagram to show two resistors R and S in parallel with each other connected to a single cell.

b) In the circuit in a), resistor R has a resistance of 2 Ω, resistor S has a resistance of 4 Ω and the cell has a potential difference of 2 V. Calculate
i) the current through resistor R,
ii) the current through resistor S,
iii) the current through the cell, in the circuit.

5 Complete the following sentences using words from the list below:

different from   equal to   the same as

a) For two components X and Y in series, the potential difference across X is ...... the potential difference across Y.

b) For two components X and Y in parallel, the potential difference across X is ...... the potential difference across Y.

EXAM-STYLE QUESTIONS

1 In a circuit diagram, symbols are used to represent different components.

Complete the table below. The first line has been done for you.

Symbol	Component	What the component does
—Ⓐ—	ammeter	Measures the current in a circuit
—Ⓥ—	voltmeter	a)
—⊣⊢—	b)	Supplies energy to a circuit
c)	diode	d)
e)	f)	Varies resistance as the temperature varies
—⊘—	g)	h)

(8)

2 A student sets up a circuit to investigate how the potential difference across a filament lamp varies with the current through it.

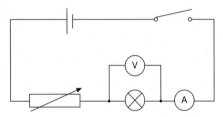

(a) How can the student vary the current through the lamp? (1)

(b) (i) Copy the axes below and sketch the shape of the graph the student would expect to obtain. (2)

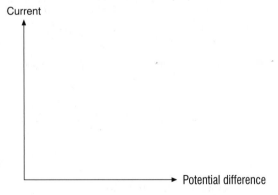

(ii) Explain the shape of the graph you have drawn. (2)

(iii) What do we call the line drawn through points on a graph plotted from experimental data which smooths out variations in measurements? (1)

3 The diagram shows an electric circuit.

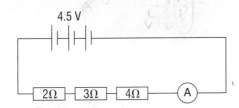

4.5 V

2Ω   3Ω   4Ω   (A)

(a) Calculate the total resistance in the circuit. (1)

(b) What is the current through the 4Ω resistor? (3)

(c) What is the potential difference across the 4Ω resistor? (2)

4 The diagram shows an electric circuit.

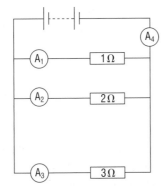

A₄

A₁   1Ω

A₂   2Ω

A₃   3Ω

The reading on ammeter A₁ is 6 A and on A₃ is 2 A.

(a) (i) What is the reading on ammeter A₂? (4)

   (ii) What is the reading on ammeter A₄? (1)

(b) The graphs **A**, **B**, **C** and **D** show how the current through a component varies with the potential difference across it.

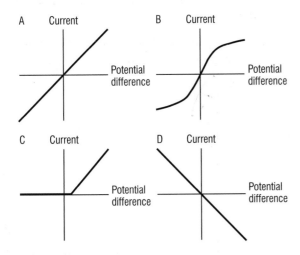

A   Current   B   Current

         Potential   Potential
         difference   difference

C   Current   D   Current

         Potential   Potential
         difference   difference

Which graph represents

(i) a resistor at constant temperature?

(ii) a diode? (2)

(c) Why can't the data in part (b) be presented as bar charts? (2)

The laboratory has just bought a new digital thermometer. It uses a thermistor to measure the temperature. It costs £35 because it is accurate and sensitive. The chief technician is very anxious to know if the thermometer works properly. She read all of the data that came with it. It claims that the thermometer will be accurate to ±0.3°C over a range of −50°C to 150°C and it will read to 0.1°C.

a) What is the range over which this instrument should work accurately? (1)

b) What might happen if you used the instrument to read temperatures below −50°C? (1)

c) What is the sensitivity of the thermometer? (1)

d) What is meant by 'the thermometer will be accurate to ±0.3°C'? (1)

The chief technician wanted to check the claims made by the company selling the thermometer. She decided to test its accuracy for herself. She set up some water baths at different temperatures. She used a £400 thermometer that measured to 0.01°C. A company specialising in testing thermometers had independently calibrated this instrument. She compared the readings given by the two thermometers. These are her results.

Thermistor	Temperature of water bath (°C)		
£400	20.15	26.78	65.43
£35	19.9	26.6	65.6

e) Why did the technician doubt the claims made by the company selling the thermometer? (1)

f) Why was the technician more confident in the expensive thermometer? (1)

g) Find the mean for each of the two sets of data? (2)

h) Suggest how the technician might have ensured that her results were valid. (1)

i) Did she choose a range of temperatures that fully tested the new thermometer? Explain your answer. (1)

j) Were her doubts about the £35 thermometer correct? Explain your answer. (1)

P2 6.1 Alternating current

LEARNING OBJECTIVES

1 What is meant by direct current and alternating current?
2 What is the frequency of the UK mains supply?
3 How do we use an oscilloscope to measure the frequency of an alternating current. [Higher]

The battery in a torch makes the current to go round the circuit in one direction only. We say the current in the circuit is a direct current (d.c.) because it is in one direction only.

When you switch a light on at home, you use alternating current (a.c.) because mains electricity is an a.c. supply.

An alternating current repeatedly reverses its direction. It flows one way then the opposite way in successive cycles. Its **frequency** is the number of cycles it passes through each second.

In the UK, the mains frequency is 50 cycles per second (or 50 Hz). A light bulb works just as well at this frequency as it would with a direct current.

a) Why would a much lower frequency than 50 Hz be unsuitable for a light bulb?

Mains circuits

Every mains circuit has a **live** wire and a **neutral** wire. The current through a mains appliance alternates because the mains supply provides an alternating potential difference between the two wires.

The neutral wire is earthed at the local sub-station. The live wire is dangerous because its potential (i.e. voltage) repeatedly changes from + to − and back every cycle. It reaches over 300 V in each direction, as shown in Figure 2.

DID YOU KNOW?

Breakdown vans usually carry a 'fast charger' to recharge a flat car battery as quickly as possible. A 'flat' battery needs a 12 V battery charger to charge it. An ordinary 'battery charger' converts a.c. from the mains to 12 V d.c. but it can take hours to recharge a flat battery.

Figure 1 A battery charger

PRACTICAL

The oscilloscope

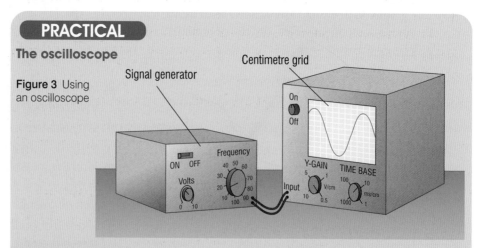

Figure 3 Using an oscilloscope

We use an oscilloscope to show how an alternating potential difference (p.d.) changes with time.

1 Connect a low voltage a.c. supply unit to an oscilloscope, as shown in Figure 3.

   – The trace on the oscilloscope screen shows that the p.d. increases and decreases continuously.
   – The highest (or 'peak') p.d is reached at each peak. Increasing the p.d. of the a.c. supply makes the waves on the screen taller.

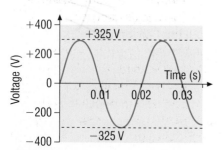

Figure 2 Mains voltage v time

PRACTICAL – continued

- Increasing the frequency of the a.c. supply increases the number of cycles you see on the screen. So the waves on the screen get squashed together.

● How would the trace change if the p.d. of the a.c. supply were reduced?

2 Connect a battery to the oscilloscope. You should see a flat line at constant potential.

● What difference is made by reversing the battery?

Measuring an alternating potential difference

We can use an oscilloscope to measure the peak p.d. and the frequency of a low voltage a.c. supply. For example, in Figure 3,

● the peak voltage is 2.1 V if the peaks are 8.4 cm above the troughs. So each peak is 4.2 cm above the middle which is at zero p.d. The **Y-gain control** at 0.5 V/cm tells us each centimetre of height is due to a p.d. of 0.5 V. So the peak p.d. is 2.1 V ($= 0.5$ V/cm $\times$ 4.2 cm).
● the frequency is 12.5 Hz if each cycle on the screen is 8 cm across. The **time base control** at 10 milliseconds per centimetre (ms/cm) tells us each centimetre across the screen is a time interval of 10 ms. So one cycle takes 80 ms ($= 10$ ms/cm $\times$ 8 cm). The frequency is therefore 12.5 Hz ($= 1/80$ ms or $1/0.08$ s).

More about mains circuits

Look at Figure 2 again. It shows how the potential of the live wire varies with time.

● The live wire alternates between +325 volts and −325 volts. In terms of electrical power, this is equivalent to a direct voltage of 230 volts. So we say the 'voltage' of the mains is 230 V.
● Each cycle takes 0.02 second. So the mains supply alternates at 50 cycles every second. The frequency of the mains supply (the number of cycles per second) is therefore 50 Hz.

b) What is the maximum potential difference between the live wire and the neutral wire?

SUMMARY QUESTIONS

1 Choose the correct potential difference from the list for each appliance a) to d).

  1.5 V   12 V   230 V   325 V

a) a car battery
b) the mains voltage
c) a torch cell
d) the maximum potential of the live wire.

2 a) In Figure 3, how would the trace on the screen change if the frequency of the a.c. supply was i) increased, ii) reduced?
b) In Figure 3, what would the frequency be if one cycle had measured 4 cm across the screen for the same time base setting? [Higher]

KEY POINTS

1 Alternating current repeatedly reverses its direction.
2 Mains electricity is an alternating current supply.
3 A mains circuit has a **live wire** which is alternately positive and negative every cycle and a **neutral wire** at zero volts. [Higher]

P2 6.2 Cables and plugs

When you plug in a heater with a metal case into a wall socket, you 'earth' the metal case automatically. This stops the metal case becoming 'live' if the live wire breaks and touches it. If the case did become 'live' and you touched it, you would be electrocuted.

Plugs, sockets and cables

The outer casings of plugs, sockets and cables of all mains circuits and appliances are made of hard-wearing electrical insulators. That's because plugs, sockets and cables contain 'live' wires.

Sockets are made of stiff plastic materials with the wires inside. Figure 1 shows part of a wall socket circuit. It has an 'earth' wire as well as a live wire and a neutral wire.

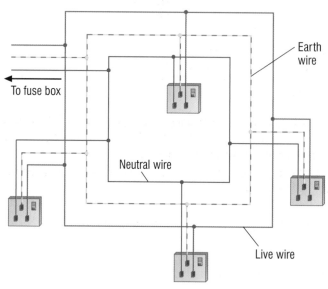

To fuse box

Earth wire

Neutral wire

Live wire

Figure 1 A 'wall socket' circuit

● The 'earth wire' of this circuit is connected to the ground at your home.
● The longest pin of a three-pin plug is designed to make contact with the 'earth wire' of a wall socket circuit. So when you plug an appliance with a metal case to a wall socket, the case is automatically earthed.

a) Why are sockets wired in parallel with each other?

Plugs have cases made of stiff plastic materials. The live pin, the neutral pin and the earth pin, stick out through the plug case. Figure 2 shows inside a three-pin plug.

● The pins are made of brass because brass is a good conductor and does not rust or oxidise. Copper isn't as hard as brass even though it conducts better.
● The case material is an electrical insulator. The inside of the case is shaped so the wires and the pins cannot touch each other when the plug is sealed.

● The plug contains a fuse between the live pin and the live wire. The fuse melts and cuts the live wire off if too much current passes through it.

b) Why is brass, an alloy of copper and zinc, better than copper or zinc for the pins of a three-pin plug?

Cables used for mains appliances (and for mains circuits) consist of two or three insulated copper wires surrounded by an outer layer of rubber or flexible plastic material.

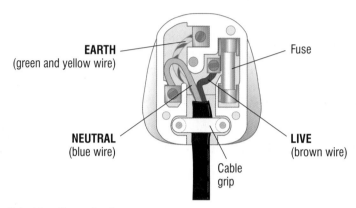

Figure 2 Inside a three-pin plug.

● The brown wire is connected to the live pin.
● The blue wire is connected to the neutral pin.
● The green-yellow wire (of a three-core cable) is connected to the earth pin. A two-core cable does not have an earth wire.

● Copper is used for the wires because it is a good electrical conductor.
● Plastic is a good electrical insulator and therefore prevents anyone touching the cable from receiving an electric shock.
● Two-core cables are used for appliances which have plastic cases (e.g. hairdryers, radios).

Figure 3 Mains cable

c) Why are cables that are worn away or damaged dangerous?

SUMMARY QUESTIONS

1 Choose words from the list to complete the sentences a) to e):

      earth   live   neutral   series   parallel

  a) The ...... wire in a mains plug is blue.
  b) If too much current passes through the fuse, it blows and cuts the ...... wire off.
  c) Appliances plugged into the same mains circuit are in ...... with each other.
  d) The metal frame of an appliance is connected to the ...... wire of a mains circuit when it is plugged in.
  e) The fuse in a plug is in ...... with the live wire.

2 a) Match the list of parts 1–4 in a three-pin plug with the list of materials A–D.

    1 cable insulation   **2** case   **3** pin   **4** wire
    A brass   **B** copper   **C** rubber   **D** stiff plastic

  b) Explain your choice of material for each part in a).

KEY POINTS

1 **Cables** consist of two or three insulated copper wires surrounded by an outer layer of flexible plastic material.
2 **Sockets** and **plugs** are made of stiff plastic materials which enclose the electrical connections.
3 In a **three-pin plug** or a three-core cable, the live wire is brown, the neutral wire is blue, the earth wire is yellow/green. The earth wire is used to earth the metal case of a mains appliance.

P2 6.3   Fuses

LEARNING OBJECTIVES

1 What do we use fuses and circuit breakers for?
2 Why is it important to use a fuse with the correct rating?
3 Why don't appliances with plastic cases need to be earthed?

DID YOU KNOW?

If a live wire inside the appliance touches a neutral wire, a very large current passes between the two wires at the point of contact. We call this **a short-circuit**. If the fuse blows, it cuts the current off.

Fuses are included in vehicle circuits too. This is because the current from a 12V vehicle battery can cause a fire if a short-circuit happens in the circuit.

If you need to buy a fuse for a mains appliance, make sure you know the fuse rating. Otherwise, the new fuse might 'blow' as soon as it is used or, even worse, it might let too much current through and cause a fire.

● A fuse contains a thin wire that heats up and melts if too much current passes through it. If this happens, we say the fuse 'blows'.
● The rating of a fuse is the maximum current that can pass through it without melting the fuse wire.

A fuse in a mains plug must always have the correct rating for the appliance.

If the rating is too large, the fuse will not blow when it should. The heating effect of the current could set the appliance on fire.

a) What would happen if the rating of the fuse was too small?

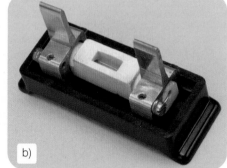

Figure 1 a) Cartridge fuses, b) a rewireable fuse

The importance of earthing

Figure 2 shows why an electric heater is made safer by earthing its frame.

In Figure 2a), the heater works normally and its frame is earthed. The frame is safe to touch.

In Figure 2b), the earth wire is broken. The frame would become live if the live wire touched it.

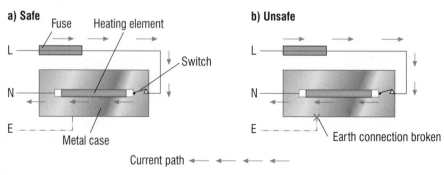

Figure 2 Earthing an electric heater

In Figure 2c), the heater element has touched the unearthed frame so the frame is live. Anyone touching it would be electrocuted. The fuse provides no protection to the user because a current of no more than 20 mA can be lethal.

In Figure 2d), the earth wire has been repaired but the heater element still touches the frame. The current is greater than normal and passes through part of the heater element via the live and the earth wires. Because the frame is earthed, anyone touching it would not be electrocuted. But Figure 2d) is still dangerous because the current might not be enough to blow the fuse and the appliance might overheat.

b) Why is the current in Figure 2d) greater than normal?

Circuit breakers

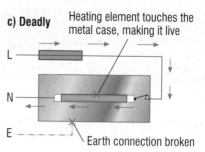

c) Deadly — Heating element touches the metal case, making it live

Earth connection broken

d) Still dangerous

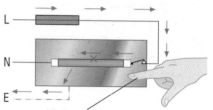

Victim touches the metal case, and if the Earth wire is broken, will conduct the current to Earth

Figure 2 (cont) Earthing an electric heater

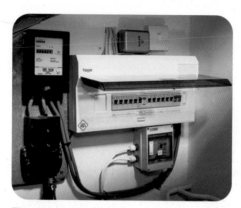

Figure 3 A circuit breaker

A circuit breaker is an electromagnetic switch that opens (i.e. 'trips') and cuts the current off if the current is greater than a certain value. It can then be reset once the fault that made it trip has been put right.

Circuit breakers are sometimes fitted in 'fuse boxes' in place of fuses. They work faster than fuses and can be reset quicker.

c) What should you do if a circuit breaker trips again after being reset?

SUMMARY QUESTIONS

1 a) What is the purpose of a fuse in a mains circuit?
   b) Why is the fuse of an appliance always on the live side?
   c) What advantages does a circuit breaker have compared with a fuse?

2 The diagram shows the circuit of an electric heater that has been wired incorrectly.

   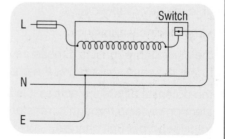

   a) Does the heater work when the switch is closed?
   b) When the switch is open, why is it dangerous to touch the element?
   c) Redraw the circuit correctly wired.

KEY POINTS

1 A **fuse** contains a thin wire that heats up and melts, cutting the current off, if too much current passes through it.
2 A **circuit breaker** is an electromagnetic switch that opens (i.e. 'trips') and cuts the current off if too much current passes through it.

P2 6.4

Electrical power and potential difference

When you use an electrical appliance, it transforms electrical energy into other forms of energy. The **power** of the appliance, in watts, is the energy it transforms, in joules, per second. We can show this as the following equation:

$$\text{Power (watts, W)} = \frac{\text{energy transformed (joules, J)}}{\text{time (seconds, s)}}$$

Worked example

A lamp bulb transforms 30 000 J of electrical energy when it is on for 300 s. Calculate its power.

Solution

$$\text{Power} = \frac{\text{energy transformed}}{\text{time}} = \frac{30\,000\,\text{J}}{300\,\text{s}} = 100\,\text{W}$$

a) The human heart transforms about 30 000 J of energy in a school day of about 8 hours. Calculate an estimate of the power of the human heart.

Figure 1 An artificial heart

Calculating power

Millions of millions of electrons pass through the circuit of an artificial heart every second. Each electron transfers a small amount of energy to it from the battery. So the total energy transferred to it each second is large enough to enable the device to work.

For any electrical appliance:

- the current through it is a measure of the number of electrons passing through it each second (i.e. the charge flow per second),
- the potential difference across it is a measure of how much energy each electron passing through it transfers to it (i.e. the electrical energy transferred per unit charge),
- the power supplied to it is the energy transferred to it each second. This is the electrical energy it transforms every second.

Therefore:

the energy transfer to $=$ the charge flow $\times$ the energy transfer
the device each second per second per unit charge

In other words:

power supplied $=$ **current** $\times$ **potential difference**
(watts, W) $\quad$ (amperes, A) $\qquad$ (volts, V)

For example, the power supplied to

- a 4 A, 12 V electric motor is 48 W ($= 4\,A \times 12\,V$),
- a 0.1 A, 3 V torch lamp is 0.3 W ($= 0.1\,A \times 3.0\,V$).

b) Calculate the power supplied to a 5 A, 230 V electric heater.

Maths note

The equation can written as:

electrical power, $P = I\,V \qquad$ where $I =$ current, and
$ V =$ potential difference

Rearranging this equation gives:

$$\text{potential difference, } V = \frac{P}{I} \quad \text{or}$$

$$\text{current, } I = \frac{P}{V}$$

Choosing a fuse

Domestic appliances are often fitted with a 3 A, or a 5 A or a 13 A fuse. If you don't know which one to use for an appliance, you can work it out from the power rating of the appliance and its potential difference (voltage).

Worked example

i) Calculate the normal current through a 500 W, 230 V heater.
ii) Which fuse, a 3 A, or a 5 A or a 13 A, would you use for the appliance?

Solution

i) $\text{Current} = \dfrac{500\,W}{230\,V} = 2.2\,A$

ii) A 3 A fuse would be needed.

---

c) Why would a 13 A fuse be unsuitable for a 230 V, 100 W table lamp?

SUMMARY QUESTIONS

1 Choose words from the list to complete sentences a) and b):

$\qquad$ **current** $\qquad$ **potential difference** $\qquad$ **power**

a) When an electrical appliance is on, …… is supplied to it as a result of …… passing through it.

b) When an electrical appliance is on, a …… is applied to it which causes …… to pass through it.

2 a) Calculate the power supplied to each of the following devices in normal use.

i) a 12 V, 3 A light bulb, $\qquad$ ii) a 230 V, 2 A heater,

b) Which type of fuse, 3 A or 5 A or 13 A, would you select for:

i) a 24 W, 12 V heater? $\qquad$ ii) a 230 V, 800 W microwave oven?

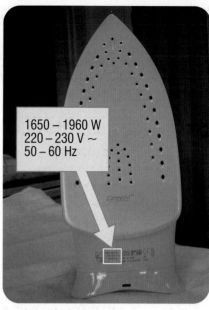

1650 – 1960 W
220 – 230 V ~
50 – 60 Hz

Figure 2 Power rating

NEXT TIME YOU…

… change a fuse, do a quick calculation to make sure its rating is correct for the appliance.

Figure 3 Changing a fuse

KEY POINTS

1 The **power** supplied to a device is the energy transfer to it each second.

2 **Electrical power** supplied (watts) $=$ current (amperes) $\times$ potential difference (volts)

P2 6.5   Electrical energy and charge

LEARNING OBJECTIVES

1 What is electric current?
2 What is the unit of electric charge?
3 What energy transformations take place when charge flows through a resistor?

Electrons

Charge flow = current × time

Figure 1 Charge and current

Calculating charge

When an electrical appliance is on, electrons are forced through the appliance by the potential difference of the voltage supply unit. The potential difference causes a flow of charge through the appliance carried by electrons. The rate of flow of charge is the electric current through the appliance.

The unit of charge, the **coulomb (C)**, is the amount of charge flowing through a wire or a component in 1 second when the current is 1 A.

The charge passing along a wire or through a component in a certain time depends on:

- the current, and
- the time.

We can calculate the charge using the equation:

$$\textbf{charge flow} = \textbf{current} \times \textbf{time}$$
$$\text{(coulombs)} \qquad \text{(amperes)} \qquad \text{(seconds)}$$

For example:

- when the current is 2 A for 5 s, the charge flow is 10 C (= 2 A × 5 s)
- when the current is 4 A for 20 s, the charge flow is 80 C (= 4 A × 20 s)

> **Worked example**
> Calculate the charge flow when the current is 8 A for 80 s.
>
> **Solution**
> Charge flow = current × time = 8 A × 80 s = 640 C.

a) Calculate the charge flowing in 50 s when the current is 3 A.

Energy and potential difference

When a resistor is connected to a battery, electrons are made to pass through the resistor by the battery. Each electron repeatedly collides with the vibrating atoms of the resistor, transferring energy to them. The atoms of the resistor therefore gain kinetic energy and vibrate even more. The resistor becomes hotter.

When charge flows through a resistor, electrical energy is transformed into heat energy.

The energy transformed in a certain time in a resistor depends on:

- the amount of charge that passes through it, and
- the potential difference across the resistor.

Because energy = power × time = potential difference × current × time, we can calculate the energy transformed using the equation

$$\textbf{energy transformed} = \textbf{potential difference} \times \textbf{charge flow}$$
$$\text{(joules, J)} \qquad\qquad \text{(volts, V)} \qquad\qquad \text{(coulombs, C)}$$

For example:

- when the charge flow is 10 C and the potential difference is 10 V, the energy transformed = 100 J (= 10 V × 10 C),
- when the charge flow is 20 C and the potential difference is 10 V, the energy transformed = 200 J (= 10 V × 20 C)

Worked example

Calculate the energy transformed in a component when the charge flow is 30 C and the potential difference is 20 V.

Solution

Energy transformed = 20 V × 30 C = 600 J.

b) Calculate the energy transformed when the charge flow is 30 C and the p.d. is 4 V.

Energy transformations in a circuit

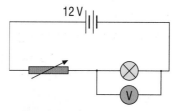

Figure 2 Energy transformations in a circuit

The circuit in Figure 2 shows a 12 V battery in series with a torch lamp and a variable resistor. When the voltmeter reads 10 V, the potential difference across the variable resistor is 2 V.

Each coulomb of charge:

- leaves the battery with 12 J of energy (because energy from the battery = charge × battery potential difference)
- delivers 10 J of energy to the torch lamp (because energy transfer to torch lamp = charge × potential difference across torch lamp). This is transformed into light and heat energy in the torch lamp.
- delivers 2 J of energy supplied to the variable resistor. This is transformed into heat energy in the variable resistor.

SUMMARY QUESTIONS

1 Choose words from the list to complete sentences a) to d):

   charge   current   energy   potential difference

   a) The coulomb is the unit of ....
   b) Charge flowing through a resistor transfers ...... to the resistor.
   c) A ...... is the rate of flow of charge.
   d) Energy transformed = ... × charge.

2 a) Calculate the charge flow for:
      i) a current of 4 A for 20 s,
      ii) a current of 0.2 A for 60 minutes,
   b) Calculate the energy transfer:
      i) for a charge flow of 20 C when the potential difference is 6.0 V,
      ii) in 20 s, for a current of 3 A that passes through a resistor when the potential difference is 5 V.

KEY POINTS

1 An electric current is the rate of flow of charge.
2 When charge flows through a resistor, electrical energy is transferred as heat.
3 Charge (coulombs) = current (amperes) × time (seconds).
4 Energy transferred (joules) = potential difference (volts) × charge flow (coulombs).

P2 6.6 | Safety matters

Spot the hazards!

Imagine you are a safety inspector who has been asked to check the electrics in Shockem Hall. How many electrical faults and hazards can you find just by looking around the main hall?

Circuit breakers for safety

A special 'RCCB' socket should be used for outdoor appliances such as lawnmowers. These sockets each contain a residual current circuit breaker instead of a fuse. This type of circuit breaker switches the current off if the live current and the neutral current differ by more than 30 mA. This can happen, for example, if the insulation of the live wire becomes worn and current 'leaks' from the live wire to 'earth'.

A residual current circuit breaker

1 What other appliances would you use an RCCB for besides a lawn mower?

List them in the table like the one below.

Appliance	Hazard	Rating
Lawnmower	The blades might cut the cable	
Electric drill		

2 Design a hazard rating icon like a star rating but use something different to stars. A '4-star hazard' doesn't sound right.

The Evening Post

Family rescued in house fire!

The Fire Service rescued two children and their parents from the upper floor of a burning house in Lower Town last night. Fortunately, all family members were safe and well. The fire spread to two neighbouring properties before being brought under control. A fire service spokesperson said the fire was caused by an electrical fault.

Cutting out the cowboys

The UK government has passed a law to stop unqualified people doing electrical work. This is because many accidents have happened due to shoddy electrical work, not just by unqualified 'cowboy' electricians but also by householders in their own homes. If you want to be an electrician, you have to train for several years as an apprentice and study for exams. When you qualify, you can register as an approved electrician.

ACTIVITY

The new law is intended to reduce accidents due to unsafe electrical work. But what other effects will it have? It might make rewiring jobs by qualified electricians too expensive and create more work for the cowboys.
Discuss whether this new law is a good law and if there are other ways of regulating electrical work.

ACTIVITY

a) What do these expressions mean? See if you and your friends can add more electrical examples.
b) Use the jargon in a discussion with your friends about something that happened in your favourite TV soap. Award one point each time jargon is used and see who wins.
c) Is jargon unsafe? Can it be misunderstood? Think of a situation where jargon is dangerous.

Electrical jargon

People often complain about jargon – the words that experts use. But sometimes, we use jargon without realising it, especially electrical jargon because we all use electricity. Sometimes, we even use it in our everyday conversations.

Here are some examples:

'Don't blow a fuse.'

'She's a sparky character.'

'Can't you short-circuit the usual procedure?'

Holiday time!

ACTIVITY

Find out what type of adaptor you would need if you go on holiday to Spain.

Holiday Essentials

When you go abroad... be careful if you intend to take mains appliances with you.

* If the voltage is not 230 V (as in the UK and Europe), the appliance must have a 'dual voltage' switch that can be changed from 230 V to the new voltage. You **must** change the switch back when you return.
* If the voltage is 230 V, you may need to take a suitable plug adaptor with you for each appliance. This is because sockets abroad may be different to those at home.
* Only use one appliance per socket or you might blow a fuse!

shavers only

115V | 230V

SUMMARY QUESTIONS

1 a) In a mains circuit, which wire:
   i) is earthed at the local sub-station,
   ii) alternates in potential?

   b) An oscilloscope is used to display the potential difference of an alternating voltage supply unit. How would the trace change if:
   i) the p.d. is increased,
   ii) the frequency is increased?

2 Complete a) and b) using words below:

   earth   live   neutral

   a) When a mains appliance is switched on, current passes through it via the …… wire and the …… wire.

   b) In a mains circuit:
   i) the …… wire is blue,
   ii) the …… wire is brown,
   iii) the …… wire is green yellow.

3 a) Complete the sentences:
   i) Wall sockets are connected in …… with each other.
   ii) A fuse in a mains plug is in …… with the appliance and cuts off the …… wire if too much current passes through the appliance.

   b) i) What is the main difference between a fuse and a circuit breaker?
   ii) Give two reasons why a circuit breaker is safer than a fuse.

4 a) i) Calculate the current in a 230 V, 2.5 kW electric kettle.
   ii) Which fuse, 3 A or 5 A or 13 A, would you fit in the kettle plug?

   b) Calculate the power supplied to a 230 V electric toaster when the current through it is 4.0 A.

5 Calculate the charge flow through a resistor when the current is 6 A for 200 s.   [Higher]

6 A 5 Ω resistor is in series with a lamp, a switch and a 12 V battery.

   a) Draw the circuit diagram.

   b) When the switch is closed for 60 seconds, a direct current of 0.6 A passes through the resistor. Calculate:
   i) the energy supplied by the battery,
   ii) the energy transformed in the resistor,
   iii) the energy transformed in the lamp.   [Higher]

EXAM-STYLE QUESTIONS

1 An electric heater is connected to a 230 V mains supply. The current flowing through the heater is 12 A.

   (a) What is the power of the heater?   (2)

   (b) The heater is switched on for 30 minutes. Calculate how much charge flows through the heater during this time and give the unit.   (4)

2 The diagram shows a three-pin plug.

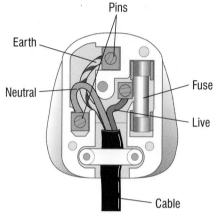

   (a) State the colour of each wire.

   Live ……… Neutral ……… Earth ………   (3)

   (b) State and explain which parts of the plug are made out of . . .

   (i) plastic   (ii) brass   (4)

3 Explain:

   (a) why appliances with metal cases need to be earthed, but appliances with plastic cases do not.   (4)

   (b) which wire in a circuit should contain the fuse.   (2)

   (c) why the rating of the fuse in an appliance should be slightly higher than the normal working current through the appliance.   (2)

4 Cells and the electrical mains are both sources of electrical energy.
   Describe the currents and potential differences from each of these types of supply.   (7)

5 Most domestic appliances are connected to the 230 V mains supply with a 3-pin plug containing a fuse. 3A, 5A and 13A fuses are available.

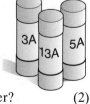

   (a) A food mixer has a normal current of 2A. What is the power of the mixer?   (2)

   (b) What fuse should be used in the plug for a 2.8 kW kettle?   (4)

(c) (i) A 9 kW shower is wired directly to the mains. It has a separate fuse in the household fuse box. Explain why? (3)

(ii) The fuse for the shower keeps melting. The householder replaces it with a nail. Why is this dangerous? (2)

6 The pictures show situations in which electricity is not being used safely.

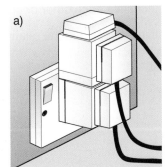
a)

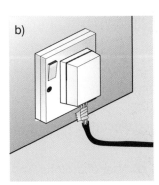
b)

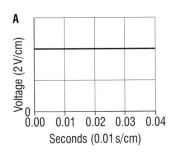

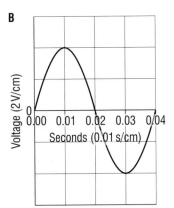
c)

For each picture (a), (b) and (c), explain how electricity is not being used safely. (6)

7 An oscilloscope can be used to measure the potential difference of different electrical supplies.

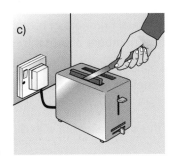

A
Voltage (2 V/cm)
0.00 0.01 0.02 0.03 0.04
Seconds (0.01 s/cm)

B
Voltage (2 V/cm)
0.00 0.01 0.02 0.03 0.04
Seconds (0.01 s/cm)

The diagrams show the traces produced on a centimetre grid by two different supplies.

(a) What is the potential difference of supply A? (3)

(b) (i) What type of supply is supply B? (1)

(ii) What is the peak potential difference of supply B? (1)

(iii) What is the frequency of supply B? (3)

[Higher]

HOW SCIENCE WORKS QUESTIONS

'There I was watching Rovers beat United, when it blew a fuse. No, it wasn't the United manager, it was the box. I reckon it was down to the United fans switching off their tellies when we scored that second goal. It must have been some sort of surge. Anyway, I fixed it before the end of the game. I put a bit of wire into where the fuse had burned and the telly worked perfectly. Unfortunately the house burned down! Anyway Rovers won and that's the important thing . . .'

a) Would you say that putting a piece of wire to replace a fuse was based on good science? Explain your answer. (1)

b) Do you think there was a link between Rovers scoring a second goal and the television fuse blowing? Was it causal, due to association or due to chance? Explain your answer. (1)

The fire brigade did a thorough investigation into the cause of the fire. They recovered a reel of the wire used in place of the 3 A fuse that should have been used. Their scientists at the Fire Service laboratory found that six equal lengths of this wire fused at currents of 6.5 A, 6.1 A, 6.2 A, 5.8 A, 6.0 A and 6.1 A. They also discovered a fault in the television had caused it to overheat. This had caused the curtains to catch fire and burn the house down.

c) i) Calculate the mean value of the measurements above. (1)

ii) Comment of the precision of the results. (1)

iii) Why did they test equal lengths? (1)

d) Is it likely that there was a causal link between the 'repair' of the fuse and the house burning down? Explain your answer. (1)

e) Why can you trust this investigation? (1)

P2 7.1   Nuclear reactions

The atom has a nucleus composed of protons and neutrons surrounded by electrons. In a nuclear reaction, neutrons and protons crash into each other and get rearranged. At speeds approaching the cosmic speed limit, the speed of light, they can even annihilate each other or create new particles.

The table gives the relative masses and the relative electric charges of a proton, a neutron and an electron.

	Relative mass	Relative charge
proton	1	+1
neutron	1	0
electron	0.0005	−1

An uncharged atom has equal numbers of protons and electrons. A charged atom, an **ion**, has unequal numbers of protons and electrons.

The atoms of the same element each have the same number of protons. The number of protons in a nucleus is denoted by **Z**. It is called the **atomic number** (or proton number).

Isotopes are atoms of the same element with different numbers of neutrons.

The number of protons and neutrons in a nucleus is called its **mass number**, denoted by **A**.

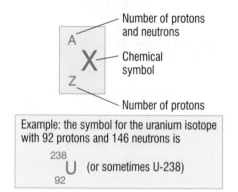

Example: the symbol for the uranium isotope with 92 protons and 146 neutrons is

$^{238}_{92}U$ (or sometimes U-238)

Figure 1 Representing an isotope

An isotope of an element X, which has Z protons and A protons and neutrons, is represented by the symbol ^A_ZX. For example, the uranium isotope $^{238}_{92}U$ contains 92 protons and 146 neutrons ($= 238 - 92$) in each nucleus. So its relative mass is 238 and its relative charge is 92.

a) How many protons and how many neutrons are in the nucleus of the uranium isotope $^{235}_{92}U$?

Radioactive decay

An unstable nucleus becomes more stable by emitting an α (alpha) or a β (beta) particle or by emitting γ (gamma) radiation.

α emission

- An α particle consists of two protons and two neutrons. Its relative mass is 4 and its relative charge is 2. So we can represent it by the symbol $^4_2\alpha$.
- When an unstable nucleus emits an α particle, its atomic number goes down by 2 and its mass number goes down by 4.

For example, the thorium isotope $^{228}_{90}Th$ decays by emitting an α particle. So it forms the radium isotope $^{224}_{88}Ra$.

b) How many protons and how many neutrons are in $^{228}_{90}Th$ and $^{224}_{88}Ra$?

The nucleus emits an α particle and forms a new nucleus

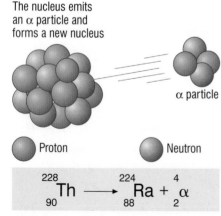

Figure 2 α emission

β emission

- A β particle is an electron created and emitted by a nucleus which has too many neutrons compared with protons. A neutron in its nucleus changes into a proton and a β particle. This is instantly emitted at high speed by the nucleus.
- The relative mass of a β particle is effectively zero and its relative charge is -1. So we can represent a β particle by the symbol $_{-1}^{0}\beta$.
- When an unstable nucleus emits a β particle, its atomic number goes up by 1 but its mass number stays the same (because the neutron changes into a proton).

For example, the potassium isotope $_{19}^{40}K$ decays by emitting a β particle. So it forms a nucleus of the calcium isotope $_{20}^{40}Ca$.

c) How many protons and how many neutrons are in $_{19}^{40}K$ and $_{20}^{40}Ca$?

γ emission

γ radiation is emitted by some unstable nuclei after an α particle or a β particle has been emitted. γ radiation is uncharged and has no mass. So it does not change the number of protons or the number of neutrons in a nucleus.

The origins of background radiation

Background radiation is ionising radiation from space (cosmic rays), from devices such as X-ray tubes and from radioactive isotopes in the environment. Some of these isotopes are present because of nuclear weapons testing and nuclear power stations. But most of it is from substances in the Earth. For example, radon gas is radioactive and is a product of the decay of uranium in rocks found in certain areas.

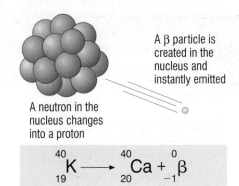

A β particle is created in the nucleus and instantly emitted

A neutron in the nucleus changes into a proton

$$_{19}^{40}K \longrightarrow {}_{20}^{40}Ca + {}_{-1}^{0}\beta$$

Figure 3 β emission

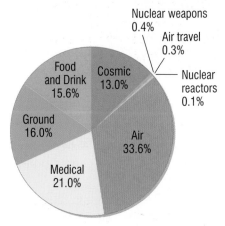

Figure 4 The origins of background radioactivity

		Change in the nucleus	Particle emitted
1	α decay	Nucleus loses 2 protons and 2 neutrons	2 protons and 2 neutrons emitted as an α particle
2	β decay	A neutron in the nucleus changes into a proton	An electron is created in the nucleus and instantly emitted

KEY POINTS

SUMMARY QUESTIONS

1 How many protons and how many neutrons are there in the nucleus of each of the following isotopes?

a) $_{6}^{12}C$

b) $_{27}^{60}Co$

c) $_{92}^{235}U$

2 A substance contains the radioactive isotope $_{92}^{238}U$, which emits alpha radiation. The product nucleus X emits beta radiation and forms a nucleus Y. How many protons and how many neutrons are present in:

a) a nucleus of $_{92}^{238}U$,

b) a nucleus of X,

c) a nucleus of Y?

P2 7.2 The discovery of the nucleus

LEARNING OBJECTIVES

1 How was the nuclear model of the atom established?
2 What other models of the atom were there?

Ernest Rutherford had already made important discoveries about radioactivity when he decided to use alpha (α) particles to probe the atom. He asked two of his research workers, Hans Geiger and Ernest Marsden, to investigate the scattering of α particles by a thin metal foil.

Figure 1 shows the arrangement they used.

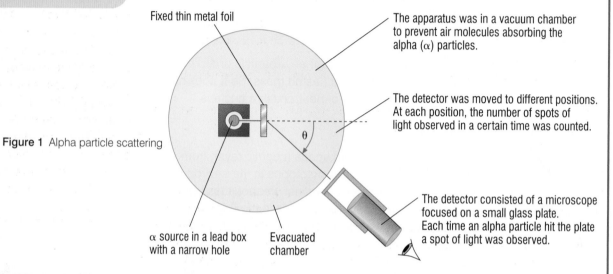

Fixed thin metal foil

The apparatus was in a vacuum chamber to prevent air molecules absorbing the alpha (α) particles.

The detector was moved to different positions. At each position, the number of spots of light observed in a certain time was counted.

Figure 1 Alpha particle scattering

θ

The detector consisted of a microscope focused on a small glass plate. Each time an alpha particle hit the plate a spot of light was observed.

α source in a lead box with a narrow hole

Evacuated chamber

PRACTICAL

Lucky strike!

Fix a small metal disc about 2 cm thick at the centre of a table. Hide the disc under a cardboard disc about 20 cm in diameter. See if you can hit the metal disc with a rolling marble.

The radioactive isotope they used had a long half life so its activity stayed the same during the experiment. They measured the number of α particles deflected per second through different angles. The results showed that:

● most of the alpha particles passed straight through the metal foil,
● the number of alpha particles deflected per minute decreased as the angle of deflection increased,
● about 1 in 10 000 alpha particles were deflected by more than 90°.

a) If you kicked a football at an empty goal and the ball bounced back at you, what would you conclude?

Rutherford was astonished by the results. He said it was like firing 'naval shells' at cardboard and discovering the occasional shell rebounds. He knew that α particles are positively charged. He deduced from the results that there is a nucleus at the centre of every atom which is:

● positively charged because it repels α particles (remember that like charges repel),
● much smaller than the atom because most α particles pass through without deflection,
● where most of the mass of the atom is located.

Using this model, Rutherford worked out the proportion of α particles that would be deflected for a given angle. He found an exact agreement with Geiger and Marsden's measurements. He used his theory to estimate the diameter of the nucleus and found it was about 100 000 times smaller than the atom.

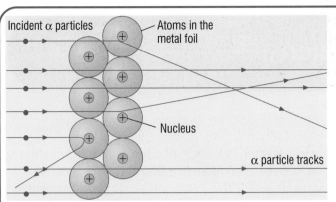

Figure 2 Alpha (α) particle paths

Rutherford's nuclear model of the atom was quickly accepted because:

- it agreed exactly with the measurements Geiger and Marsden made,
- it explains radioactivity in terms of changes that happen to an unstable nucleus when it emits radiation,
- it predicted the existence of the neutron, which was later discovered.

b) What difference would it have made if Geiger and Marsden's measurements had not fitted Rutherford's nuclear model?

Goodbye to the plum pudding atom!

Before the nucleus was discovered in 1914, scientists didn't know what the structure of the atom was. They did know atoms contained electrons and they knew these are tiny negatively charged particles. But they didn't know how the positive charge was arranged in an atom, although there were different models in circulation. Some scientists thought the atom was like a 'plum pudding' model with:

- the positively charged matter in the atom evenly spread about (like in a pudding), and
- electrons buried inside (like plums in the pudding).

Rutherford's discovery meant farewell to the 'plum pudding' atom.

> **DID YOU KNOW?**
>
> Imagine a marble at the centre of a football stadium. That's the scale of the nucleus inside the atom. Almost all the mass of the atom is in its nucleus. The density of the nucleus is about a thousand million million times the density of water. A match box of nuclear matter would weigh about a million million tonnes!

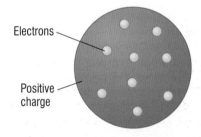

Figure 3 The plum pudding atom

SUMMARY QUESTIONS

1 Complete a) to c) using the words below:

charge   diameter   mass

a) A nucleus has the same type of …… as an alpha particle.
b) A nucleus has a much smaller …… than the atom.
c) Most of the …… of the atom is in the nucleus.

2 a) The diagram shows 4 possible paths, labelled A, B, C and D, of an alpha particle deflected by a nucleus. Which path would the alpha particle travel along?
b) Explain why each of the other paths in a) is not possible.

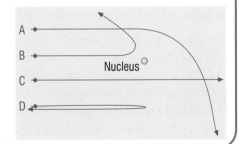

> **KEY POINTS**
>
> 1 Alpha particles in a beam are sometimes scattered through large angles when they are directed at a thin metal foil.
> 2 Rutherford used the measurements from alpha-scattering experiments to prove that an atom has a small positively charged central nucleus where most of the mass of the atom is located.

P2 7.3   Nuclear fission

Chain reactions

Energy is released in a nuclear reactor as a result of a process called **nuclear fission**. In this process, the nucleus of an atom of a fissionable substance splits into two smaller 'fragment' nuclei. This event can cause other fissionable nuclei to split, so producing a **chain reaction** of fission events.

Fission neutrons

When a nucleus undergoes fission, it releases

- two or three neutrons (referred to as 'fission' neutrons) at high speeds,
- energy in the form of radiation and kinetic energy of the fission neutrons and the fragment nuclei.

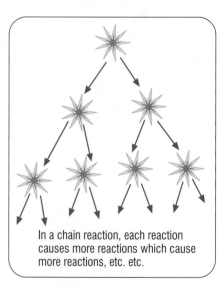

In a chain reaction, each reaction causes more reactions which cause more reactions, etc. etc.

Figure 1 A chain reaction

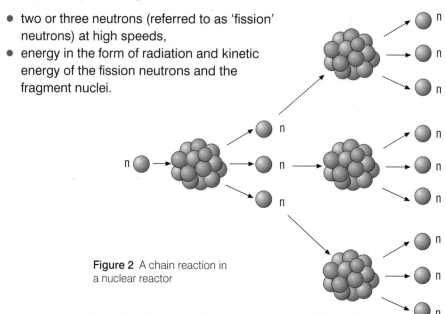

Figure 2 A chain reaction in a nuclear reactor

The fission neutrons may cause further fission resulting in a chain reaction. In a nuclear reactor, exactly one fission neutron from each fission event on average goes on to produce further fission.

a) What would happen if more than one fission neutron per event on average went on to produce further fission?

Fissionable isotopes

The fuel in a nuclear reactor must contain fissionable isotopes.

- Most reactors at the present time are designed to use 'enriched uranium' as the fuel. This consists mostly of the non-fissionable uranium isotope $^{238}_{92}U$ (U-238) and about 2–3% of the uranium isotope $^{235}_{92}U$ (U-235) which is fissionable. In comparison, natural uranium is more than 99% U-238.
- The U-238 nuclei in a nuclear reactor do not undergo fission but they change into other heavy nuclei, including plutonium-239 (the isotope $^{239}_{94}Pu$). This isotope is fissionable but not in a uranium reactor.

GET IT RIGHT!

During nuclear fission a large nucleus breaks up into two smaller nuclei. Make sure you know how to spell 'fission' – two 's's.

FOUL FACTS

A nuclear bomb is two lumps of pure U-235 or Pu-239. Each lump can't produce a chain reaction because it loses too many fission neutrons. But if you bring them together . . . !

Inside a nuclear reactor

A nuclear reactor consists of uranium fuel rods spaced evenly in the reactor core. Figure 3 shows a cross-section of a Pressurised Water Reactor (PWR).

- The reactor core is a thick steel vessel containing the fuel rods, control rods and water at high pressure. The fission neutrons are slowed down by collisions with the atoms in the water molecules. This is necessary as fast neutrons do not cause further fission of U-235. We say the water acts as a **moderator** because it slows the fission neutrons down.

- **Control rods** in the core absorb surplus neutrons. This keeps the chain reaction under control. The depth of the rods in the core is adjusted to maintain a steady chain reaction.

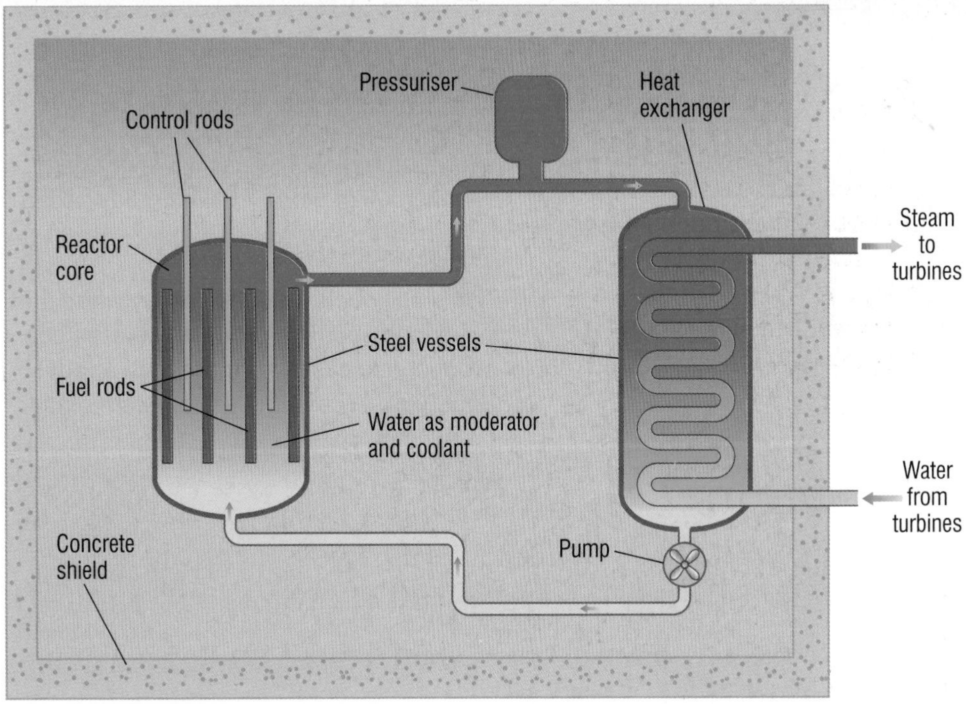

Figure 3 A nuclear reactor

- The water acts as a **coolant**. Its molecules gain kinetic energy from the neutrons and the fuel rods. The water is pumped through the core and through sealed pipes to and from a heat exchanger outside the core. The water transfers thermal energy to the heat exchanger from the core.

- The reactor core is a thick steel vessel, designed to withstand the very high temperature and pressure in the core. The core is enclosed by thick concrete walls which absorb radiation that escapes through the walls of the steel vessel.

b) What would happen if the control rods were removed from the core?

SUMMARY QUESTIONS

1 Complete a) and b) using the list below:

nucleus   uranium-235   uranium-238   plutonium-239

a) Nuclear fission happens when a …… of …… or …… splits.
b) A nucleus of …… in a nuclear reactor changes without fission into a nucleus of …… .

2 Put the statements A, B and C in the list below into the correct sequence of boxes 1–4 to describe a steady chain reaction in a nuclear reactor.

A a U-235 nucleus splits
B a neutron hits a U-235 nucleus
C neutrons are released

Steady chain reaction
1
energy is released
2
3
4

KEY POINTS

1 **Nuclear fission** occurs when a uranium-235 nucleus or a plutonium-239 nucleus splits.
2 A **chain reaction** occurs in a nuclear reactor when each fission event causes further fission events.
3 In a *nuclear reactor*, one neutron per fission on average goes on to produce further fission.

P2 7.4   Nuclear fusion

Imagine if we could get energy from water. Stars release energy as a result of fusing small nuclei like hydrogen to form larger nuclei. Water contains lots of hydrogen atoms. A glass of water could provide the same amount of energy as a tanker full of petrol – if we could make a fusion reactor here on the Earth.

Fusion reactions

Two small nuclei release energy when they are fused together to form a single larger nucleus. The process releases energy only if the relative mass of the product nucleus is no more than about 55 (about the same as an iron nucleus). Energy must be supplied to create bigger nuclei.

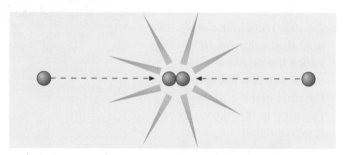

Figure 1 A fusion reaction

The Sun is mostly 75% hydrogen and about 25% helium. The core is so hot that it consists of a 'plasma' of bare nuclei with no electrons. These nuclei move about and fuse together when they collide. When they fuse, they release energy. Figure 2 shows how protons fuse together to form a $^4_2$He nucleus. Energy is released at each stage.

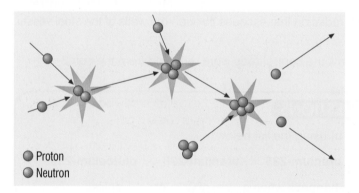

○ Proton
○ Neutron

Figure 2 Fusion reactions in the Sun

- When two protons (i.e. hydrogen nuclei) fuse, they form a 'heavy hydrogen' nucleus, $^2_1$H. A positron, the antimatter counterpart of the electron, is created and emitted at the same time.
- Two more protons collide separately with two $^2_1$H nuclei and turn them into heavier nuclei.
- The two heavier nuclei collide to form the helium nucleus $^4_2$He.
- The energy released at each stage is carried away as kinetic energy of the product nucleus and other particles emitted.

a) Look at Figure 2 and work out what is formed when a proton collides with a $^2_1$H nucleus.

Fusion reactors

There are enormous technical difficulties with fusion. The 'plasma' of light nuclei must be heated to very high temperatures before the nuclei will fuse. This is because two nuclei approaching each other will repel each other due to their positive charge. If the nuclei are moving fast enough, they can overcome the force of repulsion and fuse together.

In a fusion reactor:

- the plasma is heated by passing a very large electric current through it,
- the plasma is contained by a magnetic field so it doesn't touch the reactor walls. If it did, it would go cold and fusion would stop.

Figure 3 An experimental fusion reactor

Scientists have been working on these problems since the 1950s. A successful fusion reactor would release more energy than it uses to heat the plasma. At the present time, scientists working on experimental fusion reactors are able to do this by fusing 'heavy hydrogen' nuclei to form helium nuclei – but only for a few minutes!

b) Why is a fusion reactor unlikely to explode?

A promising future

Practical fusion reactors could meet all our energy needs.

- The fuel for fusion reactors is readily available as 'heavy hydrogen' and is present in sea water.
- The reaction product, helium, is a non-radioactive inert gas so is harmless.
- The energy released could be used to generate electricity.

SUMMARY QUESTIONS

1 Complete a) and b) using the words below:

larger   small   stable

a) When two …… nuclei moving at high speed collide, they form a …… nucleus.

b) Energy is released in nuclear fusion if the product nucleus is not as …… as an iron nucleus.

2 a) Why does the plasma of light nuclei in a fusion reactor need to be very hot?

b) Why would a fusion reactor that needs more energy than it produces not be much use?

KEY POINTS

1 Nuclear fusion occurs when two nuclei are forced close enough together so they form a single larger nucleus.

2 Energy is released when two light nuclei are fused together.

3 A fusion reactor needs to be at a very high temperature before nuclear fusion can take place.

P2 7.5   Nuclear energy issues

The Manhattan project

In the Second World War, scientists in Britain and America were recruited to work in Arizona on the Manhattan project, the project to build the first atomic bomb. They knew they would be in deadly competition with scientists in Nazi Germany. They also knew that if they lost the race, the war would be lost.

By 1945, the first atomic bomb was ready to be used. Nazi Germany had already surrendered. The allied forces were still involved in bitter fighting against Japan in the Far East. Their leaders knew the planned invasion of Japan would claim the lives of many allied troops. An atomic bomb was dropped on the Japanese city of Hiroshima to force Japan to surrender. The explosion killed 140 000 people. The Japanese government did not give in until after a second atomic bomb was dropped on the Japanese city of Nagasaki a week later.

ACTIVITY

Discuss these questions as a small group:

a) Most people think the British and American governments were right to build an atomic bomb. But do you think scientists should continue to work on deadly weapons?

b) Many people think the power of the atomic bomb should have been demonstrated to Japan by dropping it on an uninhabited island. What do you think?

Cold fusion

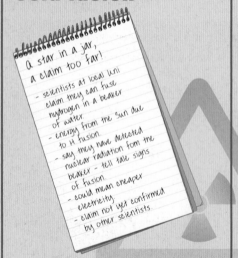

a star in a jar,
a claim too far!

- scientists at local uni claim they can fuse hydrogen in a beaker of water
- energy from the Sun due to H fusion
- say they have detected nuclear radiation from the beaker - tell tale signs of fusion
- could mean cheaper electricity
- claim not yet confirmed by other scientists

ACTIVITY

Imagine you're a journalist and you've got a 'scoop' on cold fusion. Your editor wants you to write it up for the front page – nothing too complicated. Prepare a front-page feature on your scoop. Remember the claims have not been confirmed yet.

The fast-breeder reactor

This fast-breeder reactor uses plutonium-239 as its fuel. It can 'breed' its own plutonium by fusion from uranium-238. Present and planned uranium reactors will use up the world's supply of uranium within about 200 years. Fast-breeder reactors would extend that to thousands of years. As in the uranium reactor, control rods in the reactor core are used to keep the rate of fission events constant. This ensures energy is released at a constant rate. **But** if somehow, plutonium got stuck in a pipe . . . !

ACTIVITY

a) Finish the sentence at the end of the paragraph.

b) The UK government built and tested an experimental fast-breeder reactor on the coast of Northern Scotland at Dounreay. It has now been closed. So why are many people still worried about it? Imagine you are one of them. Write a letter to your local newspaper about your concerns.

Nuclear reprocessing – a hot problem!

Used fuel rods contain uranium-238 and plutonium-239. After removal from a reactor, a used fuel rod is left to cool in a large tank of water for up to a year. Then the fuel in it is removed and the uranium and plutonium content is taken out chemically. This process is called reprocessing. The rest of the fuel is stored in sealed containers at secure sites. Reprocessed uranium and plutonium can be used in fast-breeder reactors to generate electricity. Plutonium can also be used to make nuclear bombs.

The UKs THORP reprocessing plant in Cumbria reprocesses waste from other countries as well as from the UK. Lots of scientists are employed there. It generates income but it also generates lots of controversy. Many people think it should be closed.

ACTIVITY

Should we reprocess nuclear waste for other countries? Should we reprocess our own nuclear waste or just store it? Discuss the issue as a group. Send an e-mail to your MP to tell him/her what you think.

Atom smashers

Here's something you don't need to know for your GCSE exam – yet! We now know that neutrons and protons are made of smaller particles called **quarks**. Physicists use big machines (like the one in the picture) called accelerators to make charged particles travel extremely fast. They discovered that a beam of fast-moving electrons is scattered by three small particles inside each neutron and proton. They worked out that

- a proton is made of two 'up' quarks and a 'down' quark,
- a neutron is made of two 'down' quarks and an 'up' quark.

You'll learn more about the quark family at AS level!

ACTIVITY

What conclusions can you make about the charge of an 'up' quark and the charge of a 'down' quark?

New improved nuclear reactors

Most of the world's nuclear reactors presently in use will need to be replaced in the next 20 years. They were built to last for no more than about 30 to 40 years. We all want electricity and we want it without burning fossil fuel. Reactor companies have been developing new improved 'third-generation' nuclear reactors to replace existing nuclear reactors when they are taken out of use.

These new types of reactors have:

- a standard design to cut down capital costs and construction time,
- a longer operating life – typically 60 years,
- improved safety features,
- much less effect on the environment.

Some of the new reactors are designed with 'passive' safety features, where natural processes (for example, convection of outside air through cooling panels along the reactor walls) are used to prevent accidents. Such features are additional to 'active' safety controls, such as the use of control rods and safety valves. Some scientists claim these 'new' features are about giving nuclear power a more 'positive image'.

ACTIVITY

New reactors are being built in many countries. Should new reactors be built in the UK? Discuss the benefits and the drawbacks of such a programme.

SUMMARY QUESTIONS

1 a) How many protons and how many neutrons are in a nucleus of each of the following isotopes?
   i) $^{14}_{6}C$,   ii) $^{228}_{90}Th$

b) $^{14}_{6}C$ emits a β particle and becomes an isotope of nitrogen (N).
   i) How many protons and how many neutrons are in this nitrogen isotope?
   ii) Write down the symbol for this isotope.

c) $^{228}_{90}Th$ emits an α particle and becomes an isotope of radium (Ra).
   i) How many protons and how many neutrons are in this isotope of radium?
   ii) Write down the symbol for this isotope.

2 a) Complete the sentences using words from the list.

   decreases   increases   stays the same

   When energy is released at a steady rate in a nuclear reactor,
   i) the number of fission events each second in the core ....
   ii) the amount of uranium-235 in the core ....
   iii) the number of radioactive isotopes in the fuel rods ....

b) Explain what would happen in a nuclear reactor if:
   i) the coolant fluid leaked out of the core,
   ii) the control rods were pushed further into the reactor core.

3 a) i) What do we mean by nuclear fusion?
   ii) Why do two nuclei repel each other when they get close?
   iii) Why do they need to collide at high speed in order to fuse together?

b) Give two reasons why nuclear fusion is difficult to achieve in a reactor.

4 a) Complete the sentences using words from the list.

   fission   fusion

   i) In a ...... reactor, two small nuclei join together and release energy.
   ii) In a ...... reactor, a large nucleus splits and releases energy.
   iii) The fuel in a ...... reactor contains uranium-235.

b) State two advantages that nuclear fusion reactors would have in comparison with nuclear fission reactors.

EXAM-STYLE QUESTIONS

1 The diagram shows two isotopes of the element carbon.

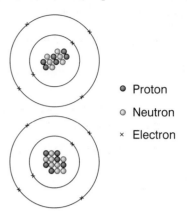

● Proton
◯ Neutron
× Electron

(a) What are isotopes of an element? (2)

(b) (i) What is the atomic number of carbon?
   (ii) What are the mass numbers of the two isotopes of carbon shown in the diagram? (3)

(c) Which of the particles ●, ◯ and ×, shown in the diagram:
   (i) has a negative charge?
   (ii) has no charge?
   (iii) has the smallest mass? (3)

2 In a nuclear reactor, energy is produced by the process of nuclear fission.

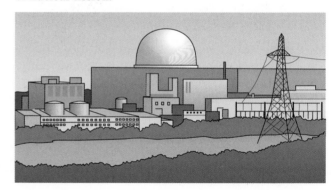

Describe as fully as you can the process of nuclear fission.

The answer has been started for you. Copy and complete:

Atoms of uranium–235 are bombarded by neutrons. .... (6)

3 Nuclear fusion is the process by which energy is released in stars.
Describe as fully as you can the process of nuclear fusion. (4)

4 (a) Radon is formed when radium-226 decays by the emission of an alpha particle.

Copy and complete the nuclear equation below.

$$^{226}_{88}\text{Ra} \longrightarrow \quad^{.......}_{.......}\text{Rn} + \quad^{......}_{......}\alpha \qquad (4)$$

(b) Nitrogen is formed when carbon-14 decays by the emission of a beta particle.

Copy and complete the nuclear equation below.

$$^{14}_{6}\text{C} \longrightarrow \quad^{.......}_{.......}\text{N} + \quad^{......}_{......}\beta \qquad (4)$$

(c) What changes take place in the carbon-14 nucleus when it decays by emitting a beta particle? (3)

5 Background radiation is with us all the time and comes from many different sources, such as radon gas.

(a) Name two other sources of background radiation. (2)

(b) Some scientists are measuring the amount of radon gas inside a house. The gas is released into the air from rocks in the ground.
Suggest what the scientists could do to make their measurements as reliable as possible. (4)

(c) The table gives some values for the dose of background radiation from the ground in different parts of the UK.

Area of UK	Dose in millisieverts per year
South west	0.35
South east	0.20
Midlands	0.25
North west	0.30
North east	0.23

(i) What type of variable is the 'Area of UK'? (1)

(ii) What would be the best way to represent this data on a bar chart or line graph? (1)

HOW SCIENCE WORKS QUESTIONS

Iodine-125 is a radioactive isotope used by doctors as a gamma emitter for measuring bone density in humans. It can also be used in the treatment of prostate cancer.

It is important to know how the activity of iodine-125 changes with time. The following measurements were taken in two identical tests of iodine-125.

Time (days)	0	50	100	150	200	250
Sample A (counts/min)	100	56	31	17	10	6
Sample B (counts/min)	100	55	31	18	9	5

a) Are the differences in activity between the two samples due to random or systematic error? Explain your answer. (1)

b) The tests were carried on for several years and the results stayed more or less constant after a couple of years. This was said to be due to the ever-present background radiation.
Explain why the background radiation introduces a systematic error into the measurements. (1)

c) What are the environmental issues involved in using this isotope? (1)

PRESS RELEASE

Fifteen-year studies of prostate cancer patients using iodine-125 have been completed. The Medical Director from a US company confirmed that results show only 4% of patients had died from the prostate cancer. A British consultant urologist said that after 5 years, 93% of patients were disease-free.

d) Suggest two questions you might want to ask the scientists who gave this press release. (2)

EXAMINATION-STYLE QUESTIONS

1 When an air-rifle is fired a small explosion takes place which pushes the pellet forwards and the air-rifle backwards.

See pages 152–3

(a) The mass of an air-rifle is 2 kg. The mass of the pellet is 0.0005 kg and its speed as it leaves the rifle is 100 m/s.

Calculate the speed with which the air-rifle moves backwards   *(3 marks)*

GET IT RIGHT!

The total momentum before the explosion is zero.

(b) The picture shows a batsman hitting a cricket ball.

The batsman 'follows through' when hitting the ball, so the force is applied to the ball for a longer time. Why does he do this?

(3 marks)
[Higher]

2 A student is investigating terminal velocity. She drops a metal ball into a tall beaker containing glycerine.

See pages 140–1

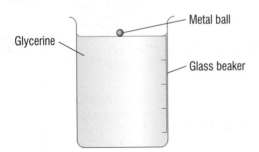

Initially the metal ball accelerates because of the force of gravity. Eventually the resultant force on the ball bearing becomes zero.

(a) Why does the resultant force become zero?   *(3 marks)*

The student watches the ball slowly moving through the glycerine. As it does, she times how long it takes to get to each mark on the beaker.

(b) Describe what precautions she should take to make her results as accurate as possible. *(2 marks)*

(c) Copy the axes below and sketch the line you would expect on the graph of speed of ball against time. *(3 marks)*

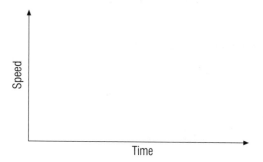

3 At one time scientists believed in a 'plum pudding' model of the atom.

See pages 200–1

(a) What is meant by the 'plum pudding' model of the atom? *(2 marks)*

(b) Rutherford and Marsden carried out an experiment that led to this model being replaced by the nuclear model.

They fired alpha particles at thin gold foil. Some of the observations from their experiment are given below.
For each observation write down the matching explanation.
One has been done for you.

Observation	Explanation
Most of the particles go straight through the gold foil without being deflected.	
Some particles are deflected through small angles.	The nucleus is charged.
A few alpha particles are deflected back through angles greater than 90°.	

(3 marks)
[Higher]

GET IT RIGHT!

There are three marks here, so try to make three points.

4 In a fitness centre people use machines containing pulleys to move 'weights'.

See pages 146–9

(a) Some of the 'weights' are marked '5 kg'.

This is incorrect physics. Explain why. *(2 marks)*

(b) Calculate the work done on a 30 N weight when one of the machines raises it 2 m. Give a unit with your answer. *(4 marks)*

(c) A running machine displays the speed a person would be travelling if they were running on the road.

Calculate the kinetic energy of a person of mass 70 kg running at a speed of 5 m/s. Give a unit with your answer. *(4 marks)*
[Higher]

GET IT RIGHT!

Remember to square the speed when calculating kinetic energy.

P3 | Further physics

Figure 1 Light travels faster than sound

What you already know

Here is a quick reminder of previous work that you will find useful in this unit:

Forces

- The gravitational pull between any two objects depends on their masses and the distance between them.
- The weight of an object is the force of gravity on the object.
- When an object is at rest or moving at constant velocity, the forces acting on it are balanced.

Light and sound

- We see objects which are not light sources because they reflect or scatter light.
- Refraction occurs when a light ray changes its direction as it passes from one transparent substance to another.
- Light travels faster than sound. Light travels through a vacuum. Sound cannot travel through a vacuum.

Magnetism

- Permanent magnets are made of steel because steel does not lose its magnetism easily.
- An electromagnet is a coil of insulated wire wrapped round an iron core. When an electric current passes through the coil, the core is magnetised. The core loses its magnetism when the current is switched off.

Space

- The Earth orbits the Sun and the Moon orbits the Earth.
- The Sun and the stars emit light. Planets and satellites are seen by reflected light from the Sun.

RECAP QUESTIONS

1 Which of the forces A–D listed below act on each of the following objects:

    A air resistance   **B force of gravity**
      C friction   **D magnetic attraction**

a) A falling ball in air

b) A paper clip lifted by a magnet

c) A cyclist stopping.

2 a) In a thunderstorm, why is there a delay between a lightning flash and hearing the thunder from the flash?

b) Why do we not hear noise from the Sun?

3 a) Why is a permanent magnet made from steel not iron?

b) Why is the core of an electromagnet made from iron not steel?

4 A **Moon** B **A communications satellite**
  C **Jupiter** D **Sun**

a) List the objects A–D in order of increasing distance from the Earth.

b) List the objects A–D in order of increasing mass.

c) Which of the objects A–D orbit the Earth?

d) Which one of the objects A–D causes a solar eclipse?

Making connections

Artificial joints

People who suffer from damaged hip joints can now have replacement joints fitted. A replacement hip joint must be carefully designed to fit the patient. The hip joint is a ball-and-socket joint. The replacement material is carefully chosen to be strong and won't wear away. It needs to last so the patient doesn't need another replacement for many years. When it is first fitted, the patient has to be very careful – one false turn can force the ball out of the socket! You'll learn more about the turning effect of a force in this unit.

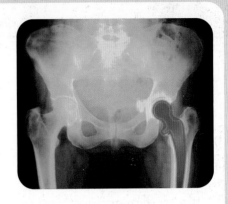

Brain waves

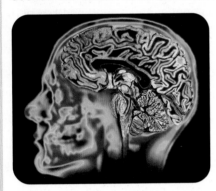

Brain scanners can now be used to locate your thoughts. The MRI scanner was invented by the American chemist, Paul Lauterbur, and the British physicist, Sir Peter Mansfield. For their invention, they were jointly awarded the 2003 Nobel Prize for medicine. MRI stands for Magnetic Resonance Imaging. Magnetic fields are used to scan the brain and make hydrogen atoms in brain tissue emit tiny radio signals. The radio signals are detected and used to produce a visual image of the brain. The images show that seeing or hearing or thinking about different things makes different parts of the brain active. You will find out more about scanners and magnetic fields in this unit.

The endoscope

Doctors use endoscopes to see directly inside the body. For example, an endoscope inserted into the oesophagus can be used to see inside the stomach if a stomach ulcer is suspected. An endoscope consists of two bundles of optical fibres, one to shine light into the body and the other to see what's inside. A tiny lens over the second bundle is used to form an image on the ends of the fibres in the bundle. The image can then be seen at the other end of the fibre bundle. You will find out more about lenses in this unit.

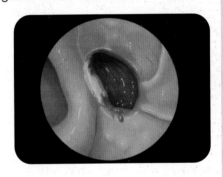

Images from space

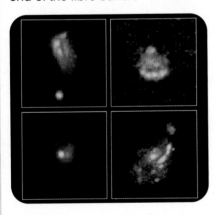

The main component of the Hubble Space Telescope (HST) is a 4.2 metre wide concave mirror. It can gather and focus light from galaxies of stars billions of light years away. Because the HST orbits the Earth high above the atmosphere, light reaching it isn't affected by the atmosphere. So HST images are clearer than images from telescopes on the ground. You will find out more about concave mirrors and stars in this unit.

ACTIVITY

Medical scanners and large telescopes use electric motors to turn heavy objects. Such objects need to be turned so they point in precise directions. Use a low-voltage electric motor to turn an object and see how well you can control the object's position.

Chapters in this unit

○——————○——————○——————○

Turning forces   Light and sound   Electromagnetism   Stars and space

P3 1.1 Moments

LEARNING OBJECTIVES

1 What is a moment and what are its units?
2 How can we calculate the moment of a force?

Figure 1 A turning effect

To undo a very tight wheel-nut on a bicycle, you need a spanner. The force you apply to the spanner has a turning effect on the nut. You couldn't undo a tight nut with your fingers but with the spanner you can undo it. The spanner exerts a much larger turning effect on the nut than the force you apply with your fingers to the spanner.

If you had a choice between a long-handled spanner and a short-handled one, which would you choose? The longer the spanner handle, the less force you need to exert on it to untighten the nut.

In this example, the turning effect of the force, called the **moment** of the force, can be increased by:

● increasing the size of the force,
● using a spanner with a longer handle.

a) What happens if a nut won't undo and you apply too much force to it?

Levers

A crowbar is a lever that can be used to shift a heavy weight. Look at Figure 2.

The weight is called the **load** and the force the person applies to the crowbar is called the **effort**. Using the crowbar, the effort needed to lift the safe is only a small fraction of its weight. The point about which the crowbar turns is called the **pivot**.

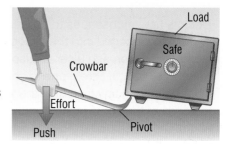

Figure 2 Using a crowbar

b) Would you choose a long crowbar or a short crowbar to shift a heavy weight?

PRACTICAL

Investigating the turning effect of a force

The diagram in Figure 3 shows one way to investigate the turning effect of a force. The weight W is moved along the metre ruler.

● How do you think the reading on the newtonmeter compares with the weight?

You should find that the newtonmeter reading (i.e. the force needed to support the ruler) increases as the weight is increased.

● How does this reading change as the weight is moved away from the pivot?

You should find that the newtonmeter reading increases as the weight is moved away from the pivot.

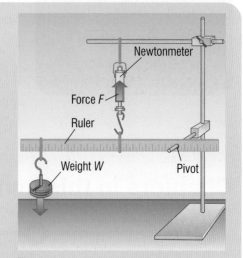

Figure 3 Investigating turning forces

You can work out the **moment** of a force using this equation:

moment = **force** × **perpendicular distance from**
(newton metres, N m)   (newtons, N)   **the pivot to the line of action**
of the force (metres, m)

Learn the definition of moment carefully. In calculations, make sure that your units are consistent.

c) How does the moment of the weight *W* in Figure 3 change as it is moved away from the pivot?

Look at Figure 4. The claw hammer is being used to remove a nail from a wooden beam.

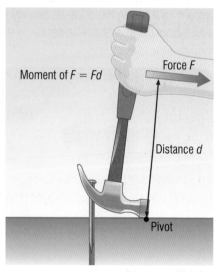

Figure 4 Using a claw hammer

- The applied force *F* on the claw hammer tries to turn it clockwise about the pivot.
- The moment of force *F* about the pivot is $F \times d$, where *d* is the perpendicular distance from the pivot to the line of action of the force.
- The effect of the moment is to cause a much larger force to be exerted on the nail.

DID YOU KNOW?

A patient fitted with a replacement hip joint has to be very careful at first. A slight movement can cause a turning effect that pulls the hip joint apart.

Worked example
A force of 50 N is exerted on a claw hammer of length 0.30 m, as shown in Figure 4. Calculate the moment of the force.

Solution
Force = 50 N × 0.30 m = 15 N m

d) Calculate the moment if the force on the claw hammer had been 70 N.

SUMMARY QUESTIONS

1 In Figure 1, a force is applied to a spanner to undo a nut. State whether the moment of the force is:

   a) clockwise or anticlockwise,
   b) increased or decreased by:
      i) increasing the force,
      ii) exerting the force nearer the nut.

2 a) Explain each of the following statements:
      i) A claw hammer is easier to use to remove a nail if the hammer has a long handle.
      ii) A door with rusty hinges is more difficult to open than a door of the same size with lubricated hinges.
   b) A spanner of length 0.25 m is used to turn a nut as in Figure 1. Calculate the force that needs to be applied to the spanner if the moment it exerts is not to be greater than 18 N m.

KEY POINT

1 The moment of a force *F* about a pivot is $F \times d$, where *d* is the perpendicular distance from the pivot to the line of action of the force.

P3 1.2

Centre of mass

The design of racing cars has changed a lot since the first models. But one thing that has not changed is the need to keep the car near the ground. The weight of the car must be as low as possible. Otherwise the car would overturn when cornering at high speeds.

Figure 1 Racing cars: a) 1920s racing car design, b) modern racing car design

We can think of the weight of an object as if it acts at a single point. This point is called the **centre of mass** (or the centre of gravity) of the object.

The centre of mass of an object is the point where its mass may be thought to be concentrated.

a) Balance a ruler on the tip of your finger. The point of balance is at the centre of mass of the ruler. How far is the centre of mass from the middle of the ruler?

PRACTICAL

Suspended equilibrium

If you suspend an object and then release it, it will come to rest with its centre of mass directly below the point of suspension, as shown in Figure 2a). The object is then in **equilibrium**. Its weight does not exert a turning effect on the object because its centre of mass is directly below the point of suspension.

If the object is turned from this position and then released, it will swing back to its equilibrium position. This is because its weight has a turning effect that returns the object to equilibrium, as shown in Figure 2b).

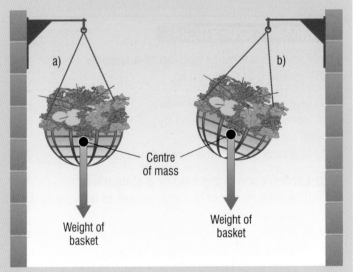

Figure 2 Suspension. a) In equilibrium, b) non-equilibrium.

The centre of mass of a symmetrical object

For a symmetrical object, its centre of mass is along the axis of symmetry. You can see this in Figure 3.

If the object has more than one axis of symmetry, its centre of mass is where the axes of symmetry meet.

- A rectangle has two axes of symmetry, as shown Figure 3a). The centre of mass is where the axes meet.
- The equilateral triangle in Figure 3b) has three axes of symmetry, each bisecting one of the angles of the triangle. The three axes meet at the same point, which is where the centre of mass of the triangle is.

PRACTICAL

A centre of mass test

Figure 4 shows how to find the centre of mass of a flat card. The card is at rest, freely suspended from a pin.

Its centre of mass is directly below the pin. A 'plumbline' can be used to draw a vertical line on the card from the pin downwards.

The procedure is repeated with the card suspended from a second point to give another similar line. The centre of mass of the card is where the two lines meet.

Test your results to see if you can balance the card at this point on the end of a pencil.

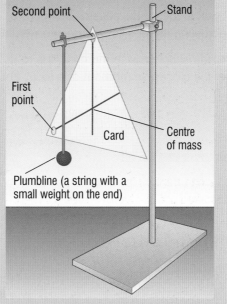

Figure 4 Finding the centre of mass of a card

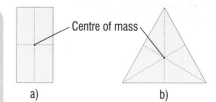

Figure 3 Symmetrical objects

GET IT RIGHT!

Make sure you can describe all the steps in the above experiment.

b) Find the centre of mass of a semicircular card of radius 100 mm.

SUMMARY QUESTIONS

1 Sketch each of the objects shown in the figure and mark its centre of mass.

a)

b)

c)

2 Explain why a child on a swing comes to rest directly below the top of the swing.

KEY POINTS

1 The centre of mass of an object is the point where its mass may be thought to be concentrated.
2 When a suspended object is in equilibrium, its centre of mass is directly beneath the point of suspension.
3 The centre of mass of a symmetrical object is along the axis of symmetry.

P3 1.3   Moments in balance

1 What can we say about the moments of the forces acting on an object that isn't turning?

2 How can we use our knowledge of forces and moments to explain why objects at rest don't turn?

A seesaw is an example in which clockwise and anticlockwise moments might balance each other out. The girl in Figure 1 sits near the pivot to balance her younger brother at the far end of the seesaw. Her brother is not as heavy as his big sister. She sits nearer the pivot than he does. That means her anticlockwise moment about the pivot balances his clockwise moment.

A model seesaw

Look at the model seesaw in Figure 2. The ruler is balanced horizontally by adjusting the position of the two weights. When it is balanced:

- the anticlockwise moment due to W_1 about the pivot = $W_1 d_1$, and
- the clockwise moment due to W_2 about the pivot = $W_2 d_2$

Figure 1 The seesaw

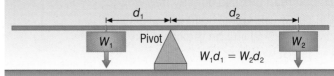

Figure 2 The principle of moments

The anticlockwise moment due to W_1 = the clockwise moment due to W_2

therefore,

$$W_1 d_1 = W_2 d_2$$

a) Use the equation to explain why the girl in Figure 1 needs to sit nearer the pivot than her younger brother.

The seesaw is an example of the **Principle of Moments**. This states that, for an object in equilibrium:

the sum of all the clockwise moments about any point = **the sum of all the anticlockwise moments about that point**

Measuring an unknown weight

You can use the arrangement in Figure 1 to find an unknown weight, W_1, if we know the other weight, W_2, and we measure the distances d_1 and d_2. Then you can calculate the unknown weight using the equation:

$$W_1 d_1 = W_2 d_2$$

Worked example

Calculate W_1 in Figure 3, if $W_2 = 4.0\,\text{N}$, $d_1 = 0.25\,\text{m}$ and $d_2 = 0.20\,\text{m}$.

Solution

Rearranging $W_1 d_1 = W_2 d_2$ gives

$$W_1 = \frac{W_2 d_2}{d_1} = \frac{4.0\,\text{N} \times 0.20\,\text{m}}{0.25\,\text{m}} = 3.2\,\text{N}$$

b) Calculate W_1, if $W_2 = 5.0\,\text{N}$, $d_1 = 0.30\,\text{m}$ and $d_2 = 0.15\,\text{m}$.

PRACTICAL

Measuring the weight of a beam

We can measure the weight of a beam by balancing it off-centre using a known weight. The weight of the beam acts at its centre of mass, which is at distance d_0 from the pivot.

- The moment of the beam about the pivot $= W_0 d_0$ clockwise, where W_0 is the weight of the beam.
- The moment of W_1 about the pivot $= W_1 d_1$ anticlockwise, where d_1 is the perpendicular distance from the pivot to the line of action of W_1.

Applying the principle of moments gives $W_1 d_1 = W_0 d_0$

So we can calculate W_0 if we know W_1 and distances d_1 and d_0.

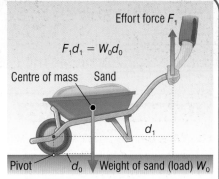

$F_1 d_1 = W_0 d_0$

Effort force F_1

Centre of mass   Sand

d_1

Pivot d_0 Weight of sand (load) W_0

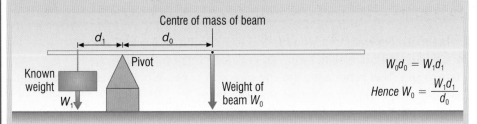

$W_0 d_0 = W_1 d_1$

Hence $W_0 = \dfrac{W_1 d_1}{d_0}$

Figure 3 Finding the weight of a beam

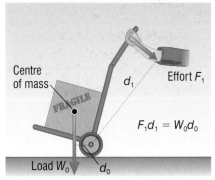

Centre of mass

FRAGILE

d_1 Effort F_1

$F_1 d_1 = W_0 d_0$

Load W_0 d_0

Figure 4 Using moments

c) Calculate the weight of the beam above if $W_1 = 2.0\,\text{N}$, $d_1 = 0.15\,\text{m}$ and $d_0 = 0.25\,\text{m}$.

d) In Figure 4 explain why the effort is smaller than the load.

NEXT TIME YOU...

. . . have to move a heavy load, think beforehand about how to make the job easier. Figure 4 shows a wheelbarrow and a trolley being used to move a load. The load (weight W_0) is lifted and moved using a much smaller effort (force F_1).

SUMMARY QUESTIONS

1 Dawn sits on a seesaw 2.50 m from the pivot. Jasmin balances the seesaw by sitting 2.00 m on the other side of the pivot.

a) Who is lighter, Dawn or Jasmin?

b) Jasmin weighs 425 N. What is Dawn's weight?

c) Dawn gets off the seesaw so John can sit on it to balance Jasmin. His weight is 450 N. How far from the pivot should he sit?

2 For each of the balanced beams in the figure, work out the unknown weight.

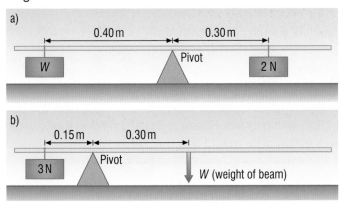

a)

0.40 m   0.30 m

Pivot

W   2 N

b)

0.15 m   0.30 m

Pivot

3 N   W (weight of beam)

GET IT RIGHT!

Make sure the units in your calculations are consistent.

KEY POINT

1 For an object in equilibrium, the sum of the anticlockwise moments about any point = the sum of the clockwise moments about that point.

P3 1.4   Stability

LEARNING OBJECTIVES

1 What factors affect the stability of an object?
2 What will make a body tend to topple?

PRACTICAL

Tilting and toppling tests

How far can you tilt something before it topples over? Figure 1 shows how you can test your ideas using a tall box or a brick on its end.

- If you tilt the brick slightly, as in Figure 1a), and release it, the turning effect of its weight returns it to its upright position.
- If you tilt the brick more, you can just about balance it on one edge, as in Figure 1b). Its centre of mass is then directly above the edge on which it balances. Its weight has no turning effect in this position.
- If you tilt the brick even more, as in Figure 1c), it will topple over if it is released. This is because the line of action of its weight is 'outside' its base. So its weight has a turning effect that makes it topple over.

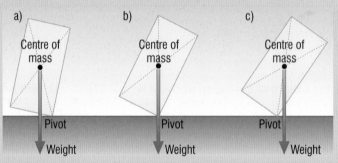

a)   b)   c)

Centre of mass   Centre of mass   Centre of mass

Pivot   Pivot   Pivot

Weight   Weight   Weight

Figure 1 Tilting and toppling. a) Tilted, b) at balance, c) toppled over.

a) Why does the weight of the brick have no turning effect in Figure 1b)?

Stability and safety

Look around you and see how many objects could topple over. Bottles, table lamps and floor-standing bookcases are just a few objects that can easily topple over. Lots of objects are designed for stability so they can't topple over easily.

b) Why do filing cabinets sometimes topple over?

1. Tractor safety

Look at the tractor on a hillside. It doesn't topple over because the line of action of its weight acts within its wheelbase. If it is tilted more, it will topple over when the line of action of its weight acts outside its wheelbase. Its weight would then give a clockwise turning effect about the lower wheel.

c) Why is the engine of a tractor as low as possible?

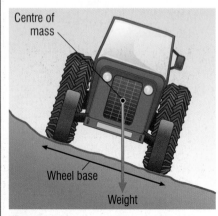

Centre of mass

Wheel base

Weight

Figure 2 Forces on a tilting tractor

2. Bus tests

Figure 3 A toppling test

Look at the double-deck bus. It is being tested to see how much it can tilt without toppling. Such tests are important to make sure buses are safe to travel on, especially when they go round bends and on hilly roads.

d) Would a double-deck bus be more stable or less stable if everyone on it sat upstairs?

3. High chairs

A high chair for a young infant needs to have a wide base. When the child is sitting in it, the centre of mass is above the seat. If the base was narrow, the chair would topple over when the child leant sideways too much.

e) Why are stabiliser wheels fitted to bicycles designed for young children?

SUMMARY QUESTIONS

1 a) Make a list of objects that are designed to be difficult to knock over?
  b) Think of an object that needs to be redesigned because it is knocked over too easily. Sketch the object and explain how it could be redesigned to make it more stable.

2 A well-designed baby chair has a wide base and a low seat.
  a) If the base of a baby chair was too narrow, why would the chair be unsafe?
  b) Why is a baby chair with a low seat safer than one with a high seat?

NEXT TIME YOU...

... go bowling, think about the shape of the pins. A bowling pin has a narrow base and a high centre of mass so it falls over if it is nudged slightly.

GET IT RIGHT!

Remember that bodies with a low centre of mass and a broad base are more stable than bodies with a high centre of mass and a narrow base.

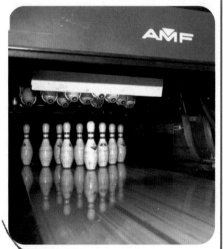

Figure 4 At the bowling alley

KEY POINTS

1 The stability of an object is increased by making its base as wide as possible and its centre of mass as low as possible.
2 An object will tend to topple over if the line of action of its weight is outside its base.

P3 1.5 Circular motion

1 How can a body moving at a steady speed be accelerating?
2 What is the direction of a centripetal force?

Figure 1 A hammer thrower

Fairground rides whirl you round in circles and make your head spin. But you don't need to go to a fairground to see objects moving in circles.

● A vehicle on a roundabout or moving round a corner travels in a circle.
● A satellite moving across the sky moves on a circular orbit round the Earth.
● An athlete throwing a 'hammer' or a discus spins round in a circle before releasing the hammer.

PRACTICAL

Testing circular motion

An object whirled round on the end of a string moves in a circle, as shown in Figure 2. The pull force on the object from the string changes the object's direction of motion.

Figure 2 Whirling an object round

For an object moving in a circle at constant speed, at any instant:

● the object's velocity is directed along a tangent to the circle,
● its velocity changes direction as it moves round,
● the change of velocity is towards the centre of the circle.

The object therefore accelerates continuously towards the centre of the circle.

So the force on the object acts towards the centre of the circle.

a) In Figure 2, which direction would the object move if the string suddenly snapped at the position shown?

Centripetal force

Any object moving in a circle must be acted on by a resultant force that acts towards the centre of the circle. We say the resultant force is a **centripetal** force because it *always* acts towards the centre of the circle.

● The centripetal force on a vehicle moving round a roundabout is due to friction between the tyres and the road.
● The centripetal force on an aircraft circling round is due to the combined effect of its weight and the lift force on it. The centripetal force is the resultant of these two forces.

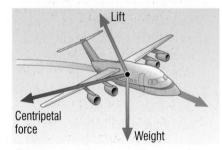

Figure 3 Circling round

b) What causes the centripetal force on a satellite moving in a circular orbit round the Earth?

Centripetal force factors

How much force is needed to keep an object moving in a circle?

You could find out using a radio-controlled model car.

Figure 4 Centripetal force factors

- If it goes too fast, it will skid off in a straight line. The centripetal force needed increases if the speed is increased.
- If the circle is too small, it will skid off. So the centripetal force needed increases if the radius of the circle is decreased.

c) Why is the speed for no skidding much less on an icy roundabout?

How does the force depend on the mass of the object?

If you whirl a rubber bung round on the end of a thread, you can feel the pull force. If you tie another rubber bung on, you will find the pull force (for the same speed and radius) has increased. This shows that the greater the mass of the object, the greater the centripetal force is.

GET IT RIGHT!

- For a body to move in a circle, there must always be a resultant force acting on the body towards the centre of the circle.
- Centripetal force is not a force in its own right; it is always provided by another force such as a gravitational force or an electric force.

SUMMARY QUESTIONS

1 The figure shows an object moving clockwise in a circle at constant speed.

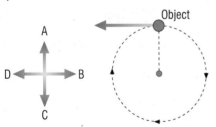

Complete the sentences using directions A, B, C or D as shown in the figure.

a) When the object is at the position shown, its velocity is in direction ...... and the force on it is in direction ....

b) When the object has moved round by 90° from the position shown in the diagram, its velocity is in direction ...... and the force on it is in direction ....

2 In each of the following situations, a single force acts as the centripetal force. Match each situation with the force, a) to d), that causes the circular motion.

    electrostatic force   friction   gravity   pull (tension)

a) A car travelling round a bend.
b) A stone being whirled round on the end of a string.
c) A planet moving round the Sun.
d) An electron orbiting the nucleus of an atom.

KEY POINT

1 For an object moving in a circle at constant speed,
- the object accelerates continuously towards the centre of the circle,
- the centripetal force needed increases, i) as the mass or the speed of the object increases, ii) as the radius of the circle decreases.

P3 1.6

Gravitational attraction

LEARNING OBJECTIVES

1 What is the force of gravity?
2 What factors affect the gravitational attraction between two objects?

What goes up must come down – unless it can overcome the force of gravity acting on it.

The Earth exerts a force of gravity on us all. In fact, any two objects exert a force of gravitational attraction on each other. The force depends on the mass of each object. The Earth is a massive object so its force of gravitational attraction on each of us keeps us on the ground.

a) What keeps the Earth moving in a circle round the Sun?

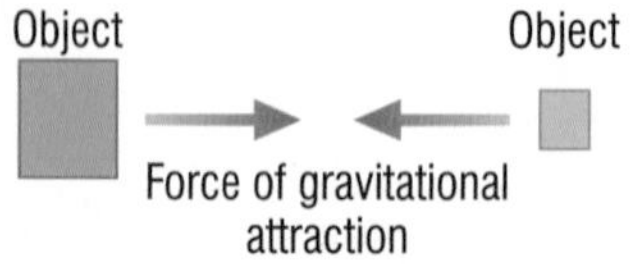

Newton's rules on gravity

Sir Isaac Newton devised the theory of gravity over 300 years ago. He used his theory to explain why the planets orbit the Sun and why the Moon orbits the Earth. He said that the force of gravity between two objects:

- is an attractive force,
- is bigger the greater the mass of each object is,
- is smaller the greater the distance between the two objects is.

He used his theory to make many successful predictions, such as the return of comets.

b) Why is the force of gravitational attraction between two objects in front of you too small to notice?

On a space journey

When a space probe moves away from the Earth towards the Moon, the force of gravity on it:

- due to the Earth decreases as it moves away from the Earth,
- due to the Moon increases as it moves towards the Moon.

c) Why would it be easier to launch a space probe from the Moon than from the Earth?

Gravitational field strength

The gravitational field strength of the Earth at its surface is 10 newtons per kilogram (N/kg).

So the force of gravity on a 50 kg person on the Earth is 500 N (= 50 kg × 10 N/kg). (Look back to page 140 if necessary.)

The gravitational field strength of the Moon at its surface is 1.6 N/kg. So the force of gravity on a 50 kg person on the Moon would be 80 N (= 50 kg × 1.6 N/kg).

Object   Object

Force of gravitational attraction

Figure 1 Gravitational attraction

GET IT RIGHT!

Remember that gravitational forces are always attractive.

DID YOU KNOW...

Gravity keeps us on the Earth without flattening us. But if a black hole came near, nothing could escape from it if it came too near. Its gravitational field would drag objects in so it would become bigger and drag even more objects in. Bursts of gamma radiation from distant galaxies might be the last sign of a star sucked in by a black hole.

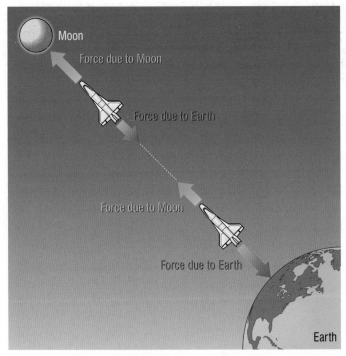

Figure 2 The forces on a space probe

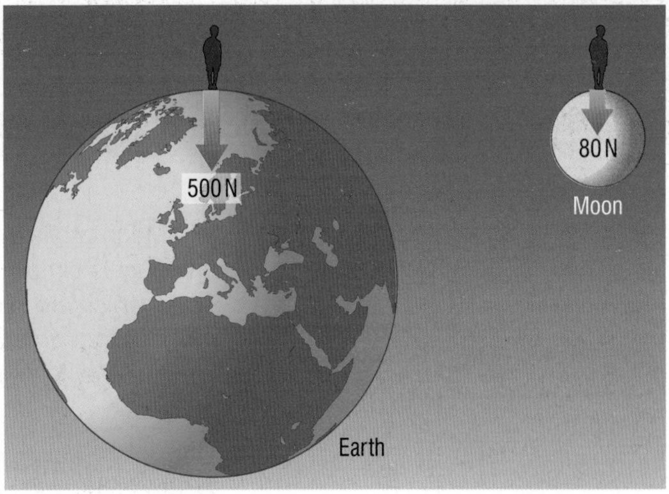

Figure 3 Gravitational field strength

Newtons to kilograms

Use weighing scales marked in newtons to weigh yourself and then work out your mass in kilograms.

Why is an object heavier on the Earth than on the Moon? The reason is that the Earth's mass is much greater so it exerts a greater force on an object on its surface than the Moon does.

d) A space probe is midway between the Earth and the Moon. Which is bigger, the force of gravity on it due to the Earth or the force of gravity due to the Moon?

SCIENCE @ WORK

The force of gravity on an object on the Earth's surface can be affected by what is underneath it. Dense rocks in the Earth would cause a tiny increase in the force of gravity on an object at the surface. By measuring the surface gravity, geophysicists can detect dense substances in the Earth.

SUMMARY QUESTIONS

1 Complete the sentences below using words from the list.

decreases   **increases**   **stays the same**

a) When a comet approaches the Sun, the force of gravity on it ....
b) When a satellite orbits the Earth at a constant height, the size of the force of gravity ....
c) When a rocket leaves the Earth, the force of gravity on it ....

2 a) Explain why an astronaut can walk more easily on the Moon than on the Earth.
b) Explain why you could throw an object higher on the Moon than on the Earth.

KEY POINT

1 The force of gravity between two objects
● is an attractive force,
● is bigger the greater the mass of each object is,
● is smaller the greater the distance between the two objects is.

P3 1.7   Planetary orbits

LEARNING OBJECTIVES

1 What provides the centripetal force that keeps planets and satellites moving in their orbits?
2 How does the time for a planet to orbit the Sun depend on its distance from the Sun?

The Moon orbits the Earth in a circular orbit. The Earth orbits the Sun in an orbit that is almost circular. In general, the planets orbit the Sun in elliptical orbits which are slightly squashed circles. In each case, an object orbits a much bigger object. The centripetal force on the orbiting object is due to the force of gravitational attraction between it and the larger object.

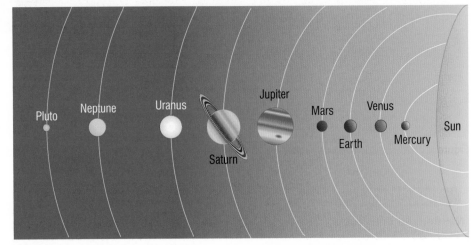

Figure 1 Planetary orbits (not to scale)

a) If the Earth's orbit were more elliptical, how would we be affected?

Look at the diagram in Figure 2. It shows the force of gravity acting on a planet in a circular (or almost circular) orbit round the Sun. The force of gravity on the planet due to the Sun acts towards the centre of the Sun. The planet's direction of motion is changed by this force so it continues to circle the Sun.

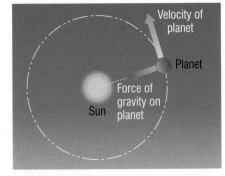

Figure 2 A circular orbit

To stay in orbit at a particular distance, a planet must move at a particular speed around the Sun.

● If its speed is too low, it will spiral into the Sun.
● If its speed is too high, it will fly off its orbit and move away from the Sun.

The further a planet is from the Sun, the less its speed is as its moves round the Sun.

This is because the force of gravity is weaker further from the Sun. So the speed of the planet needs to be less than if it were closer to the Sun. Otherwise, the planet would fly off its orbit and move away from the Sun.

The further a planet is from the Sun, the longer it takes to make a complete orbit.

This is because the distance round the orbit, i.e. the circumference, is greater and the planet moves slower. So the time for each complete orbit (= circumference ÷ speed) is longer.

b) The table shows the average radius of orbit for some of the planets and the time for each complete orbit. How does this show that the speed of Jupiter is less than the speed of the Earth?

Planet	Radius of orbit (AU)	Time for each orbit (years)
Mercury	0.39	0.24
Venus	0.72	0.61
Earth	1.00	1.00
Mars	1.52	1.88
Jupiter	5.20	11.9
Saturn	9.53	29.5

1 astronomical unit (AU) = mean distance from the Sun to the Earth

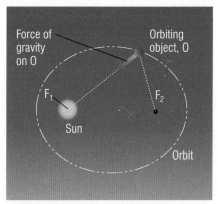

Figure 3 An elliptical orbit
1. The orbit is defined by the two 'foci' F_1 and F_2, (such that the sum of the distances OF_1 and OF_2 is constant).
2. The Sun is at one focus of the ellipse.

> **DID YOU KNOW?**
>
> Many asteroids orbit the Sun in elliptical orbits between Mars and Jupiter. Sometimes they collide and get thrown into orbits that cross the Earth's orbit. An asteroid impact with the Earth about 65 million years ago is thought to have finished off the dinosaurs. Figure 3 shows an object in an elliptical orbit around the Sun.

SUMMARY QUESTIONS

1 Choose the correct word from the list below to complete each of the sentences a) to d).

Earth   planet   satellite   Sun

a) The Moon is a natural ...... in orbit round the ....
b) A communications satellite stays in its orbit because of the force of gravity between it and the ....
c) The further a ...... is from the Earth, the slower its speed is and the longer it takes to orbit the ....
d) The orbit of a ...... is almost circular with the ...... near the centre of the orbit.

2 a) Use the information in the table above to deduce which of the three planets, Venus, Earth or Jupiter, travels
   i) slowest,
   ii) fastest on its orbit.
   b) The Earth moves in its orbit at a speed of about 30 km/s. Use the information in the table to estimate the speed of Mercury in its orbit.

> **KEY POINTS**
>
> 1 To stay in orbit at a particular distance, a small body must move at a particular speed around a larger body.
> 2 The larger an orbit is, the longer the orbiting body takes to go round the orbit.

P3 1.8 Satellites

Figure 1 A hand-held GPS receiver

If you go to a remote area or go sailing at sea, take a GPS receiver with you. Then you will know exactly where you are. Global positioning satellites (GPS) send out signals that are used by a receiver to pinpoint its position. A GPS receiver fitted to a car tells a driver exactly where the car is and which direction it is going in.

a) Why is a GPS receiver useful to a mountaineer?

Satellite orbits

Every satellite orbiting the Earth was launched into its orbit from the ground or from a space vehicle. Imagine launching a satellite into orbit from the top of a very tall mountain. Look at Figure 2.

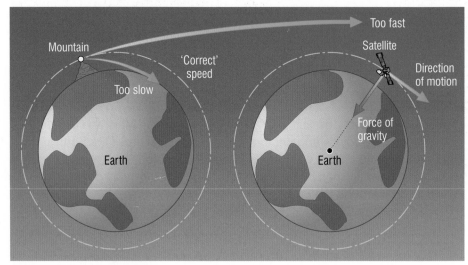

Figure 2 Launching a satellite

- If the satellite's speed is too low, it will fall to the ground.
- If its initial speed is too great, it will fly off into space.
- At the 'correct' speed, it orbits the Earth.

For two satellites in orbits at different heights, the satellite in the higher orbit moves at a slower speed and travels further on each complete orbit. So the satellite in the higher orbit takes longer than the other satellite to complete each orbit.

The period of a satellite is the time it takes to make one complete orbit.

b) A satellite has a period of 2 hours. How many complete orbits would it make in 24 hours?

Using satellites

We use satellites for communications and for monitoring.

- **Communications satellites** are usually in an orbit at a particular height above the equator so they have a period of 24 hours. They orbit the Earth in the same direction as the Earth's spin. So they stay above the same place on the Earth's surface as they go round the Earth. We describe such orbits as **geostationary**.

Geostationary orbits are about 36 000 kilometres above the Earth. The force of gravity there keeps a satellite moving in a circular orbit with a period of 24 hours.

Figure 3 A satellite in orbit

- **Monitoring satellites** are fitted with TV cameras pointing to the Earth. We use them for many purposes, including weather forecasting, military and police surveillance and for environmental monitoring. They are in much lower orbits than geostationary satellites. This is so we can see as much detail on the Earth as possible. They orbit the Earth once every two or three hours. Their orbits usually take them over the Earth's poles so they can scan the whole Earth every day.

c) Why is it not possible to put satellites into really low orbits?

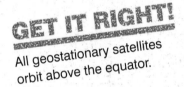

GET IT RIGHT!

All geostationary satellites orbit above the equator.

SUMMARY QUESTIONS

1 Complete the sentences below using words from the list.

equator   high   low   poles

a) A geostationary satellite is in a …… orbit that is directly above the Earth's …… .

b) A monitoring satellite is in a …… orbit that is directly above the Earth's …… .

2 GPS satellites orbit the Earth about once every 12 hours.

a) Does a GPS satellite orbit the Earth above or below i) a geostationary satellite, ii) a weather satellite that has a period of 2 hours?

b) Why are GPS satellites easier to launch than geostationary satellites?

KEY POINTS

1 A satellite in a geostationary orbit has a period of 24 hours and stays at the same position directly above the Earth's equator.

2 Geostationary orbits are usually used for communication satellites.

3 Monitoring satellites are usually in low polar orbits.

229

P3 1.9   Turning issues

Roller coaster rides

Make a rating system for fairground rides. For example,

*   a ride on a train moving at steady speed on a straight track would be suitable for infants accompanied by parents,

**   a ride on a roundabout turning at a moderate steady speed would be suitable for junior-age children,

***   etc.

You do the rest.

ACTIVITY

A risk assessment of an activity is a 'Health and Safety' assessment of all the extra possible risks compared with an 'everyday' activity. Make a risk assessment of a fairground ride and say what should be done to reduce the risk.

Artificial limbs

Modern artificial limbs are very different to the wooden limbs fitted to people long ago.

An artificial hand is fitted with sensors and lightweight motors so the wearer can use it to pick objects up, turn them over and move them about.

Many children in war-torn countries have been injured by weapons such as land mines. Although the use of land mines has been banned, many unexploded mines remain undetected – until people step on them. Non-governmental organisations (NGOs) such as 'Save the Children' work with the United Nations to help people in poor countries who need artificial limbs.

ACTIVITY

a) Do a survey to find out if
    i)   people think the issue of landmines has gone away,
    ii) the Government should make weapons manufacturers pay to help civilians injured by their weapons.

b) Design a poster to raise public awareness about landmines.

Satellite tracking – Big Brother!

In George Orwell's compelling book *Nineteen Eighty-Four*, televisions controlled by 'Big Brother' spy on people and the 'Thought Police' control what everyone thinks and does.

The UK Government wants to bring in 'road pricing' by using satellite technology to monitor motorists. Every road vehicle would be tracked and drivers made to pay for their journeys.

Motorway driving and city centre driving will cost much more than driving in rural areas. The Government claims satellites linked to computers would keep track of every vehicle.

ACTIVITY

a) At present, hand-held receivers can pick up signals from GPS satellites. Why do you think it would be more difficult for satellites to pick up signals from hand-held transmitters?

b) Some people claim that satellite tracking of vehicles could turn the country into a totalitarian 'Big Brother' state. Other people think satellite tracking is the only sensible way to cut congestion on our roads. They say 'Big Brother' concerns are a fantasy. Discuss and debate the issues with your friends.

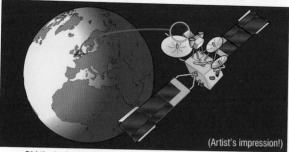

A LUCKY MISS!

(Artist's impression!)

Did the junk come from a communications satellite?

Fred Green is the luckiest person in the country. A piece of space junk dropped out of the sky and hit the ground next to him. It destroyed his favourite rose bush. A few moments earlier, he had been cutting some roses from the bush!

With more and more satellites in space, there's going to be more and more junk whirling round the Earth – used rockets, redundant satellites, solar panels that snap off. Some space junk will re-enter the atmosphere and burn up. Some of it will crash to the ground. It is not likely to go away. But should we just ignore it as more and more junk accumulates in orbits above the Earth?

Imagine we're in the 25th century and a space refuse collection service has been set up. Write a job advert for a space refuse collector, highlighting all the perks. Turn the drawbacks like cosmic radiation into 'benefits'.

Paying for space

Lots of money is spent on space exploration and space technology. Most of the money is from taxes. People have different views about paying for space.

It's good for our image.

We can track down criminals quicker.

We all benefit from space exploration and technology.

I think the money would be better spent on other things such as health.

a) With the help of your friends, list the direct benefits you get from space exploration and space technology.

b) The next big step into space will probably be to send astronauts to Mars. Would you like to go on this epic journey? Discuss your views in a small group.

231

SUMMARY QUESTIONS

1 The figure shows a toy suspended from a ceiling.

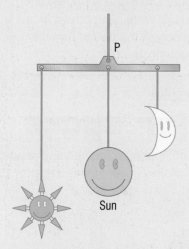

Sun

a) How would the stability of the toy be affected if the Sun was removed from it?

b) The star on the toy has a weight of 0.04 N and is a distance of 0.30 m from the point P where the thread is attached to the toy.

   Calculate the moment of the star about P.

2 The crescent moon attached to the toy in question 1 is at a distance of 0.20 m from P. Calculate the weight of the crescent. [Higher]

3 A space station and a small satellite are in the same orbit above the Earth.

   Copy and complete the following sentences using words from the list.

   greater than   less than   equal to

   a) The speed of the space station is …… the speed of the satellite.

   b) The centripetal force needed by the space station is …… the centripetal force needed by the satellite.

   c) The force of gravity on the satellite is …… the force of gravity on the space station.

   d) The time taken for the satellite to orbit the Earth once is …… the time taken by the space station to orbit the Earth once.

4 a) i) What is the period and direction of motion of a geostationary satellite?
   ii) Describe the orbit of a geostationary satellite.

   b) Explain why a geostationary satellite would be no use for weather forecasting.

EXAM-STYLE QUESTIONS

1 (a) What is meant by the *centre of mass* of an object? (1)

   (b) The drawing shows a thin sheet of card. There are holes in the card at **A** and **B**.

   Describe how you would find the centre of mass of the sheet of card.

   Include a diagram with your answer. (6)

2 The diagram shows a painter standing on a plank. The plank rests on two supports.

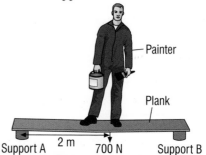

Support A   2 m   700 N   Support B

The weight of the painter is 700 N. He is standing 2 m from support **A**.

   (a) Calculate the moment of his weight about support **A**. (4)

   (b) The painter moves along the plank away from support **A**.

   State and explain what happens to the moment of his weight about support **A**. (2)

3 A teacher is talking to her class about circular motion. She demonstrates with a bung fastened to a piece of rubber tubing that she swings around in a horizontal circle.

The diagram below shows an overhead view of the bung.

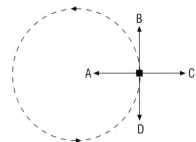

(a) (i) In which direction, **A**, **B**, **C** or **D**, does the centripetal force act?

(ii) The teacher lets go of the tubing at the instant shown in the diagram.

In which direction, **A**, **B**, **C** or **D**, does the bung move? (2)

(b) What will happen to the centripetal force if the teacher:

(i) uses a bung with a smaller mass?

(ii) swings the bung more slowly?

(iii) swings the bung on a shorter piece of tubing? (3)

(c) In each case in part (b) she keeps all the other variables constant, apart from the variable under investigation.

(i) What do we call the variables that are kept constant in an investigation? (1)

(ii) What is the general name for the 'variable under investigation'? (1)

4 There are many satellites orbiting the Earth in circular paths.

(a) (i) What force provides the centripetal force that allows satellites to maintain their circular orbits? (1)

(ii) A satellite moving at a steady speed in a circular orbit is continuously accelerating.

Explain why. (2)

(b) Some satellites are in *geostationary orbits*.

(i) What is meant by a *geostationary orbit*? (1)

(ii) What is the time period of a geostationary orbit? (1)

(iii) What type of satellite is usually put into a geostationary orbit? (1)

HOW SCIENCE WORKS

Springboards are about 5 metres long, 50 cm wide and 4 cm thick. They are made from an aluminium centre and a plastic coating. You have devised a new method of construction and you need to test your new construction. Some of the properties of the board can be tested by placing masses on the springboard and making suitable measurements.

Look at the drawing of the springboard and decide how you are to test it.

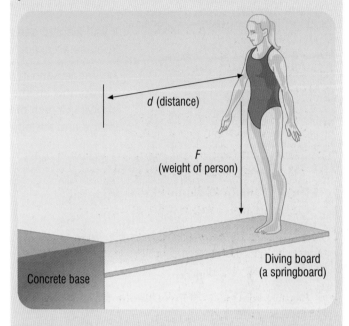

a) What will be your independent variable? (1)

b) What will be your dependent variable? (1)

c) Suggest a suitable range for your independent variable. (1)

d) Suggest a suitable number of interval measurements for the independent variable. (1)

e) What sensitivity would you require for measuring your dependent variable? (1)

f) State two control variables you should use. (2)

g) Draw a table for your results. (3)

P3 2.1   Reflection

1 What is an angle of incidence?
2 What can we say about the reflection of a light ray at a plane mirror?

If you have visited a 'Hall of Mirrors' at a funfair, you will know that the shape of a mirror affects what you see. If you see:

● a tall, thin image of yourself, you are looking in a **convex mirror**, which is one that bends out,
● a short, broad image of yourself, you are looking into a **concave mirror**, which is a mirror that bends in.

If you want to see a normal image of yourself, look in a plane (i.e. flat) mirror. You see an exact 'mirror' image of yourself.

An image seen in a mirror is due to **reflection of light** by the mirror. Figure 1b) shows how an image of a point object is formed by a plane mirror. The diagram shows the path of two light rays from the object that reflect off the mirror. The image and the object in Figure 1 are equal distances from the mirror.

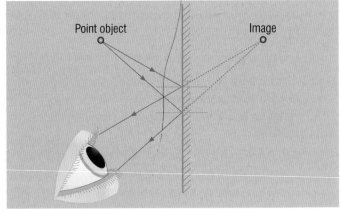

Figure 1 a) Mirror images

b) Image formation by a plane mirror

a) If you stand 0.5 m in front of a plane mirror, your image is 0.5 m behind the mirror.
What is the distance between you and your image?

Investigating the reflection of light

We can use a ray box and a plane mirror to investigate reflection, as shown in Figure 2.

● What did you find out?
● Comment on the reliability of your investigation. (See pages 5, 9 and 15.)

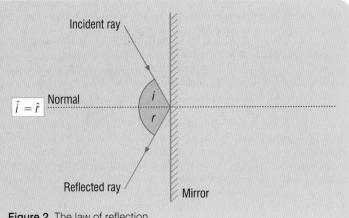

Figure 2 The law of reflection

Look at Figure 2.

The perpendicular line to the mirror is called the **normal**.

The **angle of incidence** is the angle between the incident ray and the normal.

The **angle of reflection** is the angle between the reflected ray and the normal.

Measurements show that for any light ray reflected by a mirror:

angle of incidence = angle of reflection

b) If the angle of reflection of a light ray from a plane mirror is 20°, what is:
  i) the angle of incidence,
  ii) the angle between the incident ray and the reflected ray?

Real and virtual images

The image in Figure 1 is a **virtual image**. When you look at a mirror image, the light rays that reflect off the mirror into your eye appear to come from the image. A virtual image can't be projected onto a screen like the movie images that you see at a cinema. An image like this is described as a **real image** because it is formed by focusing light rays onto a screen.

c) When you use a face mirror, is your image real or virtual?

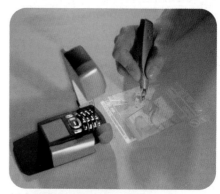

Figure 3 A real image formed by a mobile phone projector

SCIENCE @ WORK

Ambulances and police cars often carry a 'mirror image' sign at the front. This is so a driver in a vehicle in front looking into the rear-view mirror can read the sign.

Figure 4 A mirror sign on an ambulance

GET IT RIGHT!

Remember that angles of incidence, reflection and refraction are always measured between the ray and the normal.

Real images are formed where rays of light (from the same point on the object) cross, so they can be formed on a screen. Virtual images cannot be formed on a screen, they are just where rays of light appear to have come from.

SUMMARY QUESTIONS

1 Two plane mirrors are placed perpendicular to each other. Draw a ray diagram to show the path of a light ray at an angle of incidence of 60° that reflects off both mirrors.

2 A point object O is placed in front of a plane mirror, as shown:

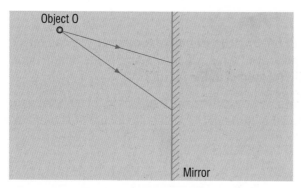

a) Copy and complete the path of the two rays from O after they have reflected off the mirror.

b) i) Use the reflected rays to locate the image of O.
   ii) Show that the image and the object are equidistant from the mirror.

KEY POINTS

1 The **normal** at a point on a mirror is perpendicular to the mirror.
2 For a light ray reflected by a mirror,
   angle of incidence = angle of reflection

P3 2.2
Curved mirrors

Figure 1 Using a concave mirror

The concave mirror

You can see some strange things when you look in a giant concave mirror.

● When you look closely at it, you should see an enlarged image of your face.
● Retreat from the mirror and your image will retreat and become blurred.
● Keep moving and your image will reappear – upside down and very small!

a) i) Is your close-up image real or virtual?
   ii) Is your upside-down image real or virtual?

Image formation by a concave mirror

Figure 2 shows how a concave mirror forms a real image of a distant object. The light rays from any point of an object are focused by the mirror to the same point.

1 **For a distant point object**, the light rays are effectively parallel when they reach the mirror. Then they are focused to the principal focus (or focal point), F, of the mirror. A real image of the object is formed here.

The distance from the mirror to the principal focus is called the **focal length**, f, of the mirror. (See Figure 2 below.)

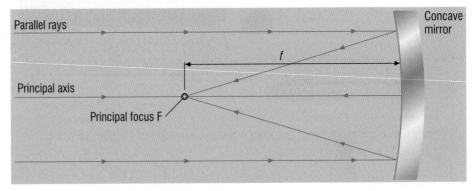

Figure 2 The focal length (f) of a concave mirror

2 **For an object beyond the principal focus**, an inverted real image is formed by the reflected rays. The position and size of the image depends on the distance from the object to the mirror.

Figure 3 shows how to draw a ray diagram to locate the image. The light rays from the tip of the object are used to locate the tip of the image.

The **magnification** of the image is:

$$\frac{\text{the image height}}{\text{the object height}}$$

b) A concave mirror is used to form a real image of a slide of height 20 mm. The height of the image is 50 mm. Calculate the magnification of the image.

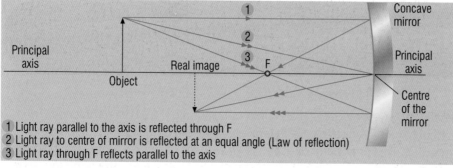

1 Light ray parallel to the axis is reflected through F
2 Light ray to centre of mirror is reflected at an equal angle (Law of reflection)
3 Light ray through F reflects parallel to the axis

Figure 3 Using a concave mirror to form a real image

3 ***For an object between the focal point and the mirror***, the reflected rays form an upright virtual image of the object. Figure 4 shows how the image is formed using 3 key construction rays. The image is magnified and is behind the mirror, as in Figure 4.

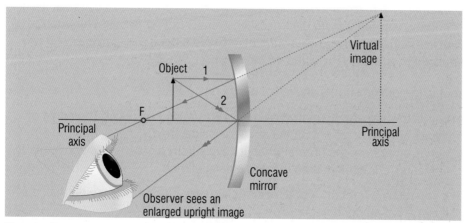

Figure 4 Using a concave mirror to form a virtual image

c) Describe the image you see when you look at yourself in a concave mirror?

The convex mirror

We use convex mirrors as rear-view mirrors in cars. The driver has a much wider field of view than with a plane mirror. Figure 5a) shows why. The image of an object viewed in a convex mirror is virtual and smaller than the object as shown in Figure 5b).

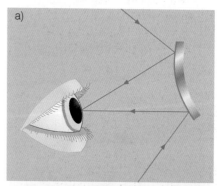

Figure 5 A rear-view mirror

SUMMARY QUESTIONS

1 Complete the following sentences using words from the list:

behind   in front   inverted   real   upright   virtual

a) The image formed by a concave mirror of a distant tree is ...... and .... The location of the image is ...... of the mirror.

b) The image formed by a convex mirror of a distant tree is ...... and .... The location of the image is ...... the mirror.

2 a) An object is placed midway between a concave mirror and its principal focus. Draw a ray diagram to show the formation by the concave mirror of the image of this object.

b) Describe the image and calculate its magnification.

KEY POINTS

1 The **principal focus** of a concave mirror is the point where parallel rays are focused to by the mirror.

2 A **concave mirror** forms:
   • a real image if the object is beyond the principal focus of the mirror,
   • a virtual image if the object is between the mirror and the principal focus.

3 A **convex mirror** always forms a virtual image of an object.

P3 2.3 Refraction

LEARNING OBJECTIVES

1 What is refraction?
2 Why does a glass prism split white light?

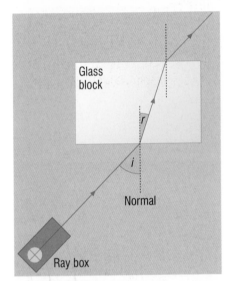

Figure 1 Refraction of light

When you have your eyes tested, the optician might test different lenses in front of each of your eyes. Each lens changes the direction of light passing through it. This change of direction is known as **refraction**. People with sharp eyes don't need extra lenses. Each eye already has a perfectly good lens in it.

PRACTICAL

Investigating refraction

You can use a ray box and a rectangular glass block to investigate refraction.

Look at Figure 1. You should find that a light ray changes its direction at the boundary between air and glass (unless it is along the normal). This change of direction happens whenever a light ray crosses a boundary between any two transparent substances (including air).

Your investigation should show that a light ray:

● bends towards the normal when it travels from air into glass. The angle of refraction, *r*, is smaller than the angle of incidence, *i*.
● bends away from the normal when it travels from glass into air. The angle of refraction, *r*, is greater than the angle of incidence, *i*.

a) If you direct a light ray into a rectangular glass block along the normal, does it come out along the normal?

Explaining refraction

Refraction is a property of all forms of waves including light and sound.

Look at Figure 2. It shows how we can demonstrate refraction using water waves in a ripple tank.

A glass plate is submerged in a ripple tank. The water above the glass plate is shallower than the water in the rest of the tank. The waves are slower in shallow water than in deep water. Because they change speed when they cross the boundary, they change direction:

● towards the normal when they cross from deep to shallow water and slow down,
● away from the normal when they cross from shallow to deep water and speed up.

b) Why do waves on a beach 'break' as they approach the shore?

The speed of light

Light travels slower in glass than in air.

● When a light ray travels from air to glass, it refracts towards the normal because it slows down on entering the glass.
● When a light ray travels from glass to air, it refracts away from the normal because it speeds up on leaving the glass.

c) Is the speed of light after it comes out of glass less than, more than, or the same as the speed before it enters the glass?

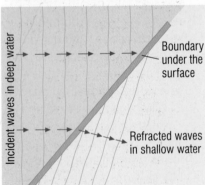

Figure 2 Refraction of water waves

PRACTICAL

Investigating refraction by a prism

If you direct a beam of white light into a glass prism, you should find that the beam is split into the colours of the spectrum.

Each colour of light is refracted slightly differently. This is because the speed of light in glass depends on the wavelength of the light.

Blue light has a shorter wavelength than red light. Blue light travels slower than red light in glass. So it is refracted more than red light.

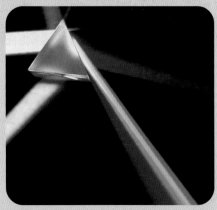

Figure 4 Refraction by a prism

- Why does the spectrum form?

d) Green light is between red and blue light in the spectrum. Does green light in glass travel faster or slower than
   i) red light,
   ii) blue light?

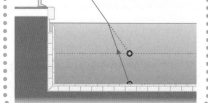
SUMMARY QUESTIONS

1 Choose words from the list to complete the sentences below.

away from   decreases   increases   towards

a) When a light ray travels from air into glass, its speed ...... and it bends ...... the normal.
b) When a light ray travels from glass into air, its speed ...... and it bends ...... the normal.
c) When a light ray travels from water into glass, it bends towards the normal and its speed ....

2 a) Copy and complete the path of the light ray through each glass object below.

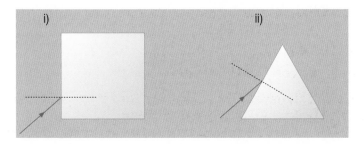

b) Explain what is observed when a beam of white light passes through a prism as in Figure 4 above.

GET IT RIGHT!

Remember that a prism bends blue light more than red light.

KEY POINT

1 Refraction of light is the change of direction of a light ray when it crosses a boundary between two transparent substances.
- If the speed is reduced, refraction is towards the normal (e.g. air to glass).
- If the speed is increased, refraction is away from the normal (e.g. glass to air).

P3 2.4   Lenses

LEARNING OBJECTIVES

1 What is a converging lens?
2 What do we use converging lenses for?
3 What is a diverging lens and what can we use it for?

Figure 1 Cameras. a) An early camera, b) a digital video camera.

SCIENCE @ WORK

A diverging lens is the opposite to a magnifying glass. It always forms a virtual image of an object and makes it appear nearer (and smaller). Opticians use them to correct eyes that can't see distant objects (short sight). A diverging lens makes a distant object nearer so the viewer sees it clearly.

Lenses are used in optical devices such as the camera. Although a digital camera is very different from the very first cameras made over 160 years ago, they both contain a lens that is used to form an image.

Types of lenses

A lens works by changing the direction of light passing through it. Figure 2 shows the effect of a lens on the light rays from a ray box. The curved shape of the lens surfaces refracts the rays so they meet at a point.

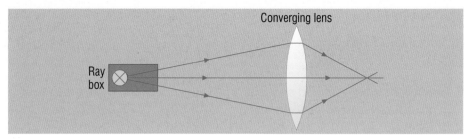

Figure 2 Investigating lenses

Different lens shapes can be tested using this arrangement.

● A **converging lens** makes parallel rays converge to a focus. The point where *parallel* rays are focused to is the **principal focus** (or focal point) of the lens.
● A **diverging lens** makes parallel rays diverge (i.e. spread out). The point where the rays appear to come from is the **principal focus** of the lens.

In both cases, the distance from the centre of the lens to the principal focus is the **focal length** of the lens.

a) Which is stronger, a lens with a focal length of 5 cm or one with a focal length of 50 cm?

PRACTICAL

Investigating the converging lens

Use the arrangement in Figure 3 to investigate the image formed by a converging lens.

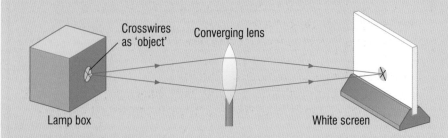

Figure 3 Investigating images

(1) With the object at different distances beyond the principal focus of the lens, adjust the position of the screen until you see a clear image of the object on it. The image is **real** because it is formed on the screen where the light rays meet.

- When the object is a long distance away, the image is formed at the principal focus of the lens. This is because the rays from any point of the object are effectively parallel to each other when they reach the lens.
- If the object is moved nearer the lens towards its principal focus, the screen must be moved further from the lens to see a clear image. The nearer the object is to the lens, the larger the image is.

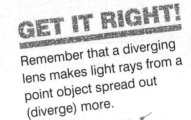

GET IT RIGHT!

Remember that a diverging lens makes light rays from a point object spread out (diverge) more.

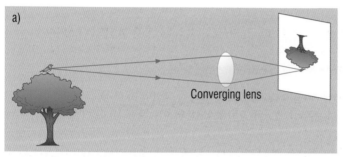

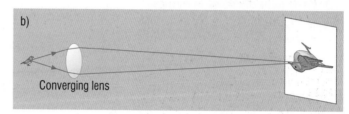

Figure 4 a) The image of a distant object, b) an enlarged image

b) Is the image inverted or upright in Figure 4a)?

(2) With the object nearer to the lens than the principal focus, a magnified virtual image is formed. But you can only see the image when you look into the lens from the other side to the object. The lens acts as a **magnifying glass** in this situation. Use the lens to magnify different objects.

c) Why is a diamond usually inspected with a magnifying glass?

SUMMARY QUESTIONS

1 Copy and complete the following sentences using words from the list.

converging   diverging   real   virtual

a) A …… lens can be used to focus light from an object on to a screen. The image of the object is a …… image.

b) A …… lens can be used to make light rays from a point object spread out more. The image of the object is a …… image.

2 a) A postage stamp is inspected using a converging lens as a magnifying glass. Describe the image.

b) A converging lens is used to form a magnified image of a slide on to a screen.

i) Describe the image formed by the lens.

ii) The screen is moved away from the lens. What adjustment must be made to the position of the slide to focus its image on the screen again?

c) Describe the image of the bird in Figure 4b) and calculate the magnification produced by the lens.

Figure 5 A magnifying glass

KEY POINTS

1 A **real image** is formed by a converging lens if the object is further away than its principal focus.

2 A **virtual image** is formed by a diverging lens and by a converging lens if the object is nearer than the principal focus.

P3 2.5 — Using lenses

The position and nature of the image formed by a lens depends on:

- the focal length of the lens, and
- the distance from the object to the lens.

If we know the focal length and the object distance, we can find the position and nature of the image by drawing a ray diagram.

Formation of a real image by a converging lens

The object must be beyond the principal focus, F, of the lens, as shown in Figure 1. The image is formed on the other side of the lens to the object.

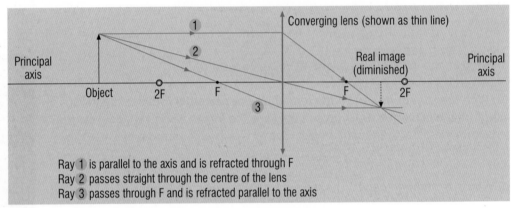

Ray **1** is parallel to the axis and is refracted through F
Ray **2** passes straight through the centre of the lens
Ray **3** passes through F and is refracted parallel to the axis

Figure 1 Formation of a real image by a converging lens

The diagram shows that:

- three key 'construction' rays from a single point of the object are used to locate the image,
- the image is real, inverted and smaller than the object.

Notice that:

1 **ray 1** is refracted through F, the principal focus of the lens, because it is parallel to the lens axis before the lens,

2 **ray 2** passes through the lens at its centre without change of direction; this is because the lens surfaces are parallel to each other at the axis,

3 **ray 3** passes through F, the principal focus of the lens, before the lens so it is refracted by the lens parallel to the axis.

The image is smaller than the object because the object distance is greater than twice the focal length (*f*) of the lens. This is how a **camera** is used.

a) i) Draw a ray diagram to show that a real, inverted and magnified image is produced if the object is between *f* and 2*f* from the lens.
   ii) What optical device projects a magnified image on to a screen?

The camera

In a camera, a converging lens is used to produce a real image of an object on a film (or on an array of 'pixels' in the case of a digital camera). The position of the lens is adjusted to focus the image on the film, according to how far away the object is.

- For a distant object, the distance from the lens to the film must be equal to the focal length of the lens.

- The nearer an object is to the lens, the greater the distance from the lens to the film.

b) If an object moves closer to the camera, does the lens of a camera need to be moved towards or away from the object?

Formation of a virtual image by a converging lens

The object must be between the lens and its principal focus, as shown in Figure 3. The image is formed on the same side of the lens as the object.

The diagram shows that the image is virtual, upright and larger than the object.

The image can only be seen by looking at it through the lens. This is how a **magnifying glass** works.

c) Why did Sherlock Holmes always carry a magnifying glass?

Formation of a virtual image by a diverging lens

The image formed by a diverging lens is always virtual, upright and smaller than the object. Figure 4 shows why.

d) Why is a diverging lens no use as a magnifying glass?

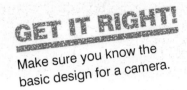
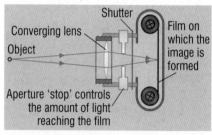

Figure 2 The camera

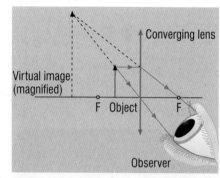

Figure 3 Formation of a virtual image by a converging lens

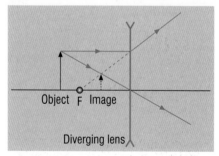

Figure 4 Image formation by a concave lens

SUMMARY QUESTIONS

1 a) Copy and complete the ray diagram to show how a converging lens in a camera forms an image of an object.

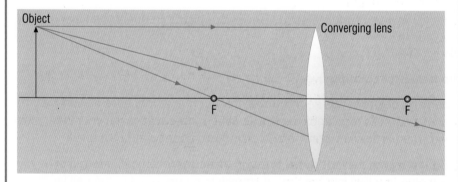

   b) State whether the image is i) real or virtual, ii) magnified or diminished, iii) upright or inverted.

2 a) Draw a ray diagram to show how a converging lens is used as a magnifying glass.
   b) State whether the image is i) real or virtual, ii) magnified or diminished, iii) upright or inverted.

KEY POINTS

1 A **camera** contains a converging lens that is used to form a real image of an object.
2 A **magnifying glass** is a converging lens that is used to form a virtual image of an object.

P3 2.6 Sound

LEARNING OBJECTIVES

1 What range of frequencies can be detected by the human ear?
2 Why can't sound travel through space?
3 What are the main differences between light and sound waves?

GET IT RIGHT!

Be sure you know the similarities and differences between light and sound.

Figure 2 Making sound waves

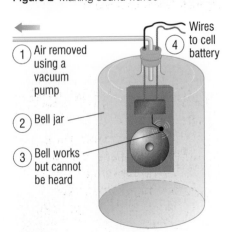

① Air removed using a vacuum pump

② Bell jar

③ Bell works but cannot be heard

④ Wires to cell battery

Figure 3 A sound test

PRACTICAL

Investigating sound waves

Sound waves are easy to produce. Your vocal cords vibrate and produce sound waves every time you speak. Any object vibrating in air creates sound waves. You can use a loudspeaker to produce sound waves by passing alternating current through it. Figure 1 shows how to do this using a signal generator. This is an alternating current supply unit with a variable frequency dial.

● If you observe the loudspeaker closely, you can see it vibrating. It pushes the surrounding air backwards and forwards.
● If the loudspeaker is connected to a 'signal generator', you can change the frequency of the sound waves it produces. The frequency of the waves gives the pitch of the sound. The higher the frequency, the higher the pitch.
● Find out the lowest and the highest frequency you can hear. Young people can usually hear sound frequencies from about 20 Hz to about 20 000 Hz. Older people in general can't hear frequencies at the higher end of this range.

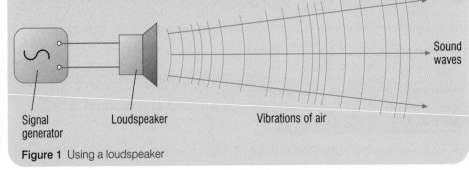

Signal generator   Loudspeaker   Vibrations of air   Sound waves

Figure 1 Using a loudspeaker

a) Which animal produces sound waves at a higher frequency, an elephant or a mouse?

The nature of sound waves

A vibrating object sends sound waves through the air because its surface pushes and pulls repeatedly on the air. When the waves reach your ears, they make your eardrums vibrate in and out so you hear sound as a result.

● **Sound waves cannot travel through a vacuum**. You can test this by listening to a bell in a 'bell jar'. As the air is pumped out of the bell jar, the ringing sound fades away.

b) What would you notice if the air is let back into the bell jar?

● **Sound waves are longitudinal waves**. The waves vibrate along the direction they travel in. Electromagnetic waves (e.g. light) are transverse waves. They vibrate at right angles to the direction they travel in.

PRACTICAL

Use a slinky spring to demonstrate how sound waves travel. If you move one end backwards and forwards, longitudinal waves travel along the slinky.

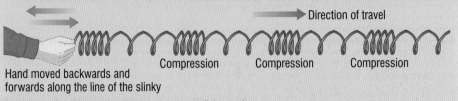

Hand moved backwards and forwards along the line of the slinky

Direction of travel

Compression   Compression   Compression

Figure 4 Making longitudinal waves in a slinky spring

● Describe the wave.

c) How would you use a slinky to demonstrate transverse waves?

Reflection of sound

A **sound echo** is an example of reflection of sound. Echoes can be heard in a large hall or gallery which has bare, smooth walls.

● If the walls are covered in soft fabric, the fabric will absorb sound instead of reflecting it and no echoes will be heard.
● If the wall surface is uneven not smooth, echoes will not be heard because the reflected sound is 'broken up'.

d) Why does a music performance at an outdoor concert sound different in an indoor hall?

Refraction of sound

At night you can hear sound a long way from the source of the sound. This is because it refracts back to the ground instead of travelling away from the ground. Refraction takes place at the boundaries between layers of air at different temperatures.

In the daytime, sound refracts upwards not downwards because the air near the ground is warmer than higher up.

e) When air refracts downwards at night, is the air near the ground warmer or colder than higher up?

SUMMARY QUESTIONS

1 Complete the sentences below using words from the list.

absorbed   reflected   refracted   scattered

a) An echo is heard when sound is …… from a bare, smooth wall.
b) Sound waves are …… by a rough wall and …… by soft fabric.
c) Sound waves may be …… when they pass from a layer of hot air into a layer of cold air.

2 a) What is the highest frequency of sound the human ear can hear?
   b) Describe how a loudspeaker produces sound waves when it vibrates.
   c) Why does a round whistle produce sound at a constant frequency when you blow steadily into it?

Figure 5 Refraction of sound

KEY POINTS

1 Sound waves
   ● can travel through liquids and gases and in solids,
   ● cannot travel in a vacuum,
   ● are longitudinal waves,
   ● can be reflected (echoes) and refracted.

P3 2.7

Musical sounds

What type of music do you like? Whatever your taste in music is, when you listen to it you usually hear sounds that are produced by instruments designed for the purpose. Even your voice is produced by a biological organ that has the job of producing sound.

- Musical notes are easy to listen to because they are rhythmic. The sound waves change smoothly and the wave pattern repeats itself regularly.
- Noise consists of sound waves that vary randomly in frequency without any pattern.

a) Name four different vehicles that produce sound through a loudspeaker or a siren?

Figure 1 Making music

PRACTICAL

Investigating different sounds

Use a microphone connected to an oscilloscope to display the waveforms of different sounds.

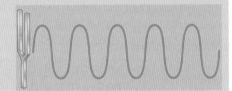

Figure 3 Tuning fork waves

Figure 2 Investigating different sound waves

1 Test a tuning fork to see the waveform of a sound of constant frequency.

2 Compare the 'pure' waveform of a tuning fork with the sound you produce when you talk or sing or when you whistle. You may be able to produce a pure waveform when you whistle or sing but not when you talk.

3 Use a signal generator connected to a loudspeaker to produce sound waves. The waveform on the oscilloscope screen should be a pure waveform.

b) What can you say about the waveform of a sound when you make the sound quieter?

Your investigations should show you that:

- *increasing the loudness of a sound* makes the waves on the screen taller. This is because the **amplitude** of the sound waves (the maximum disturbance) is bigger the louder the sound is,
- *increasing the frequency of a sound* (the number of waves per second) increases its **pitch**. This makes more waves appear on the screen.

SCIENCE @ WORK

Voice recognition

Microphones connected to computers are used to recognise individual voices. The computer is programmed to measure and recognise the frequencies in a voice waveform. However, it sometimes fails to recognise a voice if the speaker has a cold.

Figure 4 shows the waveforms for different sounds from the loudspeaker:

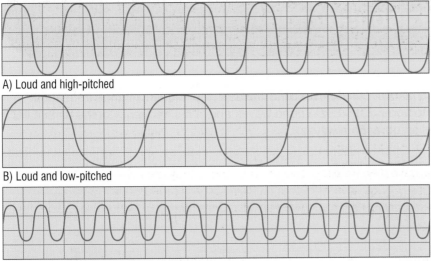

A) Loud and high-pitched

B) Loud and low-pitched

C) Quiet and high-pitched (higher pitch than A)

Figure 4 Investigating sounds

c) How would the waveform change if the loudness and the pitch are both reduced?

Musical instruments

When you play a musical instrument, you create sound waves by making the instrument and the air inside it vibrate. Each new cycle of vibrations makes the vibrations stronger at certain frequencies. We say the instrument **resonates** at these frequencies. Because the instrument and the air inside it vibrate strongly at these frequencies when it is played, we hear characteristic notes of sound from the instrument.

- A wind instrument such as a flute is designed so that the air inside resonates when it is played. You can make the air in an empty bottle resonate by blowing across the top gently.

- A string instrument such as a guitar produces sound when the strings vibrate. The vibrating strings make the surfaces of the instrument vibrate and produce sound waves in the air.

- A percussion instrument such as a drum vibrates and produces sound when it is struck.

NEXT TIME YOU...

. . . play a musical instrument, think about how it produces sound.

GET IT RIGHT!

Be sure you know the meaning of the terms frequency and amplitude

PRACTICAL

4 Test a musical instrument. Playing a flute produces a waveform that changes smoothly, as in Figure 5. However, unlike a tuning fork or signal generator waveform, the waveform is a mixture of frequencies rather than a single frequency.

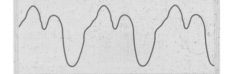

Figure 5 Flute wave pattern

SUMMARY QUESTIONS

1 A microphone and an oscilloscope are used to investigate sound from a loudspeaker connected to a signal generator. What change would you expect to see on the oscilloscope screen if the sound is
   a) made louder at the same frequency,
   b) made lower in frequency at the same loudness?

2 a) How does the note produced by a guitar string change if the string is
      i) shortened, ii) tightened?
   b) Compare the sound produced by a violin with the sound produced by a drum.

KEY POINTS

1 The **loudness** of a note depends on the amplitude of the sound waves.
2 The **pitch** of a note depends on the frequency of the sound waves.

P3 2.8   Ultrasound

LEARNING OBJECTIVES

1 What are ultrasound waves?
2 Why can ultrasonic waves be used to scan the human body?
3 How do we use ultrasonic waves to locate flaws in a metal object? [Higher]

GET IT RIGHT!

Ultrasound waves are used for pre-natal scanning because they are safer than X-rays for an unborn baby.

a)

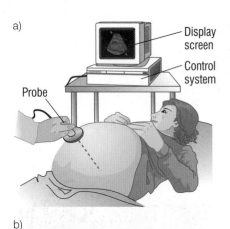

Display screen

Control system

Probe

b)

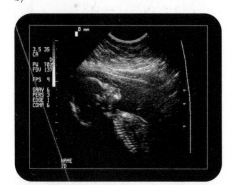

Figure 2 a) An ultrasonic scanner system, b) an ultrasonic image of a baby in the womb

The human ear can detect sound waves in the frequency range from about 20 Hz to about 20 000 Hz. Sound waves above the frequency of the human ear are called **ultrasonic** waves.

PRACTICAL

Testing ultrasound

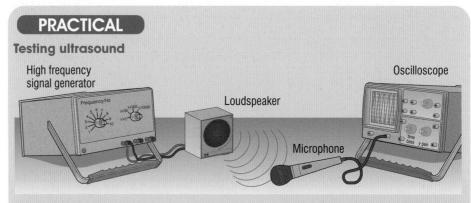

High frequency signal generator

Loudspeaker

Microphone

Oscilloscope

Figure 1 Testing ultrasounds

Use a loudspeaker connected to a signal generator to produce ultrasound waves. Connect a microphone to an oscilloscope to detect the waves and display them. You can use the apparatus to:

• measure the frequency of the ultrasound waves (see page 184 on the use of an oscilloscope if necessary),
• test different materials to see if they absorb ultrasound waves,
• show that ultrasonic waves can be reflected and refracted,
• show that ultrasonic waves can be partly reflected.

a) When a layer of material is placed between the loudspeaker and the microphone, the waves on the screen become smaller. What conclusions can you draw from this?

Uses of ultrasonics

Ultrasonic scanners

These are used to produce images of organs in the body or of a baby in the womb. A scanner consists of a probe placed on the body surface, a control unit and a display screen. The probe produces and detects pulses of ultrasonic waves.

For each pulse the probe sends out, it detects reflected pulses from the different boundaries in the path of the transmitted pulse. The probe is moved slowly over the body surface to build up an image of internal tissue boundaries on the screen.

The advantages of using ultrasonic waves instead of X-rays for medical scanning are that ultrasonic waves are:

• non-ionising, and therefore harmless when used for scanning, unlike X-rays,
• reflected at boundaries between different types of tissue (unlike X-rays) so they can be used to scan organs.

Flaws in metal castings

These can be detected using ultrasonic waves. A flaw such as an internal crack is a boundary inside the metal. The ultrasonic waves are partly reflected from the boundary. An ultrasonic transmitter on the metal surface sends pulses of ultrasonic waves into the metal object. A detector is placed on the surface next to the transmitter.

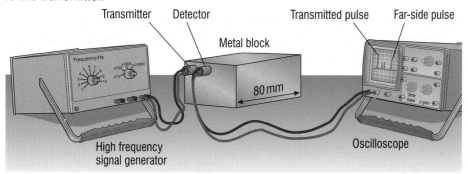

Figure 3 Detecting flaws in a metal

The detected pulses are displayed on an oscilloscope screen or on a computer monitor. The display in Figure 3 shows:

- a strong pulse due to partial reflection of the transmitted pulse at the surface, then
- some further pulses (in this case two pulses due to partial reflection at internal boundaries and the last pulse due to partial reflection at the far side of the metal object).

The further away a boundary is from the transmitter, the longer a reflected pulse takes to return.

If we know the width of the metal object, we can mark this distance on the display from the first to the last pulse. Then we can read from the display the location of each internal boundary (see question 2b below).

c) Use Figure 3 to work out how far the nearest flaw is from the transmitter?

HIGHER

SUMMARY QUESTIONS

1 a) Why are ultrasonic waves partly reflected by body organs?
   b) Why is an ultrasonic scanner better than an X-ray scanner for scanning a body organ?

2 The figure shows the screen of an oscilloscope connected to a flaw detector that uses ultrasonic waves to scan a metal block. The screen shows the reflected pulses for each transmitted pulse.

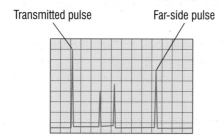

   a) How many flaws are present according to this display?
   b) The width of the metal block was 100 mm. Calculate the distance from the front of the block to each flaw. [Higher]

KEY POINTS

1 **Ultrasonic waves** are
   - sound waves that have a frequency above 18 000 kHz,
   - partly reflected at a boundary between two substances,
   - non-ionising.
2 **Uses of ultrasonic waves** include cleaning devices, flaw detectors and medical scanners.

P3 2.9   Light and sound issues

Noisy machines

Jack is very upset because the garage next door have put a car wash right next to his house. It's very noisy and it's on most of the time from 9am to 9pm. His doctor can only offer him tranquillisers to calm him down.

The noise of the machinery is driving me mad. I can't believe a company can install something like that right next to my house. If I put a machine like that in my garden the planners would be down on me like a ton of bricks.

I think you need to see a solicitor to find out why the Planning Department didn't notify you. You can make an appeal.

QUESTION

1 a) What other health hazards might be created by a car wash?

b) Discuss what else Jack can do about this problem. Could his councillor do more?

c) Find out what the law is about noisy machinery near houses and write a letter to Jack to advise him what he could do.

Sound absorbers

Music in a concert hall sounds different when the hall is full of people compared with when it is empty. People absorb sound as well as creating it. The designers of a concert hall need to make sure sound does not reflect from side to side in the hall. Soft materials are used to line the walls to stop echoes. However, the sound is deadened if too much material is used.

QUESTION

2 In a test of different absorber materials, a microphone and a loudspeaker were put in a large box at fixed positions. Different materials in turn were used to pad the box. The table shows some measurements using the loudspeaker to produce sound.

Material	Wave height (mm)	
	without material	with material
soft wallpaper	40	25
cushion fabric	40	10
plaster board	40	35
wood panel	40	45

a) Why does the sound need to be the same loudness and frequency each time a test is carried out?

b) What conclusions can you draw from these measurements?

LASERS

Surgeons use them, surveyors use them, DVD players contain them and they can be used to cut metal. Yet a laser produces no more than a narrow beam of light with a very narrow range of wavelengths.

Never look into a laser beam. It would permanently damage the light-sensitive cells at the back of the eye.

In a DVD player, a tiny laser diode produces a laser beam. The beam is focused by a lens to a tiny spot on the disc. A CD or a DVD disc stores data bits (0s and 1s) in the form of tiny pits along circular tracks on its surface.

When the disc turns, a light sensor detects pulses of light reflected from the disc as the pits move past the beam. The sensor converts the pulses of light into electrical pulses which recreate the stored data.

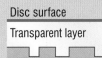

Laser diode as light source

Double prism

Light detector

Disc surface

Transparent layer

Compact disc

Music track

Using a laser diode

QUESTION

3 A DVD player contains a hard disc that stores over 40 000 megabytes of data. It can playback video for over 200 hours or music for over 1000 hours.

a) For how long could such a player give music **and** video?

b) The battery of a player lasts 3 hours. Why is the stored data unaffected when the battery runs out?

c) Find out about how recorded music used to be played back. You might need to ask your parents about cassette tapes or gramophone records.

Optoelectronics

Digital cameras have revolutionised photography – no films, no developing, instant transmission and enlargement, repeat pictures, etc., etc. Photography companies have had to adapt or close down. Newspapers and magazines can get pictures from anywhere in the world in an instant.

ACTIVITY

a) Famous people often complain when 'unauthorised' photographs of them appear in newspapers and magazines. Discuss whether or not famous people should have a greater right to privacy than everyone else.

b) The digital camera is an example of an optoelectronic device. A videophone is another example. Cost, weight and portability are important factors in developing and marketing a new device.

Imagine you are going out to buy a digital camera (or a videophone). Discuss which of the factors above or any other factors would be most important to you in choosing which make is best.

SUMMARY QUESTIONS

1 The figure shows an incomplete ray diagram of image formation by a plane mirror.

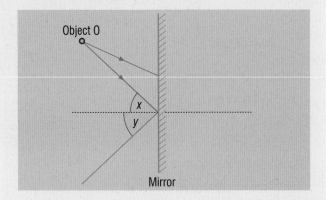

Object O

x
y

Mirror

a) What can you say about the angles *x* and *y*?
b) Complete the ray diagram to locate the image.
c) What can you say about the distance from the image to the mirror compared with the distance from the object to the mirror?

2 The figure shows an incomplete ray diagram of image formation by a lens.

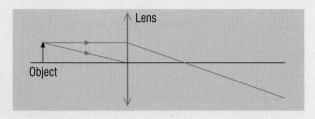

Lens

Object

a) i) What type of lens is shown in this diagram?
   ii) Mark the focal point of the lens on the diagram.
b) i) Complete the ray diagram and label the image.
   ii) Describe the image and state an application of the lens used in this way.

3 A loudspeaker is used to produce sound waves. In terms of the amplitude or frequency of the sound waves,
   a) explain why the sound is fainter further away from the loudspeaker,
   b) explain what happens to the sound waves if i) the pitch of the sound increases, ii) the sound becomes louder.

4 Ultrasonic waves used for medical scanners have a frequency of 2000 kHz.
   a) Calculate the wavelength of these ultrasonic waves in human tissue. (The speed of ultrasound in human tissue is 1500 m/s.)
   b) Ultrasonic waves of this frequency in human tissue are not absorbed much. Why is it important in a medical scanner that they are not absorbed?

EXAM-STYLE QUESTIONS

1 The diagram shows two plane mirrors being used in a periscope to allow someone to see over an obstacle.

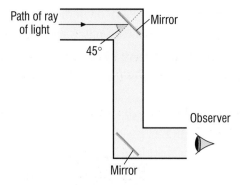

Path of ray of light — Mirror
45°
Observer
Mirror

(a) Complete the path of the ray to show how it reaches the observer. (2)

(b) The image seen in the lower mirror of the periscope is a virtual image.

   Explain the difference between a real image and a virtual image. (4)

2 (a) (i) Complete the diagram below to show what happens to the two rays of light after they enter the lens. (2)

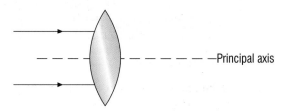

Principal axis

   (ii) Put an **F** on the diagram to label the principal focus of the lens. (1)

   (iii) What word can be used to describe this type of lens? (1)

(b) (i) Complete the diagram below to show what happens to the two rays of light after they enter the lens. (2)

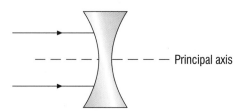

Principal axis

   (ii) Put an **F** on the diagram to label the principal focus of the lens. (1)

   (iii) What word can be used to describe this type of lens? (1)

3 This question is about sound. Sound travels as a wave.

(a) Explain why sound waves cannot travel through a vacuum. (2)

(b) What happens to the sound you hear when . . .

    (i) the frequency of the sound wave decreases?

    (ii) the amplitude of the sound wave increases? (4)

4 An *ultrasound* scan can be used to produce a picture of an unborn baby.

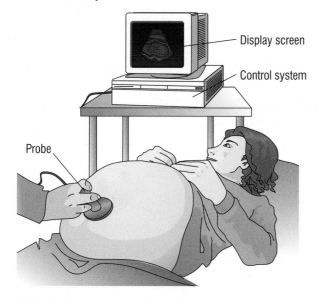

(a) What is *ultrasound*? (1)

(b) Explain how ultrasound can be used to produce a picture of an unborn baby. (3)

(c) Why are ultrasound waves used for this rather than X-rays? (2)

HOW SCIENCE WORKS

Jenny carried out an investigation into the refractive index of a piece of glass. The refractive index is a measure of how much light is refracted as it enters a transparent substance from air. The refractive index can be calculated by using the following equipment.

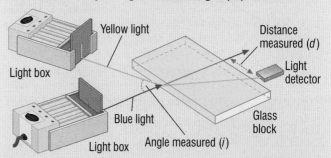

The blue light beam passes straight through the block. The narrow beam of yellow light is aimed at the point where the blue light enters. Angle *i* is measured. The light detector is used to measure exactly where the yellow light leaves the glass block and the distance from the blue to the yellow beam is measured, *d*. From these two measurements and the width of the block the refractive index can be calculated.

a) What was the advantage of using a light detector rather than her eye? (1)

b) What sensitivity would you suggest for the ruler measuring the distance *d*? (1)

c) Jenny did the measurement five times at different angles.
They should all produce the same refractive index, because the same block of glass is being used. Here are Jenny's results.

Angle of yellow to blue light, (i)	40°	42°	44°	46°	48°
Calculated refractive index	1.492	1.548	1.523	1.497	1.543

What was the range of the dependent variable? (1)

d) What was the mean of the dependent variable? (1)

e) Use the table below to decide which type of glass Jenny was using. (1)

Type of glass	Refractive index
Heaviest flint glass	1.89
Heavy flint glass	1.65
Light flint glass	1.575
Crown glass	1.52
Zinc crown glass	1.517

P3 3.1   The motor effect

LEARNING OBJECTIVES

1 When a current-carrying conductor in a magnetic field experiences a force, how can we make the force bigger?

2 When a current-carrying conductor in a magnetic field experiences a force, how can we reverse the direction of the force?

3 How do we use the motor effect to make objects move?

FOUL FACTS

An electric drill contains an electric motor. Dentists use electric drills to drill teeth. What do surgeons use electric drills for? Ugh!

PRACTICAL

Investigating the motor effect

When a current is passed along a wire in a magnetic field, a force may be exerted on the wire. This effect is known as the **motor effect**. Figure 1 shows how you can investigate it.

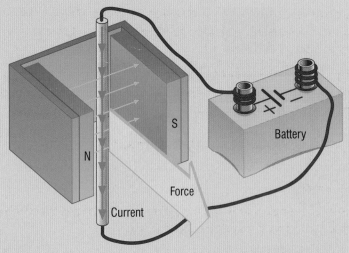

Figure 1 Investigating the motor effect

You should find that a force acts on the wire unless the wire is parallel to the magnetic field lines.

Force factors

Your investigations should show that:

● the force can be increased by:
  – increasing the current, or
  – using a stronger magnet.

● the force depends on the angle between the wire and the magnetic field lines; the force is:
  – greatest when the wire is perpendicular to the magnetic field,
  – zero when the wire is parallel to the magnetic field lines.

● the direction of the force is always at right angles to the wire and the field lines. Also, the direction of the force is reversed if the direction of the current or the magnetic field is reversed.

a) What happens if the current and the magnetic field are both reversed?

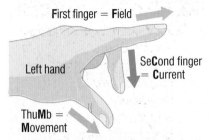

Figure 2 The left hand rule. You can use this rule to work out the direction of the force (i.e. movement) on the wire.

The electric motor

An electric motor is designed to use the motor effect. We can control the speed of an electric motor by changing the current. Also, we can reverse its turning direction by reversing the current.

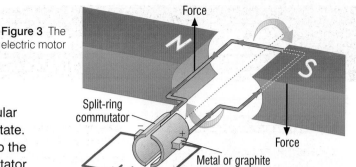

Figure 3 The electric motor

The simple motor shown in Figure 3 consists of a rectangular coil of insulated wire (the armature coil) that is forced to rotate. The coil is connected via two metal or graphite 'brushes' to the battery. The brushes press onto a metal 'split-ring' commutator fixed to the coil.

When a current is passed through the coil, the coil spins because:

- a force acts on each side of the coil due to the motor effect,
- the force on one side is in the opposite direction to the force on the other side.

The split-ring commutator reverses the current round the coil every half turn of the coil. Because the sides swap over each half-turn, the coil is pushed in the same direction every half-turn.

b) Why are the brushes made of metal or graphite?

The loudspeaker

A loudspeaker is designed to make a diaphragm attached to a coil vibrate when alternating current passes through the coil.

- When a current passes through the coil, a force due to the motor effect makes the coil move.
- Each time the current changes its direction, the force reverses its direction. So the coil is repeatedly forced backwards and forwards. This motion makes the diaphragm vibrate so sound waves are created.

c) Why does a loudspeaker not produce sound when direct current is passed through it?

DID YOU KNOW?

Graphite is a form of carbon which conducts electricity and is very slippy. It therefore causes very little friction when it is in contact with the rotating commutator.

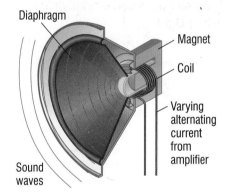

Figure 4 A loudspeaker

SUMMARY QUESTIONS

1 Choose words from the list to complete each of the sentences.

coil   current   force   magnet

a) When a ...... passes through the ...... of an electric motor, a ...... acts on each side of the ....

b) The ...... along each side is in opposite directions so the ...... is in opposite directions and the ...... turns.

2 a) Explain why a simple electric motor connected to a battery reverses if the battery connections are reversed.

b) Discuss whether or not an electric motor would run faster if the coil was wound on i) a plastic block, ii) an iron block instead of a wooden block.

KEY POINT

1 In the motor effect, the force:
- is increased if the current or the strength of the magnetic field is increased,
- is at right angles to the direction of the magnetic field and to the wire,
- is reversed if the direction of the current or the magnetic field is reversed.

P3 3.2

Electromagnetic induction

A hospital has its own electricity generator always 'on standby' in case the mains electricity supply fails. Patients' lives would be put at risk if the mains power failed and there was no standby generator.

A generator contains coils of wire that spin in a magnetic field. A potential difference (p.d.) (or voltage) is created or **induced** in the wire when it cuts across the magnetic field lines. If the wire is part of a complete circuit, the induced p.d. makes an electric current pass round the circuit.

PRACTICAL

Investigating a simple generator

Connect some insulated wire to an ammeter as shown in Figure 1. Move the wire between the poles of a U-shaped magnet and observe the ammeter. You should discover the ammeter pointer deflects as a current is generated when the wire cuts across the magnetic field.

The effect is known as the **dynamo effect**. Make the wire into a coil, and you should find the current is bigger.

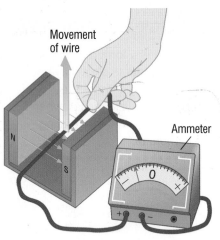

Figure 1 The dynamo effect

a) What can you say about the current if:
   i) the wire had been moved faster across the field,
   ii) the direction of motion of the wire had been reversed,
   iii) the wire had been stationary?

The cycle dynamo

Figure 2 shows the inside of a cycle dynamo.

When the magnet spins, an alternating p.d. is induced in the coil. This happens because the magnetic field lines cut across the wires of the coil. The induced p.d. makes an alternating current pass round the circuit when the lamp is on.

b) Why is it better to spin the magnet instead of the coil?

A generator test

Look at Figure 3. It shows a coil of insulated wire connected to a centre-reading ammeter. When one end of a bar magnet is pushed into the coil, the ammeter pointer deflects.

This is because:

• the movement of the bar magnet causes an induced p.d. in the coil,
• the induced p.d. causes a current, because the coil is part of a complete circuit.

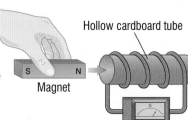

Meter pointer deflects when the magnet is pushed into the coil

c) What do you think happens if
   i) the magnet is left at rest in the coil,
   ii) the magnet is withdrawn from the coil?

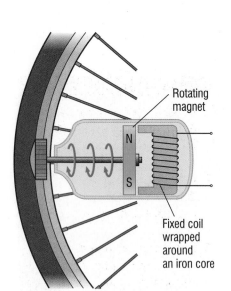

Figure 2 The dynamo

Figure 3 Testing electromagnetic induction

The alternating current generator

A simple a.c. generator consists of a rectangular coil which is forced to spin in a magnetic field. Look at Figure 4.

The coil is connected to a centre-reading meter via metal 'brushes' that press on two metal slip-rings.

When the coil turns steadily in one direction, the meter pointer deflects first one way then the opposite way then back again. This carries on as long as the coil keeps turning. The current through the meter is an alternating current.

The faster the coil rotates:

- the larger the peak value of the alternating current,
- the greater the frequency (i.e. the number of cycles per second) of the alternating current.

NEXT TIME YOU...

... cycle at night, think about why your lights are on. If your cycle lights are powered by a dynamo, pedal faster to brighten up your journey.

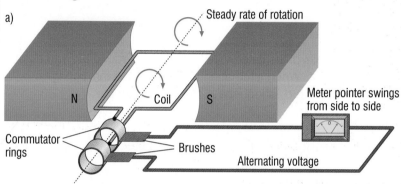

Figure 4 The a.c. generator. a) Construction. b) Alternating voltage.

SUMMARY QUESTIONS

1 A coil of wire is connected to a centre-reading ammeter. A bar magnet is inserted into the coil, making the ammeter pointer flick briefly to the right.

   What would you observe if

   a) the magnet had been inserted more slowly into the coil,
   b) the magnet was then held at rest in the coil,
   c) the magnet is withdrawn rapidly from the coil?

2 a) State two ways in which the voltage generated by a cycle dynamo could be increased.
   b) The diagram shows how the alternating voltage produced by an a.c. generator changes with time. How would the graph differ if the coil were rotated more slowly? [Higher]

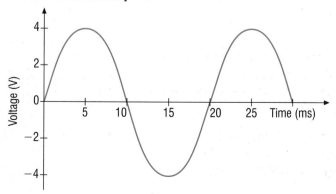

KEY POINTS

1 When a wire cuts the lines of a magnetic field, a potential difference is induced in a wire.
2 If the wire is part of a complete circuit, the induced p.d. causes a current in the circuit.
3 The current is increased if the wire moves faster or a stronger magnet is used.

P3 3.3   Transformers

A typical power station generator produces an alternating potential difference of about 25 000 volts. Mains electricity to homes and offices is at 230 volts.

When you plug a heater into the mains, electricity reaches you from a power station via a network of cables called the **National Grid**. The alternating p.d. of the cables (the grid voltage) is typically 132 000 volts.

A **transformer** is used at each stage to change the alternating p.d. We also use transformers in low-voltage supply units to step the mains p.d. down from 230 V.

How a transformer works

A transformer has two coils of insulated wire, both wound round the same iron core, as shown in Figure 1. When alternating current passes through the primary coil, an alternating p.d. is induced in the secondary coil.

This happens because:

- alternating current passing through the primary coil produces an alternating magnetic field,
- the lines of the alternating magnetic field pass through the secondary coil and induce an alternating p.d. in it.

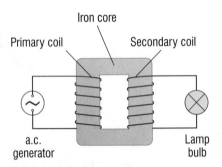

Figure 1 Transformer action

If a lamp is connected across the secondary coil, the induced p.d. causes a current in the secondary circuit. So the lamp lights up. Electrical energy is therefore transferred from the primary to the secondary coil. This happens even though they are not electrically connected in the same circuit.

a) Why would the lamp not light up as brightly if the iron core was replaced with a wooden core?
b) What happens if you wrap more turns on the secondary coil?
c) What happens if you use a 1.5 V cell instead of the 1 volt a.c. supply unit?

PRACTICAL

Make a model transformer

Wrap a coil of insulated wire round the iron core of a model transformer as the primary coil. Connect the coil to a 1 volt a.c. supply unit and connect a second length of insulated wire to a 1.5 V torch lamp. When you wrap the second wire round the iron core, the lamp should light up.

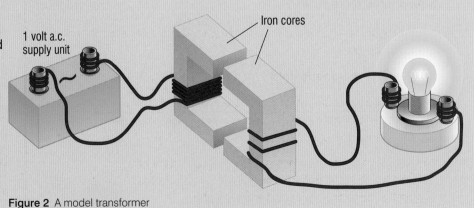

Figure 2 A model transformer

Transformers in action

Transformers only work with alternating current. With a direct current, there is no changing magnetic field so the secondary voltage is zero.

The core of the transformer 'guides' the field lines in a loop through the coils. But the field must be changing to induce a p.d. in the secondary coil.

Figure 3 shows a practical transformer.

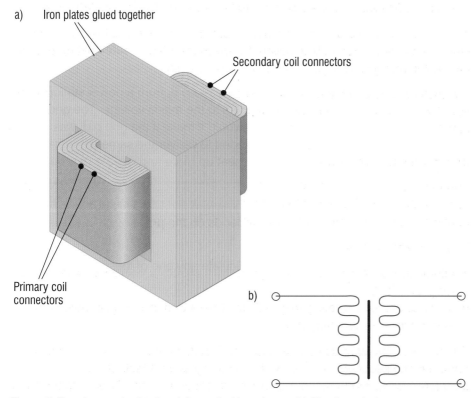

a) Iron plates glued together

Secondary coil connectors

Primary coil connectors

b)

Figure 3 Transformers in circuits. a) A practical transformer. b) Circuit symbol.

The primary and secondary coils are both wound round the same part of the core. The core is layered (laminated) to cut out induced currents in the iron layers. If it wasn't laminated, the efficiency of the transformer would be greatly reduced.

d) Why is the core made of iron not steel?

GET IT RIGHT!

Make sure you can explain how a transformer works.

SUMMARY QUESTIONS

1 Copy and complete the following sentences about a transformer using words from the list.

   current   magnetic field   p.d.   primary   secondary

   In a transformer, an alternating ...... is passed through the ...... coil. This coil creates an alternating ...... which passes through the ...... coil. As a result, an alternating ...... is induced in the ...... coil.

2 a) Why does a transformer not work with direct current?
   b) Why is it important that the coil wires of a transformer are insulated?
   c) Why is the core of a transformer made of iron?

KEY POINTS

1 A transformer consists of a primary coil and a secondary coil wrapped on the same iron core.
2 Transformers only work using alternating current.

P3 3.4   Transformers and the National Grid

LEARNING OBJECTIVES

1 Why are transformers used in the National Grid?
2 What is the difference between a step-up and a step-down transformer?
[Higher]

Figure 1 A power transformer under inspection

GET IT RIGHT!

Make sure you can describe how transformers are used in the National Grid.

When we use mains devices, the electricity is supplied to us through the National Grid from distant power stations. Figure 2 shows how the grid system is used to supply industry as well as homes.

The higher the grid p.d., the greater the efficiency of transferring electrical power through the grid.

This is why transformers are used to step up the p.d. from a power station to the grid p.d. and to step the grid p.d. down to the mains voltage. The grid p.d. is at least 132 000 V. So what difference would it make if the grid p.d. was much lower? Much more current would be needed to deliver the same amount of power. The grid cables would therefore heat up more and waste more power.

The transformer equation

The secondary p.d. of a transformer depends on the primary p.d. and the number of turns on each coil.

We can use the following equation to calculate any one of these factors if we know the other ones.

$$\frac{\text{p.d. across primary, } V_P}{\text{p.d. across secondary, } V_S} = \frac{\text{number of turns on primary, } N_P}{\text{number of turns on secondary, } N_S}$$

- **For a step-up transformer**, the number of secondary turns, N_S, is greater than the number of primary turns, N_P. Therefore V_S is greater than V_P.
- **For a step-down transformer**, the number of secondary turns, N_S, is less than the number of primary turns, N_P. Therefore V_S is less than V_P.

Worked example

A transformer is used to step a p.d. of 230 V down to 10 V. The secondary coil has 60 turns. Calculate the number of turns of the primary coil.

Solution $V_P = 230$ V, $V_S = 10$ V, $N_S = 60$ turns

Using $\dfrac{V_P}{V_S} = \dfrac{N_P}{N_S}$ gives $\dfrac{230}{10} = \dfrac{N_P}{60}$ Therefore $N_P = \dfrac{230 \times 60}{10} = 1380$ turns

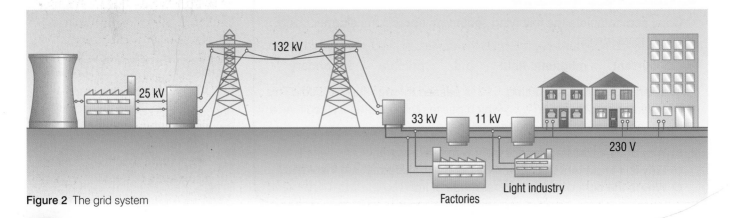

Figure 2 The grid system

a) A transformer with 1200 turns in the primary coil is used to step a p.d. of 120 V down to 6 V. Calculate the number of turns on the secondary coil.

Transformer efficiency

Transformers are almost 100% efficient. When a device is connected to the secondary coil, almost all the electrical power supplied to the transformer is delivered to the device.

- Power supplied to the transformer
  = primary current, $I_P \times$ primary p.d., V_P
- Power delivered by the transformer
  = secondary current, $I_S \times$ secondary p.d., V_S

Therefore, for 100% efficiency:

primary current $\times$ primary p.d. = secondary current $\times$ secondary p.d.

$$I_P V_P = I_S V_S$$

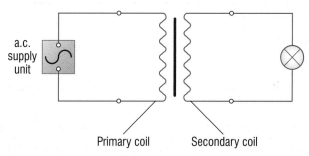

Figure 3 Transformer efficiency

b) A 230 V, 60 W lamp lights normally when it is connected to the secondary coil of a transformer and a 10 V a.c. supply is connected to the primary coil. Calculate i) the primary current, ii) the lamp current.

SUMMARY QUESTIONS

1 Choose words from the list to complete the sentences.

down   **primary**   **secondary**   **up**

a) In a step-up transformer, the p.d. across the …… coil is greater than the p.d. across the …… coil.

b) The p.d. from a power station is stepped …… so the same amount of power can be delivered through the cables as a result of stepping the current …… .

2 A transformer with a secondary coil of 100 turns is to be used to step a voltage down from 240 V to 12 V.

a) Calculate the number of turns on the primary coil of this transformer.

b) A 12 V 36 W lamp is connected to the secondary coil. Calculate the current in i) the lamp, ii) the primary coil. Assume the transformer is 100% efficient.   [Higher]

KEY POINTS

1 Transformers are used to step voltages up or down.
2 The transformer equation is:

$$\frac{\text{primary p.d., } V_P}{\text{secondary p.d., } V_S} = \frac{N_P}{N_S}$$

where N_P = number of primary turns and N_S = number of secondary turns   [Higher]

P3 3.5   More power to you

Before 1926	District power stations supply a.c. or d.c. electricity	Most power stations burn coal
1926	Grid system set up	All power stations generate 240 V,* 50 Hz a.c.
1948	Grid system and power companies nationalised	Big new power stations built including oil-fired and nuclear power stations
1990	Grid system and power companies privatised (except nuclear power)	New gas-fired power stations built
Now	Power companies such as National Grid operate internationally	Wind farms being established

(*changed to 230 V in 1994)

Alternating or direct current?

Before the National Grid was set up in 1926, electricity for each district was from a local power station. Some power stations generated alternating current and others generated direct current.

As explained on page 184, the potential of a mains live wire alternates between +325 V and −325 V. A direct potential of 230 V would deliver the same power so we say the UK mains supply is 230 V. Before d.c. power stations were converted to supply a.c.,

- some people said d.c. was safer because a live wire reaches a much higher potential with a.c. than with d.c.,
- some people said the power stations could be further away if a.c. was used instead of d.c.

ACTIVITY

Imagine you are a local newspaper reporter in 1926. You live in a d.c. town. Your editor has asked you to write a short piece (no more than 100 words) on why a.c. is better than d.c. Remember that:

- people in the rural areas don't have electricity because it's too expensive, and
- people with electricity might need to rewire their houses because alternating voltages are higher than direct voltages.

A revolutionary discoverer

I was born in 1791 and when I left school, I started an apprenticeship binding books. I was so fascinated by Sir Humphry Davy's books on science that I wrote to him at the Royal Institution in London to ask him for a job. He must have been very impressed by my enthusiasm because he took me on and trained me in science. Many years later, I followed in his footsteps and became the Director of the Royal Institution. I made lots of important scientific discoveries including how to generate electricity. Who am I?

Grid changes

New gas-fired power stations built after 1990 generate cheaper electricity than other power stations. Most oil-fired and many coal-fired power stations were closed because they were uncompetitive. North Sea gas is running out. We now need new electricity sources to reduce greenhouse gases.

ACTIVITY

Who should pay for new electricity sources, the electricity consumer or the taxpayer? Discuss the issue in your group.

Are you M . . . . . ?

Superconducting motors

A superconducting wire has no resistance. In theory, a very large current can pass through it without heating the wire. A superconducting motor would be much lighter and more efficient than an ordinary motor.

It would need:

- a rotating coil made of superconducting wires, and
- a magnetic field produced by a fixed superconducting coil.

Lighter and more efficient electric motors in cars would cut fuel usage and reduce greenhouse gases. Research scientists working on superconducting materials know their work could have a gigantic pay-off!

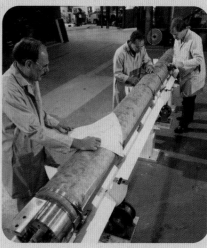

An experimental superconducting motor

QUESTION

1 Why would superconducting motors be
a) lighter, **b)** more efficient?

The Daily

GOSS

All the News...
All the Showbiz...
All the Info...
All the Time!

P.U.P.S PROTEST!

*People
Under
Powerlines
become
Pretty
Upset
Protesters!*

EXCLUSIVE REPORT!!!

People living under overhead power lines in the Hillside district marched to the Town Hall yesterday.

They want the power lines re-routed. They claim that the radiation from the power lines is a health risk.

A spokesperson said the council has agreed to a public meeting to listen to their concerns.

NEW THEORIES IN LEUKAEMIA:–
MELATONIN/MAGNETIC FIELD LINK?

Studies of illnesses in communities show there may be an increased risk of childhood leukaemia associated with exposure to 50 Hz alternating magnetic fields. The increased risk seems to be present where magnetic fields are stronger than about 0.5% of the Earth's magnetic field.

One hypothesis is that it may be due to the disruption in the night-time production of melatonin in the pineal gland at the back of the eye. Melatonin in the body is thought to sweep up the bits of damaged cells that cause cancer.

(source: *SciWorld News*, May 2005)

QUESTION

2 a) List some other causes of cancer in humans.
b) What does 'increased risk' mean?
c) The abstract puts forward the 'melatonin theory' as a hypothesis. What is a hypothesis? (See page 6.)

ACTIVITY

a) Rewrite the news report to give it a scientific flavour using the abstract – but keep it to less than 100 words.
b) If you're going to protest in a group, give yourself a better name than PUPS! Come up with something better and design a campaign poster.

SUMMARY QUESTIONS

1 Complete the following sentences using words from the list.

field   force   lines   current

a) A vertical wire is placed in a horizontal magnetic field. When a ...... is passed through the wire, a ...... acts on the wire.

b) A force acts on a wire in a magnetic field when a ...... passes along the wire and the wire is not parallel to the ...... of the ....

2 The figure shows a rectangular coil of wire in a magnetic field. When a direct current passes clockwise round the coil, an upward force acts on side X of the coil.

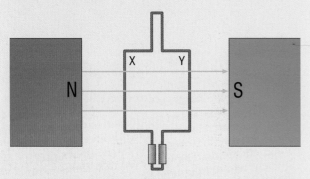

a) What is the direction of the force on side Y of the coil?

b) What can you say about the force on each side of the coil parallel to the magnetic field lines?

c) What is the effect of the forces on the coil?

3 a) Complete the sentences using words from the list.

step-down   step-up

i) A transformer that changes an alternating p.d. from 12 V to 120 V is a ...... transformer.

ii) A ...... transformer has more turns on the primary coil than on the secondary coil.

b) Explain why a transformer does not work on direct current.

4 Explain why power is transmitted through the National Grid at a high p.d. rather than a low p.d.

5 A transformer has 50 turns in its primary coil and 500 turns in its secondary coil. It is to be used to light a 120 V, 60 W lamp connected to the secondary coil.

a) Calculate the primary p.d.,

b) Calculate the current in the lamp,

c) Calculate the current in the primary coil. [Higher]

EXAM-STYLE QUESTIONS

1 The diagram shows a simple electric motor.

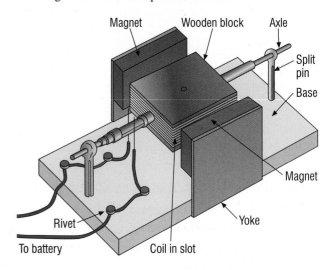

Explain why the motor turns when a current is passed through the coil. (9)

2 The diagram shows a simple generator.

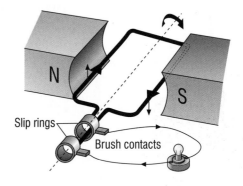

Explain why there is an alternating current in the lamp when the coil is turned. Include in your answer why the brushes and slip rings are needed. (7)
[Higher]

3 An oscilloscope is connected to an a.c. generator. The trace produced on the oscilloscope is shown below.

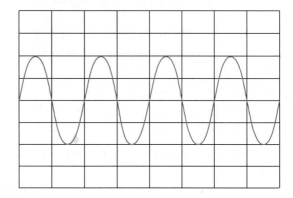

The controls of the oscilloscope are not altered.

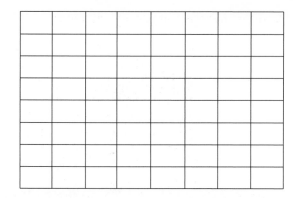

On a grid like the one shown above draw what the trace would look like if:

(a) (i) the number of turns on the coil is doubled while the speed of rotation and the magnetic field are kept constant. (3)

(ii) Why are the speed of rotation and the magnetic field kept constant in (a) part i)?

(b) the speed of rotation is doubled while the number of turns on the coil and the magnetic field are kept constant. (3)

4 The diagram shows a transformer.

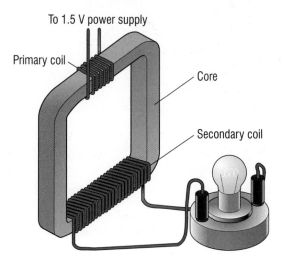

(a) Explain how an alternating current in the primary coil produces an alternating current through the lamp. (4)

(b) The potential difference across the primary coil is 1.5 V. There are 6 turns on the primary coil and 24 turns on the secondary coil.

Calculate the potential difference across the lamp. (4)

[Higher]

HOW SCIENCE WORKS

Darren had been studying electromagnetism and learned how a potential difference could be induced by the movement of a magnet through a coil. He thought that he would find out how the speed of a magnet falling through a coil would change the p.d. produced.

The equipment was set up as below. He decided to vary the speed of the magnet by adjusting the height the magnet was dropped from.

Darren predicted that there would be a directly proportional relationship between the height the magnet was dropped from and the voltage induced.

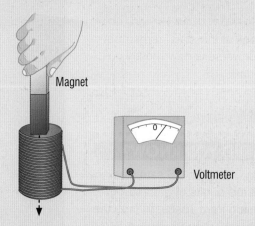

The first attempt proved impossible. The voltmeter fluttered a little as the magnet passed, but a reading could not be taken.

a) Why was this preliminary test a failure? (1)

Darren put an oscilloscope in place of the voltmeter.

b) These were his results.

Height (cm)	5	15	25	35	45	50
Voltage (V)	0.06	0.15	0.21	0.24	0.26	0.27

Draw a graph of these results (3)

c) Was Darren's prediction correct? (1)

d) What was the sensitivity of the oscilloscope? (1)

e) Was the oscilloscope sensitive enough for the range of the independent variable? (1)

f) How could Darren improve the accuracy of his results? (1)

g) How might Darren demonstrate the reliability of his results? (1)

h) What technological development might come from this idea? (1)

P3 4.1 Galaxies

LEARNING OBJECTIVES

1 What is a galaxy?
2 What is the force responsible for the formation of stars?

NEXT TIME YOU...

. . . look at the stars, remember the Universe is now mostly cold and dark.

DID YOU KNOW?

In the Cold War, US satellites detected bursts of gamma radiation from space. At first, the US military thought nuclear weapons were being tested in space by Russia. Then astronomers found the bursts were from violent events long ago in distant galaxies – maybe stars being sucked into black holes!

The Big Bang that created the Universe was about 13 thousand million (13 billion) years ago. Space, time and radiation were created in the Big Bang. At first, the Universe was a hot glowing ball of radiation and matter. As it expanded, its temperature fell. Now the Universe is cold and dark, except for hot spots we call stars.

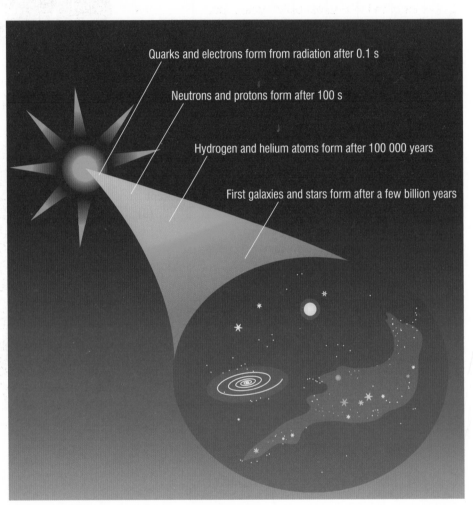

Quarks and electrons form from radiation after 0.1 s

Neutrons and protons form after 100 s

Hydrogen and helium atoms form after 100 000 years

First galaxies and stars form after a few billion years

Figure 1 Time line for the Universe

The stars we see in the night sky are all in the Milky Way galaxy, our home galaxy. The Sun is just one of billions of stars in the Milky Way galaxy. Using powerful telescopes, we can see many more stars in the Milky Way galaxy and individual stars in other galaxies.

We now know there are billions of galaxies in the Universe with vast empty space between them. Light from the furthest galaxies we can see has taken billions of years to reach us.

Figure 2 Andromeda – the nearest big galaxy to the Milky Way

a) Why do powerful telescopes give us a picture of the Universe long ago?

The Dark Age of the Universe

As the Universe expanded, it became transparent as radiation passed through the empty space between its atoms. The background microwave radiation that causes the spots on an untuned TV was released at this stage. (See page 108.) The Dark Age of the Universe had begun!

For the next few billion years, the Universe would have been a dark, patchy, expanding cloud of hydrogen and helium. Then the stars and galaxies formed and lit up the Universe!

b) How long, to the nearest billion years, has background microwave radiation been travelling for?

The force of gravity takes over

Uncharged atoms don't repel each other. But they can attract each other. During the Dark Age of the Universe, the force of gravitational attraction was at work without any opposition from repulsive forces.

As the Universe continued to expand, it become more patchy as the denser parts attracted nearby matter. Gravity pulled more matter into the denser parts and turned them into gigantic clumps.

Eventually, the force of gravity turned the clumps into galaxies and stars. A few billion years after the Big Bang, the Dark Age came to an end as the stars lit up the Universe.

c) Why would the force of gravity between two helium nuclei be unable to pull the nuclei together?

Figure 3 Arno Allan Penzias and Robert Woodrow Wilson standing on the radio antenna which unexpectedly discovered the Universe's microwave background radiation

Figure 4 The force of gravity takes over

SUMMARY QUESTIONS

1 Complete the following sentences using words from the list.

      attracted   cooled   expanded   formed

  a) As the Universe ......, it ....
  b) Uncharged atoms ...... each other.
  c) Galaxies and stars ...... from uncharged atoms.

2 a) i) Why can't we take a photo of the Milky Way galaxy from outside?
    ii) Why can't we take photos of a distant galaxy at different stages in its formation?
  b) i) Why do the stars in a galaxy not drift away from each other?
    ii) Why are there vast spaces between the galaxies?

KEY POINTS

1 As the Universe expanded, it cooled and uncharged atoms formed.
2 The force of gravity pulled matter into galaxies and stars.

P3 4.2 The life history of a star

LEARNING OBJECTIVES

1 What will eventually happen to the Sun?
2 What evidence is there for black holes?

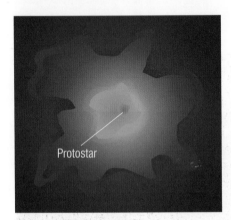

Figure 1 Star birth

Protostar

The birth of a star

Stars form out of clouds of dust and gas.

- The particles in the clouds gather together under their own gravity. The clouds merge and become more and more concentrated to form a **protostar**, the name for a star to be.
- As a 'protostar' becomes denser, it gets hotter. If it becomes hot enough, the nuclei of hydrogen atoms and other light elements **fuse** together. Energy is released in the process so the core gets hotter and brighter and starts to shine. A star is born!

a) Where does the energy to heat a protostar come from?

Shining stars

Stars like the Sun radiate energy because of hydrogen fusion in the core. This is the main stage in the life of a star. It can continue for billions of years until the star runs out of hydrogen nuclei to fuse together.

- Energy released in the core keeps the core hot so the process of fusion continues. Radiation flows out steadily from the core in all directions.
- The force of gravity that makes a star contract is balanced by the outward pressure of radiation from its core. These forces stay in balance until most of the hydrogen nuclei in the core have been fused together.

b) Why doesn't the Sun collapse under its own gravity?

The end of a star

When a star runs out of hydrogen nuclei to fuse together, it will swell out.

- As it swells, it cools down and turns red. It becomes a **red giant**. At this stage, helium and other light elements in its core fuse to form heavier elements.
- When there are no more light elements in its core, fusion stops. No more radiation is released and the star collapses on itself. As it collapses, it heats up and turns from red to yellow to white. It becomes a **white dwarf**, a hot, dense white star much smaller in diameter than it was. Stars like the Sun then fade out and go cold.

Bigger stars end their life much more dramatically. Their collapse continues past the 'white dwarf' stage then suddenly reverses in a cataclysmic explosion known as a **supernova**. Such an event can outshine an entire galaxy for several weeks.

DID YOU KNOW?

The Sun is about 5000 million years old and will probably continue to shine for another 5000 million years.

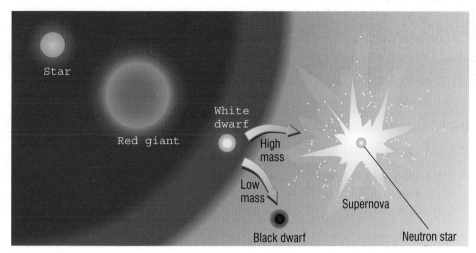

Figure 2 The end of a star

c) What force causes a red giant to collapse?

What remains after a supernova occurs?

The explosion compresses the core of the star into a **neutron star**, an extremely dense object composed only of neutrons. If the neutron star is massive enough, it becomes a **black hole**. Its gravitational field would then be so strong that nothing could escape from it, not even light or any other form of electromagnetic radiation.

d) What force causes matter to be dragged into a black hole?

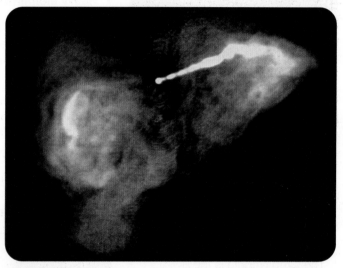

Figure 3 M87 is a galaxy that spins so fast at its centre that it is thought to contain a black hole with a billion times more mass than the Sun

SUMMARY QUESTIONS

1 a) The list below shows some of the stages in the life of a star. Put the stages in the correct sequence.

    A main stage   B protostar   C red giant   D white dwarf

  b) i) Which stage in the above list is the Sun at now?
    ii) What will happen to the Sun after it has gone through the above stages?

2 a) Complete the sentences using words from the list.

        collapse   expand   explode

    i) The Sun will eventually …… then ……. .
    ii) A white dwarf with a large enough mass will …… then ……. .
  b) i) What is the main condition needed for a neutron star to form a black hole?
    ii) Why is it not possible for light to escape from a black hole?

KEY POINTS

1 Low mass star:

    protostar → main stage → red giant → white dwarf → black dwarf

2 High mass star, after the white dwarf stage:

    white dwarf → supernova → neutron star → black hole if sufficient mass

269

P3 4.3 How the chemical elements formed

1 How were the heavy elements formed?
2 Why does the Earth contain heavy elements?

Figure 1 The Crab Nebula

DID YOU KNOW?

The Crab Nebula is the remnants of a supernova explosion that was observed in the 11th century. In 1987, a star in the southern hemisphere exploded and became the biggest supernova to be seen for four centuries. Astronomers realised that it was *Sandaluk II*, a star in the Andromeda galaxy millions of light years from Earth.

FOUL FACTS

If a star near the Sun exploded, the Earth would probably be blasted out of its orbit. We would see the explosion before the shock wave hits us.

The birthplace of the chemical elements

● *Light elements are formed as a result of fusion in stars.*

Stars like the Sun fuse hydrogen nuclei (i.e. protons) into helium and similar small nuclei, including carbon. When it becomes a red giant, it fuses helium and the other small nuclei into larger nuclei.

Nuclei larger than iron cannot be formed by this process because too much energy is needed.

● *Heavy elements are formed when a massive star collapses then explodes as a supernova.*

The enormous force of the collapse fuses small nuclei into nuclei larger than iron. The explosion scatters the star into space.

The debris from a supernova contains all the known elements from the lightest to the heaviest. Eventually, new stars form as gravity pulls the debris together.

Planets form from debris surrounding a new star. As a result, such planets will be composed of all the known elements too.

a) Lead is much heavier than iron. How did the lead we use form?

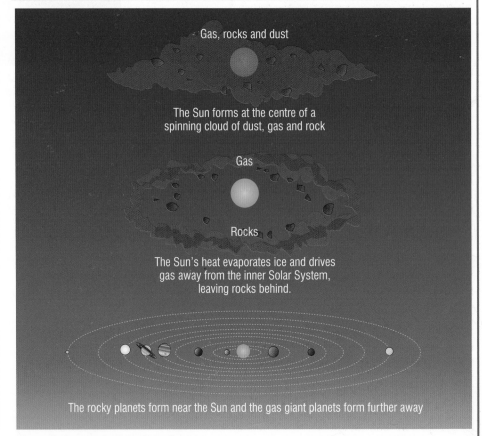

Gas, rocks and dust

The Sun forms at the centre of a spinning cloud of dust, gas and rock

Gas

Rocks

The Sun's heat evaporates ice and drives gas away from the inner Solar System, leaving rocks behind.

The rocky planets form near the Sun and the gas giant planets form further away

Figure 2 Formation of the Solar System

Planet Earth

The heaviest known natural element is uranium. It has a half life of 4500 million years. The presence of uranium in the Earth is evidence that the Solar System must have formed from the remnants of a supernova.

b) Plutonium 239 has a half life of about 24 000 years. So why is it not found naturally like uranium?

Is there or has there been life on other planets, either in our own Solar System or around other stars? Astronomers can see Earth-like planets in orbit round other stars. We know that molecules of carbon-based chemicals are present in space. Life on Earth probably developed from chemicals reacting in lightning storms.

So are we looking for any scientific evidence about life elsewhere?

Figure 3 Life on Mars?

- **Space probes sent to Mars** have tested the atmosphere, rocks and soil on Mars looking for any microbes or any chemicals that might indicate life was once present on Mars.
- **The search for extra-terrestrial intelligence,** known as **SETI**, has gone on for more than 40 years using radio telescopes. Signals from space would indicate the existence of living beings with technologies at least as advanced as our own. No signals have been detected – yet!

c) Why is carbon an important element?

SUMMARY QUESTIONS

1 Match each statement below with an element in the list.

helium   hydrogen   iron   uranium

a) Helium nuclei are formed when nuclei of this element are fused.
b) This element is formed in a supernova explosion.
c) Stars form nuclei of these two elements (and others not listed) by fusing smaller nuclei.
d) The early Universe mostly consisted of this element.

2 Choose the correct words from the list to complete each of the sentences a) to c).

galaxy   planets   stars   supernova

a) Fusion inside …… creates light elements. Fusion in a …… creates heavy elements.
b) A …… scatters the elements throughout a ……. .
c) …… and planets formed from the debris of a …… contain all the known elements.

KEY POINTS

1 Elements as heavy as iron are formed inside stars as a result of nuclear fusion.

2 Elements heavier than iron are formed in supernovas.

P3 4.4 Universal issues

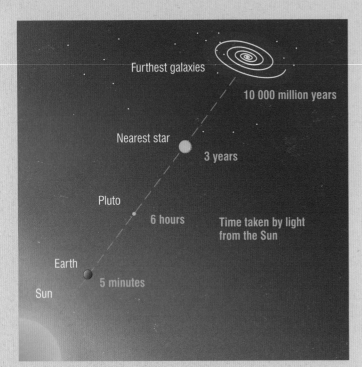

Furthest galaxies

10 000 million years

Nearest star

3 years

Pluto

6 hours

Time taken by light from the Sun

Earth

5 minutes

Sun

Light years

The light year is the distance travelled by light in 1 year. The nearest star to the Sun is about 3 light years away. The most distant galaxies are about 10 thousand million light years away. Light takes about

- 5 minutes to reach us from the Sun,
- 6 hours to reach us from Pluto, the most remote planet,
- 3 years from Proxima Centauri, the nearest star beyond the Sun,
- 100 000 years to cross the Milky Way galaxy,
- 2 million years to reach us from Andromeda, the nearest large galaxy beyond the Milky Way,
- 10 000 million years from the most distant galaxy.

QUESTION

Imagine the Sun scaled down to the size of a football. The Earth would be the size of a grain of rice about 30 metres away. Estimate how far it would be to:

a) Pluto,   **b)** the nearest star,   **c)** the furthest galaxies.

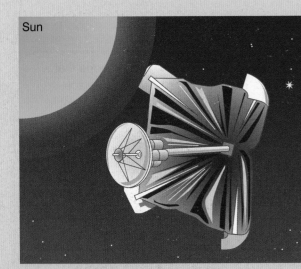

Sun

Sail to the stars

The Sun gives out a steady stream of radiation in all directions. Some scientists reckon the pressure of solar radiation could be used to carry a spaceship to the stars. The spaceship would need to have gigantic sails to catch enough solar radiation.

The force of the radiation would accelerate the spaceship almost to the speed of light. It could reach the nearest star within a few years and it could send back video pictures. The spaceship could carry a message from all the people on the Earth.

ACTIVITY

What message would you want to be carried on the spaceship? Turn your message into a poster.

Space costs

Space missions take years to plan and cost enormous sums of money. Many people argue that the money could be spent better on improving life here on Earth – ending extreme poverty in poor countries, providing better health care and housing, solving the problem of greenhouse gases, etc., etc. Others argue that scientific progress in the past has given us prosperity and living standards beyond the dreams of previous generations.

You must be joking, Columbus!

ACTIVITY

a) Imagine you are Christopher Columbus and you need to convince wealthy people to fund your project to find a sea route west to China. They think you'll drop off the edge of the world and never be seen again. Write a speech to convince them.

b) Fast-forward to the 21st century and turn your speech into an argument for a space project.

All that pollution!

Worm holes

Gravity bends light. That's what Einstein predicted in 1915. He worked out how much a ray of light would bend if it skimmed the Sun. Astronomers discovered he was right when they observed the solar eclipse of 1919. Einstein's light-bending theory also predicted black holes.

Science fiction stories often stretch Einstein's ideas to 'worm holes', 'teleportation', 'warp speeds', 'time travel', etc., etc. Step into a teleporter and you go through a wormhole to anywhere in space and time. As if!

ACTIVITY

a) Write a short news report on what you saw when you 'visited' a famous historical event.

b) Science fiction is no more scientific than 'reading your stars'. What do you think?

The 'big picture'

For many centuries, the Church held the view that the Earth is at the centre of the Universe. Galileo used his observations of stars and planets to challenge this view. Now we accept that the Earth is an insignificant planet orbiting one of the countless stars in one of countless galaxies in the Universe. But why did intelligent life develop on the Earth?

- Was it the Goldilocks theory – not too hot, not too cold, just right for life?
- Was it Intelligent Design – intelligent life needs an intelligent designer?

ACTIVITY

What do you think? Find out what other people think and debate the issue in your group.

SUMMARY QUESTIONS

1 Complete each sentence below using words from the list.

galaxy   planet   stars

a) A ...... isn't big enough to be a star.

b) The Sun is inside a ....

c) ...... became hot after they formed from matter pulled together by the force of gravity.

d) The force of gravity keeps ...... together inside a ....

2 a) What force pulls dust and gas in space?

b) Why do large planets like Jupiter not produce their own light?

c) What stops the Sun collapsing under its own weight?

d) What is the name for the type of reaction that releases energy in the core of the Sun?

3 a) The stages in the development of a star like the Sun are listed below. Put the stages in the correct sequence.

A dust and gas   B present stage
C protostar   D red giant
E white dwarf

b) After the white dwarf stage,
  i) what will happen to the Sun,
  ii) what will happen to a star that has much more mass than the Sun?

4 a) i) What is a supernova?
    ii) How could we tell the difference between a supernova and a distant star like the Sun at present?

b) i) What is a black hole?
    ii) What would happen to stars and planets near a black hole?

5 a) i) Which element as well as hydrogen formed in the early Universe?
    ii) Which of the two elements is formed from the other one in a star?

b) i) Which two of the elements listed below is not formed in a star that gives out radiation at a steady rate?

carbon   iron   lead   uranium

  ii) How do we know that the Sun formed from the debris of a supernova?

[Higher]

EXAM-STYLE QUESTIONS

1 Stars go through a life cycle. Some stars eventually become *black holes*.

(a) What type of star may eventually become a *black hole*? (2)

(b) Describe what is meant by a *black hole*. (2)

2 The sentences below describe the life cycle of a star such as the Sun.

A The star contracts to form a white dwarf.

B The star is in a stable state.

C The star expands to form a red giant.

D Gravitational forces pull dust and gas together and the star is formed.

(a) Put the sentences in the correct order. (3)

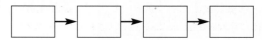

(b) At which stage in its life is the Sun, **A, B, C** or **D**? (1)

(c) What balances the gravitational forces to make a star stable? (2)

3 Describe as fully as you can what is meant by:

(a) the Milky Way (3)

(b) a neutron star (2)

(c) a supernova. (2)

4 (a) Explain how a star generates energy. (3)

(b) The early universe contained only hydrogen but now contains many heavier elements. The inner planets of the solar system contain atoms of these heavier elements.

  (i) Where did these atoms come from?

  (ii) What does this tell us about the age of the solar system? (3)

[Higher]

HOW SCIENCE WORKS

The Earth at the centre of the Universe?

A Chinese myth (600 BC) tells how the Earth was created by Phan Ku. He carved the mountains and the rivers and then created the Moon and the stars. Other cultures have their own myths of the relationship between the Earth and other 'heavenly' bodies in the sky. The word 'myth' comes from the Greek word for 'story'. Anaxagoras (fifth-century BC) claimed that the Moon and the Sun were merely rocks and not gods. This was frowned upon by the Greek authorities who exiled him from Athens. Observations clearly showed that the Moon, the Sun and the stars moved across the sky and re-appeared the next day. Therefore the Earth must be at the centre of the Universe. It was a matter of making the detailed observations and calculations fit this model. Philolaus was the first person recorded to have suggested that the Earth moved around the Sun. The Greeks concluded that this hypothesis was wrong, because if it were true, there would be a constant wind. Ptolemy (second-century AD) worked hard to support the Earth-centred theory with mathematical calculations of great complexity. Copernicus in the sixteenth century countered Ptolemy's view of the Universe by using data about the size of the Moon. Copernicus believed that

- the Earth and the planets orbited the Sun,
- the Moon orbited the Earth,
- the movement of the stars was due to the Earth rotating.

Bruno went further and suggested that the stars could have planets and these could have life on them. The Church burnt him to death in 1600 because of his religious beliefs. The Copernican view of the Universe suffered a set-back because it had been supported by Bruno. However, the Copernican model was eventually accepted – largely as a result of Galileo's astronomical observations and his long struggle with the Church to gain acceptance of the Copernican model.

Use this passage to illustrate examples of the following scientific ideas:

a) myths (1)

b) observation (1)

c) data (1)

d) hypothesis (1)

e) a theory that has been disproved (1)

f) a theory that remains to be disproved (1)

g) political influence on science. (1)

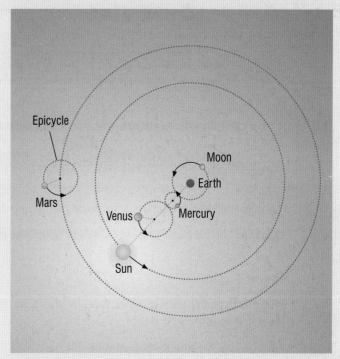

Ptolemy model

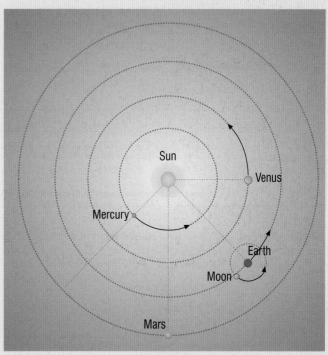

Copernican model

EXAMINATION-STYLE QUESTIONS

1 The drawing shows Aimie and Charlie sitting on a see-saw.

See pages 218–19

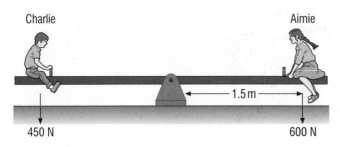

Charlie   Aimie

←— 1.5 m —→

450 N   600 N

(a) Aimie weighs 600 N and sits 1.5 m from the middle of the see-saw.

    Calculate the moment of Aimie's weight about the middle of the see-saw.

                                       (4 marks)

(b) Charlie weighs 450 N.

    How far from the middle of the see-saw must Charlie sit for the see-saw to balance horizontally?   *(4 marks)*

                                                 [Higher]

GET IT RIGHT!

Remember to state whether the moment is clockwise or anticlockwise.

2 The diagram shows a converging lens being used as a magnifying glass. The size and position of an object at **O** is shown. The points marked **F** are the principal foci of the lens.

See pages 242–3

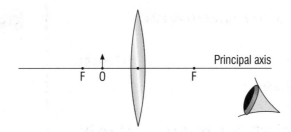

Principal axis

F O   F

(a) Copy and draw construction rays on the diagram in order to locate accurately the position and size of the image.   *(4 marks)*

(b) The same type of lens can be used in a camera to produce an image on a film.

    Describe the nature of the image that would be produced on the film

                                       (3 marks)

GET IT RIGHT!

Your construction rays must be very neat or the image will not be in the right place. Use a sharp pencil and a ruler. Remember to put arrows on the rays to show the direction of the light.

3 The diagram shows a simple a.c. generator.

See pages 256–7

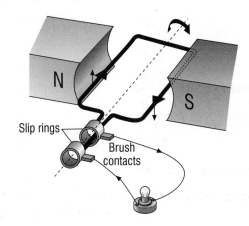

Slip rings

Brush contacts

The coil is turned as shown in the diagram.

(a) State two ways of reversing the direction (polarity) of the induced potential difference. *(2 marks)*

(b) State three ways of increasing the size of the induced potential difference.

(3 marks)
[Higher]

GET IT RIGHT!

Read the question carefully, be sure that you state what will **increase** the p.d.

4 The Earth orbits the Sun because there is an attractive force between them which provides a centripetal force.

See pages 222–8

(a) What is the name of this attractive force? *(1 mark)*

(b) What would happen to the size of this force if:
  (i) the mass of the Earth were greater?
  (ii) the distance between the Sun and the Earth were greater? *(2 marks)*

(c) What would happen to the time taken for one orbit if the distance between the Sun and the Earth were greater? *(1 mark)*

(d) How are the stars and the planets formed? *(3 marks)*

See pages 268–9

Glossary

A

Acceleration Change of velocity per second (in metres per second per second, m/s²).

Accuracy An accurate measurement is close to the true value.

Acid rain Rain that is acidic due to dissolved gases, such as sulphur dioxide, produced by the burning of fossil fuels.

Activity Number of atoms of a radioactive substance that decay each second.

Alpha emission The process in which a large unstable nucleus becomes stable by emitting an alpha particle.

Alpha particle scattering Scattering of alpha particles (usually in a narrow beam) by nuclei of the atoms of a thin metal foil.

Alpha radiation Alpha particles, each composed of two protons and two neutrons, emitted by unstable nucleus.

Amplitude The maximum disturbance of the particles in a substance (e.g. air) when sound waves pass through it.

Analogue signal A signal that varies continuously in amplitude or frequency between a maximum and minimum value.

Angle of incidence The angle between the incident ray and the normal.

Angle of reflection The angle between the reflected ray and the normal.

Anomalous A measurement that is well away from the pattern shown by other results.

Antistatic material Material that is a poor insulator and which is used to conduct charge to earth.

Atom The smallest part of an element.

Atomic nucleus Positively charged object composed of protons and neutrons at the centre of every atom with one or more electrons moving round it.

Atomic number The number of protons in a nucleus, symbol Z (also called the proton number).

B

Background microwave radiation Electromagnetic radiation emitted shortly after the Big Bang. Its discovery confirmed the Big Bang theory.

Background radioactivity Radioactivity from substances around us.

Bar charts Used when the independent variable is categoric and the dependent variable is continuous.

Beta emission A process in which a neutron-rich nucleus becomes stable as a result of a neutron changing into a proton, creating and emitting a beta particle (i.e. an electron) at the instant of change.

Beta radiation Beta particles which are high-energy electrons created in and emitted from unstable nuclei.

Bias The influence placed on scientific evidence because of: wanting to prove your own ideas; supporting the person who is paying you; political influence; the status of the experimenter.

Big Bang theory The theory that the Universe was created in a massive explosion (the Big Bang) and that the Universe has been expanding ever since.

Billion A thousand million.

Biomass fuel Fuel from plants or animal waste.

Black hole An object in space that has so much mass that nothing, not even light, can escape from its gravitational field.

Braking distance The distance travelled by a vehicle during the time its brakes act.

C

Cable Two or three insulated wires surrounded by an outer layer of rubber or flexible plastic.

Camera An instrument for photographing an object by using a converging lens to form a real image of the object on a film (or on electronic pixels) in a light-proof box.

Carrier wave Waves used to carry a signal.

Categoric variable These tell us the name of the variable, e.g. type of wire used for a resistance investigation.

Causal link One change in a variable has caused a change in another variable. You can only be reasonably certain of this when you have valid and reliable evidence. E.g. increasing the length of the wire causes an increase in resistance.

Centre of mass The point where an object's mass may be thought to be concentrated.

Centripetal force The resultant force towards the centre of a circle acting on an object moving in a circular path.

Chain reaction Reactions in which one reaction causes further reactions, which in turn cause further reactions, etc. A nuclear chain reaction occurs when fission neutrons cause further fission, so more fission neutrons are released. These go on to produce further fission.

Chance When there is no scientific link between the two variables. E.g. increased sea temperatures and increased diabetes.

Charging by friction The process of charging certain insulating materials by rubbing with a dry cloth, causing electrons to transfer between the material and the cloth.

Charging without direct contact The process in which an insulated conductor is charged without being in direct contact with a charged object.

Chip An electronic component which contains an integrated circuit.

Circuit Components connected together so that current passes through them.

Circuit breaker An electromagnetic switch that opens and cuts the current off if too much current passes through it.

Communications satellite A satellite that orbits the Earth above the equator in a circular orbit, usually with a period of 24 hours in the same direction as the Earth's spin, so it stays directly above the same place on the Earth's surface.

Component A part or device in an electric circuit.

Compound A substance made of two or more types of atom chemically joined together.

Concave mirror A curved mirror with a surface that bends in.

Conclusion A conclusion considers the results and states how those results match the hypothesis. The conclusion must not go beyond the data available.

Conduction Heat transfer in a substance due to motion of particles in the substance.

Conduction electrons Electrons that move about freely inside a metal because they are not attached to individual atoms.

Conservation of energy Energy cannot be created or destroyed.

Conservation of momentum Momentum is conserved in any collision or explosion provided no external forces act on the objects that collide or explode.

Continuous variable A continuous variable can be any numerical value, e.g. length of wire used in a resistance investigation.

Control variable These are the variables that might affect your result and therefore must be kept the same for a valid investigation. E.g. voltage used in a resistance investigation.

Control rods Metal rods (made of boron or cadmium) used to absorb excess fission neutrons in a nuclear reactor so that only one fission neutron per fission on average goes on to produce further fission.

Controlled An experiment is controlled when all variables that might affect your result (apart from the independent variable) have been kept constant.

Convection Heat transfer in a liquid or gas due to convection currents.

Convection currents The flow of a fluid due to differences in temperature. E.g. circulation of the upper part of the Earth's mantle.

Converging lens A lens that makes light rays parallel to the principal axis converge to (i.e. meet at) a point; also referred to as a convex lens.

Convex mirror A curved mirror with a surface that bends out.

Coolant Fluid in a sealed circuit pumped through the core of a nuclear reactor to remove thermal energy to a heat exchanger.

Coulomb (C) The unit of electrical charge, equal to the charge passing a point in a (direct current) circuit in 1 second when the current is 1 A.

D

Data Measurements or observations of a variable. Plural of datum.

Deceleration Change of velocity per second when an object slows down.

Density Mass per unit volume of a substance.

Dependent variable The variable that you are measuring as a result of changing the independent variable, e.g. current measured in a resistance investigation.

Diffusion Spreading out of particles away from each other.

Digital signal A signal that consists of a sequence of pulses which are at two levels only, either high (1) or low (0).

Directly proportional A graph will show this if the line of best fit is a straight line through the origin.

Discrete variable These are numerical, but can only be whole numbers, e.g. numbers of layers of insulation.

Diverging lens A lens that makes light rays parallel to the axis diverge (i.e. spread out) as if from a single point; also referred to as a concave lens.

Doppler effect The change of wavelength (and frequency) of the waves from a moving source due to the motion of the source.

Drag force A force opposing the motion of an object due to fluid (e.g. air) flowing past the object as it moves.

Dynamo effect The effect in which a potential difference is generated in a wire or coil when the wire or coil cuts across the lines of a magnetic field.

E

Earth wire A wire used to connect the metal case of an appliance to earth so that the case cannot become live.

Earthed Connected to the ground by means of a conducting lead or wire.

Economic How science affects the cost of goods and services. E.g. developing wind power might increase the cost of electricity.

Efficiency This is defined as:

$$\frac{\text{Useful energy transferred by a device}}{\text{Total energy supplied to the device}}$$

Effort The force applied to a device used to raise a weight or shift an object.

Elastic A material is elastic if it is able to regain its shape after it has been squashed or stretched.

Elastic potential energy Energy stored in an elastic object when work is done to change its shape.

Electric current The rate of flow of electric charge (in amperes, A).

Electric potential energy Energy of a charged object due to its charge (in joules, J).

Electrical energy Energy transferred by the movement of charge.

Electrical power The rate of transfer of electrical energy (in watts, W).

Electromagnetic waves Electric and magnetic disturbances that transfer energy from one place to another. The spectrum of electromagnetic waves, in order of increasing wavelength, is as follows: gamma and X-rays, ultraviolet radiation, visible light, infra-red radiation, microwaves, radio waves.

Electrons Negative particles found outside the nucleus of an atom.

Element A substance made up of only one type of element.

Energy forms Ways in which energy is stored or transferred, including **chemical energy**: energy stored in fuel; **elastic (or strain energy)**: energy stored in a squashed or stretched object; **electrical energy**: energy transferred by an electric current; **gravitational potential energy**: energy of an object due to its position, **kinetic energy**: energy of a moving object, **thermal energy**: energy of an object due to its temperature.

Energy transfer Energy transferred from one place to another.

Energy transformation Energy change from one form to another.

Ethical Whether it is 'right' or 'wrong' to do something. E.g. experimentation on nuclear weapons.

Equilibrium (of forces) The state of an object when it is at rest.

Evidence Scientific evidence should be reliable and valid. It can take many forms. It could be an observation, a measurement or data that somebody else has obtained.

Expansion of the Universe The motion of galaxies away from each other, discovered from the observations that the red shift (and therefore the speed) of the distant galaxies increases with their distance.

F

Fair test Only the independent variable is affecting your dependent variable, all other variables are kept the same.

Fluid A liquid or a gas.

Focal length The distance from the centre of a lens or a curved mirror to the point where light rays parallel to the principal axis are focused (or, in the case of a convex mirror or a diverging lens, appear to diverge from).

Force A force can change the motion of an object (in newtons, N).

Fossil fuel Coal, oil or gas or any other fuel formed long ago from the fossilised remains of dead plants or creatures.

Free electrons Electrons that move about freely inside a metal and are not held inside an atom.

Frequency The number of complete waves passing a point each second. The unit of frequency is the hertz (Hz).

Friction force A force opposing the relative motion of two surfaces where they are in contact with each other.

Fuse A fuse contains a thin wire that melts and cuts the current off if too much current passes through it.

Fusion The process in which small nuclei fuse to become larger nuclei.

G

Gamma radiation Electromagnetic radiation emitted from unstable nuclei in radioactive substances.

Geostationary satellite A satellite that orbits the Earth above the equator in a circular orbit with a period of 24 hours in the same direction as the Earth's spin so it always stays directly above the same place on the Earth's surface.

Global dimming A gradual reduction in the amount of light reaching the Earth's surface due to particles in the atmosphere.

Global warming Warming of the Earth due to greenhouse gases in the atmosphere trapping infra-red radiation from the surface.

Gravitational field strength The force of gravity on an object of mass 1 kg (in newtons per kilogram, N/kg).

Gravitational potential energy Energy of an object due to its position in a gravitational field. Near the Earth's surface, change of g.p.e. (in joules, J) = weight (in newtons, N) × vertical distance moved (in metres, m).

Greenhouse gases Gases such as carbon dioxide in the atmosphere that absorb infra-red radiation from the Earth's surface.

H

Half-life of a radioactive isotope Time taken for the number of nuclei of the isotope (or mass of the isotope) in a sample to halve.

Heat transfer Energy transfer due to a temperature difference: see thermal radiation, conduction and convection.

High mass star A star that has a much greater mass than the Sun.

Hypothesis Using theory to suggest explanations for observations, e.g. 'I think that radiation from nuclear power plants has caused mutation in fish.'

I

Impact force The force acting on an object when it collides with another object; the two objects experience equal and opposite forces.

Independent variable The variable that you have decided to change in an investigation, e.g. the length of wire used in a resistance investigation.

Induced p.d. The potential difference generated in a wire or coil when the wire or coil cuts across the lines of a magnetic field.

Infra-red radiation Electromagnetic waves between visible light and microwaves in the electromagnetic spectrum.

Interference Unwanted variations on waves carrying a signal.

Interval measurements The values of your independent variable that you choose within the range e.g. $10\,cm^3$; $20\,cm^3$; $30\,cm^3$; $40\,cm^3$; $50\,cm^3$.

Ionisation Any process in which atoms become charged.

Ionising radiation Radiation that ionises substances it passes through. Alpha, beta, gamma and X-radiation are all ionising.

Ionosphere Layer of ionised gases in the atmosphere which reflect radio waves of frequency less than 30 MHz.

Ion A charged atom.

Isotopes Atoms of an element that contain different numbers of neutrons in their nuclei.

K

Kilowatt hour (kW h) Electrical energy supplied to a 1 kW electrical device in 1 hour.

Kinetic energy Energy of a moving object due to its motion; kinetic energy (in joules, J) = $\frac{1}{2}$ × mass (in kilograms, kg) × (speed)^2 (in m^2/s^2).

L

Law of force between charged objects Like charges repel; unlike charges attract.

Limiting factors Factors which limit the rate of a reaction, e.g. photosynthesis.

Line graphs Used when the independent and the dependent variables are both continuous.

Line of best fit Used to show the underlying relationship between the independent and the dependent variables. It should fit the pattern in the results and have roughly the same number of plots on each side of the line. It could be a straight line or a curve. Remember to ignore any anomalies!

Linear These are straight line graphs that can be positive (as the length of wire increases so too does the resistance) or negative (as the time increases the velocity decreases).

Link due to association When two variables change together, but they are both linked by a third variable. E.g. air temperature and voltage produced by a photoelectric cell, both are linked to the radiation from the Sun.

Link due to chance When there is no scientific link between the two variables. E.g. increased sea temperatures and increased diabetes.

Live wire The wire of a mains circuit that has a potential that alternates from positive to negative and back each cycle.

Load The weight of an object raised by a device used to lift the object, or the force applied **by** a device when it is used to shift an object.

Loudness Depends on the amplitude of the sound waves that make up a sound.

Low mass star A star that has a much smaller mass than the Sun.

M

Magnification The image height ÷ the object height.

Magnifying glass A converging lens used to magnify a small object which must be placed between the lens and its focal point.

Mass The amount of matter in an object; a measure of the difficulty of changing the motion of an object (in kilograms, kg).

Mass number The total number of protons and neutrons in the nucleus of an atom (symbol A).

Mean Add up all of the measurements and divide by how many measurements there are. Don't forget to ignore any anomalous results.

Model Description of a theory or theories that suggests further ideas that could test those theories. E.g. 'plum pudding' model of the atom that was tested and found not to be correct. A better model was then suggested.

Moderator A solid or liquid used in a nuclear reactor to slow fission neutrons down so they can cause further fission.

Modulation The process of varying the amplitude or frequency of a carrier wave so it can carry a signal.

Moment The turning effect of a force defined by the equation Moment of a force (in newton metres) = force (in newtons) × perpendicular distance from the pivot to the line of action of the force (in metres).

Momentum Mass (in kilograms, kg) × velocity (in m/s).

Monitoring satellite A satellite in a low circular orbit that takes it over the Earth's North and South Poles in each orbit.

Motive force A force on a powered object (e.g. a vehicle) that makes it move.

Motor effect When a current is passed along a wire in a magnetic field and the wire is not parallel to the lines of the magnetic field, a force is exerted on the wire by the magnetic field.

N

National Grid The network of cables and transformers used to transfer electricity from power stations to consumers (i.e. homes, shops, offices, factories, etc.).

Net Overall.

Neutral wire The wire of a mains circuit that is earthed at the local sub-station so its potential is close to zero.

Neutron star The highly compressed core of a massive star that remains after a supernova explosion.

Neutrons Neutral particles found in the nucleus of an atom.

Normal The line perpendicular to the mirror surface (or boundary where refraction occurs) at the point of incidence of a light ray.

Nuclear energy Energy released from an unstable atom as a result of a change in its nucleus.

Nuclear fission The process in which certain nuclei (uranium 235 and plutonium 239) split into two fragments when struck by a neutron, releasing energy and two or three neutrons as a result.

Nuclear fission reactor A reactor that releases energy as a result of nuclear fission inside it.

Nuclear fusion The process in which small nuclei are forced together so they fuse with each other to form a larger nucleus, releasing energy in the process.

Nuclear model of the atom Every atom contains a positively charged nucleus consisting of neutrons and protons. This is where most of its mass is concentrated, and it is much smaller than the atom. Electrons move about in the space surrounding the nucleus.

O

Ohm's law The current through a resistor at constant temperature is directly proportional to the potential difference across the resistor.

Ohmic conductor A conductor that has a constant resistance and therefore obeys Ohm's law.

Opinion Opinions are personal judgements. Opinions can be formed from scientific evidence or non-scientific ideas.

Ordered variable Variables that can be put into an order, e.g. small, large, huge lumps of rock.

Oscilloscope A device used to display the shape of an electrical wave.

Ozone layer Layer of ozone gas in the Earth's atmosphere that absorbs ultraviolet radiation.

P

Parallel Components connected in a circuit so that the potential difference is the same across each one.

Parallel circuit rules 1. The potential difference across components in parallel is the same. 2. The total current passing through components in parallel is shared between the components.

Pay-back period (or time) Length of time for the savings from an improvement to match the actual cost of the improvement.

Period The time taken for a satellite to orbit the Earth once.

Photosynthesis The process by which plants make food using carbon dioxide, water and light energy.

Pitch depends on the frequency of the sound waves that make up a sound.

Pivot The point about which an object turns when acted on by a force that makes it turn.

Plum pudding model of the atom A model of the atom which supposed that the positive charge was evenly spread throughout its matter and the negative charge was held in tiny particles (electrons) inside the atom.

Plasma A gas consisting of bare nuclei (i.e. atoms stripped of their electrons).

Plug A plug has an insulating case and is used to connect the cable from an appliance to a socket.

Pollution The contamination of air, water or soil by substances which are harmful to living organisms.

Potential difference A measure of the difference in electric potential energy per unit charge between two charged objects (in volts, V).

Power The energy transformed per second. The unit of power is the watt (W).

Precision Where your repeat results are very close to each other. This is related to the smallest scale division on the measuring instrument used.

Prediction A hypothesis that can be used to design an investigation e.g. 'I predict that if I increase the length of wire the current will decrease'.

Principal focus The point where light rays parallel to the principal axis of a lens or curved mirror are focused (or, in the case of a convex mirror or a diverging lens, appear to diverge from).

Principle of Moments For an object in equilibrium,
The sum of all the clockwise moments about any point = the sum of all the anticlockwise moments about that point.

Proton number See **atomic number**.

Protons Positive particles found in the nucleus of an atom.

Protostar The concentration of dust clouds and gas in space that forms a star.

Pumped storage station A power station that uses electricity to store energy by pumping water uphill to an upper reservoir. Electricity is generated when water in the upper reservoir is allowed to flow downhill.

R

Radiation Energy carried by waves.

Radioactive substances Substances with unstable nuclei that emit alpha, beta or gamma radiation when they become more stable.

Radiograph An X-ray picture.

Random changes Changes that cannot be predicted.

Random error Measurements when repeated are rarely exactly the same. If they differ randomly then it is probably due to human error when carrying out the investigation.

Range The maximum and minimum values.

Real image An image formed by a lens or concave mirror that can be projected on a screen.

Red giant A star that has expanded and cooled, resulting in it becoming red and much larger and cooler than it was before it expanded.

Red shift Increase in the wavelength of electromagnetic waves emitted by a star or galaxy due to its motion away from us. The faster the speed of the star or galaxy, the greater the red shift is.

Reflection of light When a light ray is reflected from a mirror, the angle of incidence is equal to the angle of reflection.

Refraction The change of direction of a light ray when it passes across a boundary between two transparent substances (including air).

Reliability The trustworthiness of data collected.

Reliable Describes data we can trust. E.g. others can get the same results, even using different methods.

Renewable energy Energy from sources that never run out, including wind energy, wave energy, tidal energy, hydroelectricity, solar energy and geothermal energy.

Resistance Resistance (in ohms, Ω) = potential difference (in volts, V) ÷ current (in amperes, A).

Resistors in parallel Resistors in a circuit with the same potential difference across each one. The bigger the resistance of a resistor, the smaller the current that passes through it

Resistors in series Resistors in a circuit with the same current passing through them. Their combined resistance = sum of the individual resistances.

Resonates When sound vibrations build up in a musical instrument and cause the sound from the instrument to become much louder.

Resultant force The combined effect of the forces acting on an object.

S

Sankey diagram Diagram to show the energy transfer through a device.

Sensitivity The smallest change that an instrument can detect, e.g. 0.1 mm.

Series Components connected in a circuit so that the same current passes through them are in series with each other.

Series circuit rules 1. The current through components in series is the same. 2. The total potential difference across components in series is shared between the components.

SETI Search for extra-terrestrial intelligence.

Short-circuit A circuit fault in which two wires at different potentials touch and a large current passes between them at the point of contact.

Social issues How science influences and is influenced by its effects on our friends and neighbours. E.g. building a wind farm next to a village.

Socket A mains socket is used to connect the mains plug of a mains appliance to the mains circuit.

Solar cell Electrical cell that produces a voltage when in sunlight; solar cells are usually connected together in solar cell panels.

Solar heating panel Sealed panel designed to use sunlight to heat water running through it.

Sound echo Sound waves from a source of sound reflected from a smooth wall.

Speed Distance travelled per second (in metres/second, m/s).

Speed of a wave Distance travelled per second by a wave.

Static electricity Charge 'held' by an insulator or an insulated conductor.

Stopping distance Braking distance + thinking distance.

Supernova The explosion of a massive star after fusion in its core ceases and the matter surrounding its core collapses on to the core and rebounds.

Sustainable development Using natural resources in a way which also conserves them for future use.

Systematic error If the data is inaccurate in a constant way, e.g. all results are 10 mm more than they should be. This is often due to the method being routinely wrong.

T

Technology Scientific knowledge can be used to develop equipment and processes that can in turn be used for scientific work.

Telescope, optical Instrument consisting of lenses (and/or a mirror) used to make distant objects appear larger or brighter.

Telescope, radio Large concave metal dish and aerial used to detect radio waves from space.

Terminal velocity The velocity reached by an object when the drag force on it is equal and opposite to the force making it move.

Theory A theory is not a guess or a fact. It is the best way to explain why something is happening. E.g. the Big Bang theory is the best way to describe how the Universe started. Theories can be changed when better evidence is available.

Thermal radiation Energy transfer by electromagnetic waves emitted by objects due to their temperature.

Thinking distance The distance travelled by the vehicle in the time it takes the driver to react.

Three-pin plug A three-pin plug has a live pin, a neutral pin and an earth pin. The earth pin is used to earth the metal case of an appliance so the case cannot become live.

Time base control An oscilloscope control used to space the waveform out horizontally.

Transformer Electrical device used to change an (alternating) voltage. A **step-up transformer** is used to step the voltage up, e.g. from a power station to the grid voltage. A **step-down transformer** is used to step the voltage down, e.g. from the grid voltage to the mains voltage used in homes and offices.

U

Ultrasonic waves Sound waves above the frequency range of the human ear (i.e. above 18 000 Hz).

Useful energy Energy transferred to where it is wanted in the form it is wanted.

V

Valid Describes an investigation that successfully gathers the data needed to answer the original question. Data may not be valid if you have not carried out a fair test.

Valid data Evidence that can be reproduced by others and answers the original question.

Van de Graaff generator A large insulated metal dome charged by the motion of a rubber belt brushing against a friction pad.

Velocity Speed in a given direction (in metres/second, m/s).

Virtual image An image, seen in a mirror (or lens), from which light rays appear to come after being reflected by the mirror (or being refracted by the lens).

Volt (V) The unit of potential difference, equal to energy transfer per unit charge in joules per coulomb.

W

Wasted energy Energy that is not usefully transferred or transformed.

Wavelength The distance from one wave peak to the next wave peak along the waves.

Weight The force of gravity on an object (in newtons).

White dwarf A star that has collapsed from the red giant stage to become much hotter and denser than it was.

Work Energy transferred by a force, given by:
Work done (in joules, J) = force (in newtons, N) × distance moved in the direction of the force (in metres, m).

Y

Y-gain control An oscilloscope control used to adjust the height of the waveform.

Z

Zero error A systematic error, often due to the measuring instrument having an incorrect zero. E.g. forgetting that the end of the ruler is not at zero.

Index

Acknowledgements

Action+/Glyn Kirk 143tr, /Peter Tarry 221.4; **AEA Technology** 102.1; **Alamy**/Network Photographers 156bl, /**Popperfoto** 150.1, /**Steve Bloom** 24.1; **Allsport, Gary Mortimore** 222.1; **Antigua Postal Service** 18.2; **Biocor/NHF** 190.1; **Bus & Coach Weekly** 221.3; **Corbis Sean Sexton Collection** 216.1a; **Corbis/Andrew Wong/Reuters** 122.3; **Corel 231 (NT)** 216.1b; **Corel 243 (NT)** 39.4; **Corel 342 (NT)** 69.4; **Corel 414 (NT)** 153.3; **Corel 444 (NT)** 66.1; **Corel 584 (NT)** 38.1; **Corel 624 (NT)** 25b; **Corel 637 (NT)** 160.1; **Corel 640 (NT)** 40.1, 122.1, 230tl; **Corel 759 (NT)** 165.4; **Data Harvest** 124.1a; **DETR** 142tl, 156tl; **Digital Vision 1 (NT)** 6.1, 22.1, 56.1, 57.4; **Digital Vision 3 (NT)** 30.1; **Digital Vision 6 (NT)** 53.2, 77.4, 128br, 229.3; **Digital Vision 9 (NT)** 109.2, 110.1, 266.2; **Digital Vision 12 (NT)** 8.1; **Digital Vision 15 (NT)** 167b; **Doug Menuez/Photodisc 45 (NT)** 246.1; **Education Development Centre, Massachusetts** 238.2a; **Hewlett Packard** 167tr; **Image 100 22 (NT)** 80.1b, 81tr; **ImageState/Alamy** 139.3; **Jim Breithaupt** 54.1, 55.2, 191.2; **John Bailey** 5.2; **Martyn F. Chillmaid** 5.3a, 5.3b, 5.3c, 7.3, 20l, 20r, 121m, 124.1b, 143l, 175.3b, 195mr; **NASA** 110.2; **NASA Goddard Space Flight Centre** 110.3; **Nike** 149.3; **Photodisc 10 (NT)** 41.3; **Photodisc 17 (NT)** 64.1; **Photodisc 44 (NT)** 206t; **Photodisc 51 (NT)** 3.1, 146.1; **Photodisc 54 (NT)** 65.3; **Photodisc 59 (NT)** 26.1; **Photodisc 66 (NT)** 91ml; **Photodisc 67 (NT)** 53.3; **Photodisc 70 (NT)** 28.1; **Photolink/Photodisc 18 (NT)** 101mr; **PowerStudies** 52.1; **Rover Group** 164.1; **Ryan McVay/Photodisc 67 (NT)** 42.1; **S Meltzer/Photolink/Photodisc 24 (NT)** 241.5; **Shout Pictures** 235.4; **Science Photo Library** 34.2, 47.3, 112br, 212tl, /**A. Barrington Brown** 115, /**A. Crump, TDR, WHO** 80.1a, /**Alex Bartel** 70.1, 206b, /**Alfred Pasieka** 239.4, /**Andrew Lambert Photography** 187.3, 188.1a, 234.1a, /**Athenais, ISM** 80.2, /**Charles D. Winters** 184.1, /**Chris Priest & Mark Clarke** 34.3, /**Christian Darkin** 240.1b, /**Cordelia Molloy** 32.1, 51.4, 77.2, 84.1, 84.2, 86.1, 90tm, 191.3, 195b, /**Cristina Pedrazzini** 236.1, /**Custom medical Stock Photo** 19.4, /**Darwin Dale** 244.2, /**David Parker** 129t, /**EFDA-JET** 71.3, /**G. Brad Lewis** 66.3, /**James King-Holmes** 251br, /**Jason Kelvin** 137.3, /**Jerry Mason** 129mr, /**John Mead** 85.3, /**Keith Kent** 120.1, /**Ken M. Johns** 228.1, /**Martin Bond** 65.4, /**Martyn F. Chillmaid** 4.1, 50.1, 81.4, 175.3a, 251mr, /**Matt Meadows/Peter Arnold INC.** 77.3, /**Mauro Fermariello** 83.3, /**Maximilian Stock LTD** 42.2, /**Mehau Kulyk** 213tr, /**NASA** 113tl, 119ml, 119tr, 271.3, /**NASA/ESA/STScI** 106.1, 213bl, /**National Library of Medicine** 94.2, /**Nick Wall** 207r, /**NOAO/AURA/NSF** 267.4, /**Novosti** 69.3, /**NRAO/AUI/NSF** 269.3, /**Peter Menzel** 230r, /**Physics Today Collection/American Institute of Physics** 18.1, 267.3, /**R. Maisonneuve, Publiphoto diffusion** 260.1, /**Robert Brook** 62.2, /**Sheila Terry** 35tr, 36l, 188.1b, 189.3, 194m, /**Sovereign, ISM** 213ml, /**St. Bartholomew's Hospital** 213mr, /**Steve Allen** 67.5, /**Ton Kinsbergen** 240.1a, /**Tony Craddock** 25.3, 111.5, /**US Department of Energy** 263tr, /**Volker Steger** 235.3; **Steve Cole/Photodisc 59 (NT)** 248.2b; **Stocktrek/Photodisc 34 (NT)** 270.1; **Topfoto.co.uk** 7.2, /**HIP/Ann Ronan Collection** 18.3, /**FP** 273br, /**AP Photos** 102.2, /**UPPA Ltd** 155r; **Transport & Road Research Laboratory** 154.1, 156mr; **Trevor Baylis** 50.2; **UKAEA** 205.3

Picture research by Stuart Sweatmore, Science Photo Library and johnbailey@ntlworld.com.

Every effort has been made to trace all the copyright holders, but if any have been overlooked the publisher will be pleased to make the necessary arrangements at the first opportunity.